T0230182

Lecture Notes in Computer Science   3105

Commenced Publication in 1973
Founding and Former Series Editors:
Gerhard Goos, Juris Hartmanis, and Jan van Leeuwen

Springer
Berlin
Heidelberg
New York
Hong Kong
London
Milan
Paris
Tokyo

Stefan Göbel Ulrike Spierling
Anja Hoffmann Ido Iurgel
Oliver Schneider Johanna Dechau
Axel Feix (Eds.)

Technologies for Interactive Digital Storytelling and Entertainment

Second International Conference, TIDSE 2004
Darmstadt, Germany, June 24-26, 2004
Proceedings

Springer

Volume Editors

Stefan Göbel
Anja Hoffmann
Ido Iurgel
Oliver Schneider
Johanna Dechau
Axel Feix
ZGDV e.V. - Computer Graphics Center
Digital Storytelling Department
Fraunhoferstr. 5, 64283 Darmstadt, Germany
E-mail: {Stefan.Goebel,Anja.Hoffmann,
Ido.Iurgel,Oliver.Schneider,
Johanna.Dechau,Axel.Feix}@zgdv.de

Ulrike Spierling
FH Erfurt, University of Applied Sciences
Department of Architecture
Altonaer Str. 25, 99085 Erfurt, Germany
E-mail: spierling@fh-erfurt.de

Library of Congress Control Number: 2004107573

CR Subject Classification (1998): H.5, H.4, I.2, I.3, I.4, I.7, J.5

ISSN 0302-9743
ISBN 3-540-22283-9 Springer-Verlag Berlin Heidelberg New York

Springer-Verlag is a part of Springer Science+Business Media

springeronline.com

© Springer-Verlag Berlin Heidelberg 2004
Printed in Germany

Typesetting: Camera-ready by author, data conversion by PTP-Berlin, Protago-TeX-Production GmbH
Printed on acid-free paper   SPIN: 11012900   06/3142   5 4 3 2 1 0

Preface

Interactive Digital Storytelling has evolved as a prospering research topic banding together formerly disjointed disciplines stemming from the arts and humanities as well as computer science. It's tied up with the notion of storytelling as an effective means for the communication of knowledge and social values since the existence of humankind. It also builds a bridge between current academic trends investigating and formalizing computer games, and developments towards the experience-based design of human-media interaction in general.

In Darmstadt, a first national workshop on Digital Storytelling was organized by ZGDV e.V. in 2000, which at that time gave an impression about the breadth of this new research field for computer graphics (DISTEL 2000). An international follow-up was planned: the 1st International Conference on Technologies for Interactive Digital Storytelling and Entertainment (TIDSE 2003). Taking place in March 2003, it showed a more focussed range of research specifically on concepts and first prototypes for automated storytelling and autonomous characters, including modelling of emotions and the user experience.

At TIDSE 2004, an established and still-growing community of researchers gathered together to exchange results and visions. This confirms the construction of a series of European conferences on the topic – together with the International Conference on Virtual Storytelling, ICVS (conducted in 2001 and 2003 in France) – which will be further cultivated.

The TIDSE 2004 conference program provided traditional scientific talks, but also demonstrations and interactive exhibitions of computer arts. Further on, there were special tracks on Virtual Human Design (kick-off of an international network on Virtual Human Design) and Knowledge Media Design (KMD). These tracks were arranged in cooperation with the project consortium of the national R&D project "Virtual Human" (www.virtual-human.org) and the KMD Forum centered at ZGDV Darmstadt (www.kmd-forum.de) and emphasized by invited talks by Norman I. Badler, a specialist in the field of computer graphics and information science, and Ronald M. Baecker, one of the pioneers in the field of Knowledge Media Design.

Scientific Contributions

The wide range of questions, ideas, concepts and applications discussed in the contributions of this volume reflect the vitality and engagement of the storytelling community and its neighboring disciplines. The current research situation into Interactive Digital Storytelling demands interdisciplinary cooperation and mutual stimulation, since, in this emerging field, both technologies on the one hand, and new storytelling concepts and ideas for applications on the other hand, are evolving simultaneously. This accounts for the fact that some contributions address purely technological questions, whereas others present fundamental philosophical concepts. However, most authors search for a middle way that comprises both new technological and conceptual ideas.

Demos and Exhibitions

Designing and producing engaging and attractive Interactive Digital Storytelling applications requires more than the technology-driven approach. Moreover, a broad bandwidth of disciplines is involved. Artists and designers are entering the field of Interactive Digital Storytelling with an experimental and art-driven view. The exhibition was planned to encourage the interdisciplinary dialogue and open a space for approaching the fusion of art and technology in Interactive Digital Storytelling. On a more applied level, product and project demonstrations presented an overview on state-of-the-art Interactive Digital Storytelling applications.

Darmstadt, June 2004

Stefan Göbel
Ulrike Spierling
Anja Hoffmann
Ido Iurgel
Oliver Schneider
Johanna Dechau
Axel Feix

Acknowledgement and Sponsoring Institutions

The international conference series on Technologies for Interactive Digital Storytelling and Entertainment (TIDSE) was initiated by the Digital Storytelling group at ZGDV Darmstadt. Analogous to DISTEL 2000 and TIDSE 2003, the organization of TIDSE 2004 remained in the hands of that group.

However, TIDSE 2004 only came about thanks to the financial, moral and pragmatic support of various institutions: ZGDV Darmstadt e.V. hosted and sponsored the conference. The Foundation INI-GraphicsNet provided financial support for invited speakers. The Forum for Knowledge Media Design (KMD Forum) and the Virtual Human project (funded by the German Federal Ministry of Education and Research) supported the special conference topics on Virtual Human and Knowledge Media Design. ProRegio Darmstadt, as the local society for tourism marketing, and Cybernarium, the edutainment center for virtual worlds, supported the social events. Special thanks go to Hewlett-Packard and the Senckenberg Museum in Frankfurt for supporting the exhibition with appropriate hardware and a dinoskeleton prototype. Further moral support for the exhibition was provided by the European Commission in the context of the art-E-fact project. Finally we had the pleasure to welcome NVIDIA Corporation, which offered a prize for best paper. The HeyWall featured by NVIDIA Quadro FX delivered by PNY Technologies GmbH provided a great platform for high-end computer graphics presentations.

We really thank all of them for offering the opportunity to organize TIDSE 2004 in a way that provided a diversified scientific and social program. Especially we thank all members of the Scientific Board, and the Program and Exhibition Committees for their great job in defining the conference topics and reviewing the large number of submitted papers.

Zentrum für Graphische
Datenverarbeitung e.V.

INI-GraphicsNet

Committee Listings

Thomas Rist	German Research Center for Artificial Intelligence, DFKI GmbH, Saarbrücken, Germany
Andrew Stern	InteractiveStory.net, Brookline, USA
Wolfgang Wahlster	German Research Center for Artificial Intelligence, DFKI GmbH, Saarbrücken, Germany
R. Michael Young	North Carolina State University, Raleigh, USA

Program Committee

David Bearman	Archives and Museum Informatics, Toronto, Canada
Jay David Bolter	Center for New Media Research and Education, School of Literature, Communication and Culture, Atlanta, USA
Norbert Braun	Interactive Graphics System Group, Technical University of Darmstadt, Germany
Paul Brna	School of Computing and Mathematics, University of Northumbria, UK
Chris Crawford	www.erasmatazz.com, USA
Volker Coors	FH Stuttgart, University of Applied Sciences, Stuttgart, Germany
Kerstin Dautenhahn	Department of Computer Science, University of Hertfordshire, UK
Holger Diener	Fraunhofer Institut Graphische Datenverarbeitung, Rostock, Germany
Alan Dix	Computing Department, Lancaster University, UK
Ralf Dörner	Hochschule Harz, Wernigerode, Germany
Clive Fencott	University of Teesside, UK
Janet Finlay	Leeds Metropolitan University, UK
Doron Friedman	Department of Computer Science, University College London, UK
Li Gong	SAP Labs, Palo Alto, CA
Marc Hassenzahl	Technical University of Darmstadt, Germany
Xavier Marichal	alterface, Louvain-la-Neuve, Belgium
Maic Masuch	University of Magdeburg, Germany
Frank Nack	CWI, Amsterdam, The Netherlands
Stéphane Natkin	Cedric, France
Anton Nijholt	University of Twente, The Netherlands
Helmut Prendinger	University of Tokyo, Japan
Maria Roussou	makebelieve - immersive interactive new media, Athens, Greece
Leonie Schäfer	Fraunhofer Institute for Applied Information Technology, Germany
Gerard Subsol	University of Perpignan, France
Nicolas Szilas	IDtension, Paris, France

Exhibition Committee

Christian Bauer	International Center for New Media, Salzburg, Austria
Peter A. Bruck	International Center for New Media, Salzburg, Austria
Brunhild Bushoff	sagasnet, Munich, Germany
Frédéric Durieu	LeCielEstBleu, France
Susan Hazan	The Israel Museum, Jerusalem, Israel
Horst Hörtner	AEC Ars Electronica Center, Linz, Austria
Paul Kafno	HD Thames, London, UK
Lucia Leão	University of São Paulo, Brazil
Michael Lew	MIT Media Lab Europe, Dublin, Ireland
Alok Nandi	alterface, Louvain-la-Neuve, Belgium
Sally Jane Norman	École Superiéure de l'Image, Poitiers, France
Xavier Perrot	International Cultural Heritage Informatics Meeting, Paris, France
Gerfried Stocker	AEC Ars Electronica Center, Linz, Austria

Table of Contents

Authoring

Mobile

Learning

Embodied Agents and Meaningful Motion

Norman I. Badler

Computer and Information Science, Center for Human Modeling and Simulation, University of
Pennsylvania, Philadelphia, PA 19104-6389
badler@seas.upenn.edu

Abstract. We examine motion realism in terms of salient communicative features. We argue that motion is amenable to a parameterization based on Laban
Movement Analysis that yields real-time control over motion qualities, and that
these qualities carry discernable and useful non-verbal information about the
character's personality or emotional state.

Extended Abstract

The state-of-the-art in embodied agents has advanced to the point where real-time
animations of bodies and talking heads are commonplace. Our expectations for animated graphics are driven by the achievements of movie special effects and games.
These enterprises rely on talented animators who are able to imbue animated characters with personality, emotions, and intent.

Of course, such achievements whet the appetite for interactive computer-controlled
animated characters of similar quality and expressivity. Somehow that goal has been
harder to achieve. Visual realism is a natural point of attack, and modern graphics
boards and software support sufficient polygonal mesh and shader loads to produce
remarkable real-time characters (e.g., nVidia's "Dawn"). But visual realism begets
expectations that communicative intent will be equally realistic and transparent to the
viewer.

Communicative realism depends on animating body, limbs, and face to exacting
human perceptual standards. As all of us are experts in understanding the subtleties
of human movement, we are therefore equally expert in picking out anomalies and
incongruous behaviors, or else we read into it character personality. The implications
for storytelling are immense: successful games and movies tell stories with believable
or appropriate characters. To achieve the same level of storytelling veracity we need
adequate characters as well as a good story [1].

Having a longstanding interest in motion representation, we have approached it
through research into motion description systems. Among the many candidates, only
Laban Movement Analysis (LMA) has both intrigued and fascinating us for decades
[2]. Recently we built a computationally tractable real-time analog to LMA called
EMOTE [3]. EMOTE takes a movement "form" and applies "qualities" to vary its
performance; a loose comparison is that EMOTE supplies adverbs that modify actions
(verbs), though our work is quite different from Rose and Cohen's "verbs and adverbs" [4]. EMOTE can modify any virtual human limb motion, be it key-framed,
procedural, or motion captured.

S. Göbel et al. (Eds.): TIDSE 2004, LNCS 3105, pp. 1-2, 2004.

EMOTE's parameterization applies to limbs and torso motion, but from motion science we know that a character's nonverbal gestures are not just limited to its arms; rather, motion spreads throughout the body. We hypothesize that this consistency of motion is strongly supported by extending the EMOTE parameterization to other body components, such as the face [5], and prototype implementations show that this is reasonable. As we looked closer at facial animation, we discovered that better eye motions were needed, so we developed a model of eye saccades based on three states of the speaker: talking, listening, and thinking [6].

Our present work with EMOTE involves building recognizers for the EMOTE qualities from motion capture data. The motivation for this task is that people can easily observe attitudes and emotions in others, yet the vocabulary for such recognition has not been elucidated. Studies [7] of non-verbal behavior show that remarkably short exposures can yield personality assessments that strongly correlate with longer term observations. People must therefore be very good in picking up non-verbal features from thin slices (even 2 seconds!) of motion. We trained neural networks to recognize the EMOTE qualities in professional performers [8]. The initial results were quite encouraging, even if limited to one video camera view.

The significance of a computational ability to both synthesize and recognize EMOTE qualities is that it opens a wide door to the mutual understanding of non-verbal communication between real and virtual people. If we can identify, in real-time, the presence or absence of specific EMOTE qualities in a subject's movement, then we can provide virtual agents with valuable information about real people just by having them watch via motion capture or even video. The EMOTE qualities themselves are agnostic with respect to the emotion or personality tags that we place on people, and therefore we suspect that they form a less subjective movement descriptive layer to buffer between raw movement and semantic features.

References

1. Gratch, J., Rickel, J., Andre, E., Badler, N., Cassell, J., Petajan, E.: Creating interactive virtual humans: Some assembly required. IEEE Intelligent Systems (2002)
2. Badler, N.: A representation for natural human movement. In Gray, J. (ed.): Dance Technology I, AAHPERD Publications, Reston, VA (1989) 23-44
3. Chi, D., Costa, M., Zhao, L., Badler, N.: The EMOTE model for Effort and Shape. ACM SIGGRAPH, New Orleans, LA (2000) 173-182
4. Rose, C., Cohen, M., Bodenheimer, B.: Verbs and adverbs: Multidimensional motion interpolation. IEEE Comp. Graphics & Appli. 18(5) (1998) 32-40
5. Byun, M. Badler, N.: FacEMOTE: Qualitative parametric modifiers for facial animations. Symp. on Computer Animation, San Antonio, TX (2002) 65-71
6. Lee, S., Badler, J. Badler, N.: Eyes alive. ACM Trans. Graphics 21(3) (2002) 637-644
7. Ambady, N, Rosenthal, R.: Half a minute: Predicting teacher evaluations from thin slices of nonverbal behavior and physical attractiveness. J. of Personality and Social Psychology 64 (3) (1993) 431-441
8. Zhao, L., Badler, N.: Acquiring and Validating Motion Qualities from Live Limb Gestures. In review, Graphical Models

Natural Language Understanding in Façade: Surface-Text Processing

Michael Mateas*[1] and Andrew Stern*[2]

* co-authors listed alphabetically
[1] College of Computing and LCC, Georgia Tech,
michaelm@cc.gatech.edu
[2] InteractiveStory.net
andrew@interactivestory.net

1 Introduction

Façade is a real-time, first-person dramatic world in which the player, visiting the married couple Grace and Trip at their apartment, quickly becomes entangled in the high-conflict dissolution of their marriage. The *Façade* interactive drama integrates real-time, autonomous believable agents, drama management for coordinating plot-level interactivity, and broad, shallow support for natural language understanding and discourse management. In previous papers, we have described the motivation for *Façade's* interaction design and architecture [13, 14], described ABL, our believable agent language [9, 12], and presented overviews of the entire architecture [10, 11]. In this paper we focus on *Façade's* natural language processing (NLP) system, specifically the understanding (NLU) portion that extracts discourse acts from player-typed surface text.

The *Façade* NLP system accepts surface text utterances from the player and decides what reaction(s) the characters should have to the utterance. For example, if the player types "Grace isn't telling the truth", the NLP system is responsible for determining that this is a form of criticism, and deciding what reaction Grace and Trip should have to Grace being criticized in the current context. General natural language understanding is of course a notoriously difficult problem. Building a system that could understand open-ended natural language utterances would require common sense reasoning, the huge open-ended mass of sensory-motor competencies, knowledge and reasoning skills which human beings make use of in their everyday dealings with the world. While *Façade* is a micro-domain, a dramatically-heightened representation of a specific situation, not the whole world, there are still no general theories, techniques or systems which can handle the syntactic, semantic and pragmatic breadth of the language use which occurs in *Façade*. Instead, *Façade* makes use of broad, shallow, author-intensive techniques to understand natural language typed by the player.

Our approach in *Façade* it to view the natural language understanding problem as a dialog management problem, focusing on the pragmatic effects of language (what a language utterance does to the world) rather than on the syntax (the form of surface text) or semantics (meaning) of language. In dialog management systems (e.g. Collagen [19, 7], Trains [1, 4]), language use situations are seen as consisting of a discourse context within which conversants exchange speech acts. A conversant's sur face utterance is interpreted *as* a speech act in a manner dependent on the current discourse context. In *Façade*, discourse acts have been chosen that are appropriate for the conflict-filled interaction with Grace and Trip. This approach of choosing discourse acts that align with player narrative actions has similarities to the approach described in [2]. The discourse context is determined by dramatic beats, the smallest unit of dramatic action, and the "atoms" out of which *Façade* stories are constructed [10].

NLP is divided into two phases: phase 1 maps surface text into discourse acts representing the pragmatic effects of an utterance, while phase 2 maps discourse acts into one or more (joint) character responses. Where phase 1 determines, in a context specific way, *which discourse act* was produced by the player, phase 2 determines *what effect* this act will have, including, potentially, how it changes the discourse context. It is within Phase 2 that a stack of discourse contexts is actively maintained and used to determine a context-appropriate response to a given discourse act. Phase 1 only makes use of discourse contexts insofar that different collections of phase 1 rules may be turned on and off in different contexts. The rest of this paper focuses on the phase 1 (NLU) pipeline.

2 Introduction to Surface Text Rules

Forward chaining rules map surface text to discourse acts. Some rules map specific patterns of surface text directly to intermediate meaning representations, while other rules combine intermediate meanings to form more complex meanings. Eventually the process of mapping islands of surface text into intermediate representations, and combining these representations, produces the final meaning, consisting of one or more discourse acts.

```
"hello"  →  iGreet
"grace"  →  iCharacter(Grace)
iGreet AND iCharacter(?x)  →  DAGreet(?x)
```

Fig. 1. Pseudo-code for simple greeting rules

For example, imagine that the player types "Hello Grace". The first rule in Figure 1 matches on the appearance of the word "hello" anywhere in the text and asserts an iGreet intermediate fact. The second rule matches on the appearance of the word "grace" anywhere in the text and asserts an (iCharacter Grace) fact. The third rule matches on the occurrence of the two intermediate facts and asserts a (DAGreet Grace) discourse act fact, indicating that a greeting was directed at Grace. The rule makes use of a variable; ?x binds to the argument of iCharacter on the left hand side and brings this value over to the assertion of DAGreet on the right hand side of the rule. In order to capture more ways of saying hello (e.g. "how're you doing?", "how's it going?", "what's up", etc.), additional iGreet rules can be written without changing the iCharacter or DAGreet rules.

3 Discourse Acts

Our current set of discourse acts appears in table 1 below. All player utterances map into one or more of these discourse acts. Phase 1 processing is a strong many-to-few mapping – the huge, rich range of all possible strings a player could type is mapped onto this small set of discourse acts. Besides ignoring any nuance in the tone of the player's text, the system also focuses almost exclusively on the pragmatics of the utterance, ignoring most of the semantics (denotative meaning).

Table 1. *Façade* discourse acts

Representation of Discourse Acts	*Pragmatic Meaning of Discourse Acts*
(DAAgree ?char)	Agree with a character. (e.g. "certainly", no doubt", "I would love to")
(DADisagree ?char)	Disagree with a character. (e.g. "No way", "Fat chance", "Get real", "Not by a long shot")
(DAPositiveExcl ?char)	A positive exclamation, potentially directed at a character. ("Yeah", "Wow", "Breath of fresh air")
(DANegExcl ?char)	A negative exclamation, potentially directed at a character. (e.g. "Damn", "That really sucks", "How awful", "I can't stomach that", "D'oh!")
(DAExpress ?char ?type)	Express an emotion, potentially directed at a character. The emotion types are *happy* ("I'm thrilled", ":-)"), *sad* ("That bums me out", ":-("), *laughter* ("ha ha"), and angry ("It really pisses me off", "grrrr").
(DAMaybeUnsure ?char)	Unsure or indecisive, potentially directed at a character. This discourse act is usually a response to a question. (e.g. "I don't know", "maybe", "I guess so", "You've lost me")
(DAThank ?char)	Thank a character (e.g. "Thanks a lot")
(DAGreet ?char)	Greet a character. (e.g. "Hello", "What's up")
(DAAlly ?char)	Ally with a character. (e.g. "I like you", "You are my friend", "I'm here for you")
(DAOppose ?char)	Oppose a character. (e.g. "Kiss off", "You're the worst, "I hate you", "Get out of my life")
(DADontUnderstand ?char)	Don't understand a character utterance, or the current situation (e.g. "I'm confused", "I don't get it", "What are you talking about")
(DAApologize ?char)	Apologize to a character. (e.g. "I'm sorry", "My bad", "How can I make this up to you")
(DAPraise ?char)	Praise a character. (e.g. "You're a genius", "What a sweetheart you are", "You've got good ideas")
(DACriticize ?char ?level)	Criticize a character. There are two levels of criticism, *light* ("You're weird", "Don't be so up tight"), and *harsh* ("Idiot", "What a dipshit")
(DAFlirt ?char)	Flirt with a character. (e.g. "You look gorgeous", "Kiss me", "Let's get together alone sometime")
(DAPacify ?char)	Pacify a character. (e.g. "Calm down", "Relax, guys" "Keep your shirt on", "Take it easy")

Representation of Discourse Acts	*Pragmatic Meaning of Discourse Acts*
`(DAExplain ?param ?char)`	Give an explanation about the social situation to a character (e.g. "Grace is lying", "Trip is having an affair", "You're not happy together")
`(DAAdvice ?param ?char)`	Give advice to a character. (e.g. "You should get a divorce", "Try to work it out")
`(DAReferTo ?char ?obj)`	Refer to an object, potentially directed at a character. There are a number of different objects in the room, including the *couch* ("I like the couch"), the *wedding picture* ("Your wedding picture looks nice"), and *paintings* ("Where did you get these paintings").
`(DAIntimate ?char)`	Ask a character to share their thoughts or feelings with you. (e.g. "What's wrong", "Let it all out", "Talk to me")
`(DAGoodbye ?char)`	Say goodbye to a character. (e.g. "Catch you later", "So long", "I'm out of here")
`(DAInappropriate ?char)`	Utterances containing vulgar or socially inappropriate words or phrases. (e.g. "blow job", "slut")
`(DAMisc ?char ?type)`	Miscellaneous specialized discourse acts, often specific to certain beats or contexts. The *type* encodes the specialized act, e.g. *ask for drink* ("I'd like a drink"), and *should I leave* ("Is this a bad time", "Should I leave").
`(DASystemCannotUnderstand)`	Catch-all for all utterances which trigger no other discourse acts.

4 The Template Language

The rules which map surface text to discourse acts are written in a custom rule language that compiles to Jess [6], a java implementation of the CLIPS rule language [15]. The custom rule language is a superset of Jess, adding an embedded template description language that allows compact descriptions of surface text patterns to appear on the left hand side of rules. An initial implementation of the template compiler was done by Mehmet Fidanboylu, an undergraduate working under Michael's direction.

```
;; A template rule for agreement
(defrule global-agree-rule1
  (template (toc (love (to | it | that))))
 =>
(assert (iAgree)))
```

Fig. 2. Rule example using the template sublanguage

The rule in Figure 2 contains a template test on the LHS – a specification of a pattern that will be tested over the input string. If the input string matches this pattern, the RHS asserts an `iAgree` fact (an intermediate fact) that will eventually be combined with an intermediate fact indicating the character addressed (potentially the null character `none`) to produce the final `DAAgree` fact.

4.1 The Pattern Language

The sub-language for specifying template patterns consists of a combination of regular expressions and occurrence expressions. Regular expressions are sensitive to the positions of terms in a pattern – for the regular expression `(love it)` to match a string, "it" must appear right after "love" in the string. Occurrence expressions don't care about position, only term occurrence – for the expression `(tand love it)` to match a string, "love" and "it" must both appear in the string, but do not have to be contiguous and can appear in either order. Note that when an occurrence expression is embedded in a regular expression, the occurrence expression only tests across the substring delimited by the regular expression. Examples of all the template pattern language expressions appear in Table 2.

Table 2. Template pattern language expressions

Example Expressions	*Meaning*
`(X Y)`	An *and* regular expression. Matches an input string if it consists of X immediately followed by Y.
`(X | Y)`	An *or* regular expression. Matches an input string if it consists of X or Y.
`([X])`	An *optional* regular expression. Matches an input string if it consists of X or nothing.
`*`	A *match all* wildcard. Matches any number of words in an input string.
`?`	A *match one* wildcard. Matches any one word in an input string.
`(tand X Y)`	An *and* occurs expression (tand is short for template-and). Matches an input string if it contains X and Y in any order.
`(tor X Y)`	An *or* occurs expression (tor is short for template-or). Matches a input string if it contains X or Y.
`(toc X)`	An *occurrence* occurs expression (toc is short for template-occurs). Matches an input string if it contains X.
`(tnot x)`	A *not* occurs expression (tnot is short for template-not). Matches an input string if X does not occur in it.

The `tor`, `tand` and `toc` expressions are syntactic sugar for classes of regular expressions: `(tor X Y)` can be rewritten as `((* X *) | (* Y *))` (toc is a special case of `tor`), and `(tand X Y)` can be rewritten as `((* X * Y *) | (* Y * X *))`.

Of course the various expressions can be recursively nested to produce compound patterns such as (tand (X (tnot Y)) Z) or (X | ([(tor Y Z)] W)).

Individual words are not the only atomic terms in the pattern language: besides matching an individual word, one can also match a positional fact, match an entire collection of words determined by WordNet [3] expansion, and match stemmed forms of words, using a WordNet stemming package.

4.2 Matching Positional Facts

Facts asserted by template rules can be *positional facts*. A positional fact includes information about the substring range matched by the rule which asserted the fact, and, potentially, author-determined information. Positional facts can then be matched as atomic terms within other templates. An example appears in Figure 3.

The first rule, positional_Is, asserts a positional fact (iIs ?startpos ?endpos) when an "is" word is recognized, such as "is" "seems", or "looks". The appearance of the special variables ?startpos and ?endpos is what makes this a positional fact – these variables are bound to the starting and ending position of the substring matched by the template.

```
;; Rule for recognizing positional "is" fact
(defrule positional_Is
   (template (tor am are is seem seems sound sounds look
                   looks))
   =>
   (assert (iIs ?startpos ?endpos)))
;; Rule for recognizing positional "positive
;; description" fact
(defrule positional_PersonPosDesc
   (template (tor buddy comrade confidant friend genius
                   go-getter pal sweetheart))
   =>
   (assert (iPersonPosDesc ?startpos ?endpos)))
;; Rule for recognizing praise
(defrule Praise_you_are_PersonPos
   (template ({iPersonPosDesc} | (you [{iIs}] [a | my]
              {iPersonPosDesc} *)))
   =>
   (assert (iPraise)))
```

Fig. 3. Example rule for recognizing *praise* discourse act using positional facts

The second rule, positional_PersonPosDesc, asserts a positional fact when a word or phrase that is a positive description of a person appears.

The last rule, Praise_you_are_PersonPos, one of the rules for recognizing *praise* discourse acts, recognizes praises that consist of only a positive description (e.g. "friend"), or of a sentence of the form "You are <positive description>" (e.g. "You are a friend"). When an atomic term appear in curly braces, this tells the template compiler to treat the term as the name for a positional fact, and to use the positional information (start position and end position) associated with the fact to determine if the pattern matches.

Positional facts make the template language as powerful as a context free grammar – when template patterns are combined with arbitrary Jess matches on the left-hand-side, the language becomes Turing complete. However, the *spirit* of the template language is to recognize simple text patterns and map them to discourse acts, not to build grammars that accept all and only the set of grammatically correct strings. Positional rules such as those in Figure 3 can be viewed as noise-tolerant parsing rules.

4.3 Term Retraction

When a template matches terms (words and patterns) within a string, it can remove terms to prevent other templates from matching on the same terms. This is particularly useful when matching idiomatic phrases (e.g., "fat chance") that could potentially trigger other templates that match on the same words according to their more typical meanings. The retraction operator "–" can be placed in front of any term in a LHS template pattern; if the rule matches, the marked words are retracted from the internal representation of the string, and any facts that were asserted directly or indirectly from those words are also retracted (compiled template rules enforce proper truth maintenance). The retraction operator can be thought of as creating an implicit retraction action on the right hand side of the rule.

4.4 Compilation Strategy

Input strings are represented as a collection of facts, one fact for each word. Each unique word is represented as a unique word occurrence fact; each of these unique facts includes the start position and end position of the word, which are always the same[1]. For example, for performing template matching on the input string "I like it", the string is represented as a collection of three facts: (wo-i 1 1) (wo-like 2 2) (wo-it 3 3). The fact names for each word in a string are constructed by appending the word onto "wo-" (for *word occurrence*).

The template compiler compiles template patterns into collections of rules whose LHSs ultimately test word occurrence facts. Thus word occurrence (wo) facts are chained together by generated rules to produce intermediate phrase occurrence (po) facts. The intermediate phrase occurrence facts are ultimately tested on the LHS of the authored rules, which assert author defined facts (e.g. discourse acts, positional facts). By representing the individual words of an input string as word occurrence facts, and compiling templates into networks of rules which test these facts, the expensive string tests which would potentially have to be run for every template rule

---

[1] Even though words always have the same start and end position, explicitly representing the start and end position makes it easier for compiler generated rules to combine word occurrence facts with phrase facts, which *do* have different start and end positions.

LHS are eliminated. Further matching efficiencies are gained through Jess' use of the Rete [5] matching algorithm.

5 Idioms for Template Rules

The general (non-beat specific) template rules are organized in the following way. First, a collection of high salience template rules recognize generically useful patterns and synonyms. An example is the "is" rule in Figure 3; others include sets of synonyms for positive and negative words, greets, flirts, insults, curses, and so on.

Salience declarations can be used to declare that some rules should be preferred over others. We use salience to create tiers of template rules, with higher salience rules recognizing lower-level features than lower-salience rules.

After general low-level patterns, the next (lower-salience) tier of rules recognizes idiomatic expressions. Each idiomatic rule uses the retraction operator to retract the idiomatic expression once it is found – this prevents other rules from incorrectly matching on individual words in the idiomatic expression. There are generally a large number of idiomatic expression rules for each discourse act (e.g. agree) or sub-discourse act "meaning" (e.g. idioms for "person positive description", used by the praise rule in Figure 3). To compile an initial list of such idioms, we examined the phrase resources [8, 16, 17, 18] to compile a large number of expressions (~ 9000 phrases); ~1000 of these were applicable to our domain and were categorized in terms of our discourse acts.

The next tier of rules uses retraction to cancel out adjacent negative words. For example, for the surface text "you are not bad", the words "not" and "bad" get retracted and replaced with iAgree, as if the original surface text had been "you are good".

The final tier(s) of rules consists of keyword and combination rules. Keyword rules watch for individual words or short, non-idiomatic phrases that are indicative of a discourse act or sub-discourse act meanings. The positional_PersonPos Description rule in Figure 3 is an example of a sub-discourse act keyword rule. Discourse act keyword rules similarly match on words or short phrases, but directly assert a discourse act. In an attempt to reduce the number of false positives, discourse act keyword rules tend to impose a limit on the total number of words that can appear in the surface utterance. Unlike sub-discourse act keyword rules, which can depend on combination rules further along the chain to impose additional constraints, discourse act keyword rules are more likely to be fooled by a longer utterance because something else in the utterance contradicts the keyword assumption.

Combination rules, such as the Praise_you_are_PersonPos rule in Figure 3, combine intermediate positional facts, and impose constraints on the relative positions of these facts, to recognize discourse acts.

Anaphora resolution occurs by simply looking up a stored referent for each anaphoric reference. In the *Façade* architecture, the autonomous characters are responsible for updating referents as they deliver different dialog lines, particularly the referent for "it".

6   Templates and Ungrammatical Inputs

Template rules tend to be promiscuous, mapping a large number of ungrammatical inputs to discourse acts. Keyword rules, in particular, tend to produce false positives. False positives can be reduced by writing ever more elaborate combination rules (in essence, moving towards full parsing), but at the expense of increasing false negatives (player utterances that should be recognized as a discourse act but aren't).

Given this tradeoff, the template rules for *Façade* err on the side of being overly permissive. This is based on the design approach that it is more interesting for the characters to eke some meaning out of a broad set of utterances, and thus have some interesting response for this broad set, than to only have interesting responses for a narrow set, and respond with some form of "huh?" to the rest. While players will sometimes try to break the NLU by seeing what kinds of ludicrous sentences they can get the characters to respond to, the templates are designed not to robustly support this meta-activity, but rather to extract meaning from a broad a collection of "natural" utterances likely to arise during the course of playing *Façade*.

7   Relationship to Chatterbots

Our approach for mapping surface text to discourse acts, while bearing some similarities to chatterbot approaches such as AIML [20], significantly extends the capabilities of these approaches. As AIML is representative of contemporary chatterbot language processing, here we briefly summarize AIML's features. In AIML, the fundamental unit is a pattern-template pair, where patterns match player input and templates produce output text in response to the player input matching the corresponding pattern (note that in our NLU approach, we use the word "template" for what AIML calls a "pattern"). AIML pattern syntax is a subset of regular expression syntax, excluding regexp-or and optional subexpressions. Templates can recursively invoke pattern matching, potentially introducing new words into the recursively matched expression. Templates can get and set (side-effecting) the value of unary predicates; unary predicates *cannot* be accessed in patterns. AIML's support for anaphora resolution is similar to ours, using a collection of unary predicates to keep track of the current referents for he, she and it, placing the burden of maintaining the current referents on the author. Pattern matching can depend on the bot's previous utterance, introducing limited support for discourse context.

There are a number of differences between our approach and AIML.

1. Our NLU template language doesn't map surface text directly to a reaction, but rather to a discourse act; phase II of our NLP processing is responsible for selecting a reaction to the discourse act. This separation supports reasoning that can take into account more sophisticated discourse context than just the last agent utterance. When given ambiguous input, our NLU system produces all possible interpretations, letting the next layer of the NLP decide which discourse act(s) to respond to. AIML uses implementation-dependent, non-author-accessible heuristics to decide which single response to give.

2. Positional facts are the mechanism through which we introduce recursion into the NLU matching process. The support for the inclusion of author-determined

information in positional facts, plus the ability to match facts and chain variables on the left-hand-side of our NLU rules, makes our rule language more expressive than AIML. Our framework supports rule strategies ranging from simple pattern matching, through (noise tolerant) context-free and context-sensitive parsing, to arbitrary computation, all of which can co-exist within a single rule set.

3. Author-declared rule salience allows authors to specify their own tiers of rule processing. In contrast, the matching order for AIML patterns is fixed by the AIML interpreter.
4. Retraction supports more robust handling of idioms and double negatives.
5. Wordnet expansions and stemming supports the matching of a wider variety of player inputs.

8 Experiences with the Template Language

In the course of authoring *Façade* we've written ~800 template rules, which compile to ~6800 Jess rules. On a 2GHz machine, with the rest of the *Façade* AI running, as well as the animation engine, the rules fire to completion (generally proposing several discourse acts) in 300 milliseconds or less, giving us adequate real-time performance.

As we continue play testing, we use session traces to find NLU failures and modify the rules. However, preliminary play testing has found our initial set of rules to be surprisingly robust. The context of the *Façade* dramatic situation does, as we'd hoped, guide the player to use language appropriate to the situation.

References

1. Allen, J., Byron, D., Dzikovska, M, Ferguson, G., Galescu, L., and Stent, A. 1998. An Architecture for a Generic Dialog Shell. *Natural Language Engineering* 6 (3).
2. Cavazza, M., Martin, O., Charles, F., Mead, S. and Marichal, X. Users Acting in Mixed Reality Storytelling, *Second International Conference on Virtual Storytelling (ICVS 2003)*, Toulouse, France, pp. 189-197.
3. Fellbaum, C. (Ed.). 1998. Wordnet:An Electronic Lexical Database. MIT Press.
4. Ferguson, G., Allen, J. F., Miller, B. W., and Ringger, E. K. 1996. *The design and implementation of the TRAINS-96 system: A prototype mixed-initiative planning assistant.* TRAINS Technical Note 96-5, Department of Computer Science, University of Rochester, Rochester, NY.
5. Forgy, C. L. 1982. Rete: A Fast Algorithm for the Many Pattern/ Many Object Pattern Match Problem. *Artificial Intelligence* 19, 17-37.
6. Friedman-Hill, E. 1995-2003. Jess, the Rule Engine for Java. Sandia National Labs. http://herzberg.ca.sandia.gov/jess/.
7. Lesh, N., Rich, C., and Sidner, C. 1999 Using Plan Recognition in Human-Computer Collaboration. In *Proceedings of the Seventh International Conference on User Modeling.* Banff, Canada.
8. Magnuson, W. 1995-2002. English Idioms, Sayings, and Slang. http://home.t-online.de/home/toni.goeller/idiom_wm/.

9. Mateas, M. and Stern, A. 2004. A Behavior Language: Joint Action and Behavior Idioms, in Prendinger, Helmut and Ishizuka, Mitsuru (Eds.), *Life-Like Characters: Tools, Affective Functions, and Applications*, Springer-Verlag, 2004.
10. Mateas, M and Stern, A. 2003a. Integrating plot, character and natural language processing in the interactive drama *Façade*, *1ˢᵗ International Conference on Technologies for Interactive Digital Storytelling and Entertainment (TIDSE '03)*, Darmstadt, Germany , March 24 – 26, 2003 .
11. Mateas, M and Stern, A. 2003b. Façade, an experiment in building a fully-realized interactive drama, *Game Developers Conference (GDC '03)*, San Jose, CA, USA, March 4 – 8, 2003.
12. Mateas, M and Stern, A. 2002. A behavior language for story-based believable agents, *IEEE Intelligent Systems*, July/August 2002, 17 (4), 39-47.
13. Mateas, M., and Stern, A. 2001. Façade. *Digital Arts and Culture* 2001. Brown University, Providence RI. 2001.
14. Mateas, M. and Stern, A. 2000. Towards Integrating Plot and Character for Interactive Drama. In *Working notes of the Social Intelligent Agents: The Human in the Loop Symposium*. AAAI Fall Symposium Series. Menlo Park, CA: AAAI Press. 2000.
15. NASA. 1985-2002. C Language Integrated Production Systems (CLIPS). Originally developed at NASA's Johnson Space Center. http://www.ghg.net/clips/WhatIsCLIPS.html.
16. Oliver, D. 1995-2002. The ESL Idiom Page.
    http://www.eslcafe.com/idioms/id-mngs.html.
17. PhraseFinder. 2002. Phrases, Sayings, Quotes and Cliches at The Phrase Finder.
    http://phrases.shu.ac.uk/index.html.
18. Phrase Thesaurus. 2002. http://www.phrasefinder.co.uk/index.html.
19. Rich, C., and Sidner, C. 1998. COLLAGEN: A Collaboration Manager for Software Interface Agents. *User Modeling and User-Adapted Interaction*. Vol. 8, No. 3/4, pp. 315-350.
20. Wallace, R. The Anatomy of ALICE. http://www.alicebot.org/anatomy.html.

Stepping into the Interactive Drama

Nicolas Szilas

LINC – University of Paris VIII
IUT de Montreuil
140, rue de la Nouvelle France
93100 Montreuil, France
n.szilas@iut.univ-paris8.fr

Abstract. Achieving a successful Interactive Drama where the user can act as a character in the story requires not only finding an algorithmic solution for combining interactivity and narrativity, but also interfacing those algorithms with the user. This paper focuses on the way in which the user can choose the actions of the character. Three specific issues are discussed: the variety of choices proposed to the user, the need for the user to anticipate his/her future possibilities for actions and the time necessary to enter the action. This allows us to propose a taxonomy of different user interfaces and to evaluate the advantages and drawbacks of each category of interface. This should serve as a guideline for the design of user interfaces for Interactive Drama.

1 Introduction

This paper addresses the specific kind of interactive dramatic experience on the computer, where the user is a character in the drama. In short, we call this an Interactive Drama (ID), even if this term sometimes covers a larger set of experiences. Even if the idea of building an ID has arose for some years now [3,9,13] and despite some research effort on the subject [4,11,15,21,22,23], ID appears to be a quite difficult issue, which requires the collaboration of various disciplines.

Within the *IDtension* project [8], we study ID from three different but interrelated approaches [18]: the algorithmic approach [19,20,21], the author approach[18] and the user approach. This paper focuses on this last approach. In particular, it aims at providing some guidelines for the design of how the user enters his/her actions.

This topic has been rarely tackled even if several systems propose their own method for entering the action. This is certainly due to the fact that this issue is seen as a design issue, only involving an ergonomic design of the user interface. However, we believe that this issue is far more fundamental and that it is linked to the basic properties of ID.

This paper has two main goals:
-   help the design of an ID;
-   provide a set of conceptual tools to better analyze interfaces used in ID systems or related systems (like video games).

S. Göbel et al. (Eds.): TIDSE 2004, LNCS 3105, pp. 14–25, 2004.

This paper is divided into three sections, each one focuses on a specific feature of ID. From the careful examination of each feature, we draw some conclusions regarding the way to enter actions in an ID. We do not consider that we have exhausted the subject, other features of ID will be added later to this study.

2   The Variety of Choices

2.1   The Choice Problem

The most notable difference between ID and existing forms of interactive narrative (hypertext, Interactive Fiction, adventure video games, etc.) is the number of narrative actions that the user can undertake (the range of actions, to use Brenda Laurel's terminology [9 p. 20]). In an adventure video game for example, only a few actions really have a significant effect on the story (usually, only one action makes the story go forward, others are "fails"). This difference is particularly marked in the dialogs: being that a key feature of interactive drama is the dialogs, ID allows a user to have a wide range of dialog choices during the interaction [5,17,19]. For example, if one considers only one type of dialog act such as "ask for assistance", suppose that the user's character has to perform 5 tasks and that there are 5 other characters, it makes 25 possible "ask for assistance" acts. In *IDtension*, there are many types of acts. We could observe experimentally the fast growing number of choices given to the user [19].

Choosing among a large number of actions is a problem. Using a choice list of actions is obviously unsatisfactory if the number of actions exceeds 10. We call this problem the "choice problem".

In the example above, it is assumed that the algorithms for ID have the possibility to interpret all the actions and produce the expected effect. As a consequence, by giving all these meaningful choices, such an ID provides agency, as defined by J. Murray: "the satisfying power to take meaningful action and see the results of our decisions and choices" [13, p. 126]. The "choice problem" can be seen as the other side of the coin of agency in ID.

2.2   The Interface Mapping Function

In order to properly classify the various types of interfaces that can be proposed to cope with this problem, we introduce the following notions:
- when the user is to choose an action, there is a set of actions that the system can logically process as a significant input to its narrative engine. Let us call this set L.
- at the same time, there is a set of actions that the user can physically perform and which she/he can interpret as significant from a narrative point of view. Let us call this set P. For example, a simple move of the character is not part

of this set, while revealing an intention to another character would be part of this set.

- Let us define the ideal interface mapping function f the relation from the set P to the set L, which associate whenever possible the physical action to the proper logical action (see Fig. 1). By "proper" we mean that the interpretation by the machine of $f(x)$ is the same as the interpretation of x by the user, x being an element of P.

- Let us define the actual mapping function g the relation from the set P to the set L, which is implemented by the system and which associate, whenever possible, a physical action to a logical action.

The difference between f and g lies in the fact that in some cases, the theoretical function f is not easily programmed on a computer. Initially, we will consider that f and g are similar and we will only reason on f.

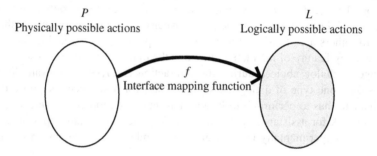

Fig. 1. The mapping function

The distinction between P and L looks similar to the distinction between perceived affordances and real affordances in ecological psychology and Human-Computer Interaction. However, we are not concerned with the immediate possibility of action like moving within the virtual world but with the higher level narrative actions, and the corresponding affordances, usually involving language. Higher level affordances have been discussed in the context of ID in terms of material and formal affordances [10]. While material affordances correspond to the set P, formal affordances, as defined by Mateas, are different from the set L, because they are linked to the *motivation* to act ("why [players] should take action within the story world *at all*").

Let us specify that f and g are effectively functions (an element cannot be in relation with two elements) because a physical action is always interpreted univocally by the computer.

Depending on the simple mathematical properties of f, one obtains various types of interfaces for an ID, as illustrated in Fig. 2.

If f is not total, that is if some physical actions cannot be associated to logical actions, then we have a *free interface*. Indeed, the user is free to perform some actions, which are not interpreted by the computer.

If f is not surjective, that is if some logical actions cannot be reached by any physical action, then we have a *filtering interface*. Indeed, the interface acts as a filter, forbidding some logical actions to be chosen by the user.

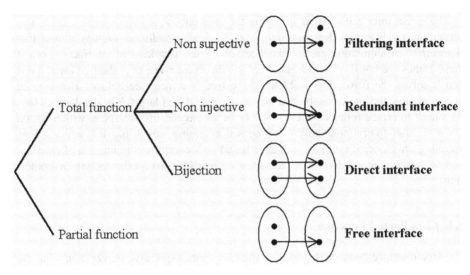

Fig. 2. Taxonomy of various interfaces for ID depending of the properties of the interface mapping function.

If f is not injective, that is if two different physical actions are associated to the same logical action, then we have a *redundant interface*.

Finally, if f is bijective (injective and surjective), that is if there is a one-to-one mapping between the physical actions and the logical actions, then we have a *direct interface*. Indeed, the proposed actions are exactly the logical actions.

In the following, we discuss in detail each of these categories of interfaces.

2.3 f Is a Total Function

If f is total, three cases are worth studying: the non surjective case, the non injective case and the bijective case (see above).

The filtering interface hides the complexity of the set L by only providing a limited set of options. Typically, it corresponds to the use of interface agents such as "wizards" or anthropomorphic agents. For example, in an ID the filtering interface consists in proposing to the user the choice of some of the most relevant actions even if the system could interpret more actions. The filtering interface solves the choice problem, because the size of L is hidden. This kind of interface, however, is problematic when the user wants to perform an action, which is not proposed. In that case, frustation takes place. We will discuss again this kind of interfaces in Section 3.

The redundant interface is classical in the design of user interfaces. However, in the case of ID, it does not solve our choice problem, because the redundancy increases the number of choices rather than decreasing it. Note that some free interfaces can have some redundancy, but it is not labeled a redundant interface in our taxonomy.

The direct interface consists in letting the user choose among a large selection of actions, through a well designed interface. Typically, real-time strategy games like *Warcraft*™ or simulation games like *The Sims*™ use that kind of interfaces, even if these games are not ID. The advantage of the direct interface over the free interface is that it solves the frustration problem of the free interface (see below). However, it does not solve the choice problem a priori, because if L is large, P is also large. Thus, the direct interface relies on the feasibility of an easy-to-use interface, which would allow the user to ergonomically select an action among tens of possible actions. Furthermore, this kind of interface, which is based on a complex combination of classical user interface components (lists, buttons, etc.) tends to disrupt the feeling of immersion.

2.4 f Is a Partial Function

The free interface consists in giving to the user more expressive power than what the machine can really interpret. Typically, this interface uses a free text or free speech interface for entering the action. This type of interface has been chosen by several research projects on ID [5,11,16].

Among free interfaces are *natural interfaces*, which use free speech, free text, body gesture, etc. and *verb-based interfaces* (there might exist other types of free interfaces that we omit or forget to mention). Verb-based interfaces are used in some adventure video games (like the *Indiana Jones* series from *LucasArt*): the interface contains a panel with several clickable verbs: to choose the action, the user clicks on a verb, then on a point on the screen. For example, the user would click on "Push" and click on an object, to move it. These verb-based interfaces are free interfaces because the user could produce many more actions that the game could interpret.

The main advantage of the free interface is that it allows the user to easily choose among a large set of actions since the interface is closer to the human means of expression (especially for natural interfaces).

The problem of the free interface is that the user can choose an action that the machine cannot take into account. One can only hope that in the future with the improvement of narrative engines the set L will become larger, however, it will never cover the range of a free text or a free speech interface. Note that this problem is independent of the limitation of the language technology used to decode the user input (it remains even if f and g are identical).

With the free interface, the user has to control and limit his/her language to what the machine understands. The question is whether the user will manage to do this naturally or if this will provoke a feeling of frustration. This is related to the design of the free interface, whether it affords actions in P that are in L or not. By proposing two explicitly choices which are not in L , the verb-based interface typically generates bad perceived affordances.

Note that the classical turnaround of this problem is to add a special element in L which means "I don't understand", and which encourages the user to change or rephrase his/her action. While video games have used this technique in a basic way, there exists a more subtle way to do it which consists in having numerous general reactions to a non interpreted event [17].

It is formally possible for free interfaces also to distinguish the non-injective and non-surjective cases. Practically, the free interfaces aim to be surjective (no filtering): it is their raison d'être (even if g could be non-surjective, for technical problems or limitations). The natural interfaces are redundant (f is not injective) while the verb-based interfaces are not (f is injective).

2.5 Conclusion on the Taxonomy

Until now, we have only considered a single mapping function f, hence a single type of interface. However, it is conceivable that a more complex interface could combine several modes of interaction. To each mode is associated a set P and a mapping function f. For example, the user is proposed a small set of actions, (filtering interface) if no action is satisfactory, he/she will switch to a text field to type another action (natural free interface). Such "hybrid" interfaces might be interesting to explore in order to combine some advantages of the various types of interfaces mentioned above.

The rigorous study of the mapping function has allowed us to classify the interfaces regarding how they tackle the choice problem. However, we need a deeper analysis to better understand the differences and limitations of those various types if interfaces. Some elements of such an analysis are proposed in the next section.

3 The Anticipation of Action

3.1 Anticipation in Classical and Interactive Narratives

The force of any narrative lies in the way the audience's expectations are handled.
Umberto Eco's "inferential walks" refer to the various paths the reader imagines at a given point of a narrative [6]. At each path is associated a subjective judgment of possibility. The author activity consists in planning the reader's inferences in order to maintain his/her interest. The reader tries to anticipate the evolution of the story, making good and bad guesses, which provides for an enjoyable and playful experience.
Narrative effects like suspense or surprise are directly related to this play. These inferences are performed according to some sort of rules, most of which do not show in the narrative itself: the reader uses his/her own encyclopedia, which contains all his/her knowledge of the real world, on the genre and on other narratives [6]. Thus, during the narrative, the audience is constantly making anticipations on what could happen, both immediately and on a longer period of time.

In ID, where the narrative becomes interactive, we estimate that this essential feature of narrative must be preserved. This means that the user must be able to anticipate events and actions including his/her own actions because the user is a character.

Because the user's actions are mediated through the interface, this necessity of anticipation has consequences on the design and understanding of the interface.

The rules used by the user to anticipate what he/she will be able to do later are
contained not only in the "encyclopedia" of the user but also in the "rules of the
game", which are set before or during the interactive drama. For example, in *GTA III*,
the user can anticipate that his/her character will steal a car later in the game. However, he/she cannot anticipate that the character will invite passengers in the car because she has internalized the possibilities and impossibilities in the game at a given
moment in the play.

3.2 Consequence on the Filtering Interfaces

It is necessary that the user anticipate which possibilities he/she will be given later in
the game. Given this principle, some interfaces mentioned above appear not to be
suitable to ID. Indeed, filtering interfaces where only a subset of logically possible
actions are presented to the user make the anticipation of action impossible. The systems chooses a limited set of possible actions and the user cannot anticipate which
actions will be possible, and which ones will not be (the user cannot anticipate the
content of the set P, even if L is predictable). Typically, in many adventure video
games, the user has to choose among a small set of possibilities. In this situation,
he/she discovers these possibilities as they appear on the screen: he/she could have
anticipated these possibilities or not. More importantly, the user could have planned
to perform an action but this particular action would have not been proposed as a
choice. This makes the adventure game genre a narrative genre where the user is still
in the position of a person to whom the story is being told. He/she is being given
some successive choices in the narrative, which are sequentially defined by the
author. Being unable to anticipate the choices, the user is not capable of building a
kind of strategy: he/she is no longer a character. Note that this critic on adventure
video games is independent of the limited algorithmic possibilities of these games, in
terms of management of user choices: this is an interface problem that would occur in
an AI-based ID that would make use of a filtering interface.

3.3 About Stability ...

In this discussion, we have argued that the user should be able to anticipate the set P
of physically possible actions. This is also true for the set L. This means that the set of
possible actions must be relatively stable during the narrative.

It also means that the user must perceive this stability. For the direct interface (see
previous section), this stability is perceived through the stability of the user interface
itself. This task is more difficult when it comes to the free interface: it is central for
this kind of interfaces that the user expresses him/herself within the proper range, so
that his/her actions are understood. After an initial period of trial and errors combined
with a playful behavior of testing the limits of the systems, the user has to implicitly
understand the size of the set L. From an authoring point of view, it is necessary for

the author to accurately guess the possible behaviors of the user in order to design the set *L*. We find here a process similar to the classical authoring of text as described in [6]. Instead of predicting internal inferential paths (classical story) the author predicts an actual action of the user. This is more critical because a bad prediction can lead to a failed action and to corresponding frustration.

The anticipation of action also has an impact on short-term interaction. When the user has to act, if he/she already knows (has anticipated) the possible actions then the interaction becomes user friendly. For example, in a filtering interface again, the user has to read the proposed choices, whereas in other interfaces because of their stability the user already has his/her internal representations of the set of possible actions.

3.4 And Surprise!

The argument of stability is in contradiction with the idea of surprise: if the user can expect all possibilities of action, he/she cannot be surprised by a new way of acting (he/she can still be surprised by the outcomes of the actions, actions of others characters, and by events). That is why we propose to weaken the stability constraint by allowing the inclusion of new possibilities of actions, at any given moment in the narrative. This is typical in strategic and adventure games: new "powers", new tools, new buildings are given to the user to act, and sometimes the user does not expect these new possibilities. Two important constraints must, however, be followed in order to maintain the anticipation of action:

- once the new possibility to act is added, it should remain (which is the case in the video games);
- the pace of the adding of new and unexpected possibilities of action must be slow.

This second condition is necessary so that these new actions are not taken into account in the "inferential walks" of the users. If new possibilities of action appeared often, then the user would implicitly tell him/herself "If I do this, may be I will be given new possibilities, maybe not"... which is disturbing.

*

To sum up , the extension of the fundamental narrative notion of anticipation to the field of interactive narrative has allowed us to better analyze and understand various user interfaces for ID. Interestingly, this study also shed a new light on some existing game interfaces.

4   The Duration of Interaction

4.1   The Problem

Another fundamental difference between many current real-time 3D video games and ID is the amount of time given to the user to act. While in real-time 3D video games the fundamental action is to move the character through the virtual space, in ID, the idea is to *think* for the character. The time scale is different between the two experiences: in action games, the user reacts in a tenth of a second, while in ID, several seconds are available to act.

This amount of time is useful for two reasons:
- some dramatic situations are complex and ask for a certain reasoning, especially for conflicting situations;
- the user interface can be complex, especially if a direct interface is chosen.

In ID, the time scale to act is thus longer than the time scale of the virtual world. Emblematic to this problem is the so called *waiting animation* in video games, where the character is having some various futile gestures either realistic (looking around), or humorous (playing basketball with its body, *Rayman*™).

It could be argued that this is a transitory problem due to the limitations of the current interfacing technologies. With a perfect speech and body gesture recognition system, the user would be able to interact and think continuously as he/she does in real life. However, we still consider that the problem of the duration of interaction must be seriously considered, for the following reasons:
- currently, we do not have such "perfect technology", yet we wish to produce some good examples of ID;
- discarding the problem returns to discard direct interfaces, which have some advantages to be explored (see Section 2);
- it might be stressful to ask the user to make all the choices in real-time and we want to explore the case where the user does have time to think of his/her actions.

4.2 Classical Solutions

In order to compensate this difference of scale, there are two classical solutions:
- freeze the fictional time during the interaction.
- Fill in the time to act by a neutral activity, that is an activity that has no significant influence on the narrative.

The first solution has the drawback to disrupt the immersion.

The second solution consists in having some waiting animations as mentioned above. It works up to a certain point but it is obviously unnatural to have your character looking around for 5 or 10 seconds...

4.3 The Semi-autonomy

Another solution consists in letting the user's character take actions. The character is then semi-autonomous [14]. This solution, which amends the very definition of ID presents several difficulties because the user is not fully responsible for his/her character:
- where to draw the limit between autonomous and controlled behaviors?
- would the user appreciate the lack of control over his/her character's behavior?
- how to design the communication between the sometimes autonomous character and the user?

Thus, the solution of semi-autonomous is interesting to "fill in" the duration of interaction but it is certainly quite difficult to design.

4.4 From Immersive to Elliptic ID

There is a last solution that we would like to consider here. It consists in freezing the time during interaction as mentioned above but not necessarily restarting the fictional time exactly where it stopped. For example, the user would choose to "leave the house", and after entering his/her action, the character would be in the garden. This mechanism is well known in various narrative forms and is called an *ellipsis*. The idea here is not to undergo the interruption caused by the duration of interaction but conversely to take advantage of it by transforming it into an ellipsis.

Such use of an ellipsis in ID is certainly a breach of the classical vision of ID as it has been conveyed by J. Murray in [13]. Indeed, this vision considers Virtual Reality as the ideal medium for ID, and Virtual Reality is fundamentally real-time, a characteristic that must be taken into account in order to design an ID for this media [2]. In a more general approach to ID, however, we must consider the computer as a system for Virtual Reality applications and other applications. In that context the use of the ellipsis in ID should be taken into consideration.

The classical theories of narrative consider two times: the narrative or discursive time, which corresponds to the time of the narration process, and the story time, which correspond to the time of the world of the story (diegesis) [7]. An ellipsis is a typical relation of duration between those two times (other relations being a descriptive pause, a summary, etc.). The ID introduces very naturally a third time, the time of (inter) action, which is a sub-category of the narrative time. In other forms of interactive narratives, like hypertext, this third time has less importance because it does not conflict with other times. But in ID, because of the very nature of drama which consists in showing characters acting (the mimesis [1]), the duration of interaction is to be taken into account. In drama, within a scene, the narrative time and the story time run in parallel. In ID, the introduction of the interaction time disrupts this parallel evolution and possibly injects ellipses at the heart of drama.

There exists a well-known form of drama (drama being defined as a mimetic narrative form) which uses ellipses intensively: comics. In comics, the interstice between two boxes usually represents a time ellipsis between the events described in the boxes. This suggests that while cinema is the most common media of reference in ID [2], some interesting forms of ID could also derive from comics. It does not mean that it would be made of fixed images (although this option is to be considered) but that some forms of ID might also be some "sequential art", as defined in [12].

5 Conclusion

Starting from features specific to ID we have proposed a taxonomy of input interfaces for ID and raised a certain number of issues regarding the design of the interaction.

We have tried to be objective and not to bias our study towards a certain type of interface. Practically, we conclude that the viable solutions are the following:

- the free interface (if the technical issue and the user frustration issue are reasonably solved);
- the direct interface (if a user-friendly interface is found, and the disruption of immersion made acceptable);
- the filtering interface, only in combination with one of the above interfaces.

For the *IDtension* engine [8], we have chosen a direct interface and we are currently designing the interface.

Interestingly, the specific issue of the duration of interaction in the virtual world has led us to propose alternative forms of ID, which would be inspired more by comics than movies or theatre. By their elliptic nature these forms challenge in someway the widespread vision of ID, the "Holodeck vision" [13].

References

1.   Aristotle, 330 BC. *La Poétique (The Poetics)*
2.   Aylett, R., Louchart, S. Towards a narrative theory of Virtual Reality. Virtual Reality, 7(1), 2-9, Dec. 2003
3.   Bates, J. Virtual Reality, Art, and Entertainment. In Presence: The Journal of Teleoperators and Virtual Environments. Vol. 1. No. 1. MIT Press. (Winter 1992)
4.   Cavazza, M., Charles, F., Mead, S. J.: Characters in Search of an author: AI-based Virtual Storytelling. In Proceedings of the First International Conference on Virtual Storytelling (ICVS 2001). Lecture Notes in Computer Science 2197, Springer Verlag (2001) 145-154
5.   Cavazza, M., Martin, O., Charles, F., Mead, S. J. Marichal, X. User Acting in Mixed Reality Interactive Storytelling. In Proceedings of the Second International Conference on Virtual Storytelling (ICVS 2003), Toulouse, France, Lecture Notes in Computer Science, n. 2897, Springer Verlag, 189-197 (2003)
6.   Eco, U.: Lector in Fabula.. Bompiani, Milano (1979)
7.   Genette, G. Figure III. Paris, Le Seuil (1972)
8.   IDtension. http://www.idtension.com
9.   Laurel, B.: Computers as Theatre. Addison-Wesley, Reading Harlow Menlo Park Berkeley Don Mills Sydney Amsterdam Tokyo Mexico (1993)
10. Mateas, M. A preliminary Poetics for Interactive Drama and Games. Digital Creativity, 12 (3), 2001, 140-152
11. Mateas, M., Stern, A.: Towards Integrating Plots and Characters for Interactive Drama. in Proc. AAAI Fall Symposium on Socially Intelligent Agents: The Human in the Loop (North Falmouth MA, November 2000), AAAI Press (2000)
12. McCloud S. Understanding Comics: The invisible Art. HarperCollins, Publishers, Inc., New York (1993)
13. Murray J. Hamlet on the Holodeck. The future of narrative in the cyberspace. Free Press, New York (1997)
14. Portugal, J.-N. Environnement narratif: une approche pour la fiction interactive, appliquée au jeu The Insider. Imagina'99 (1999)
15. Sgouros, N. M. Dynamic, User-Centered Resolution in Interactive Stories. In *Proc. IJCAI'97* (1997)

16. Spierling, U., I. Iurgel. "Just Talking about Art" – Creating Virtual Storytelling Experiences in Mixed Reality. In Proceedings of the Second International Conference on Virtual Storytelling (ICVS 2003), Toulouse, France, Lecture Notes in Computer Science, n. 2897, Springer Verlag, 179-188 (2003).

17. Stern A., Mateas M.: Integrating Plot, Character and Natural Language Processing in the Interactive Drama Façade. In Göbel et al. (eds) Proc. TIDSE'03. Frauenhofer IRB Verlag, (2003)

18. Szilas, N., Marty, O., Rety, J.-H. Authoring Highly Generative Interactive Drama. In Proceedings of the Second International Conference on Virtual Storytelling (ICVS 2003), Toulouse, France, Lecture Notes in Computer Science, n. 2897, Springer Verlag, 37-46 (2003)

19. Szilas, N.: IDtension: a narrative engine for Interactive Drama. In Göbel et al. (eds) Proc. TIDSE'03. Frauenhofer IRB Verlag, (2003)

20. Szilas, N.: A New Approach to Interactive Drama: From Intelligent Characters to an Intelligent Virtual Narrator. In Proc. of the Spring Symposium on Artificial Intelligence and Interactive Entertainment (Stanford CA, March 2001), AAAI Press, 72-76 (2001)

21. Szilas, N.: Interactive Drama on Computer: Beyond Linear Narrative. In Papers from the AAAI Fall Symposium on Narrative Intelligence, Technical Report FS-99-01. AAAI, Press Menlo Park (1999) 150-156

22. Weyhrauch, P. Guiding Interactive Drama. Ph.D. Dissertation, Tech report CMUCS-97-109, Carnegie Mellon University (1997)

23. Young, R.M.: Notes on the Use of Plan Structure in the Creation of Interactive Plot. In Papers from the AAAI Fall Symposium on Narrative Intelligence, Technical Report FS-99-01. AAAI, Press Menlo Park (1999) 164-167

From Another Point of View: Art-E-Fact

Ido Iurgel

ZGDV e.V., Fraunhoferstr. 5, 64283 Darmstadt, Germany
ido.iurgel@zgdv.de
www.zgdv.de

Abstract. This paper presents the EU funded project Art-E-Fact and goes into details of the dialogue management module, showing that a directed graph approach is appropriate if certain measures are taken. In this project, a software environment with designated authoring tools is being developed for the creation of narrative, interactive discussion groups of virtual characters. Interaction comprises chatting with a keyboard and the use of specialized devices, e.g. gesture recognition. Target use groups are visitors of a museum who will get interpretations of works of art form different points of view.

1 Introduction

1.1 The Settings of the Project "Art-E-Fact"

Art-E-Fact[1] is an EU funded project which aims to provide culturally enriching, but also entertaining experiences to museum visitors through interactive installations related to the artworks.

These installations are composed of stories which engage the user in dialogs with virtual characters. The user interacts with the characters through keyboard input as well as various special interactive devices. Other interactive devices allow the user to inspect the art more closely so that they come to a greater understanding of the artwork.

The knowledge of the multifaceted and deeply personal aspects of art are transferred to the user through conversations with well informed albeit virtual characters. The discussions between these characters are embedded in a story which unfolds against the personal background of each character. This is a model for a new kind of interactive storytelling which places emphasis on a narrative, interactive presentation of a theme through a discussion group.

One could imagine a coffee table discussion about an art exhibition as a fitting metaphor for Art-E-Fact, but also a Platonic dialogue (cf. [3]).

---

[1] IST-2001 37924, cf. www.art-e-fact.org.

S. Göbel et al. (Eds.): TIDSE 2004, LNCS 3105, pp. 26–35, 2004.

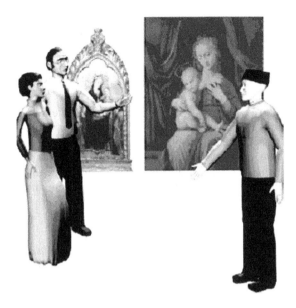

Fig. 1. A group of virtual characters discuss religious icons.

Users interact with devices such as a 'magic eraser' to uncover hidden layers of painting as well as e.g. a virtual magnifying glass. Both employ gesture recognition. The keyboard is used to chat with the virtual characters.

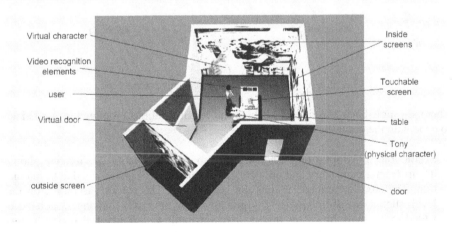

Fig. 2. A possible use of the Art-E-Fact platform with projections[2]

A key requirement of the project is creative flexibility. As an authoring tool, Art-E-Fact enables the creation of installations e.g. with any number or kind of virtual characters, using a deliberate number of displays, and with either real or virtual works of art as part of the installation.

---

[2] An idea by M. Burgos and J. M. 'hafo', arteleku, Spain.

Figure 2 shows a potential use for an Art-E-Fact installation using several displays and a separated room inside the museum.

1.2   Challenges

The challenge of Art-E-Fact, as with all interactive storytelling, is in conflicting requirements. There is a permanent conflict between the story line, freedom of interaction, the virtual characters believability, and accessibility of the authoring process. Interaction threatens the story line, which in its turn may require a behavior from the virtual characters that is not believable at a certain situation, and exploding complexity due to anticipation of user interaction may result in unmanageability of the authoring of an engaging story.

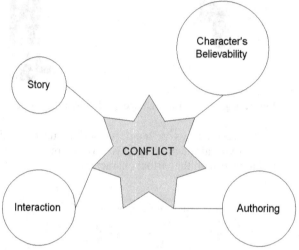

Fig. 3. Several conflicts exist in interactive storytelling.

There are some basic assumptions behind the actual solutions promoted in Art-E-Fact to cope with these conflicts:

- **Scene Based Adaptation.** Since interaction threatens story quality, we should depart from a main story and allow only for variations of this story, due to interaction. The story experience is thus not "emergent". The story's variations, on this level, should be *scene based*, i.e. segments of the story are exchanged, deleted or added to the main line. This process is comparable to a director changing a story script, e.g. for user adaptation, when the system detects that the visitor is more interested in, say, history of art rather than color analysis. Scene based variation is especially important to control total interaction time, i.e. a story will be shortened or elongated depending on how long a visitor remains in a single scene. Interaction within a scene lays the ground for the consecutive choice of further scenes. In Art-E-Fact, a story engine selects the appropriate scenes.
- **Improvisation Based Adaptation.** At this level, the virtual actors adapt their behavior to cope with interaction, given a certain leeway of the scene directions. In

general, improvisation implies autonomy of the virtual characters. In Art-E-Fact, improvisation exists in the sense that the virtual characters may perform the same direction displaying different personal emotions, as a result of past interaction. The content of the story remains unchanged, but *how* the story is told changes. Also, in Art-E-Fact, the possibility of chatting with the characters may count as improvisation, since the chat normally does not affect the story progression.

- **Levels of Anticipation.** Anticipation of user interaction easily leads to exploding complexity, especially if keyboard interaction is employed, disallowing the creation of a good story. Therefore, authoring issues must be considered from scratch on. It is advantageous to allow for different levels of anticipation, and distinguish between "normal" and "abnormal" user input. Thus, a cooperative user will often – though not always - obtain a very good reaction of the system, if the input is exactly as expected. In Art-E-Fact, different levels of anticipation are employed, such as explicit transitions for exact anticipation and generally evocable response patterns in case the more precise anticipation fails.

Another considerable challenge is the use of keyboard interaction. No current "deep" dialogue management system is able to handle the wide range of responses and input possible in storytelling. Since the demand was for a pragmatic solution that would enable the visitor also to gather additional information about artworks, we've chosen to integrate the efficient, successful and simple chatbot ALICE[3]. ALICE performs shallow natural language processing and, in spite of some clever advanced features, basically outputs repetitive responses to input that matches certain patterns. The task then was to mediate between the (almost) state memory free responses of ALICE and the requirements of an ongoing story. Some of the solutions are explained in chapter 4.2.

2 Related Work

Art-E-Fact has many parallels with the work of Mateas and Stern [4]; on the one hand, and with research by André et al. [1] on the other. Similar to Façade, the user is generally not the main person. Rather, he is involved in the story of the virtual persons. With the context being edutainment, Art-E-Fact dictates the use of the keyboard interaction in the manner of a chatbot, to enable the visitor to gather information about works of art.

André et al. have developed a group of virtual characters for presentation. They use neither narration nor interaction, but share with us the idea of using characters to elucidate different perspectives of a subject.

An example of a setting without educational components, but within the context of storytelling and natural language interaction, is currently being followed by Cavazza (cf. [2]) using hierarchic planning.

The amount and variety of chatbots is growing significantly. We have chosen ALICE due to the fact that it is free, simple to author and has proven results in the Loebner-context[4].

---

[3] Cf. www.alicebot.org
[4] Cf. web.infoave.net/~kbcowart and www.loebner.net.

3 Architecture

Figure 4 depicts the architecture and shows the main content bases. The core module is the Dialogue Engine, which controls the visible actions and immediate reactions of the system, including the text and the gestures of the virtual characters. The Story Engine is a module that accesses a pool of scenes and uses a declarative model of the story structure to choose the next scene depending on interaction results. The interaction results are logged by the Dialogue Engine and passed over to the Narration Engine (cf. [5]) after the end of a scene.

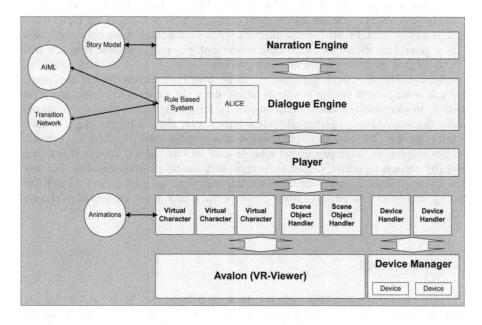

Fig. 4. Architecture of Art-E-Fact

The Dialogue Manager issues commands for the virtual characters, devices and the environment. It determines what the characters say and how they say it. The Player distributes the commands to the subordinate components. The virtual character modules receive commands in a dedicated XML language derived from RRL[5], enabling precise alignment of gestures, events and spoken words.

In addition to executing the commands issued by the Dialogue Engine and displaying random behavior, the virtual characters can display variations in the emotional expressiveness of their movements. The emotional models increase believability (cf. [3]).

---

[5] Cf. www.ai.univie.ac.at/NECA/RRL

4 Dialogue Management

The Dialog Engine was built around a directed graph ("bubbles and arrows") because it is necessary to take the authoring process from scratch into account. Visual representation of authoring tools for a directed graph still are the most intuitive interface for non-programmers.

4.1 Reducing Complexity of Connections

However, the main shortcoming of a directed graph approach for handling interaction is the well known tendency of the number of connections to explode. To handle this problem, two related measures were taken: (i) Composite states were used, and (ii) rule based state changes without explicit transitions were introduced.

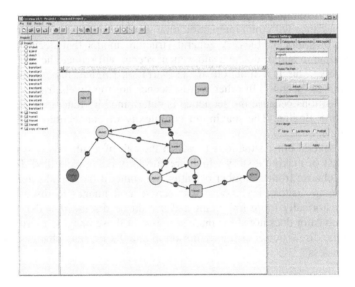

Fig. 5. A screenshot of the authoring tool

4.1.1 Composite States

Composite States are well known e.g. from state chart diagrams. A composite state is a container of elementary states or further composite states which enables the grouping of scenes and the use of a single free transition that is applicable to all the immediate sub-states. A typical case is a break-condition that interrupts the ongoing story segment, whatever the active inner state. Further on, memory states can be accessed to pilot to the last active sub-state of a composite state, in case that the composite state is repeatedly deactivated and activated.

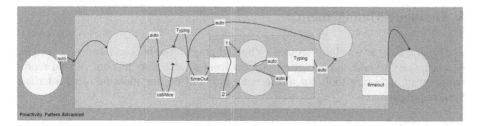

Fig. 6. An example for the use of composite states

4.1.2 Rule-Based State Changes

Some situations reoccur among different installations that would lead to similar, complex patterns of connections between states. This complexity can be reduced if a rule based system is called from within the state graph to control the state changes. For example, a transition graph for a story that is shortened or prolonged with facultative scenes in accordance with total interaction time would result in a tremendous complex system or arrows and bubbles. A general structure model that decides, after each scene if it is time to add or delete a subsequent scene, will reduce the graph complexity considerably. This is a function of the Narration Engine; thus, some composite states function as "scenes". In other words, scenes are top levels frames that are not linked by transitions because the sequence is determined by function calls to the rule based Narration Engine. The maximum complexity of connections is found at the level of a single scene.

There are several other situations in which the call of a rule based system simplifies the process of making a story which are currently being examined. For example, the user may choose from a number of paths, but some of those paths are mandatory. E.g. the museum visitor may choose between several images to discuss, but some images are historically more important and should be discussed under any circumstances. If the visitor does not show interest in one of those images, a virtual character will initiate the discussion. For the definition of rule based state changes, we use the expert system Jess[6].

4.2 Integration of Chatting into the Directed Graph

The integration of a chatbot with an unfolding story is achieved with the help of two measures: Selective call of the chatbot with thematic constraints from within the state graph (cf. figure 7), and use of the chatbot in the conditions of the transitions of the graph (cf. figure 9). In particular in the second case, the bot is not used to generate a response directly, but its extended pattern matching faculties are employed to detect the meaning of the input.

---

[6] Cf. herzberg.ca.sandia.gov/jess.

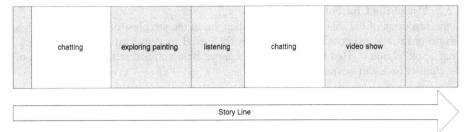

Fig. 7. Chat can be allowed periodically

4.2.1 Selective Call of the Chatbot

One way to use the chatbot consists in calling it explicitly from within the Dialogue Engine, restricting the range of patterns and answers. If no matching pattern is found within one range, a second range can be called, resulting in priorities of thematic fields (cf. figure 8). The chat period finishes when a certain condition is met, e.g. after a timeout. This results in delimited chatting periods.

When certain responses of the chatbot are desirable or necessary for the continuation of the session, e.g. if certain information about a work of art must be provided to continue the story, the system can be made to check if the chatbot has provided the information. If necessary, another virtual character can be made to pose a question that leads to the desired information. Expert system rules are being developed for such cases.

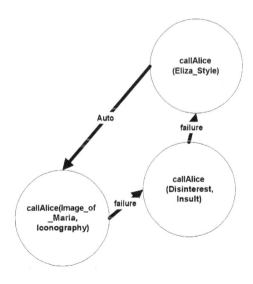

Fig. 8. Subsequential calls of ALICE data bases

4.2.2 Use of the Chatbot in Transitions

Some reactions of the visitor are very predicable, in the simplest of cases e.g. when a yes-no-answer is expected. The chatbot is then used to detect equivalent input, e.g. "yes", "ok", "fine". This function can, of course, be combined with selective calls of the chatbot to detect deviant input.

Fig. 9. ALICE used in the transitions. The tag "Speechact" calls the chatbot to resolve the input

5   Forthcoming Issues

Currently, artists are creating stories with the platform and exploring its possibilities. Their experiences shall result in further adaptation of the dialogue manager and detection of further specific patterns that can be simplified with functions. Especially abrupt changes of theme by the visitor need currently very complex connections between states, composite states and calls of the chatbot to produce sensible results, and we expect to detect additional connection patterns that can be simplified with the use of rules.

A natural extension of the project's idea would consist in using mobile devices to enable the visitor to take some preferred character along with him to comment every part of the exhibition, using the main installation as a kind of center of encounters, where different virtual characters and visitors share their impressions and opinions and "tell their stories".

An obvious application field for the Art-E-Fact software is education. First tests with the platform for teaching mathematics in primary school were very motivating. Additionally, a web based version is being developed which could be used by web museums or for marketing.

A task for future research will certainly be increasing the autonomy of the virtual actors, transforming them into veritable actors with deeper natural language processing and complex, intelligent behavior patterns. But not only natural language and AI technology pose difficult challenges. Also, the dramatic concepts and virtual character acting ideas have to evolve in parallel with technology, since interactive storytelling is currently in a situation were not only wanting technology prevents realization, but where there is also a lack in proven dramatic concepts.

6 Conclusion

The project Art-E-Fact provides authoring tools for interactive, narrative discussion groups for educational museum installations. A directed graph approach is advantageous for authoring given the present project settings and can sensibly be used if supplemented with rules for implicit state changes and with composite states to reduce the complexity of the connections. The chatbot ALICE can be used in combination with these features to enable chatting with the characters if chatting is employed during delimited episodes of the unfolding story and complemented with pattern anticipation on the level of transitions of the graph.

References

1. André, E., Klesen, M., Gebhard, P., Allen S., Rist, Th.: Exploiting Models of Personality and Emotions to Control the Behavior of Animated Interface Agents. In: Jeff Rickel (eds.), Proceedings of the workshop on "Achieving Human-Like Behavior in Interactive Animated Agents", in conjunction with the Fourth International Conference on Autonomous Agents, pp. 3-7, Barcelona, June (2000)
2. Cavazza, M., Martin, O., Charles, F., Mead, S. J., Marichal, X.: Interacting with Virtual Agents in Mixed Reality Interactive Storytelling. In: Thomas Rist, Ruth Aylett, Daniel Ballin, and Jeff Rickel (Eds.). Proceedings of the 4th International Workshop on Intelligent Virtual Agents, IVA 2003, Kloster Irsee, September (2003) 231-235.
3. Iurgel, I.: Emotional interaction in a hybrid conversational group. In: Prendiger, H. (ed.): International Workshop on Lifelike Animated Agents. Working Notes in Proceedings PRICAI-02, Tokyo, Japan (2002) 52-57
4. Mateas, M., Stern, A.: Integrating Plot, Character and Natural Language Processing in the Interactive Drama Façade. In: Proceedings of TIDSE 2003, Darmstadt, March 24-26 (2003) 139-151
5. Spierling, U., Grasbon, D., Braun, N., Iurgel, I.: Setting the Scene: Playing Digital Director in Interactive Storytelling and Creation. In: Computers & Graphics (2002) 26, 31-44

1, 2, 3 …. Action! Directing Real Actors and Virtual Characters

Isabel Machado[1], Paul Brna[2], and Ana Paiva[3]

[1] ISCTE, University of Leeds & INESC-ID. Rua Alves Redol, 9 1000 – 029 Lisbon, Portugal
Isabel.Machado@ inesc-id.pt
[2] School of Informatics, Northumbria University. Ellison Building, Newcastle upon Tyne. NE1 8ST – UK
Paul.Brna@unn.ac.uk
[3] IST & INESC-ID. Rua Alves Redol, 9 1000 – 029 Lisbon, Portugal
Ana.Paiva@inesc-id.pt

Abstract. The new interactive ways of storytelling, which can be realised as interactive narratives, virtual storytelling, interactive fiction, interactive drama, are often regarded as a significant break from traditional storytelling methods. In this paper we focus on the role of a person in an interactive storytelling context who facilitates the story construction process, the *Director*. The term *Director* is often associated with roles such as theatre director, stage director, film director or even television director. The meaning usually assigned to this concept is of someone who: *"oversees and orchestrates the mounting of a play by unifying various endeavours and aspects of production. The director's function is to ensure the quality and completeness of a theatrical product"*. In our research, the concept of a *Director* is extended and does not only have the role of supervising the acting in a play where every actor knows his/her role in a well-known plot, but to supervise the role being played by a set of autonomous virtual characters and to provide support to the users that engage in the story by controlling and commanding virtual actors. In our view, our concept of a *Director* is challenging because its role is vital in the sense that it does not only supervise a set of synthetic characters but has to accommodate the choices made by the users, within our context children, and at the same time guarantee that the coherence of the story is maintained.

1 Related Research

In the past few years several researchers have conducted their research in the area of storytelling and many of them have one of the typical problems of interactive narratives/stories – *the higher degree of freedom that is given to the user to intervene in the narrative flow, the weaker is the power given to the author to decide on the progress of the story* [2].

The approaches taken to solve this problem follow, in the majority of the cases, two strategies: a plot based or a character-based strategy. The first strategy divides the story in several pieces and some relational/causal relations are established between them. The segmentation of the story has assumed several formats: N. Sgouros followed the dramatic structure defined by Aristotle and based the modelling on the

S. Göbel et al. (Eds.): TIDSE 2004, LNCS 3105, pp. 36–41, 2004.

conflicts that raise between the characters [4]; Mateas & Stern developed an interactive virtual world based on units called beats which are the grains of the plot itself and the basis for interaction [5], etc. The second strategy considers that the plot is encoded in the character's behaviour and the plot emerges from the interactions being established between such characters – the achievement of the story is guaranteed by the assumption that each character stays in character during the interaction [3]. In this case, for a successful achievement of the plot the ways in which the characters present their actions and interact with the user assume a very important weight. This need can be translated into the concept of a believable character [6], which should have the ability of engaging in a fluid conversation and interaction with the user - see the work of J. Cassell *et al.* on embodied conversational agents [7], and have coherent animation procedures which resemble the behaviour of a real actor [8]. Both approaches turn out to be extremely demanding for the author of the story. In the first strategy, the author would have to parameterise the characters to such a level that they would be able to respond to any interaction with the user and at the same time maintain a coherent plot, and in the second strategy, the author would also have a giant task, since he would have to define his story in such a way that every piece that composes the plot should be able to take into account any way that the story might develop that is reasonably coherent or at least chosen by the user.

In our research, we tried to avoid this common problem by assuming that the story being *created* and *told* is not predefined manually, and the users that interact with the autonomous characters collaboratively play the role of the author. This approach merges the actor, author and spectator roles, since the users are invited *to act* in an interactive story along with synthetic characters, to create/author such story by acting in it and to understand the others characters' actions – being a spectator – in order to respond to their behaviours. In the light of this, the *Director* assumes a very important role in the task of guiding the accomplishment of a meaningful story.

2 Context

The *Director Agent* was developed as component of *SAGA*, which is an *open architecture[1]* that can receive information from an external story creation application, in real-time, and processes such information and suggests support and guidance directives back to such application [9]. The development of *SAGA* was carried out with the goal of providing its *services* to applications that have children as users.

The main goals of *SAGA* are achieved through the integration of different components, which have different roles throughout the story creation activity: such as a dynamic scriptwriter; a narrative guidance engine; a drama manager – the director; and a reflection engine (see Fig. 1).

---

[1] The concept of an open architecture stands for a software architecture, which allows the usage of its services by any story creation application that follows the interface rules defined by it.

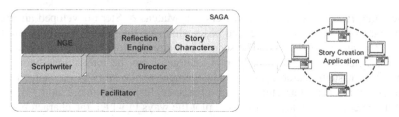

Fig. 1. Support And Guidance Architecture (**SAGA**).

3 Director Agent

To understand how the *Director Agent* performs its task, it is necessary to introduce first some of the theories explored within SAGA and which are the crucial for the work carried by the *Director Agent*. One of the most important concepts is that associated with the *story*. The theory behind the definition of such concept has its roots in Propp's narrative morphology [10].

The story definition stands for a variable sequence of two different constituents: an *initial story situation* and *variable story schema*. The first can be seen as the situation in which the characters and their inter-relations are introduced, the story is situated in terms of temporal and spatial localisation, the initial positioning of the characters, and the definition of the goal of the story. The *variable story schema* is a sequence of functions[2]- each of them represented by a letter-, which starts with a villainy (*A*) or with a lack (*a*), and may develop accordingly along the upper or the lower branch of the schema, meaning that it is characterised: by the existence of a struggle (*H*) and a victory over the villain (*I*) – in this case the sequence should start with a villainy; or, by the existence of a difficult task (*M*) and the solution of such a task (*N*) – in this case the sequence should start with a lack (see below).

$$(A|a)C{\uparrow}DEFG \ \underline{HJI} \ K{\downarrow}PrRsExUW$$
$$\underline{M.N}$$

The next step for the application of this *variable story schema* is the interpretation of what each function means and how can it be applied in an interactive context. To do this, we extended the concept of *function* to *plot point* – an important moment in the story [11]. Each *plot point* is then represented by a set of *generic goals*, and each of them is equally valid for reaching such particular plot point. Taking for example, the plot point *villainy* can be decomposed in five different generic goals: *theft, kidnapping someone, casting of a spell, imprisonment* or *order to kill someone*. Although, these different generic goals are quite specific and folktale oriented, it is always possible to generalise them and apply them to a more realistic and modern context. Each *generic goal* is translated into a *plan* that guarantees the achievement of the *plot point*. Each *plan* is a hierarchical representation of goals and actions - similar to

---

[2] A *function* can be understood as both the actions of the characters and the consequences of these actions in the story.

the work conducted by Cavazza [14] -, i.e., which can be decomposed into a set of sub-goals and ultimately into a set of atomic actions (the actions performed by the characters in the story world) - see Table 1 for an example of a schema associated with the generic goal *kidnapping someone*).

Table 1. Generic Goal: **Kidnapping someone.**

GENERIC GOAL	SCHEMA
KIDNAPPING SOMEONE: It is considered that entity being kidnapped is one member of the others role (the beloved character) or another hero character in the story. To do this the villain character uses a magical entity that turns the beloved entity invisible. The invisibility is achieved through the energy dimension.	DECOMPOSE(KIDNAPPINGSOMEONE(BELOVED ENTITY), PLAN(STEPS: { S_1: LOOKFOR(MAGICAL PROP); S_2: GET(MAGICAL PROP); S_3: LOOKFOR(BELOVED ENTITY); S_4: WALKTO(BELOVED ENTITY); S_5: USE(MAGICAL PROP, BELOVED ENTITY)}, ORDERINGS: {$S_1 \rightarrow S_2, S_2 \rightarrow S_4$, $S_3 \rightarrow S_4, S_4 \rightarrow S_5$}, BINDINGS: { S_5: (BELOVED ENTITY)$_{ENERGY}$ = INVISIBLE^3}, LINKS: {$S_2 \rightarrow^{MAGICAL\ PROP} S_5$}^{4}))

Another important aspect that derives from the application of Propp's theory is the implicit definition of roles associated with the characters – which are named by him as *dramatis personae*. Following Propp's perspective, each of the dramatis personae has a specific set of functions associated, which determines when such character must intervene in the story. After having established a common ground, we have now the conditions to present the functioning and the specifications associated with the *Director Agent*.

The *Director Agent* follows the specification of a narrative agent and complies with Dautenhahn's type IV models of a narrative agent [13]. Our agent fits this categorisation because it uses its memory – the *narrative memory* - to interact with the story characters and respond with support and guidance directives not only to those characters but also to the children. Nevertheless, we opted not to call autobiographic to our agent's memory because it does not have the capability to learn from the facts collected from the stories. However, our agent does not limit itself to collect and store the information from the stories, but organises such information in accordance with the several perspectives of the different dramatis personae.

The *narrative memory* is organised in the form of episodes. Each episode is constituted by three important events: crisis, climax and resolution [1] and are organised in a temporal sequence and with cause-effect links.

The *Director Agent* creates its *narrative memory* by analysing the current goals of each story character. This analysis consists on the investigation of which story character may have suffered a change of its fortune. At the end of the story creation activ-

---

^{3} S_i: (XPTO)$_x$ = Y, which is read as in step S_i the variable **x** of character **xpto** assumes the value **y**.

^{4} $S_i \rightarrow^c S_j$, which is read as S_i achieves c for S_j.

ity, the *Director Agent* can use the various character-centred stories stored in its memory to generate a unique story that reflects the overall experience of the story creation activity.

In order to perform its task, the *Director* maintains an internal model of the story world and implements a *mind* associated with each story character[5]. The specification of the rules and functioning of such *minds* is determined according to the roles played by each character in the story. During the story creation process, the *Director Agent* has four different activities: (1) to update the internal world model and investigate the possibility of generating an episode. To do this, the *Director Agent* inspects the characters' goals in order to find conflicts among characters. When it detects a conflict of goals between two characters, it inspects the possibility to add a new episode to its narrative memory. This update task happens whenever the *Director Agent* receives information from the Facilitator component; (2) to check whether the current plot point has been achieved, in order to make sure that the story progresses. In case of success the *Director Agent* asks the Narrative Guidance Engine (NGE) for the next plot point; (3) to check the need to trigger a reflection event. This reflection event happens when there is a conflict between the actions/behaviour performed by the child and her character's role or a conflict in terms of emotional behaviour – which is detected through the comparison with what the story character is supposed to be doing, i.e., the story character's mind kept by the *Director Agent*. To trigger this reflection event the *Director Agent* asks the Reflection Engine Component to generate an appropriate interaction with the child, and; (4) to check the need to introduce a new story element (character or object) in order to enrich the story or to overcome some children disagreement with her/his character's role.

4 Results

The *Director Agent*, together with *SAGA*, has been integrated with a previously developed application, *Teatrix*. *Teatrix* is a collaborative virtual environment for story creation which does not include any support and guidance mechanism. In this application children have the opportunity to create their own stories by controlling the story characters. By plugging in *SAGA* into *Teatrix*, we provided the children with a support and guiding mechanism during their story creation activities. An evaluation study was conducted in a real classroom scenario and the results showed that children felt more immersed in the story world when received the support and guidance directives from the *Director Agent*.

These directives offered the children with the possibility to see the story through their character's eyes, understand what was happening on their minds and respond emotionally to the actions being performed. By giving the children the opportunity to reflect during the story creation, they are empowered with further knowledge about their character and the others in world to better comprehend the interactions and fully enjoy this kind of role-playing and role-taking situations ([9],[12]). These results show that the task being performed by the *Director* facilitates the work being carried by the children and the reward and level of understanding of the story also improves.

---

[5] This concept of *mind* is associated with the mind of a software agent, which is responsible for the reasoning process.

References

1. Freytag, G.. Freytag's technique of the drama: an exposition of dramatic composition and art, Scott, Foresman, Chicago, 1900.
2. Clarke, A., Mitchell, G.: Film and Development of Interactive Narrative. In Proceedings of the International Conference in Virtual Storytelling – LNCS 2197. Springer, 2001.
3. Hayes-Roth, B.: Acting in character. In R. Trappl and P. Petta (eds.), Creating Personalities for Synthetic Actors: Towards Autonomous Personality Agents. Springer Lecture Notes in Artificial Intelligence 1195, Springer Verlag, Heidelberg/New York, pp. 120-165, 1997.
4. Sgouros, N.: Dynamic generation, management and resolution of interactive plots. Aritificial Intelligence, 107(1), pp. 29—62, 1999.
5. Mateas, M., Stern, A.: Towards Integrating Plot and Character for Interactive Drama. In Dautenhahn, K., Bond, A., Cañamero, D. and Edmonds, B. (eds.) Socially Intelligent Agents - creating relationships with computers and robots of the Multiagent Systems, Artificial Societies, and Simulated Organizations Series, Kluwer, 2002.
6. Bates, J.: The Role of Emotion in Believable Agents, Technical Report CMU–CS–94–136, Carnegie Mellon University, 1994.
7. Cassell, J., Vilhjalmsson, H.: Fully embodied conversational avatars: Making communicative behaviours autonomous. In Autonomous agents and Multi-Agent Systems, volume 2(1), 1999.
8. Perlin, K., Goldberg, A.: Improv: a system for scripting interactive actors in virtual worlds. Computer Graphics, 24(3), 1996.
9. Machado, I., Paiva, A., Brna, p.: Real characters in Virtual Stories. In Proceedings of the International Conference in Virtual Storytelling – LNCS 2197. Springer, 2001.
10. Propp, V.: Morphology of the folktale, Austin: University of Texas Press, 1968.
11. Mateas, M.: An oz-centric review of interactive drama and believable agents. In M. Wooldridge and M. Veloso, (Eds.), AI Today: Recent Trends and Developments. Lecture Notes in AI 1600. Berlin, NY: Springer. 1999.
12. Machado, I., Paiva, A., Prada, R.: Is the wolf angry or … just hungry? – Inspecting, disclosing and modifying characters' minds. In the Proceedings of the 5th International Conference on Autonomous Agents, ACM Press, 2001.
13. Dautenhahn, K., Coles, S.: Narrative Intelligence from the Bottom Up: A Computational Framework for the Study of Story-Telling in Autonomous Agents, The Journal of Artificial Societies and Social Simulation, Special Issue on *Starting from Society - the application of social analogies to computational systems*, 2001.
14. Cavazza, M., Charles, F., Mead S.J.: Agent's Interaction in Virtual Storytelling. In Proceedings of the International Conference of Intelligent Virtual Agents – LNAI 2190, Springer, 2001.

Object Oriented Prompted Play (O2P2): A Pragmatic Approach to Interactive Narrative

Daniel Roberts and Mark Wright

EdVEC (Edinburgh Virtual Environment Centre)
The University of Edinburgh, Edinburgh EH9 3JZ, UK
{Daniel.Roberts, Mark.Wright}@ed.ac.uk
www.edvec.ed.ac.uk

Abstract. We describe an interactive narrative system that embodies *Object Oriented Prompted Play* (O2P2). This means that behaviours, attributes, and crucially *stories* are attached to objects in the story world. The approach is inspired by children's social play where narrative emerges from collaborative, improvised negotiation. The object oriented architecture is appropriate for improvisation, imposing little predefined structure. Our goal is not the modelling, understanding and generation of narrative but the *computer aided support for the improvisation process from which narrative emerges*. Although based on play and children's material, we believe the system is applicable more widely. Ours is a pragmatic approach that strikes a balance between the culturally fundamental activities of "play" and "story telling".

1 Introduction

In this paper we describe a system that represents a new approach to interactive narrative: Object Oriented Prompted Play (O2P2). This paradigm occupies the middle ground between open-ended play and structured narrative. Our goal is not to create a system which encodes, models, understands or generates a definitive narrative, but to create a system that facilitates collaborative play from which improvised narrative emerges. The narrative is *object oriented* in the sense that behaviours, attributes, and most importantly, stories are attached to objects in the scene. An object oriented architecture is appropriate for improvisation because its distributed nature does not impose much pre-defined structure. In principle, any type of story could be attached to an object, but we envisage them as being low-level subplots involving the object and one or more characters. For example, a seesaw may have a story attached that involves two characters playing together, or using the seesaw as a lever. The user is able to introduce new objects to the scene, with subplots attached that are integrated in to the template plot. The user controls the characters in the story, and, through them, can interact with the objects that are present. *Prompted play* is inspired by the research and observations of children's 'collaborative play'[7]. Such play is a *socially embedded* stream of interactions [2]. Narrative *emerges* during such play as the result of an unpredictable, improvised and constantly renegotiated process.

S. Göbel et al. (Eds.): TIDSE 2004, LNCS 3105, pp. 42–47, 2004.

There is no master script, no child or other agent is totally in control of this process. The embedded, distributed and unpredictable nature of the interactions and the narrative which emerges means that the application of traditional global structural reductionist approaches of deconstruction, analysis and modelling are problematic. We therefore focus not on narrative modelling, understanding and generation but on *computer aided support for the improvisation process.*

Another insight we use from research on play, is that global coherence of these emergent narratives is aided by *scaffolding*, where gross context is provided, and that local sequential coherence is aided by *metaplay* or *dialogic* strategies, where children narrate in or out of character to facilitate negotiation of the direction of the narrative.

Our system aims to aid the improvisation process by embodying the principles of scaffolding, metaplay and dialogic processes. The system as a whole is a kind of 'play facilitator' - a good analogy is that of a kindergarten assistant who suggests an initial context and scenario (scaffolding), moves things on when a scenario finishes, and ensures that the narrative doesn't flag, either by taking over and telling the story for a while, or by prompting the children (or user) with new ideas. The embedding of stories and behaviours in objects facilitates improvisation as well as allowing the system to engage in metaplay/dialogic contributions to affect the flow of the narrative.

2   Related Work

State of the art approaches to interactive narrative aim to solve perennial problems of the field - high level issues of linguistic comprehension, narrative coherence, and dramatic tension. These are constant themes, running from Propp's work on modelling the grammar of narrative [5], through to present day systems such as Mateas and Stern's Facade [3] and Szilas' IDTension [8]. Both of these are sophisticated systems that aim to provide a structured narrative experience analogous to that of a good novel or movie - one that follows the traditional 'dramatic arc'. Parallels can be drawn between our system and theirs: in our system, a conflict must be resolved before another can start, and the actions of the user dictate which conflict/resolution pair occurs next. Facade functions in a similar way - input from the user affects the actions of the other characters in the interactive drama, and determines which 'beat' happens next. IDTension has as a component a 'narrative logic' that presents to the user all possible actions that are available to him. This is similar to our concept of a narrator who suggests actions to the user at appropriate junctures in the plot.

However, despite these similarities, our approaches are fundamentally different. We are not aiming for a narrative experience that approximates that of a film or a book. Rather, we hope to create an experience that is closer to the narrative that emerges from play. By aiming for a different, less stringent kind of narrative, namely the kind that emerges from collaborative play, we hope to avoid the strictures of more conventional narrative modalities. There is no 'master plot' in our system; simply a 'template plot' that, in conjunction with

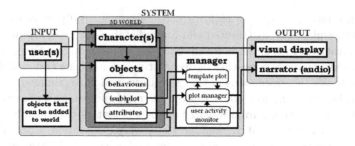

Fig. 1. Architecture of the system

prompts from the narrator and subplots added by the user, provides a loose narrative context within which the user can play.

Systems which also aim to involve play in the interactive narrative experience include StoryMat [6], a playmat that records the verbally improvised stories of children, and plays back those recorded by others at appropriate junctures. StoryMat shares our desire to mediate improvisational play, but comes at the problem from a different angle. The KidsRoom [1] was an interactive, narrative playspace for children. The actions of the children, who were in a real bedroom overlooked by several video cameras, were interpreted by computer vision tracking and action recognition algorithms. Recognition of the movements initiated a structured narrative experience, in which the scope for improvisation was limited. In Computer-Animated Improvisational Theater [4], the improvisation is performed by the *system* rather than the *user*. The user gives directions to the animated characters - these directions can be anywhere between very specific ("hop over there energetically") and very general ("move over there in whatever way you want"). A general instruction means that, in the case of the examples given, the character must improvise the method of locomotion.

3   Sketch of the System

Figure 1 is a schematic representation of our interactive narrative system. Below is an explanation of how the system will work. Figure 2 gives an example of a user's experience of the system, using a plot based on a Tiny Planets episode.

User Agency - The user's agency in the system consists of two components: firstly, the ability to control the character or characters that are present in the world; secondly, the ability to add new objects (with subplots attached) to the world. The addition of new objects to the world takes place as a drag-and-drop operation from a menu of objects appropriate to the current world state. The user does not design the plots attached to objects, or indeed the objects themselves. In our system the plots, objects and characters are taken from the TV series Tiny Planets. A conventional author/3D modeller who was familiar with our system could just as easily design them.

The 3D Virtual World - All action that takes place in a plot is represented in a 3D virtual world, consisting of the characters and objects involved. The

Initial plot (below) is attached to the Seasons Machine and the tree, and inserted in to the template plot at the start of the episode.

```
[Bing moves to seasons machine
Bing presses spring button
Flowers grow on tree
Cloud arrives over Bing, rains     CONFLICT 1
Bing moves around scene
Bing moves to seasons machine
Bing presses summer button
Rain stops, cloud leaves    RESOLUTION 1
Fruit grows on tree     CONFLICT 2
Bing moves to tree
Bing jumps
Bing moves to seasons machine
Bing presses autumn button
Fruit falls
Bing moves to fruit
Bing eats fruit    RESOLUTION 2]
```

User starts by moving Bing close to the seasons machine and clicking on the spring button. This triggers the arrival of the raincloud. Plot manager is sent a message by the raincloud saying that among its attributes are that it is now visible and raining on Bing. Plot manager activates CONFLICT 1 and sends a message to the narrator to let it know. Narrator says "Oh no! Bing is getting wet. Can you find a way to help him?" User tries moving Bing to get him away from the cloud, but the cloud follows him everywhere he goes. If user has not resolved the conflict after (say) 30 seconds the narrator will prompt him: "Why don't you try using the seasons machine? Or if you would like Bing to help, just don't click the mouse". User doesn't click the mouse - the user activity monitor senses this, so the system takes over. The system knows that CONFLICT 1 has not been resolved, so takes action to resolve it by enacting the template plot from after the initialising event of CONFLICT 1. Bing is moved around the scene, and then to the seasons machine. The summer button is pressed, the raincloud disappears, and a message is sent by the rain cloud to the plot manager telling it that one of its attributes is that it is now invisible and not raining on Bing. Thus, the plot manager is aware that RESOLUTION 1 has occurred, and sends a message to the narrator saying so. Narrator says "Hurray! Bing is dry". Since user is still inactive, the next event in the template plot is enacted: fruit grows on the tree. Tree sends a message to the plot manager that it has grown fruit - plot manager activates CONFLICT 2 and send a message to the narrator telling it so. Narrator says "Look! There's some fruit on the tree. Can you help Bing eat the fruit?" User becomes active again, so control is relinquished by the system. User moves Bing close to the tree, and makes Bing jump to reach the fruit. This doesn't work, so the user becomes bored, and introduces a new object, a bouncy ball, to the scene. CONFLICT 2 is still active, so the ball's subplot (shown below) is inserted in to the template plot after RESOLUTION 2.

```
[ Bing moves to ball
Bing touches ball
Ball bounces away from Bing        SUBCONFLICT
Bing follows ball
Bing catches ball        SUBRESOLUTION ]
```

Narrator is sent a message by the plot manager to say that a new subplot has been inserted but CONFLICT 2 is still active. Narrator says "Help Bing eat the fruit first". User moves Bing to the seasons machine, and presses the autumn button. Tree's fruit drops, and the user helps Bing to eat it. Tree sends a message to the plot manager to let it know that its fruit has been eaten, the necessary condition for the resolution of CONFLICT 2. Plot manager sends a message to the narrator to say that CONFLICT 2 has been resolved - narrator says "Well done! Bing has eaten the fruit". User is now able to fully interact with the ball, and when he does, it will bounce away from him. When he catches it, all conflicts will have been resolved, and the episode will end with a concluding message from the narrator, e.g. "Now its time for Bing to go. Goodbye!". (Note that the conflicts in the template plot do not necessarily have to occur in the order described above - CONFLICT 2 could be activated and resolved before CONFLICT 1 under the assumptions governing our system).

Fig. 2. Walkthrough of user experience

objects in the world have *behaviours*, *attributes*, and *plots* attached. Behaviours, as the name suggests, dictate the behaviour of an object in certain situations. These behaviours alter the attributes of the object. The plot attached to an object become part of the template plot when the object is introduced to the world.

Representation Of Plot - A plot is modelled as a linear list of events. These events in the list correspond to animations that are played in the 3D virtual world. Some events are triggers for behaviours (*trigger events*), and need to be initiated by the plot manager. The rest (*behaviour events*) occur as a result of these triggers, and are part of a behaviour, meaning that they do not need to be initiated by the plot manager. As already mentioned, plots are attached to objects in the scene. The template plot is initialised as the list of events that is attached to objects present in the world at the commencement of the story. Within the list of events that constitutes a plot, certain events are identified as the initiation of a conflict, and others as the resolution of a conflict.

Management Of Plot - To make the management of the plot more tractable, two simplifying assumptions have been made: firstly, that no more than one conflict can be 'active' (i.e. unresolved) at any one time; secondly, that the order in which conflict/resolution pairs occur is unimportant. These assumptions may seem naive, but they are not unreasonable in the context of the simple, problem-solving narratives of the Tiny Planets series. Once our system has been validated using these initial simplifying assumptions, they will be discarded in favour of a more realistic approach.

The plot manager takes care of the interplay between user, system and template plot. When the user is active, the plot manager keeps track of any conflicts or resolutions from the template plot that the user may trigger, and keeps him updated on the situation via the narrator. When the user is inactive, the plot manager steps through the template plot until he becomes active again. The functioning of the plot manager is made clearer by the example in Figure 2.

Introduction Of New Objects/Subplots - A subplot attached to a newly introduced object is represented (like the template plot) as a list of events. This list is inserted in to the template plot list either immediately after the current event (if no conflict is active), or after the event that resolves the current conflict (if a conflict is active).

The Narrator - The narrator gives verbal prompts to the user, as well as a more brief text prompt at the bottom of the screen. It can be viewed as the 'voice' of the kindergarten assistant described in the introduction - it mediates the processes of scaffolding and metaplay.

4 Conclusions and Future Work

In this paper, we have described a new approach to interactive narrative, Object Oriented Prompted Play (O2P2). We have also given a sketch of an interactive narrative system that implements this concept. Our pragmatic approach avoids difficult issues of narrative coherence and understanding by fashioning an experience in which play is the primary constituent. The stories attached to the objects in the 3D virtual world, along with prompts from the narrator, apply a narrative structure to this play, resulting in a system that combines the desirable attributes of open-ended play with those of structured narrative. We are applying this system to short, simple narratives of a problem solving nature, but we see it as having applications in many different situations.

At present, we have implemented an interactive pilot of the 3D Tiny Planets world, with behaviours embedded in objects and narrator functionality. Work for the immediate future includes following this implementation through to completion, and testing the system on users. More distant goals are to investigate how the system would work if we removed the simplifying assumptions that were made, to explore character intelligence and growth throughout the narrative, and to deal with the issue of the management of the system's growth as new objects are added by the user.

Finally, we believe that the key to providing more engaging experiences from interactive media in the future is to strike a balance between the culturally fundamental activities of "story telling" and "play". Object Oriented Prompted Play (O2P2) is a paradigm which offers such a balance.

Acknowledgements. TINY-IN is funded by EPSRC grant GR/R54361/01 under the DTI Broadcast Link initiative. Collaborators are KMi (Open University), R. Joiner (University of Bath) and Pepper's Ghost Productions. Thanks to Carl Goodman (PGP), Peter Stansfield (Wavecrest Systems Ltd.) and Criterion Software Inc. for the use of RenderWare^{TM}.

References

1. Bobick, A.F., Intille, S.S., Davis, J.W., Baird, F., Pinhanez, C.S., Campbell, L.W., Ivanov, Y.A., Schutte, A. and Wilson, A.: Perceptual User Interfaces: the KidsRoom. In Communications of the ACM 43(3) (March 2000) 60–61
2. Dourish, P.: Where the Action Is: The Foundations of Embodied Interaction. Massachusetts Institute of Technology (2001)
3. Mateas, M. and Stern, A.: Architecture, Authorial Idioms and Early Observation of the Interactive Drama Facade. Tech Report CMU-CS-02-198, School of Computer Science, Carnegie Mellon University, Pittsburgh, PA (December 2002)
4. Hayes-Roth, B., Brownston, L., and van Gent, R.: Multiagent collaboration in directed improvisation. Stanford University Report KSL-94-69 (1994)
5. Propp, V.: Morphology of the Folktale. In International Journal of American Linguistics, Vol. 24, Nr. 4, Part III, Bloomington, IN, (1958)
6. Ryokai, K. and Cassell, J.: Computer Support for Children's Collaborative Fantasy Play and Storytelling. In Proceedings of CSCL '99 (1999)
7. Sawyer, R.K.: Improvisation and Narrative. In Narrative Inquiry, 12(2), John Benjamins B.V. Amsterdam (2002) 319–349
8. Szilas, N.: IDtension: a narrative engine for Interactive Drama. In Proc. of TIDSE 2003 (Darmstadt, Germany), AAAI Press, 72-76(March 2003) 72–76

Transferring Game Mastering Laws to Interactive Digital Storytelling

Federico Peinado and Pablo Gervás

Dep. Sistemas Informáticos y Programación
Universidad Complutense de Madrid, Spain
fpeinado@fdi.ucm.es pgervas@sip.ucm.es
http://gaia.sip.ucm.es

Abstract. The Interactive Dilemma is the inevitable conflict between author's determinism and interactor's freedom. There are some approaches that try to tackle it, using strategies and heuristic rules that can combine on the fly the previously designed author material with the run-time decisions of the interactor. Interactive Narrative is a relatively new field and it is difficult to find formal studies that shows how to create this kind of art. Our proposal is based on the theoretical study of table-top Role-Playing Games and it involves the practical implementation of those ideas for managing the interaction in a simple text adventure game. Game Masters are the best models we have found in real life for designing and directing interactive stories. In this paper we transfer their player modeling, their rules for interaction management and their improvising algorithms from the real world to a new Interactive Storytelling system.

1 Introduction

The main problem of Interactive Digital Storytelling (IDS) design is structuring an intensive and meaningful interactive experience at the same time as enabling the development of a good pre-authored plot. This is a real dilemma, because while the interactor is taking a lot of decisions about the performance of his character that change the plot development, the author's plan may have been developed according to a different storyline.

Many approaches are found in the literature that try to solve this conflict in an automated or semi-automated way. Basically, they make interactive storylines by adapting author's plot units or other pre-established resources to the interactor behaviour at run-time. This task requires a computational solution that can react appropriately to "unexpected" user behavior.

Because Interactive Narrative is a relatively new field and it is difficult to find formal studies about interactive plot development, we have done a review over the pen-and-paper methodology of Role-Playing Games (RPGs) and now we are coding a practical implementation of these ideas in a textual game.

S. Göbel et al. (Eds.): TIDSE 2004, LNCS 3105, pp. 48–54, 2004.
© Springer-Verlag Berlin Heidelberg 2004

2   The Main Pillars of Our Approach

Our approach is based on developing a Case-Based Reasoning (CBR) model of a particular set of algorithms and heuristics for role-playing game mastering, and applying this model to drive the interactions in a multiplayer i-fiction engine.

2.1   Case-Based Reasoning in Interactive Storytelling

In searching for the right computational solution, widely different approaches have been proposed by researchers in the area. For example, there are proposals based on dynamic behavior of non-player characters that achieve dramatic goals [1,10]. Other approaches give more responsibility to a central dramatic planning algorithm, using directable non-player characters [5,2] or just a stand-alone dramatic planner that controls the most important narrative elements, like characters [6] or the whole fictional world [3]. In the work of [2] the CBR full life cycle -retrieval, adaptation, reuse and repair of previous solutions for new problems- is used for storyline representation and a strategy formalization that allows for storyline adaptation.

2.2   Role-Playing Game Mastering

Tabletop RPGs are exercises in intellect and imagination: a group of players sitting around a table, rolling dices and playing out an imaginary role in a complex shared fantasy, true collaborative narrative.

The Game Master (GM) is a special kind of player, he is the "interactive storyteller". He designs all the elements of the story and he manage all the possible events that can occur in its development, improvising the dialogue contributions of non-player characters, resolving players actions, etc.

The degree of interactivity in RPG can be enormous, limited only by the players imagination. This implies that no GM, however experienced, can have a deep enough plan to react appropriately to all the possible actions that players can come up with in the world of fiction. To operate successfully without such a plan, GMs must use their imagination, improvise adequate solutions, and continuously rewrite their plots on the fly.

The figure of GM is the best model we have found in real life for designing and directing interactive stories. For the development of the work presented here we have used the description of the relevant heuristics given by Robin Laws [4].

Player Models and Plot Hooks. Laws identifies seven basic types of role-players according to their motivation and the sort of characteristics that they expect of a game in order to consider satisfactory. These motivation characteristics are referred to as *plot hooks*.

Power Gamer searches for new abilities and special equipment.
Butt-Kicker always waits for a chance to fight with someone else.

Tactician feels happy in the anticlimax scenes, thinking about logical obstacles to overcome.

Specialist just wants to do the things that his favorite character do.

Method Actor needs situations that test his personality traits.

Storyteller looks for complex plot threads and action movement.

Casual Gamer remains in the background (and has a very low degree of participation in general).

Improvising Algorithm. According to Laws, the decisions that a GM must take to achieve a satisfactory game of all his players must take into account the player models into which he has classified them and the particular plot hooks that these models require. This is achieved by applying an *improvising algorithm* that must guide the choices that a GM makes in response to a game situation.

1. Imagine the most obvious result.
2. Imagine the most challenging result[1].
3. Imagine the most surprising result.
4. Imagine the result most pleasing to the players.
5. Pick the one that feels right[2]. This may be done at random, though some weighting should be applied to preserve credibility.
6. Think of consequences[3]. If the consequences seem bad, try another choice.

2.3   Internet Adventure Game Engine

Text Adventure Games, broadly known as the Interactive Fiction genre, appeared as the first narrative games at the end of 70's. Originally, interactive fictions are like interactive books, only made of text chunks. They have complex plots and offers a narrative presentation to the player. In this kind of games, story and world simulation are tightly coupled.

Internet Adventure Game Engine (IAGE [9]) is a Java Open Source project for the development of a multiplayer interactive fiction system. In contrast to Massive Multiplayer Online Role-Playing Games (MMORPGs), which maintain a lot of players playing at the same time, with as many ongoing stories as users connected to the server, IAGE allows one pre-authored storyline with the added possibility of having more than one player immersed in the same story. IAGE can be also used to create single player adventures like traditional systems as Inform [7].

---

[1] Find a challenge based on the goals of the PC that has had the least spotlight-time in the recent interactions.

[2] Maybe two or more at the same time.

[3] A choice should not endanger the success of a climax that had been previously planned by the GM.

3   Our Computational Model of Interactive Storytelling

We are trying to design a Multiplayer & Directed Interactive Fiction Engine driven by Role-Playing Heuristic Rules. We propose a Knowledge Intensive CBR (KI-CBR) approach to the problem of generating interactive stories from the game state and a set of cases specifying how the next scene will be performed. In our model of Interactive Storytelling, adapted from the original RPG conventions, we separate the world simulation from the story control. The IDS system that we are considering has a narrative environment with a high level of interactivity (textual commands) and uses IAGE as a low level world simulator. Over that we have a CBR system that can guide the development of plot, building creative new situations on the fly from the case base.

Our system involves a certain amount of explicit knowledge, an heuristic for assigning player models, and a plot driving algorithm.

Explicit Knowlege: the Ontology and the Case Base. For the development of our system structuralist models of conventional narratives have been used. In particular, the character functions of is Vladimir Propp's Morphology of the Folk Tale [8] are used as basic recurrent units of a plot. In order to be able to use them computationally, they have been translated into an ontology that gives semantic coherence and structure to our cases. The case base is built by the game author using these functions as building blocks.

An additional ontology provides the background knowledge required by the system, as well as the respective information about characters, places and objects of our world. This is used to measure the semantical distance between similar cases or situations, and maintaining a independent story structure from the simulated world. The domain knowledge of our application is the classic might-and-magic world with magicians, warriors, thieves, princesses, etc.

The author fills the case base with scenes that contain preconditions and postconditions. Each case is structured in terms of an ontology of domain knowledge: character, places, models of players, etc. The semantic constraints between scene transitions are loosely based on the ordering and co-occurrence constraints established between Proppian functions. Because the case base is made using cases proposed by the author, we know that the system makes variants of the same "interactive plot" so the author creativity (at the scene-level) is preserved.

Interactor Models and Scene Postconditions. In order to apply the algorithm described above, it is crucial to identify correctly the character profile of the player. In a RPG, this task must be carried out based on limited information like the description of the character explicitly required by the rules, observation of the player's reactions, and possibly the player's record in previous games. To simulate this dynamically in an interactive system is the next step of this study. For our current purposes, it is enough to provide players with a set of seven predefined characters, such that each one of them is related with a specific interactor model. It is hoped that players of a specific model will under such conditions choose the type of character most related to their preferences in playing. The initial adscription of player model to character type will be used by the system to assign player models to the players.

The plot hooks for Power Gamers, Butt-Kickers, Tacticians and Specialists are the easiest to implement. If a scene involves obtaining special abilities, engaging in combat, solving logical puzzles, or displaying particular skills - like magic in the case of magicians, for instance -, this appears explicitly in the postcondition of the scene. This means that the scene cannot finish unless at least one player carries out the postcondition.

In the case of Method Actors and Storytellers, their plot hooks are more complex because they require that not only the choice of content for particular scenes but also the structure of the ongoing story be modified to fulfill their particular requests. When players of one of these models take part, the system must retrieve a sequence of scenes marked as interesting for the model involved. For instance, the system would retrieve for a Method Actor a sequence that involves the development of a moral conflict, and one that introduces a secondary plot for a Storyteller.

In the application of the current version of the plot driving algorithm, the system does not take into account Casual Gamers that take part in the story.

Plot Driving Algorithm. Our Algorithm is very similar to Law's one. The case retrieval takes place using similarity assessment over the case base.

The CBR system uses two similarity functions. The first one is used to recover the scene that leads to the most obvious transition from the current scene. The inverse of this similarity function is used to find the scene that provides the most surprising transition.

The second similarity function is used to retrieve the scene that involves the most pleasing transition from the current scene. The definition of *how pleasing a scene is* is given by the number of easy tasks matching the players plot hooks that appear - and disappear - in the transition. The inverse function is used to find the scene that provides the most challenging transition, one which involves the appearance of a high number of difficult tasks that also match the plot hooks of the players.

In this way the algorithm includes a number of obvious paths and other paths that may progressively get more positive for the players interests. Additionally, it may include surprising or negative scenes.

An Example of Scene Transition Selection. Group of players: 2 Butt-Kickers, 1 Storyteller and 1 Causal Gamer.

- Scene A: The adventure starts.
- Preconditions: none.
- Description: Players are in a pub, drinking beer and talking about their adventures. There are at least two different non-player characters that have a mission for them.
- Postcondition: accept a mission.

When the algorithm is executed, it decides to select a surprising scene transition. The system retrieves a scene from the case base and the following scene is obtained:

- Scene N: Surprise attack by orcs.
- Preconditions: the previous scene did not involve combat.
- Description: Orcs appear suddenly and attack the players with no motive.
- Postcondition: all the orcs are killed.

By virtue of a heuristic defined by the author, no enemies may appear in the story before the fourth scene. This invalidates the retrieved scene as a possible continuation, so it is rejected and another one is retrieved from the case base.

This time the algorithm chooses and obvious transition, a scene is retrieved and the system comes up with:

- Scene N: The mission starts with a journey.
- Preconditions: players have accepted the mission.
- Description: A long trip must be undertaken to the place where the mission will take place.
- Postcondition: arrive at the journey's end.

The presence of two Butt-Kickers in the group implies that scene N is topped up with arbitrary combats during the journey. This is possible because the scenes in the case base only specify partial descriptions of their content, and the algorithm must fill them in dynamically during the adaptation stage of the CBR cycle. As described, this is done taking the players preferences into account.

For instance, the fact that there is a Storyteller in the group requires the system to carry out additionally some long term planning before it can fill in the scene. In this case, the man that offers the players a mission also charges them with carrying a mysterious box to their journey's end, a box that may not be opened at any time. This introduces the seed of a possible secondary plot that the system can use at later stages to satisfy the plot hooks of the Storyteller.

The presence of a Casual Gamer has played no part in the algorithm.

4   Conclusions

Although the system is not fully-implemented yet, the progress so far points to a reasonable solution to the Interactive Dilemma. Once it is fully developed, our approach has applications for every project that is looking for heuristics and algorithms to tackle the interactive dilemma on IDS systems.

We intend to make the system available on the web to let the people play and study the effects of the automated director on the game.

Acknowledgements. The first author is supported by a FPI Predoctoral Grant from Complutense University of Madrid. The work was partially funded by the Spanish Committee of Science & Technology (TIC2002-01961).

References

1. M. Cavazza, F. Charles, and S. J. Mead. Character based interactive storytelling. *IEEE Intelligent Systems*, 17:17–22, 2002.
2. C. Fairclough and P. Cunningham. A multiplayer case based story engine. In *GAME-ON Conference*, pages 41–, 2003.
3. A. S. Gordon and N. V. Iuppa. Experience management using storyline adaptation strategies. In *First International Conference on Technologies for Digital Storytelling and Entertainment*, Darmstadt, Germany, 2003.
4. R. D. Laws. *Robin's Laws of Good Game Mastering*. Steve Jackson Games, first edition, 2002.
5. S. C. Marsella, W. L. Johnson, and L. Catherine. Interactive pedagogical drama. In C. Sierra, M. Gini, and J. S. Rosenschein, editors, *Fourth International Conference on Autonomous Agents*, pages 301–308, Barcelona, Spain, 2000. ACM Press.
6. M. Mateas and A. Stern. Façade: An experiment in building a fully-realized interactive drama. In *Game Developers Conference, Game Design track*, 2003.
7. G. Nelson. *Inform Manual*. Interactive Fiction Library, USA, fourth edition, 2001. http://www.inform-fiction.org/.
8. V. Propp. *Morphology of the Folktale*. University of Texas Press, Austin, 1968.
9. R. Rawson-Tetley. Internet adventure game engine (IAGE), 2002. http://www.ifarchive.org/if-archive/programming/iage/.
10. R. M. Young. Notes on the use of plan structure in the creation of interactive plot. Technical Report FS-99-01, AAAI Fall Symposium on Narrative Intelligence, AAAI Press, Menlo Park, 1999.

Narrativity of User Experience

Presence as Transportation in IVE Based Narrative Systems

Shachindra Nath

Central Saint Martin's College of Art and Design
University of the Arts London
s.nath@synesis.tv

Abstract. This paper discusses how the concept of *narrativity* can be applied to the nature of the performative experience in IVE based participative story systems. VR technology affords an experience that has a strong narrative potential provided the design and evaluation are done from a user centred perspective. The concept of *presence* is discussed in relation to literary, film and performance theories' explanation of *transportation* in a fictional world.

1 Introduction

The key aspect this paper will address concerns the measure of narrativity in user experience. In the study of IVEs the closest concept and measure for the purpose is that of *presence*. As a concept *presence* enables us to understand the experiential peculiarities of the VR medium. As a measure it indicates the overall quality and success / failure of the experience created in VR. The central thesis of this paper is that in the context of IVE based narrative systems the study of presence needs to be viewed differently. Amongst the objective measures of presence, technologies of measuring affective states can not only provide a strong indication of the quality of the experience, but also provide a basis for real-time management of narrative order.

2 Presence, Transportation, and Narrative Potential

An important prerequisite for narrativity in the fictional world is the embodied sense of being the character performed, and the sense of being there in the fictional world[1]. This aspect of the experience of narrative fiction has been referred to by the use of the term *transportation* as indicative of *immersion* in the fictional world. The prime experiential characteristic of experience in IVEs, the concept and measure of *presence*, indicates an encouraging possibility of *transportation*. For the purpose of discussion,

---

[1] In performance an individual takes on the identity of the character while simultaneously lending her identity to the character. Being 'in character' is not just identifying with the role but embodying and inhabiting it [21].

S. Göbel et al. (Eds.): TIDSE 2004, LNCS 3105, pp. 55–60, 2004.

in this paper, I will use the term *transportation* to indicate *presence* in a fictional world, and distinguish it from the latter on the issue of assumption of a character identity.

The assumption of the 'spirit' of the character role played by the user is a fundamental aspect of narrative experience. It is related to potentiality of action and its meaningfulness. It is both the object and the result of *transportation*. It is intimately related to our sense of being there and makes the fictional virtual space 'a place'[2].

In VR, user experience is characterised by being enveloped in a 3D space (*immersion*) inducing sense of presence. The highly nebulous concept and empirical measure of *presence* is used to indicate *transportation* [25]. *Transportation* in presence studies has mostly to do with the sense of being physically relocated in a virtual environment [2], [5], [10], [22], [27], [29]. The concept of presence, however, extends beyond just the sensory perception of being in an other-than-real space. As Biocca puts it "at one point in time, users can be said to feel as if they are physically present in only one of the three places: the physical environment, the virtual environment, or the imaginal environment. Presence oscillates between these three poles." [2]. O'Brien et al. have linked presence to the concept of inter-subjectivity [18], [25]. Presence needs to be viewed and measured in the context of the user's assumption of a virtual identity and 'imaginal' persona, in other words it needs to be viewed in relation to *transportation* into a fictional world.

Psychologist Richard Gerrig presents a metaphorical account of the 'performative' act of reading that is indicative of the story experience as a journey [7]. I will build on Marie-Laure Ryan's discussion [20:93-94] of Gerrig's metaphor in relation to views on *presence*. Gerrig explains the concept of transportation in terms of the experiencer travelling [7:10-11] to the fictional world:

1. *the traveller is transported…* the reader is taken to a story world, and 'the text determines his role in this world, thereby shaping his textual identity' [20:93]. The extension of the sense of being there to the sense of 'inhabiting' a position in that 'place' is necessary to defining and measuring presence in narrative systems.

2. *by some means of transportation…* the mediation becomes the means of this transportation. The identity and the role are determined by the affordances [8], [25], [33] in the environment. Current VR technologies can be categorised in terms of the possibilities and constraints offered by the input and output devices [23:25-43]. The four main categories are Desktop VR, Binocular Omni-Orientation Monitor (BOOM), CAVE and Head Mounted Displays (HMD). These offer three types of embodied experiences:

   a. Disembodied: e.g. multiple camera angle views of the protagonist and her actions in her environment

   b. Embodied There-body: e.g. over the shoulder view or camera following protagonist sort of visual perspective of the protagonists world.

---

[2] "Space lies open; it suggests the future and invites action. Enclosed and humanised space is place" [30:54]

c. Embodied Here-body: e.g. first person view from inside the body of the protagonist.

VR technologies need also be viewed in terms of the degree of virtual embodiment (the replacement of the real with a virtual body). The CAVE, then would require a higher willingness on the part of the user in the assumption of a fictional identity. HMDs are inherent with the possibilities of a stronger sense of virtual embodiment [12] and presence. It can be argued that the possibility of a virtual body supports *transportation* in the same way as the adornment of costume and make-up increasing the creative possibilities of the narrative experience. It is clear that the degree and nature of virtual embodiment has a direct impact on the degree and nature of *narrativity in performance*. The degree of virtual embodiment as representative of the quality of narrative experience may, however, not be related to the awareness of technological mediation [33].

3. *as a result of performing certain actions...*the experience of transportation is not passive, but is determined by her actions. 'The reader's enjoyment thus depends on his own performance.' [20:94]. The quality of the experience and its narrativity depend on the user's actions and desire within the 'laws' of the story world [25], [33]. This, however, does not mean that the VE should mimic everyday reality; the VE should enable the formulation of a reality construct [17] or a 'world' [11:90-91]. *Transportation* then, extends Witmer and Singer's involvement and immersion based concept of presence [31] and includes Schubert et al.'s conceptualisation of *embodied presence* [24]. This indicates that a fundamental aspect of achieving *transportation* is being able to conceptualise the laws governing the story world. Our reconstruction of the laws governing the fictional world will be formed not so much by information (pre-briefing) as by 'making things happen' and humanising the events.

4. *The traveller goes some distance from his or her world of origin, which makes some aspects of the world of origin inaccessible...* she 'adapts to the laws of this world, which differ to various degrees from the laws of his native world'. The construct of the story world specifies 'the rules that guide the construction of a valid reality model' [20:95]. *Transportation,* then, implies not just the degree of sensory deprivation [12] of real world stimulus, it also implies a surrender to the virtual one. Whether we call this 'the willingness to suspend disbelief' [29] or the active creation of belief [16], it indicates the psychological dimension of *exclusive presence* [28]. *Transportation* implies presence in the fictional world effected by a willing act of *suspending the real*, leaving it behind as it were.

5. *The traveller returns to the world of origin, somewhat changed by the journey.* Schechner while discussing performances in theatre, distinguishes them into 'transformation' - wherein performers are changed, and, 'transportation' - wherein performers and audience are "taken somewhere" into a different virtual world, but return back to ordinary life at the end [21]. Experiences of fiction are characterised by the awareness of fictionality, at some level we know that we will return to the real world. Thus, presence is never complete and this awareness of the impending reality has a part to play in the whole experience.

In the above discussion we have seen that a high degree of presence can be related to the potentiality of narrative. However, perhaps a well rounded concept of presence, one more indicative of *transportation*, will be necessary for systems aiming to provide narrative experiences. It is also evident that *transportation* might not be immediate, and would require 'warming up' before the system and user plunge into narrative emergence. Another inherent implication of narrative emergence is that a measure of presence will be critical in maintaining / ensuring the narrativity of emergence. In the following section of this paper I will use the term *presence* as inclusive of *transportation* in a story world.

2.1 Measuring Presence

Most theories of *presence* agree that it indicates a subjective sensation of "being there", consequently most commonly used measures are based on subjective ratings based on self-reporting. While such measures elucidate the phenomenology of immersive experiences, they remain post-test measures dependent on memory of an event [4]. In the context of emergent narrative systems, such measures are not much help. In participative emergence, a system needs to guide the progressive adaptation of *narrative state* in relation to the *user state* [17], it needs a continuous measure of presence *during* the experience. Dillon et al. [4] suggest objective measures to study presence during the experience.

Since people tend to respond to mediated stimuli as if it were unmediated when they experience high levels of presence, observation and inference of their behaviour could provide an objective measure of presence [19], [25]. While it is true that *presence* is a complex mental manifestation and physiological measurement can not capture its entirety [26], research has attempted to link specific behaviours or mental phenomena to the occurrence or non-occurrence of specific physiological patterns [3], [14], [15]. Measuring Electrodermal activity (EDA), cardiovascular activity through Electrocardiogram (ECG), muscle tension through Electromyogram (EMG), changes in Blood Volume Pressure (BVP), respiration, and recognising emotions through involuntary facial muscle activity can also be used to indicate intensity and 'family' of emotion. [1], [4], [6], [9], [13], [32]. Emotional engagement is an unfailing indicator of presence. Emotions viewed in the context in which occur is an unfailing indicator of the process of meaning creation (transportation).

3 Conclusion

In this paper I have looked at the core aspects of narrativity in the context of user experience in IVEs. We have also seen that the pre-requisite to narrativity in participative emergence is presence (transportation) in the narrative world. In so much as emotion is a basic factor in the creation of meaning, and constitutes the most plausible measure of presence, emotional engagement becomes the prime concern in the narrative process. The narrative potential of experiences in the medium are related to the kind and degree of virtual embodiment, and character identification made available. Creators of such systems therefore need to consider user emotion and its contextual role in the performative position the mediating technology affords. The coherence of the 'reality' construct of the narrative world is also critical in maintaining and enhancing presence in such systems.

References

1. Bernstein, A. S.: The orienting response and direction of stimulus change, Psychonomic Science, Vol. 12, No. 4, pp. 127-128. 1968
2. Biocca, F.: The Cyborg's Dilemma: Progressive Embodiment in Virtual Environments, in Journal of Computer-Mediated Communication, vol. 3 no. 2. 1997
3. Cacioppo, J.T. and L.G. Tassinary: Inferring Psychological Significance from Physiological Signals, in American Psychologist, vol. 45, p.p. 16-18. 1990
4. Dillon, Cath, Ed Keogh, Jonathan Freeman and Jules Davidoff: Aroused and Immersed: The Psychophysiology of Presence. Goldsmith College / Independent Television Commission (UK). 2000
5. Ditton, T. and M. Lombard: At the Heart of It All: The Concept of Presence, in Journal of Computer-Mediated Communication, vol. 3 no. 2. 1997.
6. Ekman, P. and E. Rosenberg: What the Face Reveals: Basic and Applied Studies of Spontaneous Expression Using the Facial Action Coding System. Oxford University Press, Oxford. 1998.
7. Gerrig, Richard J. Experiencing Narrative Worlds: On the Psychological Activities of Reading. Yale University Press, New Haven. 1993.
8. Gibson, J.J. The Ecological Approach to Visual Perception, Houghton Mifflin. 1979
9. Greenwald, M.K., E.W. Cook and P.J. Lang.: Affective Judgement and Psychophysiological Response. Dimensional Covariation in the Evaluation of Pictorial Stimuli, in Journal of Psychophysiology, vol. 3, p.p. 51-64. 1989.
10. Heeter, C.: Being There: The Subjective Experience of Presence, in Presence, vol.1 no.2. 1992.
11. Heim, Michael. Virtual Realism. Oxford University Press, NY, Oxford. 1998
12. Ihde, Don: Bodies, Virtual Bodies and Technology, in Donn Welton ed. Body and Flesh: A Philosophical Reader. p.p. 349-357, Blackwell, 1998
13. Izard, C.E.: Innate and Universal Facial Expressions: Evidence from Developmental and Cross Cultural Research, in Psychological Bulletin, vol. 115, p.p. 288-299. 1994.
14. Lang, P.J., M.K. Greenwald, M.M. Bradley and A.O. Hamm: Looking at Pictures: Affective, Facial, Visceral and Behavioural Reactions, in Psychophysiology, vol. 30, p.p. 261-273. 1993.
15. Levenson, R.W.: Autonomic Nervous System Differences among Emotions, in Psychological Science, vol. 3, p.p. 23-27. 1992.
16. Murray, Janet H.: Hamlet on the Holodeck: The Future of Narrative in Cyberspace. Free Press, 1997
17. Nath, S.: Story, Plot and Character Action: Narrative Experience as an Emotional Braid, in S. Göbel, N. Braun, U. Spirling, J. Dechau and Holger Diener eds. Proceedings of the Technologies for Interactive Digital Storytelling and Entertainment (TIDSE) Conference 2003, p.p. 1-18. Fraunhofer IRB Verlag, Darmstadt. 2003.

18. O'Brien, J., M. Büscher, T. Rodden, J. Trevor: Red is Behind You: The Experience of Presence in Shared Virtual Environments paper presented at the Workshop on Presence in Shared Virtual Environments 1998.
19. Prothero, J.D., D.E. Parker, T. Furness III.: Towards a Robust, Quantitative Measure for Presence in Proceedings of the Conference on Experimental Analysis and Measurement of Situation Awareness, p.p. 359-366. 1995.
20. Ryan, Marie-Laure. Narrative as Virtual Reality: Immersion and Interactivity in Literature and Electronic Media. The Johns Hopkins University Press, Baltimore, London. 2001
21. Schechner, Richard. Performative Circumstances from the Avant Garde to Ramlila. Seagull Books, 1983
22. Schloerb, D.W.: A Quantitative Measure of Presence, in Presence, vol.4 no.1. 1995.
23. Schroeder, Ralph. PossibleWorlds: The Social Dynamic of Virtual Reality. Westview Press. 1996
24. Schubert, T.W., F. Friedmann and H.T. Regenbrecht: Embodied Presence in Virtual Environments, in Visual Representations and Interpretations, p.p. 268-278. Springer-Verlag, London. 1999.
25. Schuemie, Martin J., Peter van der Straaten, Merel Krijn and Charles A.P.G. van der Mast: Research on Presence in VR: a Survey, in Cyberpsychology and Behaviour, Jan 2001.
26. Sheridan, T.B.: Descartes, Heidegger, Gibson, and God: Towards an Eclectic Ontology of Presence, in Presence, vol.8 no.5, p.p. 551-559. 1999.
27. Slater, M. and M. Usoh: Representation Systems, Perceptual Positions, and Presence in Immersive Virtual Environments, in Presence, vol. 3 no. 2, p.p. 130-144. 1993
28. Slater, M., M. Usoh and A. Steed: Depth of Presence in Virtual Environments, in Presence, vol.3 no.6, p.p. 130-144. 1994.
29. Steuer, Jonathan: Defining Virtual reality: Dimensions Determining Telepresence. SRTC paper 104. 1993
30. Tuan, Y.F.: Space and Place: The Perspective of Experience. University of Minnesota Press, Minneapolis. 1974
31. Witmer, B.G. and M.J. Singer.: Measuring Presence in Virtual Environments: A Presence Questionnaire, in Presence, vol.7 no.3. 1998
32. Yaremko, R.M., M.W. Blair and B.T. Leckhart: The Orienting Reflex to Changes in Conceptual Stimulus Dimension, in Psychonomic Science, vol.5, p.p. 317-318. 1970
33. Zahorik, P. and R.L. Jenison: Presence as Being-In-The-World, in Presence, vol.7 no.1. 1998.

Integrated Decision Points for Interactive Movies

Gabriela Tully and Susan Turner

School of Computing, Napier University, Edinburgh, EH10 5DT, UK.
{g.tully, s.turner}@napier.ac.uk

Abstract We describe a study which explores alternative means of communicating decision points in an interactive movie. The two variants used novel, non-disruptive cues embedded in the movie itself: a fade to black and white and a zoom effect accompanied by subtle sound cues. Both the interactivity and its presentation were received very positively in trials and perceived to enhancing the experience of the movie greatly, despite the fact that not all viewers recognised interaction points easily.

1 Introduction

Interactive movies have been produced since the at least early 1990s. Their development has, however, save a few exceptions, been frustrated by a combination of technological limitations and by the competing possibility of more powerful engagement and illusion of control over storyworlds, promised by virtual reality (VR) storytelling environments. Today, the delay in VR materialising as an accessible form of entertainment and technological advances have seen the re-emergence of interactive movies as a significant entertainment possibility. Further, in a world where entertainment is no longer seen as a passive experience, but also as exercising the power of transformation, the idea of personalised experiences of dramatic movies appears a natural progression from traditional film storytelling.

The new format brings with it creative possibilities, but also some significant challenges. In order to make its experience worthwhile, it is necessary to understand the elements which can make it enjoyable, the implications of adding the power of interaction to a traditionally unilateral activity (viewing), and finally how design solutions work best to tie narrative, filmic representation and interaction together.

The current research combines concepts from film and interaction design to investigate a selection of such issues. In particular, it examines whether and how an interactive movie interface can preserve the pleasure of involvement in narrative worlds, associated with traditional movies, whilst supporting the participation of viewers in the shaping of their own experience of these worlds and the overall story. By its very nature, interaction in movies is disruptive to narrative immersion: viewers are distracted from the story and their involvement in the storyworld to focus on decision making and subsequent possibilities The usual approach to interactive movie interfaces increases further the effects of interruption by stopping the narrative and waiting for interaction, and by adding graphical artefacts to alert viewers of decision points.

S. Göbel et al. (Eds.): TIDSE 2004, LNCS 3105, pp. 61–67, 2004.

One of the aims of this work is to explore alternatives to interruptive decision points, and to establish whether these alternatives can provide for better overall experiences of the interactive movie format.

2 Non-intrusive Interaction for Interactive Movies

This section briefly discusses the work of the few designers of interactive movies who have explored interaction mediated without explicit cues. Favre, for example, suggests that, in parallel narratives, the cue for interactivity could be a character leaving a scene, giving the viewer the opportunity to follow or stay with the remaining character(s) [1]. Guy Vardi [2] explored a similar notion: by clicking on characters, viewers can see a story through their point of view. This idea of turning characters into links in parallel narratives is also present in Margi Szperling's interactive movie *Uncompressed* [3]. Interaction here is possible only with visually "active" characters: they "pulsate" from a bright to a normal colour, indicating decision points.

Perhaps the most prolific designer of innovative interactive interfaces for movies is artist Chris Hales. Hales has developed a series of interactive movies, in installations and CD-ROM, which convey interaction in differing, original ways. In a series of pieces produced between 1995 and 2000 [4], he explored the idea of turning scene objects, people and the whole filmic frame into links. These are active only at brief, key times, and clicking on them (or touching, in the case of installations) causes the movie to respond. Cues are given through sounds, colourful, vibrating "things" against a duller background, focus and point of view metaphors, special effects   or split screens, or are not provided at all: viewers are informed that some things are interactive and are left to explore the movie frame looking for them. Hales' approaches propose innovations which explore how better to utilise interaction to transmit a message, to provoke insights, to challenge what movies should be, to tell stories through viewer participation and response.

The current research explores further how some of these solutions cue viewers for interaction without inserting elements exterior to the movie world; and, more specifically, whether this approach, applied to more complete dramatic narrative structures, can reduce interruption to narrative immersion during decision points. It also provides an account of viewer's reactions to these concepts, an element which is missing from published accounts of most of the work just discussed.

3 The Integrated Interface and Its Evaluation

The intention of the design and evaluation work was to explore the general potential and challenges of the integrated interface approach in an interactive movie, *Embora*. We should acknowledge that this is not a finished interactive movie, but a "study" piece, constrained by implementation time, the creative talent and amateur filmmaking skills of the first author and the talent of the volunteer actors. *Embora* is a branched, node-based (see [5], for a comparison of narrative structures) interactive movie depicting the story of two people struggling to cope with their relationship. Events, rather than temporal sequence, are the key to an understanding of the characters' trials and tribulations. As the story progresses, causal relationships between events can be inferred. In the last two scenes, however, a temporal perspective provides closure to the preceding events.

The story is viewed as a sequence of nodes of approximately two minutes each - the first and last nodes being exceptions (3 and 1 min. respectively). The movie has ten nodes in total, six being viewable in any one session, lasting a total of 12 minutes. The intention is to provide well-rounded segments of information before every interaction point. The opening node familiarises viewers with the main female character and allows them to 'recentre' their world around the characters' own. The subsequent nodes, which compose the story's development *per se*, are organised in two default routes. These culminate in the same closing scene. At the end of each node a decision point is reached: viewers may remain passive and view the next default segment, or interact and view an alternative node, as shown in Figure 1. The plot itself remains unchanged; what varies is the information presented to viewers. After experiencing the movie a first time, viewers may decide to re-experience it by interacting at different points, filling the gaps as in a jigsaw puzzle. In total there are 16 possible viewing combinations. The movie uses DVD technology and responds to a single press on the OK button (or ENTER, depending on player) on the remote control (or on-screen control if viewing on a computer).

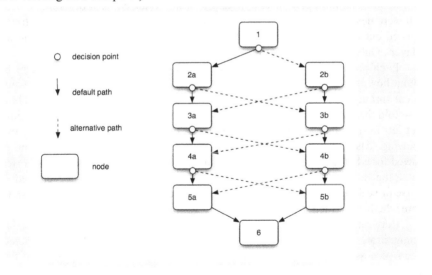

Fig. 1. The structure of the movie

Two main different versions of the movie were developed, with differing integrated interface solutions for decision points but following the overall structure described above. The two are referred to here by names mirroring their approach: "Black and

White", and "Zoom". A third version, "Cuts" was also produced, but the effects proved too subtle to attract notice in a pilot trial and was not pursued further.

In the "Black and White" version, at the end of nodes the camera focuses on a significant object in the scene from different angles, in a montage of reasonably fast shots – c. 1.5 to 2 seconds. The pictures fade from colour to black and white. At the end of eight to ten seconds the pictures fade out altogether, and the decision point ends. In the "Zoom" version, as the camera frames the significant object, it steadily zooms in until the image loses focus and fades out. Simultaneously, sounds representing "echoes" from the alternative scene can be heard. The intention here is to reinforce decision points, and hint at the contents of the alternative scene. Since this solution is visually subtle, and the sound might initially cause confusion, decision points are longer in the first scenes of the movie, giving viewers time to perceive and interpret the pattern change.

3.1 Evaluation Procedure

The objective of these trials was to gather qualitative data which could help to establish (a) whether subtle decision points could be implemented which did not disrupt narrative flow and consequently involvement; (b) whether the interaction itself was engaging; and (c) whether the overall result was enjoyable. Ten volunteers of mixed age and gender participated. None had seen an interactive movie with narrative based interaction, and most had only slight appreciation of the concept of interactive movies. All were nevertheless familiar with interactive applications in general. The trials were carried out in a room equipped with a comfortable seat, a television set and a DVD player . Only one viewer was in the room at one time,

Each participant viewed *one* version of the movie *twice*, Viewers were briefed about how to use the remote control, and advised that cues for interaction would not occur through interface graphics, but through changes in the movie itself. They were also told that the movie would be played twice, and interaction would not be enforced, but left to their discretion. The intention was to approximate the conditions of home viewing. Also, taking into account the brief duration of the movie, a second run allowed for a higher involvement with - and understanding of - the story. The researcher sat at the back of the room, so that viewers would not be distracted or tempted to converse or seek reassurance. At decision points, the route the story followed – and therefore whether interaction had taken place – was noted.

Between viewings semi-open questions were asked to explore viewers' level of recognition of cues. These related to whether they thought they had interacted (and been successful), when they thought they had interacted, and whether they felt they had recognised decision points. Also at this point all volunteers were offered the chance to either skip the title sequence of the opening scene or play the movie again from the very beginning. After the second viewing, further semi-open questions gathered information as to viewers' overall impressions, feelings of enjoyment and involvement, and specific reactions to the way in which interaction was mediated.

4   Results and Discussion

At first sight, recognition of the decision points in the Black and White (BW) version seems to have been more successful than in the Zoom version. Four viewers recognised the BW decision points against three of the Zoom; two viewers recognised the BW decision points in their first occurrence, as opposed to one viewer for the Zoom version. However, the data are inconclusive. The apparent advantage of BW is based mainly on one viewer, who recognised cues on first appearance, but from changes to narrative pace. This could be interpreted as showing that the solutions are relatively similar in terms of overall subtlety. Nevertheless, qualitative data does indicate a difference in response to BW and Zoom versions. One viewer described the BW solution as being too obvious – no similar comments came from viewers of the other. Also, more viewers from the Zoom version said they would have benefited from some prior indication as to what to look for than from the BW. No viewers thought the cues themselves were distracting. Most viewers volunteered that paying close attention to the story and trying to recognise cues created a deeper sense of involvement. This was one of the most unexpected and valuable findings from the exercise, in terms of illustrating the potential of the approach.

Viewing-to-viewing comparison reveals a considerable variation in reported experience. In general, viewers described having greater involvement with the characters and the story on the second viewing, when they had understood the nature of the experience and had had time to connect (or re-centre).

4.1   The Integrated Interface

There were both positive and negative reactions to the interactive interface itself Of the negative points –the time it took to identify clues, and not knowing what to look for –unfamiliarity with both the notion of a graphic-less interface, and the format itself, may have contributed to the difficulties found. The graphical user interface, described by Johnson (1997) as the "dominant artistic form" of the digital age, is dominates expectations of what interactivity "looks" like - still strongly associated with computers and their graphic icons, buttons and metaphors. "Users" are also accustomed to be shown clearly what to do. It is therefore to be expected that a first encounter with a different approach to the interface, and consequently a different concept of interaction, must require a certain adjustment.

As to the format itself, the lack of previous knowledge carried with it few (or mixed) expectations about how viewers could effect change and shape their own experiences. This meant that viewers experienced the movie with fresh eyes, but also that perception of messages and design intentions was open to equivocal interpretations. What viewers perceived as cues varied from individual to individual. Some noticed the photographic techniques, others the change in pace, others the prolonged attention given to storyworld elements, others "natural" points such as ends of scenes). Some found cues where there were none, and a few completely missed the real cues for interaction. A few non-interactive instances seemed to invite tentative action. In the very first scene, as the main character enters her home, the viewer is taken on a tour of her private life via rooms and objects which testify to the existence of a relationship, for example. While the intention was to familiarize the audience with the character's world, the attention pictures and objects received may have seemed to indicate added value, and most viewers seem to have perceived them as natural points for investigation. This illustrates just how critical the overall consistency of treatment is when creating interactive movies with integrated interfaces, but it highlights numerous, exciting creative possibilities.

The absence of an extra visual interaction layer seemed, with one exception, to have been received very positively. Not only were the integrated solutions said to "belong" and to pose no interruptive effect; but they were also rated as providing a challenging, involving and engaging experience, contributing to the enjoyment of the movie as a whole. Participation, through the perception of meaningful events in the story as cues, seemed to be the key. This was an extremely promising response, considering the limited quality and experimental nature of the production. The differing levels of perception from individual to individual are, however, a great challenge in deciding what can successfully convey interaction while still maintaining the excitement of the "personal" discovery of cues. What is too subtle for some is too obvious for others. This may be mitigated, in less artificial contexts, by the fact that viewers would usually have access to some prior information about the movie they chose to experience.

5 Conclusions

These conclusions are necessarily restricted by the scale of the exercise and the qualities of both the *Embora* movie itself and the small number of viewers involved in the trials. However limited, the findings do nevertheless provide some valid information for understanding the potential of the integrated interface approach:

- Overall, the integrated interface approach does have the potential to minimise interruption. Not only that, it can stimulate viewers to be more involved with the story and engaged in interaction, playing a great part in the pleasure viewers take from the experience.
- Differences between versions themselves did not conclusively affect immersion and engagement. However viewers' responses seem to suggest that the subtler of the two, the Zoom, presented a higher level of "distraction" on the first viewing, due to difficulties in recognising cues.
- The recognition of cues seems to be, in general, influenced by prior knowledge and expectations of viewers; additionally viewers had different views regarding how difficult they wanted recognition of cues to be. This presents, potentially, the greatest challenge for authors trying to reach wide audiences.
- The enjoyment of the interactive movie experience is strongly related to how successfully the different component elements are combined.

Finally, viewers were excited by the possibilities of the format itself, intrigued by the idea of participation, and keen to experience more. Also, the commercial potential of the format for DVD delivery was highlighted, as viewers showed interest in being able to take the movie home and explore all interactive possibilities, experiencing the story in full. This is a very promising prospect indeed, considering around 40% of Hollywood's revenue in 2003 came from DVD sales and rental alone.

References

1. Favre, J., 2002. "Formats in interactive fiction", parts 1-7.
    http://www.iemmys.tv/itvi/features_archives.html [24.10.2003]
2. Vardi, G., 1999. Navigation scheme for interactive movies with linear narrative, Proc. 10th ACM Conference on Hypertext and hypermedia, Darmstadt.
3. Szperling, Margi 2001. Choose your own adventure. Moviemaker [electronic version] http://www.moviemaker.com/issues/44/cinevation.html [28.10.2003]
4. Hales, C. (n.d.) Summaries and workshop notes published on the www:
    http://csw.art.pl/new/99/7e_heldl.html,
    http://interactionmasters.uiah.fi/notes/chrishales.htm [1.11.2003]
5. Ryan, M-L., 2000. Narrative as Virtual Reality: Immersion and Interactivity in Literature and Electronic Media. Baltimore: Johns Hopkins University Press.

Autonomous Virtual Actors

Stéphane Sanchez[1,2], Olivier Balet[2], Hervé Luga[1], and Yves Duthen[1]

[1] Université Toulouse 1/IRIT, Allées de Brienne, 31042 Toulouse cedex, France
{Sanchez, Luga, Duthen}@irit.fr
[2] Virtual Reality Department, C-S, Toulouse, France
{Stephane.Sanchez, Olivier.Balet}@c-s.fr

Abstract. This paper presents the VIBES (Virtual Behaviors) framework used to simulate a "virtual brain" capable of generating, in real time, behaviors for virtual characters. The main originality of VIBES is to combine usual behavioral animation techniques with a learning engine based on Learning Classifiers Systems in order to obtain actors that can learn how to adapt to their dynamic environment and how to efficiently combine known tasks in order to perform the user's tasks. VIBES is a module of the V-Man [1] character animation system developed in the frame of the V-Man project supported by the European Commission in the frame of the 5th framework program.

1   Introduction

One important objective of the research in virtual storytelling is to provide intuitive systems to direct virtual actors. This can be done by using highly scripted scenarios, usually assisted by reactive systems for motion, that accurately drive both the animation and the behavior of the actors [9,12]. The results of such approaches have been proven to be fairly correct and the actors are usually perceived as rather autonomous and intelligent because they are able to plan a more or less complex course of actions. However, these behaviors are mainly generated deterministically. There might be some cases where the actors cannot respond correctly to the user's expectations. If they encounter any situation that is unexpected by the scripted behavior, they can not choose an action that is consistent with the user's directions. They can not really adapt. In order to offer them this aptitude, we must introduce a way to make them learn how to act coherently (in accordance with their capabilities and their environment) to fulfill the operator's orders in any situation. Besides, extending the autonomy of the actors with adaptation capabilities allows the process of directing to be performed at a higher level (the user can provide fuzzy goals such as "go near the window") because the actor might be able to determine the necessary actions.

Our approach is to build a framework that represents a "virtual brain" for virtual actors. This architecture is called VIBES (Virtual Behaviors) for its main purpose is to make the actors behave in an autonomous and intelligent-like way. Its content and structure are inspired by the abilities of real humans and attempt to deal with some of the constraints any real being could face.

To this "virtual brain" we add learning aptitude based on the perception of the virtual world and the evaluation of its states against the actions that the virtual actor decides

S. Göbel et al. (Eds.): TIDSE 2004, LNCS 3105, pp. 68–78, 2004.

to perform in order to complete a particular task. The chosen learning technique is an evolutionist system known as Learning Classifier System that as been successfully used in some behavioral animation projects [5,11,21].

This paper first gives a brief overview of the VIBES framework introducing its four main components and their respective role in order to simulate the perception and the cognitive activity of the virtual actor. Then, it presents the proposed learning method and how it is integrated in the VIBES framework. Finally, the results section shows the behaviors produced by the association of the VIBES framework and the learning engine based on Learning Classifier Systems.

2 VIBES Overview

2.1 The Virtual World

The virtual world of the virtual actor can consist of various kinds of elements. These elements can represent anything from a contextual information (this zone is the kitchen, it is cold here, a sound), to another actor and its related data (size, designation, abilities ...) or any element of the set (props, background, walls, etc.). The main function of the virtual world is to maintain the list of these elements up to date, taking into account the activity of the world entities (i.e. actors) or the user. The way the virtual world will be perceived and interpreted by the virtual actors will only depend on their perceptual abilities.

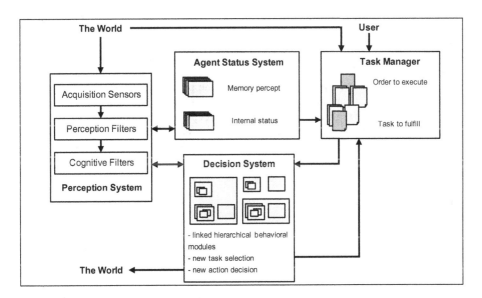

Fig. 1. The VIBES framework

The figure 1 shows the virtual behavior engine for a unique virtual actor. This engine is actually a sort of virtual brain organized in four main elements that communicate with each others via appropriate communication slots. Its main goal is to produce actions that the virtual actor must execute within the world in order to fulfill any understandable order given by the user, any other virtual entity or resulting from its internal activity.

2.2 The Task Manager

The role of the task manager is to control the virtual behavior engine by collecting and handling orders from the possible sources and by triggering their completion process in a coherent and consistent way. There are three distinct sorts of sources for orders. The first one is the *user of the application*, the second is *another actor or another element* of the virtual world, and the last one is the *virtual actor* himself. The task manager stores the orders or list of orders in a tree-like structure as and when they are collected. Then, it triggers the activation of the decision-making process linked to the first eligible order (i.e. the first order that is coherent and relevant with the current course of actions). If the processing of this order generates new tasks to complete, they are stored as children and become the next eligible ones. An order is considered as processed if it is successfully performed or if an exception has been thrown by the decision engine. Finally, a *subsumption* engine [2] allows the actor to prioritize or arbitrate the processing of competitive orders, if necessary.

2.3 The Perception System

As for any "intelligent" system, the virtual actor must have a set of well defined sensors through which the environmental information is gathered then processed in order to be correctly interpreted by the decision system. The perception system consists of three parts. The *acquisition sensors* ensure the integrity the world-agent separation by creating an abstract description of the world in a formalism that the decision system can understand. The *perception filters* simulate the physical sensors that are required to sense (see, touch, hear, smell). It is also possible to add more sophisticated sensors in order to simulate night vision or altered perception for example. The *cognitive filters* are strongly bound to the decision making system: they will analyze and compute data received from the perception sensors in order to only provide the decision making system with the data that are relevant for the completion of the current task.

2.4 The Memory System

The memory system has two main functions. First it stores, as "percept objects", any information acquired about the elements of the world. This constitutes the actor's representation of the world and the knowledge he has acquired. Besides, we introduce a notion of persistence and believing that will be useful for learning routines.

Then, it keeps a record of the consecutive internal states of the virtual actor, essentially the answers to the questions: "What do I want to do?', "What am I doing?", "How do I feel?", and "What do I like?" This is essential to trigger new behaviors due to inner stimuli (like hunger or borrow) or to maintain consistence while executing complex tasks involving the sequencing of many actions.

2.5 The Decision System

The decision-making engine is the core of the virtual behavior. Its purpose is to determine a set of tasks or actions to perform in order to fulfill the orders collected by the task manager. It consists of a set of stand-alone behavioral modules dedicated to the completion of a unique associated order. Considering that "intelligence" is the confluent effect of many unintelligent components [20], the decision system is built as a bottom-up architecture [2] that can not only support elementary reactive behaviors ("do a step", "grab the ball") but also allow them to coexist and to communicate coherently in order to generate much more complex ones ("Play football", "Feed"). Thus, the decision system can be considered as a complex task network [23] of behavioral modules that can trigger each other in order to complete their own associated task.

3 Learning in a Virtual Environment

Under the user's directions, an autonomous virtual actor will have to decide which course of actions to take in order to comply consistently with the operator's expectations and within the virtual environment. Usually, behavioral frameworks for autonomous agents frequently use both reactive and deterministic systems to animate virtual agents. These systems give generally good results but lack of adaptation capabilities. Indeed, a virtual agent ruled by deterministic or reactive behaviors can not adapt to unexpected situations or a dynamic world that might not fit exactly with the solving method or the forecasted situations. Introducing a learning mechanism to generate complex behaviors allows actors to adapt to their environment in order to find by themselves, using their known capabilities, how to perform (or not) the requested task. Two principal kinds of adaptive learning systems are usually used to generate behaviors in dynamic virtual worlds, at interactive frame rate: the Neural Networks and the Learning Classifiers Systems (LCS).

3.1 Neural Networks

Based on the concept of connectionism, neural networks are a biological metaphor resulting from work in cybernetics [17]. They have been successfully used by K. Sims [22] and D. Terzopoulos [13] to animate virtual entities whose behaviors appear of a surprising realism. Unfortunately, this research also showed the limits of this technique. Developing a behavior cannot be done in a deterministic way and necessarily goes through a phase of training that is not easily controllable.
Besides, the performances in term of training fall dramatically if the desired behavior becomes too complex. Finally, a neural network, even if it stands for a robust behavior, remains desperately "opaque". The impossibility of extracting the least information from it makes it hardly scalable and seldom reusable.

3.2 Learning Classifier System

A Learning Classifiers System [6,7] is an evolutionary computing system that uses a Genetic Algorithm [7] over a population of production rules (a.k.a. classifiers) in order to identify a sub-set of rules that can co-operate to solve a given task. A covering system [15] allows adaptation to unexpected situations, the modification of accuracy and pertinence of the rules applying the Q-Learning concept [14] ensures the learning process of the system, and the Genetic Algorithm improves its efficiency producing potentially more adapted classifiers.

Several factors have motivated the choice of LCS as a learning system. First, as a rule-based system, the LCS stores its knowledge explicitly. This allows the user to analyze the rules for simulation interpretation purposes or, in a more technical way, to manually add or modify the set of rules in order to compensate a failure in the improvement (GA) or in the adaptation (covering) process. Besides, a slight period of learning could contribute to improve a handmade a-priori set of rules that uses the LCS formalism. Secondly, a LCS is likely to be used as an efficient memory system. Indeed, in addition to the set of rules, a LCS stores the strength record of each classifier: this determines which rule is good or bad according to the current state of the environment, the task to perform and, eventually, the social rules of the agents' virtual world. Thirdly, a LCS can solve classification problems (ex: help the actor determine with which entity of the world he has to interact with) as well as task planning ones (ex: what the actor must do next to fully perform a task). Afterwards, while conceiving a behavioral module to complete a complex task (pushing an object in a crowded dynamic environment from A to B for example) it could be more convenient to create a set of trials and let the virtual agent learn by itself how to do it, than to implement an inference engine (or any other deterministic system) that computes all the situations that the agent might encounter. Besides, when the user considers that the learning process is completed, the LCS can be transformed into a simple inference engine similar to an expert system or in a finite state machine. Obviously, converting the LCS into an inference engine or an automaton provides VIBES with some strong advantages (mainly the computing speed required for real time applications) but it also implies to cope with the drawbacks (particularly determinism) of these systems. Finally, using such a learning system is interesting as it enables to provide the virtual agent with some personality. Indeed, there could be many ways to fulfill a complex task and there is quite a small chance that a classifiers system randomly generated and evolving with a genetic algorithm only corresponds to a subset of them. Therefore, even if it uses the same wide variety of trials to solve a particular task, the learning engine can generate slightly different behavioral modules. Applying these modules to different agents in the world grants them a bit of personality as they do not exactly act as their neighbors in the same situation.

3.3 Integration in VIBES Environment

Learning Classifier Systems are integrated in VIBES as stand alone behavioral modules in the *Decision System*. The *Perception System* provides them with the state of the virtual environment. It scans entities as well as the virtual actor inner state in order to create the message that will be compared to the condition part of classifiers. According to the provided message, the LCS produces a new action to perform or a new task to complete. During the learning phase, the *Task Manager* evaluates the quality of the planned course of actions and tasks and gives the appropriate reward to the *Decision System*. In running mode, once the learning phase is completed, the *Perception System* still produces messages from the environment but the LCS in the *Decision System* acts as a finite state machine, or an automaton, because it only produces the best learned actions (the ones that received the best marks) until the task fulfillment.

3.4   Learning a New Behavior

As it has been said before, the decision system (that drives the virtual actor) is a highly modular system consisting in a hierarchical network of behavioral modules. The goal of each behavioral module is to complete a unique task that the user may give. The completion strategy, inspired from Minsky's work [20], and in accordance with the bottom-up architecture of the Decision Making system, is similar to the one used in dynamic story-telling systems, such as Hierarchical Task Networks [23]: the task to complete is decomposed in a set of subtasks (usually these tasks are said to have a lower level of abstraction, the lesser one being the simple reactive action as "make a step" for example) that must be fulfilled until the completion of the main one.

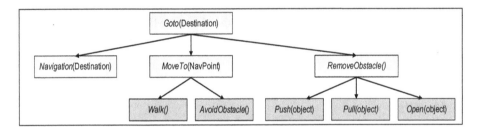

Fig. 2. Subdivision of "GoTo" task

The figure 2 shows one of the hierarchical decomposition for the "GoTo" module. This module is composed of three sub-modules: one to find the path to the destination, another to make the actor move between the navigation points of the computed path and the last to make him remove any unavoidable obstacle. The figure 3 shows how these modules are combined together to make the actor go to the requested destination using the actions he knows ("walk", "avoid obstacle", "push", "pull" and "open").

The main idea behind the Learning Classifiers System is to generate a new behavior that lets the virtual actor learn how to coherently select and combine the different behavioral modules at its disposal in order to generate a plan of actions. The learning system must be able to choose among the existing behaviors the ones that can fulfill the task and it must also plan a correct and minimal sequence of orders to achieve its goal. This is ensured by the combined effects of the LCS selection strategy, the application of Q-Learning principle and the rewarding scheme. Given a configuration of

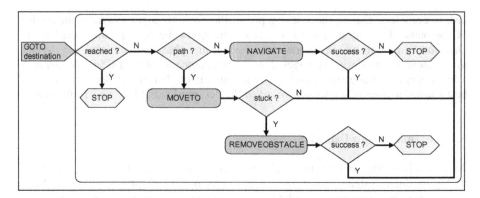

Fig. 3. Processing diagram of "GoTo" behavioral module

task to complete and the rules of the virtual world. A correct action implies a positive mark and, on the contrary, an incorrect one produces a penalty. This reward, or this penalty, is added to the strength of the classifier that has produced the action. As the LCS proceeds through its learning phase, the selection rate of good actions increases (because of the reinforcement of the strength of the production rules) while the incorrect ones are more and more ignored. Finally, the rewarding system grants a bonus reward according to the number of steps required to achieve the intended goal. Granting a higher bonus to the shortest plans of actions allows the LCS to converge towards a minimal sequence that avoids inappropriate or useless sub-courses.

4 Results

The first step in the implementation of VIBES has been to produce a set of elementary behavioral modules in order to validate the architecture. The first results only use basic behaviors such as navigation, collision avoidance and simple interaction with objects selected by user. The following results are the integration of the learning system in VIBES with the solving of a simple task: the virtual actor must, according to its hunger and tastes, find a way to feed himself. In order to succeed, the actor will have to find appropriate food, find a way to obtain it and, if necessary, cook it before consuming it.

To complete this task we have used two Learning Classifiers Systems, one to solve the quest for food and the other to determine which course of actions in case it needs to cook the aliment. These LCS are based on an extension of Zeroth level Classifiers Systems (ZCS) [15]. The extended system, called GZCS [5], is a generalization of the ZCS formalism in order to allow any kind of data (integers, real, intervals, bits or trits) to be used as heterogeneous components of condition and action parts of the classifiers. The override of the usual bit formalism used with homogeneous conditions and actions allows easing the definition of complex problems.

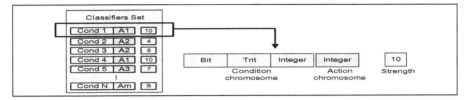

Fig. 4. Chromosomal representation of a classifier for the EatSomething LCS: the condition chromosome represents the relevant data of the world for the completion of the task. It consists of a Bit gene that indicates if the agent has selected an aliment to eat (0:false, 1:true), a trit gene that indicates if it has grabbed the selected food (0:false, 1:true, #:whatever or irrelevant), and finally an integer that indicates the state of the held aliment (0:unknown, 1:uneatable, 2:raw, 3:cooked, 4:eatable). The action chromosome consists of one integer gene that identifies the next indexed action to execute. For convergence matters, the selected action only applies to the object of attention of the virtual actor.

Using this natural representation of the problem simplifies the interpretation of the production rules obtained at the end of the learning process. The end of the learning process is determined when the LCS always answers accurately (i.e. rate of achieving success or determining unavoidable failure = 100%). The figures 5 and 6 show the generated automatons once each classifiers system has completed the learning phase. Both classifiers receive as entries the state of the environment (white boxes) and produce the relevant action (grey boxes) to modify the current state of the virtual world according to its specifications.

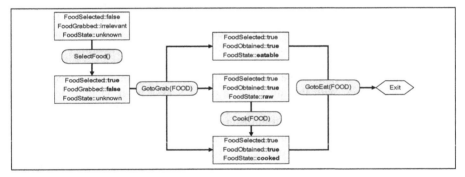

Fig. 5. EatSomething Automaton

These results show several interesting facts. First, the two automatons, especially the first one, prove that, with a correct set of simple rules within the world (for example, "to eat something you must hold it"), the LCS can select and combine a minimal set of actions to complete the associated task. Indeed, in the first case, the LCS generates an automaton consisting of only four tasks amongst the twenty available behavioral modules. The second interesting thing is that we can obtain complex scheduling of tasks: in the second automaton, if the actor chooses to cook its food in an oven, it learns how to put the food in it to cook it. Besides, the system has also been able to generate a loop of wait actions in order to let the time to the food to be cooked. Finally, it is interesting to note that a skilled user can implement such problems in about one hour and a half and that the converging time of both LCS is about ten minutes on Pentium IV 2.4 GHz.

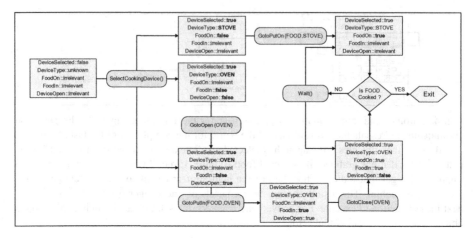

Fig. 6. Cook(FOOD) Automaton

5 Conclusion

VIBES complies with several different goals. First, it is compliant with interactive frame rate applications and animations while being scalable enough to control a reasonable number of virtual actors in the virtual world. It also supports the different methods usually used in the field of autonomous agents to generate more or less complex behaviors: reactive methods [2,13,10], deterministic ones such as scripts [9,12] or finite state machines [3], and finally evolutionist ones such as Learning Classifiers Systems. The system can process each behavior as a stand alone unit but it also allows them to coexist and communicate coherently in order to perform complex courses of action. Then, VIBES, with the introduction of LCS as a main adaptive technique, allows the learning. Virtual actors can adapt their behavior according to the user's expectations and to the marking system using a set of "social rules" within the virtual world. Finally, the highly modular bottom-up architecture allows the creation of seamless complex behaviors and offers a high expandability to the system.

However, the VIBES framework has some drawbacks. First, the respect of the real time constraint is really dependant on the selected solving method. A badly optimized algorithm or an inefficient method can considerably slow down the behavioral engine and the overall system. Then, the learning system is based on an evolutionist technique. So, the convergence of the system toward an optimal set of rules to fulfill the task is never guaranteed. Besides, the modeling of the problem to solve and the conception of the learning trials must be done with particular care because an incorrect modeling or an inappropriate set of trials may not produce the expected results: even if the LCS seems to converge towards a solution, the produced behavior will probably be incoherent and irrelevant to the task to achieve. Finally, the system currently only generates individual behaviors, it is now essential to generate group and team behaviors in order to extend the range of applications.

Acknowledgments. VIBES (Virtual Behaviours) is a module of the V-Man character animation system developed in the frame of the V-Man IST project [IST-2000-28094]. This project is supported by the European Commission and gathers industrial and academic partners in a consortium striving toward the realisation of an intuitive authoring tool allowing non-computer specialists to create, animate, control and interact with autonomous virtual characters.

References

1. Menou E., Philippon L., Sanchez S., Duchon J., Balet O.,"The V-Man Project: towards autonomous virtual characters", Second International Conference on Virtual Storytelling, Published in Lecture Notes in Computer Science, Springer, Vol. 2897, 2003
2. Brooks, R., Intelligence Without Reason, "Computers and Thought" IJCAI 1991.
3. Donikian S., « HPTS: a Behaviour Modelling Language for Autonomous Agents », in Fifth International Conference on Autonomous Agents, Montreal, Canada, May 2001.
4. Funge J., Tu X., and Terzopoulos D. "Cognitive Modelling: Knowledge, Reasoning and Planning for Intelligent Characters", SIGGRAPH 99, Los Angeles, CA, August 11-13, 1999
5. Heguy O., Sanza C., Berro A., Duthen Y. "GXCS: A Generic Classifier System and its application in a Real Time Cooperative Behavior Simulations", International Symposium and School on Advanced Distributed System (ISSADS'02), p. , November 11-15 2002
6. Holland J.H., "Adaptation in Natural and Artificial Systems", University of Michigan Press, Ann Arbor, 1975. Republished by the MIT Press, 1992.
7. Holland J. H., "Adaptive Algorithms for Discovering and Using General Patterns in Growing Knowledge Bases", International Journal for Policy Analysis and Informations Systems, vol 4, no 3, p 245-268, 1980.
8. Iglesias A., Luengo F. "Behavioral Animation of Virtual Agents". 3IA'2003 The 6th International Conference on Computer Graphics and Artificial Intelligence, Limoges(France), May 2003
9. Perlin K., Goldberg A. "Improv: a system for scripting interactive actors in virtual worlds", proceedings of SIGGRAPH'96, 1996, New Orleans, 205-216
10. Reynolds C.W. "Steering Behaviors for autonomous Characters" in Game Developper Conference, 1999 San José(USA)
11. Sanza C., "Evolution d'entités virtuelles coopératives par systèmes de classifieurs', Thèse de Doctorat, Université Paul Sabatier (Toulouse), june 2001.
12. Thalmann D., Musse S.R. and Kallmann M "Virtual Humans' Behavior : Individuals, Group and Crowds " Proceedings of Digital Media Futures International Conference. 1999. Bradford (United Kingdom).
13. Tu, X., Terzopoulos D., Artificial Fishes: Physics, Locomotion, Perception, Behavior, SIGGRAPH 1993.
14. Watkins C., and Dayan   P. Technical Note: "Q-Learning", Machine Learning, 8, 279-292, 1992.
15. Wilson S.W. "ZCS : A Zeroth level Classifier System". Evolutionary computation, 2(1), pp 1-18, 1994.
16. Norbet Wiener. Cybernetics; or, control and communication in the animal and the machine. Wiley, 1948.
17. W. S. Mc Culloch and W. Pitts. A logical calculus of the ideas immanent in nervous activity. Bulletin of Mathematical Biophysics, 5:115-133, 1943.
18. Franck Rosenblatt. The Perceptron : probabilistic model for information storage and organization in the brain. Psychological Review, 65:386-408, 1958.
19. Donald O. Hebb. The organisation of behavior. Wiley, 1949.

20. Minsky M. A Framework for Representing Knowledge, in: The Psychology of Computer, Vision, P.Winston, McGraw-Hill, NY,pp.211-277, 1975.
21. Luga H., Panatier C., Balet O., Torguet P. & Duthen Y. "Collective Behaviour and Adaptive Interaction in a Distributed Virtual Reality System,", Proceedings of ROMAN'98, IEEE International Workshop on Robot and Human Communication, 1998.
22. Sims, K. Evolving virtual creatures. In Proceedings of SIGGRAPH'94 (Orlando, Fla., July 24–29). ACM Press, New York, 1994, pp. 15–22.
23. Charles, F., Cavazza, M., and Mead, S.J.: Generating Dynamic Storylines Through Characters' Interactions. International Journal on Intelligent Games and Simulation, vol. 1, no. 1, pp. 5-11, March, 2002.

Virtual Human: Storytelling and Computer Graphics for a Virtual Human Platform

Stefan Göbel[1], Oliver Schneider[1], Ido Iurgel[1], Axel Feix[1],
Christian Knöpfle[2], and Alexander Rettig[2]

[1] ZGDV Darmstadt e.V., Digital Storytelling Department,
64283 Darmstadt, Germany
{Stefan.Goebel, Oliver.Schneider, Axel.Feix, Ido.Iurgel}@zgdv.de
http://www.zgdv.de/distel/
[2] Fraunhofer IGD, Department Virtual & Augmented Reality,
64283 Darmstadt, Germany
{Christian.Knoepfle, Alexander.Rettig}@igd.fraunhofer.de
http://www.igd.fhg.de/igd-a4

Abstract. This paper describes the usage of Computer Graphics and Interactive, Digital Storytelling Concepts within the Virtual Human project and its technical platform. Based on a brief overview of the Virtual Human approach, global aims and first R&D results, the Virtual Human platform is introduced. Hereby, methods and concepts for the authoring environment, the narration engine and the avalon player as rendering platform are provided as well as an overview of the Direction and Player Markup Language used for interfaces purposes between these components. Finally, our current Virtual Human demonstrator recently presented at CeBIT 2004 in Hannover using these methods and concepts is described and further R&D activities are pointed out within a brief summary and outlook.

1 Motivation

Virtual Human [11] has been initiated as research project funded by the Federal Ministry of Education and Research. The global aim of Virtual Human is to combine Computer Graphics technology provided by the INI-GraphicsNet (Fraunhofer IGD, ZGDV Darmstadt and TU Darmstadt) with speech and dialogue processing technology provided by the German Research Center for Artificial Intelligence (DFKI) in order to develop methods and concepts for "realistic" anthropomorphic interaction agents. In addition, the third major project partner Fraunhofer IMK is responsible for the domain model of the Virtual Human application scenario.

Whereas interactive storytelling techniques are primarily used for the dialogue and narration engine as control unit of the Virtual Human run-time environment, computer graphics technology is used for photo-realistic rendering and appearance of Virtual Human characters within the Virtual Human rendering platform.

S. Göbel et al. (Eds.): TIDSE 2004, LNCS 3105, pp. 79–88, 2004.

Since the Virtual Human project start in late 2002, an early demonstrator has been set up for summer 2003 indicating the basic principles of Virtual Human components. Another major step represented the first integrated Virtual Human demonstrator presented at the CeBIT 2004 exhibition fair in Hannover providing an eLearning scenario.

Fig. 1. Virtual Human presented to the german chancellor Gerhard Schröder and Edelgard Bulmahn, minister of the Federal Ministry of Education and Research at CeBIT 2004

2 Virtual Human Platform

From the technical point of view, figure 2 provides an overview of the major components of the Virtual Human platform and indicates partner responsibilities:

- The content layer consists of a domain model providing geometry, story models and character models, pedagogic models, media, etc.. Furthermore, Virtual Human editors are used to create application scenarios and stories. The output of the content layer is a story board.
- The narration engine consists of a story engine [3] controlling a scene engine [8] and an improvisation module [5]. The output of the story engine are directions coded in Direction ML for ...
- ... the dialog engine. Here, dialogues among virtual characters are generated during run-time and sent to the player component in form of Player ML scripts.
- Finally, the player component based on Avalon [1] creates/renders the 3D environment and sends corresponding data to the visualization platform.
- Possible peculiarities of visualization platforms range from simple monitors or web-based application scenarios up to high-level rendering applications to be shown on a Powerwall.

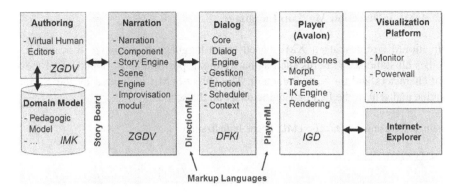

Fig. 2. Virtual Human Platform – Component based Architecture

The following sections describe these major components of the Virtual Human platform in detail.

2.1 Authoring

Apart from basic Virtual Human editors to control virtual characters, ZGDV in collaboration with Fraunhofer IGD Rostock establish a comprehensive authoring environment enabling authors to configure application scenarios, create stories and characters (inclusive behavior and characteristics of virtual humans) or define interaction metaphors among virtual humans and between users and the VH system.

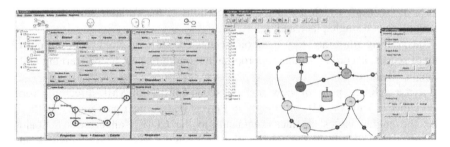

Fig. 3. Virtual Human Editors – First version providing form based editors (left) and second version using graph based hierarchic visualization techniques (right)

In addition to methods and concepts developed for the Virtual Human editors within the VH project, ZGDV Darmstadt and Fraunhofer IGD Rostock bring in results of their own strategic research in the field of graph based visualization techniques for the creation of storytelling based edutainment applications respectively methods and concepts for game based interfaces for authoring environments [7].

2.2 DML – Direction Markup Language

DirectionML represents a XML-based script-language to initialize a scene. It describes all static scene items such as background, position and orientation of the virtual characters and the virtual camera. The DirectionML is created by the Narration Engine and sent to the Dialog Engine to set up the scene.

Example for using the Direction ML: Scene Initialization

```
<directionML>
  <object id="Background"> ....</object>
  <user id="User"> ... </user>
  <character id="Tina">
    <position type="absolute"> <point x="-1" y="1"/>
      <direction> <user id="user"/> </direction>
    </position>
  </character>
  <character id="Ritchie"> ...</character>
  <light> ... </light> < camera > ... </camera>
  <scene name="greet_user">... </scene>
</directionML>
```

2.3 Narration Engine

The Narration Engine controls both the narrative and the didactic progress of a session. For this, the Narration Engine executes concurrently declarative story and learning models, which are represented as XML documents. Those models guide the choice of "scenes", which are elementary portions of the variable story line, usually taking place at a single place and time.

Thus, during run-time story creation, scenes are subsequentially chosen out of a pool of scenes, according to their appropriateness with respect to the learning and the dramatic situation.

From a technical point of view, a single scene consists of XML-directions, formulated either in DirectionML or directly in PlayerML (see next paragraph). In the first case, the engine issues abstract commands to the CDE (Conversational Dialogue Engine), which then leads the conversation accordingly, assembling sentences out of data base information. E.g., a direction to the CDE could have the meaning of "*discuss the composition of the sun in an Q/A-manner in 2 minutes.*" In the second case, the directions are concrete dialogue acts, together with corresponding animations, which are displayed without further refinement. This is especially important for sections where the author wants to define every detail of the gestures and words of the virtual humans, or for dialogues and events which cannot be appropriately generated by the CDE.

2.4 PML – Player Markup Language

The Player Markup Language (PML) is a XML based Markup Language which takes up concepts from the RRL (rich representation language) [10]. PML defines a format for sending instructions (commands) from the dialog-manager to a 3D virtual reality system (VR player Avalon [1]). Additionally it defines a message format which can be sent to a player or received from it.

PML scripts are strictly scene-based. A scene describes the 3 dimensional space containing objects and virtual characters as well as all possible actions for objects or characters (e.g. movement, animation, interaction).

At the beginning of a new scene all static objects and characters are defined by sceneDefinition scripts. During the scene actions scripts describe all run-time dependent actions depending on their temporal appearance. PML distinguishes between SceneActions, CharacterActions and WorldQueries. Hereby, SceneActions represent actions depending on the virtual environment (e.g. fade-in or fade-out of Objects). CharacterAnimations are actions which a virtual character can achieve (e.g. talking, smiling, walking).

Altogether, PML is an abstract specification language. It is independent of the implementation of the VR player and the virtual environment. But any players used have to convert the abstract definitions of PML to their own set of commands.

PML is used as descriptive interface markup language between a dialog creating environment (dialog engine) and the VR player and synchronizes all steps of dialog-generation. In the first step a very common representation of the dialog is generated. In the next step additional information (e.g. emotion, timing for lip-synchronization) augments the dialog-skeleton. In the third step the dialog is enhanced by using fitting animations like mimic and other animations. The result is a script with abstract commands to the player which is sent by the scheduler to the player.

The following example shows a slightly simplified PML actions script. The animation tags refer to preloaded animations, which are referenced by their name. In complete PML the tag sentence would contain a list of phonemes including their duration, which are mapped by the system to facial animations, as well as a source URL of an audio file, which contains generated speech.

```
<playerML id="s1">
  <actions>
    <characterAct id="ca2">
      <character refName="Sven"/>
      <animation id="a3" refName="pride"/>
      <sentence id="s4">
        <text>This sentence shall be spoken proudly.
        </text>
      </sentence>
      <animation id="a5" refName="progress"/>
      <temporalOrder>
        <seq>
```

```
<par>
  <act refId="a3" begin="0" dur="4000"/>
  <act refId="s4" begin="300" dur="3700"/>
</par>
<act refId="a5" begin="0" dur="2000"/>
    </seq>
  </temporalOrder>
</characterAct>
<temporalOrder>
  <seq>
    <act refId="ca2"/>
  </seq>
</temporalOrder>
</actions>
</playerML>
```

2.5 Avalon Player

Avalon is a component based Virtual and Augmented Reality system developed and maintained at ZGDV Darmstadt and Fraunhofer IGD. Within Avalon the behavior of the virtual world is defined by a scene graph following and extending the concepts of VRML/X3D [2]: The scenegraph describes the geometric and graphical properties of the scene as well as it's behavior. Each component in the system is instantiated as a node, which has specific input and output slots. Via connections between the slots of the nodes (called routes), events are propagated, which lead to state changes both in the behavior graph and usually in the visible representation from render frame to render frame. Events are generated by different sensor nodes exclusively, which may receive data from input devices controlled by the user and from internal sensors like CollisionSensors, which can detect collisions of objects or - most important for animations - the TimeSensor, which can generate timer events every frame. The rendering backend of Avalon is OpenSG [6], an open source high performance and high quality scenegraph renderer, which has been developed in majority by members of the INI-Graphics Net since 2001.

One major advantage of the architecture of Avalon is that new functionality can be integrated quite easily by adding respective nodes. For the Virtual Human prototype a few nodes needed to be written. Almost all the animation and sound replay stuff could be done with the already existing nodes. One new node, the PmlInterface node, performs the parsing of PML and constructing the appropriate behavior sub-graphs accordingly (mainly a time graph). For the time graph we implemented a node type TimeContainer (the naming follows the SMIL 2.0 standard [9]). This node performs the conversion between the respective local times up to the mapping of the final animation duration time to the fraction of the key frame interval, which is used to play the VRML animations.

The following figure shows the time graph corresponding to the PML example above to illustrate the mapping to VRML-like data structures.

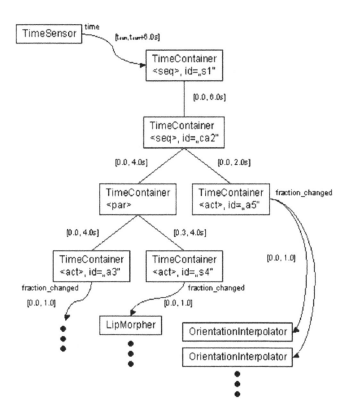

Fig. 4. Example of a time graph. *Square brackets* contain the relative time as mapped by the respective TimeContainers (note that PML describes time in milliseconds, whereas Avalon uses the VRML compliant unit second). *Arrows* resemble routes, which connect the time graph with other nodes in the behavior graph as e.g. Interpolators, which hold animation data

3 Virtual Human Demonstrator

The Virtual Human platform in some way is very generic allowing to re-place/exchange components by other components providing the same functionality and following the well-defined interfaces. Further on, it is scalable referring to the intelligence of the system. Subsequently, their different "levels of intelligence" for Virtual Human demonstrators and prototypes, see figure 5:

1. The most simple level consists of predefined scenes and dialogues created within in the authoring environment and directly sent to the player. In a second step predefined scripts are smoothly modified (assembled) and processed by the Narration Engine as control unit of the VH platform. No interaction is possible in this level.

2. Using the Dialog Engine to create dialogues during run-time, intelligence is brought into the system. Thus it is possible to generate very free commands by the Narration Engine such as "Tina is talking to a user" or "Ritchie is greeting the user". Hereby, commands are coded in Direction ML and sent to the Dialog Engine. The Dialog Engine generates commands such as speech acts (Tina says "My friend Ritchie and me welcome you!..") and send these commands to the Player using Player ML.

    Within this second level, predefined interactions are possible.

3. In a third intelligence level, bidirectional communication between the VH components is enabled taking into account events caused by user interactions. Hence, the story becomes very variable and users are totally involved in the application and become "authors of their own story". In this sense Virtual Human represents a platform for Interactive Storytelling applications.

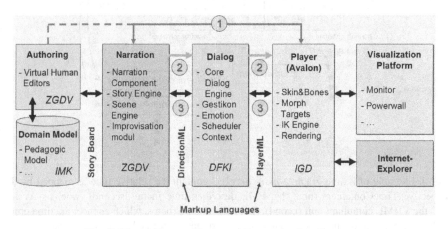

Fig. 5. Virtual Human Platform – Interaction level concept

Since project start in 2002, various VH demonstrators have been established, for example for the CeBIT 2004 a Virtual Human system consististing of a Dialog Engine from the DFKI and Avalon as player component was presented. Hereby, the virtual characters are realistic models designed by Charamel in 3ds max / character studio, which have been exported with a VRML exporter provided by INI-Graphics Net resulting in H|Anim 2001 [4] humanoids to be used within the Avalon VR player. In this scenario, user interaction is limited to multiple choice selections.

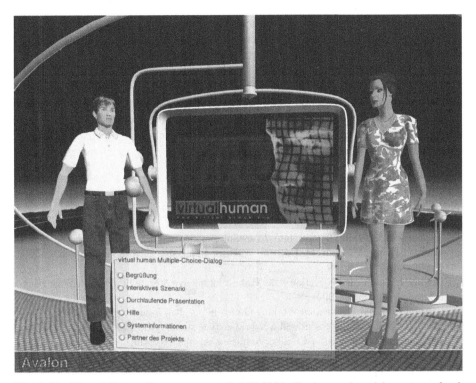

Fig. 6. The Virtual Human Demonstrator at CeBIT 2004. (Background model courtesy of rmh new media GmbH, Character models courtesy of Charamel Software GmbH)

4 Summary and Outlook

By the cooperation of leading research groups in Germany in the research fields of computer graphics and multi-modal user interfaces, a world-wide leading position in the development of virtual characters as personal dialogue partners is aspired.

Since project start in November 2002, a global architecture of a Virtual Human platform consisting of different components and interfaces have been established. First demonstrators indicate the enormous potential of Virtual Human concepts and usage in a wide-spread range of application scenarios. For example, the project team has successfully presented a Virtual Human learning scenario at CeBIT 2004, which was presented both on a traditional and simple physical setup with a PC and usual monitor but also on a high-end Powerwall providing appropriate visualizations for high-resolution images and photo-realistic Virtual Humans.

Within Virtual Human, at ZGDV and Fraunhofer IGD current research effort is spent on the definition of Direction and Player ML, the development of the Narration Engine and its integration with the Dialog Engine, the integration of dynamic hair simulation, realistic real time skin and hair rendering, inverse kinematics for humanoids or seamless motion blending with multiple animation channels. Further aspects, methods and concepts are brought in by the Virtual Human project partners resulting in a very interesting and promising project with fruitful collaboration among all partners and enormous results.

Whereas the project team has been concentrated on the establishment of early demonstrators and a stable application scenario for eLearning during the first project phase, now the focus is settled on integration issues and the adaptation of the Virtual Human platform for additional application scenarios such as interactive game/quiz shows, personal service or management training.

References

1. Avalon Virtual Reality System, http://www.ini-graphics.net/~avalon
2. Behr, J., Dähne, P., Roth, M.:Utilizing X3D for Immersive Environments. Web3D 2004 Symposium, Monterey
3. Braun, N.: Automated Narration – the Path to Interactive Storytelling. Proceedings NILE, Edinburgh, Scotland (2002) 38-46
4. H|Anim Humanoid Animation Working Group, http://www.h-anim.org
5. Iurgel, I.: Emotional interaction in a hybrid conversational group. In: Prendiger, H. (ed.): International Workshop on Lifelike Animated Agents. Working Notes in Proceedings PRICAI-02, Tokyo, Japan (2002) 52-57
6. OpenSG, an open source scenegraph renderer, http://www.opensg.org
7. Schneider, O.: Storyworld creation: Authoring for Interactive Storytelling. Journal of the WSCG, Plzen, Czech (2003) 405-412
8. Schneider, O., Braun, N.: Content Presentation in Augmented Spaces by the Narration of Interactive Scenes. Proceedings AVIR, Geneva, Swiss (2003) 43-44
9. Synchronized Multimedia Integration Language (SMIL 2.0), http://www.w3.org/TR/smil20
10. The NECA RRL, Information on Neca's Rich Representation Language, http://www.ai.univie.ac.at/NECA/RRL
11. Virtual Human Project, http://www.virtual-human.org

Evaluation of a Virtual Narrator's Expressiveness in Terms of Suspense Signaling

Norbert Braun and Thomas Rieger

GRIS, Informatik, TU-Darmstadt
64283 Darmstadt, Germany
{Nbraun, Rieger}@GRIS.Informatik.TU-Darmstadt.de

Abstract. In this paper, we describe the results of the evaluation of a Virtual Character, used as a human-like, automated narrator with focus on the signaling of suspenseful situations within stories to the Virtual Narrator's audience. Signaling is done via facial expression and gestures, driven by an underlying story examination mechanism. This mechanism uses an automatic generated story to get points of suspense progression, conflicts between story actors, and the relevance of story fragments. It indicates these points to an expressiveness module, which assigns expressiveness states to the Virtual Narrator.

1 Introduction

How can a Virtual Narrator adapt its narrative expressiveness to a story? We got the answer to this question while investigating interactive storytelling for Information Systems, Education and Interactive Storys for children. We developed a story processing unit, the so called Story Engine (see [2], [3], and a discussion of the literary aspects of the approach can be found in [1]), which is based on the semiotic principles of story as they are told by V. Propp [6], a Russian formalist of literary of the early 20th Century. His semiotics is based on morphologic functions (story fragments in a semiotic sense), roles (dramatis personae) and dependencies between morphological functions, loops (repetitions of concatenated story fragments) and moves (insertion of not previously played, concatenated story fragments). Following this approach we derived our Story Engine, enhanced by so called polymorphic functions (morphologic functions that change their outcome in relation to user interaction) to generate an interactive adaptable story from a set of story fragments. The story engine is used in several projects, but soon we found that there is a difference between having a story and *narrating* the story. Even if the story fragments are known, the story structure is well defined and the story progress is interactive affected by the user, we had problems to control the narrative expressiveness of the Virtual Characters presenting the story. We used scripts to control the narration of story fragments [8]. Therefore, most of the acting of the Virtual Characters is predefined, they do not have a *knowledge* of the story structure, every expressiveness and acting has to be handmade by 3D Animators. To overcome this situation, we concentrated on the art of narration: the user

S. Göbel et al. (Eds.): TIDSE 2004, LNCS 3105, pp. 89–94, 2004.
© Springer-Verlag Berlin Heidelberg 2004

should definitely get the point about the suspense in the story. For the first evaluation, we concentrated on the effects of one Virtual Narrator on the audience.

2 Related Work in the Field of Automated Narration

Virtual storytelling systems are typically distinguished in character-based plot development and script based plot development, see [12]. Closely related to our approach is the work of Silva et al [9]. In the Papous project, they presented a virtual storyteller whose hand gestures and facial expression are defined via tags by the author of the story. In opposite to this approach, we use meta information about suspense to calculate gestures and facial expression by the system itself.

Another approach, closely related to ours, is the work of Szilas, see [10] and [11]. He defined several narrative criteria around the personal conflicts of the actors of a story. However, our approach concentrates on suspense as the major factor of narration, as we find in personal conflicts one of the factors of suspense.

To get more into narrative details, we start with the principles of narration in the next paragraph.

3 The System

A typical constellation of raising suspense is a danger situation or problems situation, which keeps the audience in hope to experience the solving of the problems while the story continues. The situation has to be common to the audience, the audience should ask themselves how they would handle the situation or how they wish the hero of the story should handle the situation.

The approach discussed in this work uses the danger- or problems situation to catch the audience's attention for the story. The suspense is raising in relation to the problems that occur to the hero and the way he solves the problems. The Virtual Narrator has to understand the ongoing actions and situations of the story, in order to increase or decrease aspects of the story. We use three concepts to understand the ongoing actions in a story.

The first one is based on the morphology of the story we use. We identify the aspects of the actions in the story and indicate suspense points for several morphological functions and the concatenation of these functions. For example, a 'fight of the hero' against his opponent is one of the most suspenseful functions of a story. The 'victory of the hero' is also suspenseful, but not as suspenseful as the fight itself. Therefore we use annotations called *Suspense Progression*.

The second concept uses the conflict potential between several roles of a story. The situation, where a conflict initialises, rises, escalates and is solved, are aspects of a story that should be highlighted by a narrator. These aspects are more substantial for the story than the actions that are used to keep the plausibility of the story on track. We call these annotations *Narrative Conflict*.

The third concept takes into account the relevance of a function for the ongoing story. For example, if the audience did not get the birds eating the bread of Hänsel and Gretel (remember the tale!), they do not know why the kids are lost in the dark forest. The narrator should use this accentuation to raise the audience expectations. The annotation is called *Narrative Relevance*.

These three concepts are used to give the Virtual Narrator an understanding of the story. With this understanding, it can adapt its expressiveness to the story, and, consequently, its speech, gaze, facial expression, head movement and gestures.

In this paper we give an overview of the system architecture, for more details refer to Rieger and Braun [7].

The system contains three general parts:

- The story part, given as the story model, the story content and the story engine.
- The behaviour part, given as the story examination module as well as the behaviour manager (coupled with behaviour rules) and the gesture manager (coupled with gesture meta data).
- The Virtual Character with a text to speech system and synchronised lip movement, facial expression and hand gestures, like shown in Fig. 1..

The information (the content) is stored in a Story Content DB as scenes. These scenes are selected by a Story Engine, enriched with suspense annotations by a story examination mechanism and transferred to the behaviour manager. There, the suspense information is calculated as an expressiveness value within the interval [0..1] and used to control the Virtual Character's behavior.

Fig. 1. The Virtual Narrator, for the evaluation of the system its graphics was reduced to facial expression / gestures

4 Evaluation

The evaluation of the Virtual Narrator was done with the following questions to be answered: Are the gesture and facial expressions of the Virtual Narrator adequate to the suspense of the narrated situations?

To answer the question, we choose the story of Jorinde and Joringel, see [5], to be narrated by the Virtual Narrator.

We prepared two tests:

The first test (Test 1) presented the whole Jorinde and Joringel story, this to get a rating of the narrative quality of the Virtual Narrator.

The second test (Test 2) presented two scenes of the story in five different expressive states of the Virtual Narrator, this to verify which kind of expressiveness the audience would like to see within the scene.

Then we invited 14 persons to the evaluation and split them in two groups:

Group A got the first test (Test 1) with a given emotional facial expression and with randomly selected gestures.

Group B got the first test (Test 1) with system-calculated facial expression and gestures.

The facial expression and gestures vary in 5 categories: expecting, normal, sad, angry and merry. Their intensity varies between high, medium and low.

The groups got the same content of the story, as well as they got the same voice of the virtual character. Also, we reduced the visual presentation to a generic face and hands, this to limit the variables of the evaluation.

The second test (Test 2) was the same for both groups.

The Virtual Narrator itself was presented on a simple PC with speakers and the common interaction facilities of keyboard and mouse.

The evaluation audience had to rate the system with a so called think aloud test – the test persons tolf their impression while being exposed to the test, their impressions were written down by a test coordinator, they also were able to write notes by their self.

4.1 Evaluation Test Results

For the first test, Test 1, we got the following results:

Group A described the presentation of the system as monotonous.

Group B gave a lot of positive critics to the presentation of the system. As a little drawback, the notes of the users are mostly related to single scenes and not to the presentation over all. Both groups related any gesture of the Virtual Narrator to the content, presented by the system. We had few gestures related to no content, only given between the (very short) loading between scenes (idle behavior). Even these gestures were related to content by the users of both groups.

For the second test, Test 2, we got the following results:

For the first scene (Scene 1), the system calculated a merry expressiveness with a medium intensity. For the second scene (Scene 2), the system calculated a normal expressiveness with a medium intensity.

The users ranked the general expressiveness of the scenes:

Scene 1: 60 % of the users voted for the system calculated expressiveness.

Scene 2: 30 % of the users voted for the system calculated expressiveness.

The intensity of the narrative expressiveness was also ranked by the users.

Scene 1: 15 % of the users voted for the system calculated expressiveness.

Scene 2: 50% of the users voted for the system calculated expressiveness.

If we segment the evaluation data to facial expression results and gesture results, the overall rating was different:

Regarding the facial expressions, 60 % of the users voted the same expressiveness as calculated by the system for the first scene; 75 % of the users for the expressiveness calculated for the second scene.

Regarding the hand gestures of Scene 1, 60 % of the users voted for a lower gesture intensity than the expressiveness proposed by the system. 55% of the users of the Scene 2 voted for a gesture intensity equal to the expressiveness proposed by the system.

4.2 Interpretation of the Evaluation Results

The result of Test 1 show an advancement of the presentation, when using the Virtual Character as a suspense controlled Virtual Narrator. The audience has more fun with the story, when getting it with expressive gestures that combine well with the current suspense level of the story.

The second test showed, regarding the users expectations, a mismatch between facial emotion and gestures. Even when the majority of users voted for the system calculated facial expression and gestures, the users did not vote for the match of both, regarding the narrative expressiveness of the Virtual Narrator. It seems that the narrative expressiveness in regard to the combination of facial expression and gesture needs to be advanced.

5 Conclusion

We presented evaluation details of a Virtual Narrator system. The system is able to control the narrative expressiveness of a Virtual Narrator by the usage of three suspense categories (suspense progression, narrative conflict and narrative relevance). An automated process derives these categories from a story processing unit.

Our results show that users understand, generally, the promotion of suspenseful points of a story by a Virtual Narrator's facial expression and gestures.

References

1. Braun, N. Automated Narration, the Path to Interactive Storytelling, Workshop on Narrative and Interactive Learning Environments, Edinburgh, Scotland, 2002.
2. Braun, N. Storytelling in Collaborative Augmented Reality Environments, Proceedings of the WSCG, Plzen, Czech, 2003.
3. Braun, N. Storytelling and Conversation to Improve the Fun Factor in Software Applications, in: Mark A. Blythe, Andrew F. Monk, Kees Overbeeke, and Peter C. Wright (ed.): Funology, From Usability to Enjoyment , Chapter 19, Kluwer Academic Publishers, Dordrecht, ISBN 1-4020-1252-7, 2003.
4. Braun, N. and T. Rieger Expressiveness Generation for Virtual Characters, based on the Principles of Suspense Progression and Narrative Conflict, International Workshop on Mobile Computing, IMC 2003, Rostock, Germany, 2003
5. Gebrüder Grimm Jorinde and Joringel, provided by Rick Walton's Online Library, http://www.rickwalton.com/ , 2003.
6. Propp, V. Morphology of the folktale, University of Texas Press, 2nd edition, 1968.
7. Rieger, T., and Braun, N. Narrative Use of Sign Language by a Virtual Character for the Hearing Impaired. Proc. of Eurographics 2003, Granada (Spain), September, 2003.
8. Schneider, O. and N. Braun Content Presentation in Augmented Spaces by the Narration of Interactive Scenes, in First Research Workshop on Augmented Virtual Reality AVIR03, University of Geneva, Switzerland, 2003.
9. Silva, A., Vala, M. and A. Paiva Papous: The Virtual Storyteller, Proc. Of Intelligent Virtual Agents, Third International Workshop, IVA 2001, Madrid, Spain, 2001.
10. Szilas, N. A New Approach to Interactive Drama: From Intelligent Characters to an Intelligent Virtual Narrator, in: Proc. Of the 2001 Spring Spymposium on AI and Interactive Entertainment, Stanford, USA, 2001.
11. Szilas, N. Idtension: a narrative engine for Interactive Drama, , in Goebel, Braun, Spierling, Dechau, Diener (eds.): Technologies for Interactive Storytelling and Entertainement, Computer Graphic edition Band 9, 2003.
12. Theune, M., Faas, S. Nijholt, A. and D. Heylen The Virtual Storyteller: Story Creation by Intelligent Agents, in Goebel, Braun, Spierling, Dechau, Diener (eds.): Technologies for Interactive Storytelling and Entertainement, Computer Graphic edition Band 9, 2003.

Emotional Characters for Automatic Plot Creation

Mariët Theune, Sander Rensen, Rieks op den Akker, Dirk Heylen, and
Anton Nijholt

University of Twente, PO Box 217, 7500 AE Enschede, The Netherlands
{theune|rensen|infrieks|heylen|anijholt}@cs.utwente.nl

Abstract. The Virtual Storyteller is a multi-agent framework for automatic story generation. In this paper we describe how plots emerge from the actions of semi-autonomous character agents, focusing on the influence of the characters' emotions on plot development.

1 Introduction

The Virtual Storyteller is a multi-agent framework for automatic story generation. Its functionality includes plot creation, narration and presentation. Plots are automatically created by semi-autonomous character agents that carry out different actions to achieve their goals. To guarantee that the resulting plots will be well-structured, the characters are guided by a director agent, who provides (some of) them with specific goals, and who can forbid their actions if they do not fit into the general plot structure. The resulting plot is converted into a natural language text by a narrator agent, and presented to the user by an embodied, speaking presentation agent. The global architecture of the Virtual Storyteller is shown in Fig. 1.

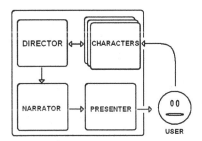

Fig. 1. Architecture of the Virtual Storyteller

With the first version of the Virtual Storyteller [12] we aimed at meeting two basic plot requirements: consistency at the level of character actions (through the use of goal-oriented characters) and well-structuredness (through the use of

S. Göbel et al. (Eds.): TIDSE 2004, LNCS 3105, pp. 95–100, 2004.

a director agent). Another storytelling system that combines a character-based appproach with the use of a virtual director is Teatrix, which is aimed at aiding story creation by children [3]. In the Oz project [4], a 'drama manager' was used to ensure the occurrence of some essential plot points during interactive story creation. The ACONF system [8] uses a different approach: here, a coherent plot structure is achieved by representing the plot as a partial-order plan, which is constructed by a group of expert systems representing the story characters.

Consistency and well-structuredness are essential for achieving a well-formed plot, but do not guarantee that the resulting story will be entertaining. For that, a plot should have additional properties such as unexpectedness, suspense and the presence of believable characters. A common approach to make character agents believable is to provide them with emotions. Most computational models of personality and emotion are based on Ortony, Clore and Collins' event appraisal theory, known as the OCC-model [6]. Examples are Elliott's Affective Reasoner [1] and Neal Reilly's Em system [5]. A simplified version of Em was incorporated in Loyall's Hap architecture for believable agents [2], used in the Oz project. This work was the main source of inspiration for our recent extension of the Virtual Storyteller with an emotion model for the characters.

In the following sections, first we briefly sketch the emotion model used in the current version of the Virtual Storyteller. Then we discuss the influence of the character's emotions on plot creation, showing how the characters' ability to adopt goals that are based on their emotions, rather than dictated by the general storyline, increases their believability and may give rise to unexpected (but nevertheless consistent) plot twists. We illustrate this with an example.

2   Emotions and Actions

In the Virtual Storyteller, the emotional state of an agent is represented by pairs of corresponding positive and negative emotions and their intensities. Emotions that are directed at the agent itself are hope-fear, joy-distress, and pride-shame. Emotions directed at other agents include admiration-reproach, hope-fear, and love-hate. Each emotion pair has an intensity value, represented by a natural number on a scale from -100 to 100. For example, a value of 20 for hope-fear means that the character experiences hope with an intensity of 20 (and no fear); a value of -20 means exactly the opposite.

Following the OCC-model [6], the emotional state of an agent changes in reaction to events, actions and objects. If an agent comes close to achieving its goal, it experiences hope, and if its current goal proves to be unachievable, the agent experiences distress. If an agent performs an action meeting its own standards (which are part of its personality model), the agent experiences pride. If an agent meets another agent which it likes (also part of the personality model), it experiences joy. The intensity and duration of these emotional effects depend on the personality parameters of the agent, which can be changed by the user. For example, some characters may be frightened more easily than others, or may forget their anger more quickly.

Based on its emotional state, a character may develop certain action tendencies such as friendly or unfriendly, aggressive or passive behaviour (cf. the mapping of emotions to action styles in Hap [2]). The action tendencies in their turn influence the importance a character attaches to certain goals. The relation between the emotions and the action tendencies of a specific character is laid down in a number of action tendency scripts, which are part of the character's personality model. For instance, strong fear could lead to passive behaviour in one character (increasing the importance of the goal to flee) and to aggressive behaviour in another (increasing the importance of attacking the object of fear).

3   Plot Creation Using Episodes

The Virtual Storyteller is aimed at the generation of short stories in the fairy tale domain. An advantage of this domain is that most fairytales have a common, fairly simple plot structure. The stories generated by the Virtual Storyteller consist of four global episodes, which are loosely based on Greimas' reformulation of Propp's story functions [7]:

1. initial state of equilibrium (a description of the initial setting of the story)
2. disruption of the state of equilibrium (something bad happens)
3. mission of the hero (the hero tries to restore the state of equilibrium)
4. return to state of equilibrium (or not, if the hero fails)

At the start of the story generation process, the director lays the basis for each of the episodes by selecting four 'episodic scripts' from a database. An episodic script contains information about the setting, goals and constraints of an episode. The setting specifies which locations, objects and characters are present in the episode. The episodic goals are goals which must be reached within the episode by (some of) the characters. Typically, episodic scripts of type 2 (disruption) will involve a villainous character with the episodic goal of performing some evil deed, and episodic scripts of type 3 (mission of the hero) will involve a character with the episodic goal of putting things right again. Finally, the episodic constraints specify certain actions that are not allowed in the episode. For example, it might be disallowed to kill a certain character before its episodic goal is reached. These three episode properties define the limits within which the character agents are allowed to act while constructing the episode.

After the episodic scripts have been selected, a story world is created according to the specified setting, and the character agents are initialized. The actual episode is then created by the characters carrying out actions to reach their individual goals. These goals can be the episodic goals that have been assigned to them by the director, but they can also be goals that were spontaneously adopted, based on the character's emotions (see section 4). Before a character can carry out a planned action, it must ask the director for permission. The director checks if the action violates any episodic constraints, or any global constraints (for instance, the director might forbid numerous repetitions of an action because they would make the story boring). If no constraints are violated, the character is allowed to carry on with its action, and the story world is updated accordingly. When one of the characters reaches its episodic goal, the episode ends. Because the characters can also adopt goals other than the episodic goal, there are many different ways in which an episodic script can develop before an episodic goal is reached. This variation can be further increased by changing the personality parameters of the characters (see section 2). Still, all variations will respect the global plot structure, because of the fixed order of episodes in combination with the local episodic goals and constraints.

In our current set-up, the episodic scripts are created and combined by a human author.[1] In terms of the 'scalable autonomy' approach of Spierling *et al.* [9], this means that there is no autonomy at the story level: the global plot structure is predefined. However, there is high autonomy at the scene (episode) and character levels: the actions carried out within an episode are not specified in advance, and the characters can make their own decisions (guided by the director, which is itself an autonomous agent).

4   Goal Selection: Emotions Taking Over

In the Virtual Storyteller, each character agent has a fixed set of potential goals. The importance that a character attaches to these goals varies depending on its action tendencies (see section 2). In addition, one of its goals may have the status of 'episodic goal', in which case it has a very high importance (90 out of 100) throughout the episode. Instead of having a character simply adopt the goal with the highest importance, we use a probabilistic approach to goal selection, where a goal's importance corresponds to the probability that it will be adopted. In other words, an episodic goal has a 90% chance of being selected for pursuit, but some 'emotional' goals may also have a high probability, due to the character's emotion-induced action tendencies. This means that a cowardly hero with the episodic goal of killing the villain could be equally likely to adopt the goal of running away from the villain because of its fear.

As we will illustrate with some examples below, probabilistic goal selection leads to variation and unexpectedness in the generated stories. However, there is risk of 'overdoing' it by having too much random switching between goals. Therefore, if a character has already carried out the first step of a plan towards achieving some goal, that goal will be maintained until it is reached (or made unreachable by changes in the story world). The goal is only abandoned if the character's emotions run so high that they cause the importance of some other goal (e.g., fleeing from an enemy) to exceed a pre-specified high value. Another risk of our approach is that a character's sudden change in behaviour, due to the adoption of a new goal, may seem incomprehensible to the user [10]. In the

---

[1] As our script database grows, it will become more important to have a proper, automatic selection mechanism that only combines compatible scripts. Also, in the future we would like to distinguish more than four types of episodes, by including more of Propp's functions. The sophisticated, real-time scene selection mechanism of the GEIST system [9] could serve as an example here.

Virtual Storyteller, we can solve this by having the narrator explicitly describe the character's motivation. Currently, this is only done to a very limited extent, and further work on this is required.

5   An Example

Here we illustrate the plot creation process by describing the different realisations of a simple script of type 2(disruption). The script involves two characters, a princess (Diana) and a villain (Brutus), who hate each other. Diana fears Brutus, but Brutus does not fear her. Diana has the episodic goal to kill Brutus, and Brutus has the episodic goal to capture Diana. Initally, the characters are in different locations. In yet another location, a sword can be found. We first discuss what happens given the default, rather stereotypical action tendency scripts of the princess and the villain. These scripts specify (among other things) that Diana is likely to behave passively when experiencing emotions such as fear and hate, whereas these same emotions trigger aggressive behaviour in Brutus.

In most episodes that were generated on the basis of this script, the characters immediately start pursuing their episodic goals: Brutus starts walking towards Diana to capture her, and she sets out to get the sword, needed to kill Brutus. Occasionally, one of the characters adopts another, emotionally motivated goal instead, such as singing out of joy. This occurs rarely, however, because initially the character's emotions have low intensity, so the importance of the associated goals is also relatively low. Whatever goal they start out with, the two characters eventually meet each other. When meeting Brutus, Diana is usually overcome by fear, causing her to abandon her episodic goal (even if she has already found the sword) and to run away instead. Brutus, who will act aggressively even if Diana has the sword, will follow her, either to capture or to attack her (the latter goal being motivated by his aggression). In the end, Diana is inevitably cornered by Brutus without any possibility to flee. If she has the sword, she is very likely to use it now, since killing Brutus is now her highest priority goal that can be attained. Otherwise, she is most likely to scream, because this is the only passive behaviour left open to her. If she does not have the sword, Diana may also go for the less likely goal of attacking Brutus by hitting or kicking him, but Brutus is stronger and will eventually capture her anyway.

We have also tested what happens, given the same episode script, if the action tendency scripts of the two characters are exchanged. In that case, the division of power is more equal, because although Brutus may be stronger than Diana, he is now more fearful and passive than she is. This leads to longer episodes involving more chase sequences and mutual attacks. In the end, as in the first version, the outcome depends on whether Diana manages to get to the sword in time or not. All in all, a large variety of episodes can be generated based on the same script. The probabilistic goal selection may give rise to unexpected character actions, but these actions can always be traced back to the character's emotions. Properly expressing these inner motivations in the narration of the plot will be our next challenge.

6   Conclusions and Future Work

The version of the Virtual Storyteller we have described here has been fully implemented, albeit with a limited set of rules and episodes. However, our experiences so far indicate that even with this limited implementation, a large number of different stories can be created. Further extension of the system with more possible goals, actions and objects is needed to show the full potential of our approach. As pointed out above, another important area of further work is the conversion of the plot into natural language, so that the underlying motivations of the characters are properly put across. With respect to presentation, we are currently working on the automatic generation of 'storytelling prosody' and on the conversion of abstract plots to 2D animations, as an alternative presentation mode for the Virtual Storyteller. Finally, in the longer run we want to extend the Virtual Storyteller so that the emotions of the user can be taken into account too, by learning rules to predict the effect on the user of different character actions. These rules can then be used to guide the decisions of the director (cf. the narrative sequencer employed in IDtension [11]).

References

1. C. Elliott. *The Affective Reasoner: A Process Model of Emotions in a Multi-Agent System.*, Ph.D. thesis, Northwestern University, 1992.
2. B. Loyall. *Believable Agents: Building Interactive Personalities.* Ph.D. thesis CMU-CS-97-123, Carnegie Mellon University, 1997.
3. I. Machado, R. Prada, and A. Paiva. Bringing drama into a virtual stage. *Proceedings of the Third International Conference on Collaborative Virtual Environments (CVE 2000)*, ACM Press, 2000.
4. M. Mateas. *An Oz-Centric Review of Interactive Drama and Believable Agents.* Technical Report CMU-CS-97-156, Carnegie Mellon University, 1997.
5. S. Neal Reilly. *Believable Social and Emotional Agents*, Ph.D. thesis CMU-CS-96-138, Carnegie Mellon University, 1996.
6. A. Ortony, G.L. Clore and A. Collins. *The Cognitive Structure of Emotions.* Cambridge University Press, 1988.
7. V. Propp. *Morphology of the Folktale.* University of Texas Press, 1968.
8. M. Riedl and R.M. Young. Character-focused narrative generation for execution in virtual worlds. *Proceedings of the International Conference on Virtual Storytelling*, 47-56, 2003.
9. U. Spierling, D. Grasbon, N. Braun and I. Iurgel. Setting the scene: Playing digital director in interactive storytelling and creation. *Computers & Graphics 26*, 31-44, 2002.
10. P. Sengers. Designing comprehensible agents. *Proceedings of the 16th International Joint Conference of Artificial Intelligence (IJCAI)*, 1227-1232, 1999.
11. N. Szilas. IDTension: A narrative engine for interactive drama. *Proceedings of the Technologies for Interactive Digital Storytelling and Entertainment (TIDSE) Conference*, 187-203, 2003.
12. M. Theune, S. Faas, A. Nijholt and D. Heylen. The Virtual Storyteller: Story creation by intelligent agents. *Proceedings of the Technologies for Interactive Digital Storytelling and Entertainment (TIDSE) Conference*, 204-215, 2003.

Writing Interactive Fiction Scenarii with DraMachina

Stéphane Donikian[1] and Jean-Noël Portugal[2]

[1] IRISA/CNRS, UMR 6074
Campus de Beaulieu
35042 Rennes, France
donikian@irisa.fr
http://www.irisa.fr/prive/donikian
[2] Dæsign
21 avenue François Favre
74000 Annecy, France
jnportugal@daesign.com
http://www.daesign.com

Abstract. This paper presents DraMachina, an authoring tool dedicated to authors of interactive fictions. An interactive fiction is an extension of classical narrative media as it supposes a direct implication of spectators during the story evolution. Writing such a story is much more complex than a classical one, and tools at the disposal of writers remain very limited compared to the evolution of technology. With DraMachina, we propose an authoring tool dedicated to the description of narrative elements composing an interactive fiction. It also automatize the exchange of information between writers and production teams.

1 Introduction

As opposed to classical literary, cinema, theatre or choreographic works, spectators of an interactive fiction are not passive as they can directly influence the story evolution. The central idea of Interactive Drama is to abolish the difference between author, spectator, actor, and character[Rya97]. It requires to use the potential of different technologies to allow the spectator to become co-author, actor and character. Interactive Fiction can be regarded as a new genre, deriving both from video games and from cinema. When *Immersion* is the basic quality players request from the former field, *identification* stands as the cornerstone of the later. Identification is only made possible when the interactor is able to witness human-like characters, endowed with a personality, and facing conflicts which he/she can potentially share and acknowledge as familiar [Lav97]. Therefore, when writing for interactive fiction, the author does not only have to describe settings, a plot, and potential ways to solve it, but he must also account for motivation, tastes, personality and consistency of the characters. Whatever degree of interactivity, freedom, and non linearity might be provided, the role that the interactor is assigned to play always has to remain inside the boundaries thus defined by the author, and which convey the essence of the work itself.

S. Göbel et al. (Eds.): TIDSE 2004, LNCS 3105, pp. 101–112, 2004.

This brings an extra level of complexity for writers, when tools at their disposal - word processors and graphical representations of a story decomposed into a tree diagram of scenes - remain limited compared to technological evolutions. DraMachina contributes to amend this situation. The goal is to design a tool that authors can use to create narrative environments by directly handling the tale's key elements - places, characters, roles, relationships and actions. A writing methodology analysis performed by Dæsign was studied to propose a more ambitious representation model, capable of specifying various types of interactive fictions or dramatic frameworks defined by literary theorists[Pro68,Bre73, Gre66,Tod69].

The DraMachina program is a partnership between IRISA[1] and the Dæsign company[2]. DraMachina was supported by the RNTL (French National Network for Research and Innovation in Software Technology) during two years until march 2003. This program develops an authoring tool dedicated to the description of narrative elements composing an interactive fiction. This tool is connected to an "interactive fiction engine" developed by Dæsign. This engine is intended for the fiction production team. By using the DraMachina tool and the database it generates, the engine considerably shorten the analysis and synthesis of documents supplied by the writer.

2   Related Works

2.1   Narrative Structure

The narrative is a statement of real and imaginary facts. Each fact can cover two kinds of reality, event and action, which are both referring to the modification of the natural course of things. An action is characterized by the presence of an anthropomorphic agent who will cause the change, while an event will arise under the effect of causes which are not outcoming from the intentional intervention of an agent. It is important to distinguish the two notions of cause and motive. In the case of a relationship between cause and effect, the antecedent is logically distinct from the consequent. On the other hand, the motive does not have any proper existence and is only thinkable from the action, as it concerns the reasons who will determine or permit to explain an act or a behaviour. The Hero of a story is driven by a motive to realize his quest.

To situate temporally and geographically a narrative, some descriptions should be given: character description (moral, physical, psychological portrayals), places and their topography, living and inert objects and last but not least the time(s) of the story. Each narrative is characterized by two bounds: the initial and final situations, and by a transformation relation between them. If each narrative possesses a transformational structure, each transformation between two states could not be assimilated to a narrative. It is necessary to take into account the notion of plot. In [AriBC], Aristotle defined the structure of a tragic

---

[1] Mixed Research Unit between INRIA, CNRS, University of Rennes 1 and INSA
[2] formerly known as Dramæra

plot in two parts: the complication and the denouement. The complication extends from the beginning of the action to the part which marks the turning-point to good or bad fortune, while the denouement extends from that point to the end. The Aristotelian curve of tension underlies millions of narratives from Greek tragedy to modern soap opera.

A global action is generally decomposed in a sequence of smaller action units. Such series should follow a chronological order but also a causal chain: there is a necessary link of logical causality between facts. Vladimir Propp[Pro68] had broken down a large number of Russian folk tale into their smallest narrative units to arrive at a typology of narrative structures. His conclusion was that there were only thirty-one generic units in the Russian folk tale. Even if they are not all present in each narrative, he found that all the tales he analyzed displayed the functions in unvarying sequence. Propp proposed also a repartition of functions between the seven main kinds of characters. There is not a unique distribution of functions: one character can accomplish more than one group of functions and a group of functions can be accomplished by more than one character inside the category. Campbell[Cam49] observed that the same stories has been told continually along the history of humanity, whatever is the culture but of course with different details and character names. He traces the story of the hero's journey and transformation through virtually all the mythologies of the world. Influenced by Propp, A.J. Greimas [Gre66] proposes the Actant Model which describes the dynamic forces and their position inside the narrative. Actants are not the same as actors, they function at the level of the text not of character. Several characters in a narrative may consolidate a single actant. Actant is a name of a fundamental Role at the level of deep structures. The Actant Model is based on six categories of agents (subject, object, sender, receiver, helper, opponent) organized on three axes: project, conflict and communication. The project-axis depicts the subject and its project, its endeavours to appropriate the coveted object. The conflict-axis depicts a helper who promotes and an opponent who opposes the subject's project. Finally the communication-axis depicts the action which is decisive for the accomplishment of the project, the sender and its doing which transfers the object to the receiver. The Actant Model permits a formalization of the partial propositions of the narrative development.

From the analysis of a hundred short stories contained in *The Decameron*, written by G. Boccaccio, T. Todorov [Tod69] proposes to describe narrative laws, to encode their expression and to build the basis of a new science: the narratology. He describes three levels: semantic, syntaxic and verbal. In his work he mainly focuses on the syntaxic level which corresponds to the combination of basic narrative units depending on their relationships, each narrative unit corresponding to an action performed by a human or anthropomorphic character. He defines a set of logic connectors to express different kinds of relations between those units. For Bremond [Bre73], Propp Narrative structure is too simplistic: a narrative may have more than one point of view. In the Propp model, there is only one hero and everything is defined from its point of view. For Bremond, functions are grouped in sequence, whose structure is fixed, but that can be organized in various ways (superpose, interlace, knot, ...). He criticizes also Todorov, saying that his model did not take into account means of actions. His own narrative structure is based on rôle distribution and on implication and exclusion relations: an event B presupposes a past event A and makes possible a future event C while it makes impossible another potential event D. He also introduces a logical model of a sequence: a situation opens the possibility of an action which can either become an action or not, and this action can either succeed or fail.

2.2   Interactive Dramas

Interactive Drama is a new media based on several other ones: the narrative branch (Literature, Theatre, Cinema) and the interactive branch (Video Games, Virtual Reality). The main problem concerns the merging of narration and interactivity, without decreasing the force of narration and the strength of interactivity. The script limits the freedom of the user, but it also maximizes the chances of a pleasurable performance. As illustrated on figure 1 there is a bidirectional link between the theatre world and the story world. The story should react to the actions of the audience (the action feedback) while also the audience should react to the narration (the emotional feedback).

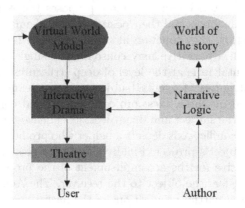

Fig. 1. Architecture of an Interactive Fiction.

Models proposed by structuralists has been used to structure interactive drama models: Propp[IMP01,SGBI02], Greimas [MKL01], Bremond [Szi03]. Another approach consists in restricting a narrative to a sequence of actions and to use AI planning techniques for interactive storytelling[CLM+03]. Facade, developed by Mateas and Stern[MS02] integrates both the story and the character levels, including drama management, autonomous character behaviour and natural language processing for the interaction with the user playing the rôle of one character in the story. Our objective with DraMachina is not to produce a drama manager and to make choice between the different models proposed in the narrative theories, but to help an author to write an interactive fiction. The main input remains the natural language directly connected, thanks to hyper-links, to the key elements of the drama, including its narrative structure, rôle distribution and character description.

3   The Authoring Tool

3.1   Introduction

DraMachina is an interactive application mainly based on text edition. An au-thor of a classical linear story would have the ability to write the story, including characters description and linear dialogs edition. A scenarist of an interactive fiction will also be able to describe the skeleton of a story at different levels (pe-riod, act, scene, action) and to specify relations between these elements. He will as well be free to specify a more complete dialog structure including user choices and branching depending on specific parameters. As summarized by Marie-Laure Ryan[Rya97], different architectures are possible for an interactive fiction. We have decided not to make a choice between these possible architectures, but to let authors writing stories with a low-constrained approach.

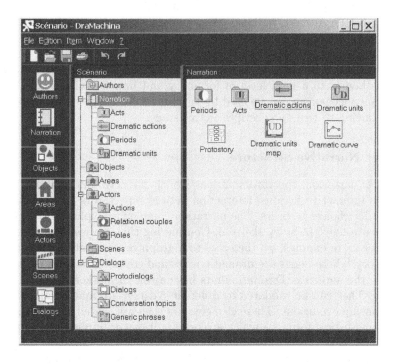

Fig. 2. Hierarchical structure of objects manipulated inside DraMachina.

The main window (cf figure 2) allows authors to access to the story elements, and is structured by using the file/directory metaphor. The main elements are:

Authors directory : each author can enter his own reference.

Narration directory : this directory includes acts, periods, dramatic actions and units description.

Objects directory : description of objects important in the course of the story.

Areas directory : description of locations of the story.

Actors directory : this directory includes elements related to the description of characters, which is composed of their characteristics, psychology, actions they can perform, roles they can play and relationships between actors.

Scenes directory : detailed description of scenes.

Dialogs directory : dialog edition based on protodialog patterns.

This logical description is based on a structural analysis, not only of drama, but also of film *morphology*. It allows the author to set up a series of criteria which will determine a *virtual director's cut* each time the interactive fiction is performed. For example, a Scene object is logically described as the combination of current setting / actors on stage / Dramatic Action currently going on / and present state of the Dramatic Units map. Entrance of a character, change of Dramatic Action... will automatically change the Scene Object and thus its parameters such as Mood / Ambience, Level of Formality, Rhythm of Action, Actions Allowed, etc. For example, we can imagine two generals, character A and character B (the Actors), walking along a palace's corridor (Setting), leading to the throne hall. They are toughly arguing about waging war on another country (Dramatic Action). A tries to argue B out of this project. In all cases, their dispute will automatically end as soon as they enter the throne hall, if this setting is bound to a high level of formality and imposes silence and respect. This simple mechanism can be used by authors to determine directing patterns, without having to write any scripts at this stage.

3.2 The Narrative Structure

In classical narration, spectators are passive, they receive informations without acting. In interactive fictions, interaction between spectators and narration implies to offer choices to users. The narration complexity explosion then force to structure strongly the story skeleton. Considering that stories have a beginning and one or more endings, we then face to a graph representation of main times of this story, where nodes are dramatic units and edges the narration directions offered to the audience. Dramatic units have a role of markers of the narration evolution. They can be validated by different events as dramatic actions, dialogs or relationship evolutions. These elements are then associated to dramatic units by declaring logical formulas which are preconditions or implications of the dramatic units, such as the Bremond logical model [Bre73]. Links between nodes of the drama unit map are then extracted from these logical formulas and a drama map can be constructed. Analyzing this drama map by detecting cycles

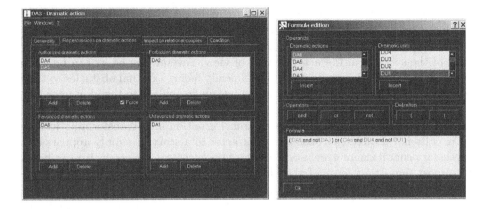

Fig. 3. Dramatic action repercussions and condition edition.

or non-linked nodes is then possible and helps authors to identify problems in the logical structure of their scenario.

3.3   Actor Description

Psychological description of characters is a delicate and important point. Classical psychoanalytical theories do not offer an approach suitable for computer abilities. Transactional theory is a social psychology developed by E. Berne[Ber61] which is devoted to the global understanding of interpersonal transactions. In this theory, the human being is globally categorized in three ego states : parent, adult and child. A human being can address to another one from any of his ego states to a specific state of the receiver, who can reply in turn: this exchange is a transaction. If the response is not given from the same state than the targeted one, there is an imbalance in the transaction. During a transaction, each one signals recognition of the other and returns that recognition; any act of recognition is a stroke. Berne observed also that people need strokes, the units of interpersonal recognition, to survive and thrive. By reproducing this mechanism while writing dialogs, an author could tag each retort by indicating the source and target ego states. In DraMachina we decide to focus on strokes. Each stroke has an impact, which could be either positive (caress) or negative (blow), and a duration on the receiver (cf figure 4). Declaring strokes that characters received before the start of a story helps to represent the characters' initial psychological state. We decomposed it in a description, a duration value from seconds to whole life and an impact value from traumatism to happiness.

Other characteristics could be given to complete the description of an actor, such as the speaking and listening focus, the accepted distance to other people in a discussion, the normal walking speed. We can also describe lists of actions and roles that the actor will be able to perform. Of course the author has also the ability to give a natural language description of the actor and to write its biography. Again however, logical description of the actors is critical, as it is meant to have a direct impact on the course of drama. Each character is endowed with a role, which itself contains a goal and potential actions. The goal is the concrete purpose of the actor, the realization of which would mark the positive end of the story from the actor's point of view. Several characters can be given identical or conflicting goals, thus mechanically facing external obstacles to their quest. These concrete goals are the only ones made obvious to the interactor but, from the author's point of view, a key dramatic objective still underlies them: reaching the peak of each character's transformation arc. Transforming himself is usually not a direct purpose for a character in a story; it simply appears as a necessary condition, or even a side effect, of his success. Conversely, it is probably the most important lever of the identification process. DraMachina allows the description of both paths.

The goal can only be reached by performing *dramatic actions*, which themselves result in sequences of more simple actions. Some of these actions may contradict the character's system of values, (this being highly recommended for the sake of dramatic tension!). Finding ways to achieve the goal without generating unbearable internal conflict for the character, or building up enough pressure to bring the character to a point where self-transgression becomes possible (and witnessing the consequences...), are the two main ways offered for interaction in DraMachina based gameplays.

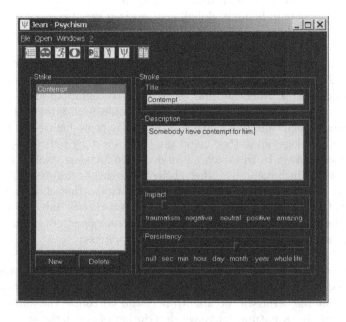

Fig. 4. The Inner Mind Edition Window.

3.4 Dialogs Writing Method

The protodialog edition window (cf figure 5) is a graph based structure including nodes, arcs and three kinds of branching - binary, ternary and unbounded. Protodialogs are used to characterize different dialog structures. Branching nodes can either correspond to a conditional expression on variables of the story or a question/answer interaction phase with spectators. All classical style characteristics can be specified for each element of the graph. Cyclic subgraphs can be detected and overviewed.

As shown on figure 5, specific patterns can be introduced in the text of transitions to give automatically information to the dialog manager. No specific protocol is defined, it is of the responsibility of the development team to define its own writing protocol with the author. A dialog structure is then based on one of the protodialogs available. Protodialogs can be created or modified interactively during a dialog edition. Figure 6 shows a dialog edition window based on the protodialog shown in figure 5. A dialog is also defined by its protagonists and each node of the protodialog can correspond to a sequence of one's lines. For example, in figure 6 the first node of the protodialog is corresponding in the dialog to four one's lines said alternately by two characters. Moreover, DraMachina provides the author with a helpful methodology to further the reuse of

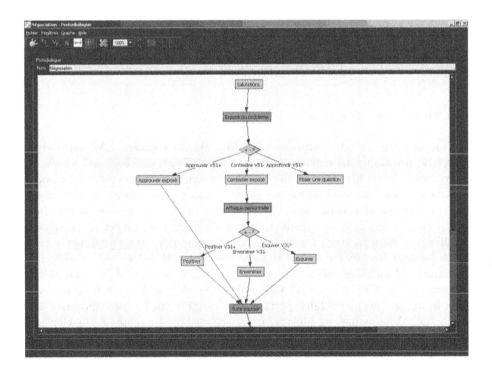

Fig. 5. The Protodialog Edition Window.

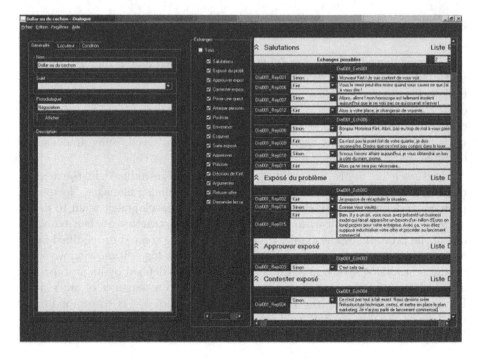

Fig. 6. The Dialog Edition Window.

sentences, expressions, locutions or set phrases stored in the database, in order to build up a variety of original and dynamic dialogs.

3.5   DraMachina Output

The internal file format is expressed in XML. We have chosen XML as it gives easily the possibility to export data to other applications. Figure 7 shows an excerpt of a XML file. During the DOM tree generation process, an optional functionality can be used which consists in syntaxic and semantic analysis of phrases. The result consists in a decomposition of each character's action into several parameters : nature, manner, source and target of the action. Verbs are classified in different categories (action, dialog, motion) by using available corpus. These data can be very interesting to integrate in an action databasis, and permit to extract informations about actions that can be performed by each of the characters. The XML file is read and analysed inside the AVA environment and by now, dialog and protodialog parts of the scenario can be used automatically inside the AVA engine, as illustrated by screenshots of figure 8. In the first picture, labels of the different choices above the frame are corresponding to those given in the protodialog shown on figure 5.

```
<?xml version="1.0" encoding="iso-8859-1"?>        </NarrativeEnvironment>
<!DOCTYPE DraMachina_scenario>                    <ActorsEnvironment>
<Scenario title="Scenario" >                       <RoleList/>
 <Authors/>                                         <ActionList/>
 <NarrativeEnvironment>                             <RelationalCouplesList/>
  <Story title="Story n1" />                        <ActorList/>
  <ProtoStory text="Once upon a time..." />         <DramaActionList>
  <ObjectList/>                                       <DramaAction name="DA1"
  <AreaList/>                                                  description="" >
  <ActList/>                                           <DramaUnitList/>
  <PeriodList/>                                        <AuthorizeList/>
  <DramaMap>                                           <ForbidList/>
   <UDList/>                                           <FavorizeList/>
    <UD name="DU1" description="" />                   <UnfavorizeList/>
   </UDList>                                           <ForceList/>
  </DramaMap>                                          <ImpactOnRelationList/>
  <Dialogs>                                            <TalnExtraction/>
   <DialogList/>                                      </DramaAction>
   <ProtoDialogList/>                                </DramaActionList>
  </Dialogs>                                        </ActorsEnvironment>
  <SceneList/>                                      </Scenario>
```

Fig. 7. Excerpt of a DraMachina XML file.

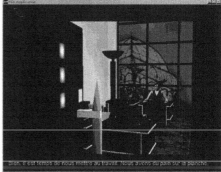

Fig. 8. Some screenshots of the corresponding AVA simulation.

4   Conclusion

What is at stake with DraMachina is to provide simple and efficient ways of writing such a complex works as interactive fictions. The variety of authors, of plots, of contexts, of interactive gameplays, etc., imposes the tool to be very generic and adaptable. Therefore, we based it on a low level analysis of the elements of fiction, bridging a gap between computer science and structural theory applied to literature, myth, and storytelling. We took advantage of available results in this lively research field, to make a clear separation between logical items which directly influence the course of the story (roles, motivations, values, preconditions of actions, actions, consequences of actions...), and *cosmetic* items such as settings, physical description of characters, elements of *style*, etc. We also provided general background patterns, like time or dramatic structures (based on different combinations of dramatic nodes), which the author can use as skeletons or guidelines. DraMachina can also be regarded as a linear screenplay laboratory as it allows the author to first describe the atomic components of the story, before experimenting several dramatic developments and conclusions. DraMachina's attempt to achieve an in depth conceptualization of a story and to display it under simple, logical and graphic appearance, is also a step in the description of complex narrative environments and story based virtual worlds.

References

[AriBC]   Aristotle. *Poetics (translation S.H. Butcher)*. Hill and Wang, 350BC.
[Ber61]   Eric Berne. *Transactional Analysis in Psychotherapy*. Ballantine Books (new edition), 1961.
[Bre73]   C. Bremond. *Logique du récit*. collection Poétique. Editions du Seuil, 1973.
[Cam49]   J. Campbell. *the hero with a thousand faces*. Bollingen Foundation Inc., New York, 1949.
[CLM⁺ 03]   F. Charles, M. Lozano, S.J. Mead, A.F. Bisquerra, and M. Cavazza. Planning formalisms and authoring in interactive storytelling. In *TIDSE'03, Technologies for Interactive Digital Storytelling and Entertainment*, pages 216–225, Darmstadt, Germany, 2003.
[Gre66]   A.J. Greimas. *Sémantique structurale : recherche de méthode*. Collection Langue et langage. Larousse, Paris, 1966.
[IMP01]   A. Paiva I. Machado and R. Prada. Is the wolf angry or... just hungry? In *International Conference on Autonomous Agents*, pages 370–376, Montreal, Canada, 2001.
[Lav97]   Y. Lavandier. *La dramaturgie*. Eds Le clown et l'enfant, 1997.
[MKL01]   J. Szatkowski M. Klesen and N. Lehmann. A dramatised actant model for interactive improvisational plays. In R. Aylett A. de Antonio and D. Ballins, editors, *IVA2001*, LNAI 2190, pages 181–194. Springer-Verlag, 2001.
[MS02]   M. Mateas and A. Stern. Architecture, authorial idioms and early observations of the interactive drama façade. Technical Report CMU-CS-02-198, Carnegie Mellon University, December 2002.
[Pro68]   V. Propp. *Morphology of the Folktale*. University of Texas Press, 1968.
[Rya97]   M.L. Ryan. Interactive drama: Narrativity in a highly interactive environment. *Modern Fiction Studies*, 43(3):677–707, 1997.
[SGBI02]   U. Spierling, D. Grasbon, N. Braun, and I. Iurgel. Setting the scene: playing digital director in interactive storytelling and creation. *Computer & Graphics*, 26(1):31–44, February 2002.
[Szi03]   N. Szilas. Idtension: a narrative engine for interactive drama. In *TIDSE'03, Technologies for Interactive Digital Storytelling and Entertainment*, pages 187–203, Darmstadt, Germany, 2003.
[Tod69]   T. Todorov. *Grammaire du décaméron*. Mouton, La Haie, 1969.

A Toolkit for Authoring Non-linear Storytelling Environments Using Mixed Reality

Daniel F. Abawi, Silvan Reinhold, and Ralf Dörner

Professur Graphische Datenverarbeitung, Johann Wolfgang Goethe-Universität,
Varrentrappstr. 40-42, 60486 Frankfurt am Main, Germany
{abawi,sreinhold,doerner}@gdv.cs.uni-frankfurt.de
http://www.gdv.cs.uni-frankfurt.de/

Abstract. Efficient creation of high-quality Mixed Reality (MR) content is challenging today due to a variety of difficult problems not only on a technological level. As a consequence, authoring problems prevent a more widespread usage of MR in digital storytelling. We present a novel authoring toolkit that allows an efficient integration of MR technology in various interactive non-linear storytelling applications. We demonstrate its usage in an example use case that represents typical MR-related authoring tasks like the calibration of real and virtual objects or the specification of their semantic relationship. As a peculiarity, a seamless provision of the MR authoring toolkit together with the storytelling application is conceptually and technically supported. Thus, we show how authors, even without technical background, who want to create MR-enriched storytelling experiences, can be adequately supported. The underlying concepts for an efficient implementation of our proposed authoring toolkit are briefly described.

1 Introduction

Mixed Reality technology allows blending interactive virtual objects in the real world to build a continuum between reality and virtual reality [6]. Being able to bridge the gap between computer-created realities and the physical world as well as to digitally enrich the ambience and create interaction spaces, Mixed Reality (MR) has in principle a high potential for realizing a wide range of applications in the area of non-linear storytelling. Yet this potential is limited, since the complexity of MR technology is an obstacle for a widespread use of MR. Thus, sophisticated concepts are needed to enable developers who are non-experts in MR to integrate this technology in their applications. However, it is most important to adequately address the authoring problem associated with MR content production: software should not only support the presentation of MR, but also allow for authors with different backgrounds to create MR environments [4]. This is not trivial as MR-specific authoring tasks (like calibration) need to be supported. Although it is desirable to perform the authoring in an MR-enhanced environment [1], some authoring tasks prove to be difficult to accomplish in the Mixed Reality itself. In addition, the author is not always able to share the

S. Göbel et al. (Eds.): TIDSE 2004, LNCS 3105, pp. 113–118, 2004.
© Springer-Verlag Berlin Heidelberg 2004

view of the end-user on the MR ("preview problem"), for instance because the author is at a different physical location than the user.

In this paper, we analyze the MR content creation problem in the context of non-linear storytelling. We also take a step towards solving this problem by proposing a concept for content creation. Beside a component-based authoring process with clearly defined author roles and a dedicated framework of software tools to support the author, one major idea in our concept is the usage of MR methodology itself for authoring applications. The concepts and implementation presented have been developed in the European project AMIRE (Authoring Mixed Reality) [3] where MR-based e-learning applications for an oil refinery in Austria and narrative environments for the Guggenheim Museum in Spain are built to validate the approach.

The paper is organized as follows: The next section gives an outline of how a framework and component-based approach to authoring can support the Storyteller in creating story templates for Mixed Reality applications. Section 3 illustrates how typical authoring tasks can be accomplished with our authoring tool prototype. Before we conclude, we sketch the underlying component and framework based concepts that we used to implement our demonstrator in section 4.

2   Components and Story Patterns

Our approach to authoring Mixed Reality applications is based on a framework concept, and on components that are used within this framework. Each component can have its own visual representation, as well as a certain behavior. This way, the approach enforces a distributed (decentralized) implementation of the underlying story, behaviors, and of the application logic. Inherently facilitated by the framework and component paradigms, any of the participating components can additionally be replaced or reused elsewhere, be it in the same sub-story or within a completely different context. The versatility of such an approach and corresponding construction kit becomes evident when we consider that this architecture allows for a very flexible implementation of a story:

Components used in one sub-story can be reused either in the same, or in a different sub-story—even as part of a completely different overall story—along with their behavior and interactive capabilities. In turn, this allows the introduction of Story Patterns: the story teller builds the structure for a particular story, which can then be implemented within an MR application using the appropriate objects and their behavior, or logic. An author may now identify arbitrary objects contained in the MR application, and replace them using other (potentially more appropriate) objects, without changing the overall structure, or context, of the story itself. The one thing that remains unchanged is the overall story, or underlying structure, providing a pattern for other contexts of use. Any of the objects used to implement the application may change or be replaced dynamically, depending on the story teller's or the author's requirements.

One application for Story Patterns is the provision of story templates, which story tellers can create to provide a certain structure and course of action or suspense. A particular story structure, course of action or suspense may be appropriate for varying areas of use or application domains, and it might, therefore, be appropriate to conceive and author it only once, and to then offer it as a best practice example to other authors. The author himself, then, does not need to create an underlying structure from scratch, but can fall back on a story template. The relevant tasks that the author has to fulfill are then reduced to his core domain and competencies, which include selecting and combining components, adapting multimedia content, and calibrating visual representations of components with the appropriate real world objects.

3   Using the Authoring Toolkit

In general, even a component-based approach will not facilitate application development to the extent that all an author has to do is plug the components into the framework and run the application.

Using a structured workflow as the basis for the authoring process, we can identify four main tasks that must be performed by an author:

- qualification of MR components
- adaptation of the selected MR components
- combination of the MR components to allow interaction between them
- calibration of real objects and the virtual objects in the application

In the qualification phase, the author selects, or qualifies, those components that are needed to assemble the MR application, from a hierarchically organized repository. In order to display multimedia content, 3D geometries, or text in a scene, the author might include a placeholder object such as an image loader, a geometry loader, or a text component. Such components allow a quick exchange of their visual representation without removing the components themselves from the scene.

As a component is usually not a special purpose object with respect to the actual context it will be used in, some adaptation will always be necessary. For example, the author may have qualified a branch component to implement a part of the application logic: a switch clause might check whether the user is closer to a real object in the scene than a certain threshold will allow, and branch into a separate sub-story whenever the distance of the user falls below that threshold. The same clause might invoke a different sub-story when the user moves away too far from the same object. The generic branch component itself must be adapted, because the author will need to set the corresponding threshold values and branch targets (i.e. the sub-stories) to be invoked. To support adaptation without passing any information about their implementation to the outside, components have properties, which can be accessed through property editors. This also allows on-the-fly adaptation of components, which means that modifications to the application or the story itself can be made in real time. An adaptation tool within the toolkit allows the author to change specific properties.

In the combination phase, components participating in a story can be connected to interact with each other. In the framework architecture discussed here, each component has so-called in-slots and out-slots, which are used for receiving and sending information, respectively. Connecting two components is simply a matter of connecting the out-slot of one component with an appropriate in-slot of another one. As described earlier, there may be components specifically singled out to be sub-story connectors; therefore, using such a component to connect two parts of a story means to connect two threads of the overall story.

Our concept of building abstract MR application descriptions has the benefit that third party applications can be integrated into the development process. Fig. 1 illustrates an example, the integration of Microsoft Visio as a tool for the combination phase. Microsoft Visio is specialized on schematic drawings; Fig. 1 shows two sub-stories (marked blue and green, respectively) connected with an MR component that switches between those threads of the story.

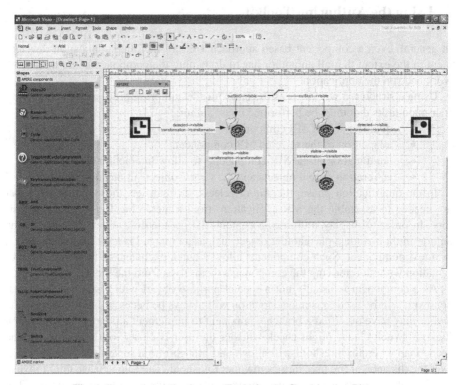

Fig. 1. External Applications as Tools for the Combination Phase

One crucial factor in Mixed Reality applications is the alignment of virtual objects such as text, video, annotations, or 3D geometries, with reference points in real space. This task is generally referred to as calibration, and must be specifically addressed by dedicated tools within the toolkit. In order to address different groups of authors adequately, we have more than one tool for this MR specific task. For instance, one tool is based on the manipulation of the orientation and position of real objects [2]. Fig. 2 depicts the calibration of a virtual object (blue boxed) with a specific calibration tool.

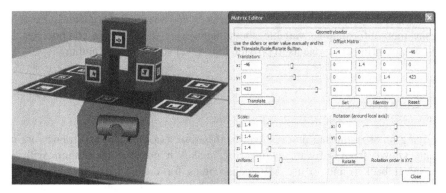

Fig. 2. Calibration of Virtual Objects

4   Implementing the Toolkit

For the realization of our authoring toolkit we use component and object-oriented framework concepts [4,5]. This greatly reduces the complexity of MR application development and has several additional advantages (like increasing efficiency, extensibility and adaptability). Our idea is to use one single framework - both for the application and the authoring toolkit. The authoring toolkit is obtained by just adding special authoring functionalities (like a calibration component that offers the calibration functionality described in section 3, [2]) to the framework; this authoring functionality is encapsulated in dedicated authoring components. A major advantage is that content built in such an environment exposes the same behavior during authoring and during presentation – without any inconsistencies. This mitigates the preview problem of MR content creation.

We not only provide the authoring functionality in the form of *authoring components* but also the following other entities are represented as components:

- *Visually represented Components*, like real world objects (e.g. a car, a painting or a chair), virtual objects (e.g. Mickey Mouse) or annotation objects that augment the real world in the MR scene with additional information, e.g. text, pictures, schemas, videos or sounds).
- *Conceptually represented components*: like context sensing components (e.g. for collision detection), interaction components responsible for interactions with the user of the MR application or behavior model components; these components are a model of a specific behavior. (e.g. a simple Boolean AND operation or a complex simulator).
- *MR System Components* that are high-level representations of MR-specific devices and technologies (like cameras, see-through glasses, head mounted displays, marker or object recognition algorithms).

Authoring components are able to manipulate these components and are able to offer the author access since all components are connected by the same framework, since all components possess well-defined interfaces and since all components are able to make meta-information available about themselves to authoring components. This allows authoring components to provide high-level support to the author.

5 Conclusion

Relying on an authoring process that itself bases on component and framework concepts known from software engineering, makes it possible for authors with non-technical background to use MR technologies for creating non-linear storytelling applications. Major advantages are the specification of the behavior of a non-linear story at a high abstraction level, the ability to divide this behavior description and associate its parts with real or virtual objects, the provision of MR representations of story patterns, the ability to toggle between author and user view, and the possibility to immediately view results of modifications. The description of how typical MR-related authoring tasks can be supported by our prototypical toolkit shows the potential and the level of support authors can expect from our approach to MR authoring.

Acknowledgements. This research was partly funded by the European Commission under the fifth framework programme, project AMIRE (IST-2001-34024). We would like to acknowledge the valuable contribution of all AMIRE project partners.

References

1. Abawi, D. F., Dörner, R., Geiger, C., Grimm, P., Haller, M., Hartmann, W., Reinhold, S., Zauner, J.: Mixed Reality – A Source for New Authoring Methodologies? ACM SIG-GRAPH Workshop Proceedings Production Process of 3D Computer Graphics Applications, Shaker 2002, pp. 9-16. (2002)
2. Abawi, D. F., Dörner, R., Haller M., Zauner J.: Efficient Mixed Reality Application Development. Visual Media Production Conference 2004 (CVMP 2004), London. (2004)
3. AMIRE Project Homepage: http://www.amire.net
4. Dörner, R., Grimm, P., Abawi, D. F.: Synergies between Interactive Training Simulations and Digital Storytelling: a Component-based Framework. Computer & Graphics 26, 2002, pp. 45-55. (2002)
5. Haines, G., Carney, D., Foreman, J.: Component Based Software Development / COTS Integration, Software Technology Review (draft), Revision 97a, Carnegie Mellon University SEL 1997. (1997)
6. Milgram, P. and Kishino, F.: A Taxonomy of Mixed Reality Visual Displays, IEICE Transactions on Information Systems, Vol. E77-D, no. 12, Dec. 1994. (1994)

Learning from the Movie Industry:
Adapting Production Processes for Storytelling in VR

Richard Wages[1], Benno Grützmacher[1], and Stefan Conrad[2]

[1] Laboratory for Mixed Realities, Schaafenstr. 25, D - 50676 Cologne, Germany
{wages, gruetzmacher}@lmr.khm.de
[2] Fraunhofer IMK, Schloss Birlinghoven, D - 53754 Sankt Augustin, Germany
stefan.conrad@imk.fraunhofer.de

Abstract. Any movie production needs a whole group of contributing authors and creative artists from various fields. The same should obviously be true for the making of a compelling VR scenario. Hence artists need to have direct access to the VR production process itself. In the VR domain however artistic and computational challenges are usually still severely interwoven. Thus nearly all of the (art) work is currently done by computer experts due to the unstructured workflow and the lack of creative tools for authors. In this paper we present two novel tools which we developed to adopt movie production procedures namely the VR Authoring Tool and the VR Tuner. The first is a tool to create a *nonlinear* screenplay and storyboard analogue to the beginning of every movie production. The second tool, the VR Tuner, facilitates editing and post-production of VR scenarios for the first time. We conclude with a brief description of our experiences during a first evaluation of the tools.

1 Introduction

Within the comparatively young field of highly immersive VR environments one can observe a steady improvement of display systems and interaction devices. On the software side sophisticated tools are available to create imagery and sound. But can this be enough to produce the best possible VR scenarios? Compared to the (Hollywood) film industry this would mean that the production of a movie starts with building up the scenery and filming right away and using the unaltered results as the final product. After more than a century of experience in movie production the film industry has developed a well-defined modular workflow. The procedure starts with the story outline, followed by the writing of the screenplay, casting and staging, filming and directing and finally the post-production with the editing of the film material. Each step is considered as an art form of its own with its specific refinements and own professionals.

In current VR productions however certain specific artists are still more or less excluded from most of the production process. It is the programmers who have to do the main work and hence have the strongest influence when it comes to the modeling of the story process and editing. The reasons for this are obvious, since the computers

S. Göbel et al. (Eds.): TIDSE 2004, LNCS 3105, pp. 119–125, 2004.

experts are usually the only ones who are able to put all the pieces for a working VR scenario together. Since they cannot rely on decades of experience in interactive storytelling, each VR installation is usually build up from scratch and 'en bloc'.

Authors of VR scenarios can only communicate their vision of scenery and story progress in written form and hope that they are fully understood. A clearly defined platform does not exist. Once the VR scenario is completed and running for the first time it might be comparable to the 'rough cut' in movie productions. At this late point major changes in the VR production are usually impossible and even smaller improvements (editing) are tedious and again can only be done by programmers. But the flexibility to make these changes and refinements will mark the difference between an acceptable and an exceptional production. An audience will less likely complain about shortcomings in technologies than about imperfect content. Hence it is time to enable authors and artists better of full access to this production process. We believe that this can only be done by the development of creative tools for these artists who for the most part not have programming skills. Our presented tools – the VR Authoring Tool and the VR Tuner facilitate important steps at the beginning and at the final stage of a VR scenario production, namely screenplay, storyboarding and post production with editing.

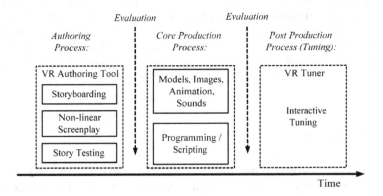

Fig. 1. The proposed production process of a VR scenario. The core production process is completed by a well-defined authoring and a post-production process. Every phase of this production process leads to a result which can be evaluated on its own

2   A Tool to Support the VR Authoring Process

The goal of the presented VR Authoring Tool is to enable creative authors with no programming experience to create a *non-linear script* defining the whole story structure including all possible forms of interaction and progression through the story without the help of programmers or technical experts. This script can be created and even tested with an integrated story player before the production of models, images and sound for the scenario has started. Beside the modeling of the story structure this tool also provides the functionality of a non-linear storyboard, where the author can communicate ideas about the presentation of the scenario to the VR production team.

2.1 Non-linear Story Structure

The concept of non-linear scenarios used for this VR Authoring Tool is based on parallel hierarchical graph structures. Graph structures are very intuitive and easy to grasp for authors which is demonstrated by the fact that they are typically used to illustrate and discuss non-linear processes [3, 4]. Furthermore they are widely used for authoring in different applications like an AI Editor [6], a Hypertext tool [2] and indirectly also in a storytelling tool [5]. The limitations of a single graph to model a complex non-linear scenario are obvious, because an author is forced to define all possible paths through the story in detail. But this argument does not hold when several graphs are introduced as parallel entities which are at first independent of each other but can be brought in context through an own scripting logic. While one central graph - the *storygraph* - roughly represents the overall progression of the story the other parallel graphs represent visible (e.g. scenery, doors, characters,...) as well as invisible (e.g. camera, timeline, apertures, plots...) objects. Every node of an object graph represents a certain state of that object. The overall state of the story is not defined by the actual state of the storygraph alone but by the actual states of *all* graphs. When we are talking of states we think of story relevant states rather than of physics and geometry. In huge VR environments – in our case the CAVE or the i-CONE – a single state might enclose options for impressive spatial navigation. Nevertheless this could be a completely irrelevant fact from a storytelling point of view. The connectors between the nodes imply possible transition inside a graph. Every node can be filled by the author with references to other objects as well as *Event Scripts* to define interdependencies between the referenced objects. An Event Script consists of a simple If-Then relation where a set of conditions (e.g. a state of a referenced object) must be fulfilled to execute a set of results (e.g. a state of a referenced object or a transition to a adjacent node).

Since there are basically no restrictions on how complex a story can be, the tool also offers the possibility to encapsulate entire parts of the story (e.g. self-contained story parts) within a - in that case - hierarchical higher node. Thus modeling of complex scenarios can be arranged more concisely by the author while the scenario structure itself gains stability and manageability for the associated story engine.

2.2 Non-linear Storyboard

Within each node, event specific information describing the scene or the object appearance can be deposited by the author. This information – pure descriptive text and attached sample sounds, pictures or movies – serves as illustrative material for the modelers of the virtual world. The internal media player of the Authoring Tool enables the author to access the attached files for the most common media file formats.

2.3 Testing with an Integrated Story Player

A non-linear script can not just be read straight forward for evaluation as a linear movie script but entails different forms of progression and experience depending on the user's interaction. Therefore an integrated *Story Player* is provided in this tool. This player enables the author to progress through the scenario and to simulate all the possible user interaction in order to test the behavior of the scenario. Cause the player provides the information about the story progress in a kind of debug mode, a scenario can be tested on the basis of the non-linear script alone, before any modeling or programming has started. For more information on the story player see [8].

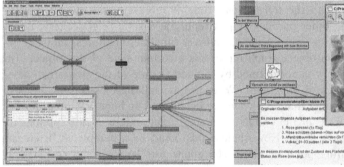
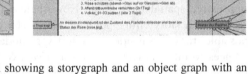

Fig. 2. *(left side)* The VR Authoring Tool showing a storygraph and an object graph with an opened node. *(right side)* storyboard information of a node

2.4 The Authoring Tool in the Further Workflow

The benefit of the Authoring Tool is not limited to the authoring process in the beginning of a VR production. Assumed that the story engine of the target platform provides an adequate interpreter, the non-linear script which consists of a very rigid xml structure can be used to control the progression of the scenario in real time. Consequently changes on the script which are made with the VR Authoring Tool will directly effect the presentation of the scenario on the target platform. Hence last minute modifications and versioning is convenient and even possible for non-programmers.

3   A Tool for Editing and Post-production

According to the role of the VR Authoring Tool for story design and screenplay writing, the VR Tuner provides functionality for fine tuning of an already produced VR story. In analogy to the post-production step in movie production the VR Tuner is used to apply changes to a story after the main development has already been concluded. The user is presented an interface combined of a 2D GUI on a wearable touchscreen computer and a set of hardware motor faders in a mixer console (see fig.3). The devices are brought into the immersive projection environment which makes them available in a running VR story. The touchscreen device can be detached from the mixer and carried around independently. For 3D interaction the touchscreen has a spatial tracker sensor attached. Being spatial aware, the touchscreens can be used like a scanner by pointing with it directly on 3D objects to retrieve their list properties. Selecting an object in 3D or in a 2D scenegraph and storygraph browser on the touchscreen computer, brings a list of the tunable properties of this object on the touchscreen. In addition, certain object parameters are assigned to motor faders. Using 2D controls on the screen and the motor faders, the user can now change the behavior and presentation of story objects. Tunable are for example light colors, material properties and the pose of geometrical objects, volume and effects of sound objects, but also parameters of abstract objects like the behavior of the mover model, which is used in the story.

Fig. 3. The VR-Tuner hardware within an immersive projection environment

After the story representation has been changed according to the user needs, all tuned parameters are made persistent in an XML based file format. Different sets of tunings can be loaded again at runtime to overwrite the original settings from the main development. The VR Tuner enables creative professionals who do not necessarily have to be VR or programming experts to tweak an already produced story. Small changes can be applied in a WYSIWYG manner, without the time consuming indirection via a programmer or modeler. The interface has been designed for ease of use which has already been verified by professionals from stage productions who especially appreciated the use of the mixer as an intuitive, well known interaction method.

4 Conclusion

In this paper we argued for the necessities to modularize the process of VR productions and to give non-programmers a stronger influence on this process to improve the quality of VR scenarios. We believe the best way to meet both necessities is the development of specific creative tools which flank the work of the VR programmers. We presented our two tools, the VR Authoring Tool for the creation of a non-linear screenplay and in advance testing of the VR scenario and the VR Tuner for the on site editing of a running scenario within a CAVE or i-CONE. First reactions of non-programming artists who tried to create non-linear screenplays for VR scenarios and computer games ranged from complete refusal to enthusiasm. It became apparent that support for authors is crucial when they engage in working with the tool for the first time due to the unfamiliar way of writing down stories. This initial blockage was easily overcome by even the shortest workshop, after that authors used the Authoring Tool and the story player in a playful way. On the long run we are expecting them to come up with completely novel types of interactive scenarios. The tools themselves have proven to run soundly in a first small test scenario 'Taking care of the Little Prince's planet'. One of the major advantages for the production process is for example the chance to make working scenario progress alterations in less than a minute by simply modifying the storygraph with the help of the VR Authoring Tool – before that the modification of source code could easily last for hours. At present the tools are evaluated further under realistic commercial production conditions for the i-CONE VR game 'Entropy' which runs on the AVANGO VR platform [1, 7] and will be a permanent installation in the Technical Museum Vienna from May 2004 on.

Acknowledgements. This work was supported by the Ministry of Education and Research (BMBF) under grant No. 01IRA06A within the 'Virtual and Augmented Reality' project framework.

References

1. Beckhaus, S., Lechner, A., Mostafawy, S., Trogemann, G., Wages, R.: alVRed: Methods and Tools for Storytelling, International VR/AR Status Conference, February 19-20, 2004, Leipzig, Germany
2. Eastgate Systems, Inc.: Storyspace, http://www.eastgate.com/Storyspace.html
3. Ryan, M.-L.: Narrative as Virtual Reality, The Johns Hopkins University Press, Baltimore (2001)
4. Samsel, J., Wimberley, D.: Writing for Interactive Media, Allworth Press, New York, (1998)

5. Silverman, B.G., Johns, M., Weaver, R., Mosley, J.: Authoring Edutainment Stories for Online Players (AESOP): Introducing Gameplay into Interactive Dramas. ICVS 2003: 2nd International Conference of Virtual Storytelling, November 20-21, 2003, Toulouse, France

6. Stottler Henke Associates, Inc.: SimBionic, http://www.simbionic.com/overview.htm

7. Tramberend, H.: A Distributed Virtual Reality Framework, in Rosenblum, L., Astheimer, P., Teichmann, D. (eds.): Proceedings Virtual Reality 99, IEEE Computer Society Press, Conference, Houston, Texas (1999)

8. Wages, R., Grützmacher, B., Trogemann G.: A Formalism and a Tool for Diverging Requirements in VR Scenario Modeling, ICAT 2003: 13th International Conference on Artificial Reality and Telexistence, December 3-5, 2003, Tokyo, Japan

A System to Compose Movies for Cross-Cultural Storytelling: Textable Movie

Catherine Vaucelle[1] and Glorianna Davenport[2]

[1] Media Lab Europe, Sugar House Lane, Dublin 8, Ireland,
`Cati.Vaucelle@medialabeurope.org`
[2] MIT Media Lab, 20, Ames Street, Cambridge 02139, USA,
`gid@media.mit.edu`

Abstract. This paper presents *Textable Movie*, an open-ended interface that allows anyone to become "video-jockey." In the framework of computational storytelling, Textable Movie promotes the idea of maker controlled media and can be contrasted to automatic presentation systems. Its graphical interface takes text as input and allows users to improvise a movie in real-time based on the content of what they are writing. Media segments are selected according to how the users label their personal audio and video database. As the user types in a story, the media segments appear on the screen, connecting writers to their past experiences and inviting further story-telling. By improvising movie-stories created from their personal video database and by suddenly being projected into someone else's video database during the same story, young adults are challenged in their beliefs about other communities.

1 Introduction

We imagine a world in which children play, create and exchange visual narratives with ease and transparency. Textable Movie explores a graphical language and interface that can invite storytellers of any age to compose and visualize movies, images and sound environments while writing a story; the system self-selects and edits images in real time based on textual input of the teller. While Textable Movie was first inspired by an application for annotating images [2], during pilot studies with teenagers, we have found that its power is maximized when it becomes a presentation system. Makers first create their own media, e.g. pictures, sounds, movie segments, based on stories they wish to recall; they then use a text driven presentation mode which allows the maker to shape a story fluidly while writing a story. By creating a movie-editing paradigm in which text leads and image follows, Textable Movie provides a very natural, fun and immediate interface to story-making. This approach creates a symbiotic relationship between the author's imagination and the stories that she wishes to tell and supports a diverse set of activities that foster narrative co-construction.

S. Göbel et al. (Eds.): TIDSE 2004, LNCS 3105, pp. 126–131, 2004.

2 Application Domain

In proposing a text-led interaction and presentation system, we redress a limitation of traditional editing and draw on observation and previous research that relates verbal and image exploration [1, 2]. In traditional "random access" video editing systems, the interaction paradigm is a timeline; the objective is to make an immutable "final" cut of a movie. The author can only see the whole once she renders the time line. The audience sees only the final version of the object. How can we turn this paradigm on its head? How can we bring the imagination of the projectionist or the audience in closer synchronicity with the "movie" output? Ironically, the very nature of digital architecture begs us to make a shift from final object to process. Why should we treat a collection of digital clips stored in a database with the rules that shaped the continuous material substrate of celluloid? Why not call chunks from the database in real time? When images or movie chunks are stored, they are generally identified with digital "metadata" including a name. Can we take advantage of the naming process?

Previous research and observation together lead to the idea that text could drive a "projection paradigm" where the projection is sequenced by the projectionist/viewer/maker in viewing time through verbal input. Early testing with this paradigm using footage of the application author uncovered a basic limitation: how would the projectionist/viewer know what words to use? This resulted in the idea that the players -- be they a small group focusing on an authored project or casual visitors to a waiting space -- submit and name their own images. The Textable Movie application thus came to serve as a platform for multiple video-oriented interactions along the lines of the play described in the scenario. By encouraging associative thinking in the verbal domain, the application leads participants into a new realm of story making. Participant "projectionists" use Textable Movie to drive a movie experience made up of the story text and the association between particular words in the text and video clips stored in the database.

Textable Movie [9] retrieves movie segments and sounds in a specified database, from analyzing textual input. It loads and plays them in real time while the story is being typed. Consequently, a novel movie gets created and generated in a very transparent, and easy manner. The simplicity of use and immediate response can help the user/projectionist focus on the story rather than on the technical concerns of editing. The system can easily be connected to any personal movie database. For example, the following short keyword sequence [forest, nature, tree, wood, leaves, Yosemite] could describe a personal 10-second video clip of the Yosemite park, called "forest.mov" The personal labelling is important as it allows the users to give the medium their own meaning. A series of simple commands add instant manipulations of the movie being played (see Figure 1.). These commands are typed directly in the text, and by deleting the text-command, the effect disappears, e.g. to zoom: [closeup], to change the speed rate [faster], to alter the overall coloration of the image [winter].

in the forest...   cover a giant rock.   giant rock [closeup]   It was cold [winter]

Fig. 1. Video segments play instantly following the story typed. A set of commands modify in real-time the video segments, e.g. [closeup], [winter].

3 Contribution to the Digital Storytelling Community

We explore a video-based interface that empowers people in discovering new ideas, and that involves them in challenging their assumptions about their surrounding environment during storytelling. While previous systems have been built for dynamic video sequence generation by secondary image selection [4], or textual specification [3], Textable Movie provides sequencing by textual and spoken text input. Textable Movie is a natural language system for a spontaneous approach to the interface. Using language as an interface allows a natural approach to story building and play for both the person who is trying to understand the world and for the person who engages in improvisational storytelling with someone else using the system.

We play, learn and exchange ideas about our identity using stories. For many centuries, the letter has been a dominant form, from family letters to pen pals. Today communications technology, with its spectrum of media potential, expands the resources we have at our disposal for exploring and sharing identity. Therefore we propose that such real-time movie-making devices could have potential in cross-cultural exploration, investigating multi-dimensional approaches to express and exchange identity. Can young adults, by sharing images and stories across borders, gain a deeper sense into cultural identity? Textable Movie is a tool that might engage people in relationships where they exchange and transfer a sense of culture through play, collaboration, and storytelling. Cultural as well as personal production of media can be shared over media spaces as a means of understanding relationships with others, their communities, their rules, their habits, and their references to the world. With new technologies, we are moving away from the letter-form into a creative and collaborative world in which images and sounds can mix with local language. Textable Movie is a movie-making device to engage people in exploring multi-dimensional approaches to expressing and exchanging identity.

In a world in which media is everywhere, media creation can provide a means of exploring self-identity both through individual sharing and group construction of media spaces. Constructionists have suggested that users could benefit from systems that support self-expression rather than create content for the user. With Textable Movie, our focus is to empower people to express what they think is meaningful in their culture, and what is optimally challenging to them. We base this research on the body of work regarding digital stories for documenting culture. A network of media could allow users to master the art of digital media for their own expression, developing powerful ideas through the presentation of interactive videos representing their own lives for the purposes of cross-cultural exchange. This would allow remote peers to reflect on their assumptions about other cultures through experiencing these videos, and instructive installations.

4 User Study

While our interface paradigm is specific, it was inspired by the need to make visual storytelling more accessible, engaging, and powerful for young people [7]. In that interest, we have designed an international workshop that focuses on visual storytelling using Textable Movie. Teenagers participating in these workshops go through the process of putting together a piece by first storyboarding, then shooting, editing, and projecting a video-story. We have started to plan a global strategy, which will allow us to compare how teenagers use this system across cultures. We observed teenagers create their own video database about Dublin.

Textable Movie acts as a projection device for a storyteller. It is specifically a tool for improvisational storytelling, and not a regular editing tool. It is based on the theory that people learn by constructing their knowledge [6], and that people are engaged in the process because they have fun, because they are challenged, and because they expect an audience for their creation. The extension of the constructionist field we explore comes from the Community Art notion of « challenging » the audience by the object created. In this workshop, we observe how teenagers can be empowered in the sense of involving them in creating pieces to challenge their recipient about their assumptions. These assumptions can be about their environment, their identities, and also their culture. The core issue of the research is to focus on storytelling in order to bring to light contradictions and resolve them. We are particularly working with teenagers because they are in an intermediate stage where they are questioning the contradictions in their environment.

4.1 Methodology

A one-week user study has been held at the Ark, Dublin, in Ireland with 11 teenagers. We divided the week into different activities: each day, the teenagers experimented with our video tools for 3-4 hours. Around ten adult mentors interacted with the teens, helping them to use the video equipment and Textable Movie, and making sure each teenager explored the equipment, and understood its features. We have first familiarized the teenagers with the traditional methods of movie making and documentary making. The teenagers had a hands-on introduction to the video equipment. We have introduced the notion of new ways of movie making by assembling video clips in a specific order, and new forms of stories by remixing them together. We have quickly shown Textable Movie in use for such purposes. They first created a storyboard telling a story about the building in which they were in. They filmed their own movie based on it, and used the Apple software iMovie to assemble their movies.

4.2 Results

The teenagers have segmented their own movie, creating a palette of keywords to explore their movie. The immediate response from the system made it comparable to a video game, and not an editing tool. The teenagers were excited to "play" with Textable Movie, and wanted more videos about themselves. They were thinking about ways to connect their facial expressions to Textable Movie. We ended up with a palette of heads and the names of the teenagers as keywords. They wanted to redo more of their own footage for the system. We have explained the intent of the workshop as a way for teenagers from other countries to navigate through their life. To this end, we have asked the participants to shoot in the city as a reporter of their environment. They shoot elements presenting their city and what they liked or disliked in it, e.g. mobile phone conversations, couples kissing, fights. They watched their video, and decide how they will cut it for the interactive projection. For instance, one of the editor said : *"Oh, this is you here! We could make it so that when "Tom Cruise" is mentioned during the projection, then you appear on the screen!"*. One participant was designated to be the projectionist creating the city story using Textable Movie. However, all the others were 'shouting' the keywords they wanted him to type in order to have surprising footage. We have found that they exclusively used Textable Movie as a tool to show others short stories in real-time and make surprise effects by creatively associating keywords to visuals. They consistently gravitated towards iMovie and its timeline to create an edited movie for export. They never used the functionality of Textable Movie to create a whole movie out of the story segments. We can deduce that the specific utility of Textable Movie is to provide a response to the user input in real-time and then act as a projection device. A more quantitative analysis could support these results; however, we found very informative that, in a one week workshop in which the teenagers felt challenged by the activities, all of them have looked at Textable Movie as a real time projection device, and each has pushed the limits of its functionality, e.g. by making surprise effects. Thus, we have found it important in imagining a set of video editing tools that this set should include a regular editing tool, e.g. iMovie, as well as an interactive projection tool, e.g. Textable Movie. We finally observed that the teenagers were constantly into creating specific content for their audience, and were excited about sharing their database with other countries. From the beginning, one of our goals for this tool was to encourage teenagers from around the world to share views of their world with each other.

5 Future Work

We found that Textable Movie is a natural tool for improvisation and projecting audio-visuals while telling a story, and we have also begun a new multi-cultural database of teenagers in their environment. We have prepared the setup for use in different countries where equivalent workshops will take place, and the cooperative results will be a permanent kiosk to navigate among other's culture. In its future versions, our system will be networked, and used as a multimedia tool to reflect into someone else's culture. Our plans include a further analysis of the new possibilities created for participants of different countries who share a database of clips from different places, installed in the form of a kiosk in children's museums internationally. Textable Movie will also be part of the worldwide activities of Pangaea [5] that aim to let children around the world feel "bonds" personally.

6 Conclusion

In this paper we argued that there is a need for an alternative framework for video editing and storytelling. The need is motivated by the desire to reproduce the playful improvisational environment of child storytelling. We have outlined the specifications of Textable Movie during a workshop. It informed us that Textable Movie engages teenagers to become video-jockey by allowing projection of media during storytelling in front of an audience. The power and flexibility of Textable Movie can be evaluated in part based on applications that we have created which we did not initially envision. For instance, Textable Game extends the concept to the realm of video games. This application aims to engage teenagers in building their own games, e.g. action games, exploration games, mystery games, using their own footage and sounds, and allowing them to create their own rules and scenarios.

References

1. Davis, M. (1995). *Media Streams: An Iconic Visual Language for Video Representation.* In: Readings in Human-Computer Interaction: Toward the Year 2000, Morgan Kaufmann Publishers.
2. Lieberman, H. & Liu H. (2002). *Adaptive Linking between Text and Photos Using Common Sense Reasoning*, Conference on Adaptive Hypermedia and Adaptive Web Systems.
3. Lindley C. A. (2001). *A Video Annotation Methodology for Interactive Video Sequence Generation*, Digital Content Creation, Earnshaw R. and Vince J. (eds).
4. Murtaugh, M. (1996). *The Automatist Storytelling System*, M.S. MIT Media Lab.
5. PANGAEA. (2003). http://www.pangaean.org/
6. Papert, S. (1991). *Situating constructionism.* In Papert & Harel, Eds., Constructionism. Cambridge, MA: MIT Press.
7. Resnick, M. (2002). *Rethinking Learning in the Digital Age.* In The Global Information Technology Report: Readiness for the Networked World, Oxford University Press.
8. Vaucelle, C., Davenport, G., and Jehan, T. (2003). *Textable Movie: improvising with a personal movie database*, Siggraph, Conference Abstracts and Applications.

Hopstory: An Interactive, Location-Based Narrative Distributed in Space and Time

Valentina Nisi, Alison Wood, Glorianna Davenport, and Ian Oakley

MediaLabEurope, Sugarhouse Lane, Bellevue, Dublin 8, Ireland
{vnisi,woodsy,gid,ian}@mle.ie

Abstract. As computing and communications technologies evolve, there is the potential for new forms of digitally orchestrated interactive narratives to emerge. In this process, balanced attention has to be paid to audience experience, creative constraints, and presence and role of the enabling technology. This paper describes the implementation of HopStory, an interactive, location-based narrative distributed in space and time, which was designed with this balance in mind. In HopStory, cinematic media is housed within wireless sculptures distributed throughout a building. The audience, through physical contact with a sculpture, collects scenes for later viewing. Inspired by the history of the installation space the narrative relates a day in the life of four characters. By binding the story to local time and space and inviting the audience to wander, we amplify the meaning and impact of the HopStory content and introduce an innovative approach to a day-in-the-life story structure.

1 Introduction

Over the past few decades, researchers and artists have explored computation as a storytelling medium, resulting in an explosion of eye-catching interactive media experiments. While many hypermedia stories have been published as CD-ROMs or on the WWW, success has been limited suggesting they lack the compelling depth of more traditional linear media. Meanwhile less commercially focused explorations have taken place in research laboratories and under the direction of individual artists. Many of these experiments propose novel interfaces or extend the reach of computation into the presentation form or navigational paradigm. However we are concerned with the structure of the story itself, with what makes a "good" computational story. One lesson that rings true from the previous research is that the opportunity for digital interaction with story content alone does not constitute a meaningful narrative experience.

As Kearney [1] points out, every story is told by someone to someone else. He develops this argument, suggesting that innovation in storytelling depends on both the medium and the story being told. Non-linear, computationally-augmented storytelling is still in its infancy. Over the past 15 years, most research has been tethered to a technological resource: link-based hypermedia and other script-based computational

S. Göbel et al. (Eds.): TIDSE 2004, LNCS 3105, pp. 132–141, 2004.
© Springer-Verlag Berlin Heidelberg 2004

frameworks have been used to publish fiction [2], documentary [3] and a variety of histories. While many interactive fictions have been published on CD-ROM, few continue to be referenced. With a few notable exceptions (such as Myst), those works that lock viewers into a single user, screen-based interaction seem to be limited in their ability to deeply engage and touch.

Many factors may account for this unsatisfactory experience: choice of story, style of telling, conflict between the physical act of interaction and the mental processing of story, the promise of non-linear infinitude and the expectation of catharsis. Despite these difficulties, more thoughtful structures for computational stories are slowly emerging. Over the past few years, wearable computers and PDA's with GPS or other location sensors have made it possible to construct location-based cinematic narratives. In this form, the audience members receive narrative elements as they physically navigate through a geographical story space [4],[5].

Extending this work, the installation discussed in this paper, HopStory, describes the implementation of a novel location based narrative. This approach takes a digitally-enhanced story beyond the computational desktop and distributes it in a physical space that humans navigate in day to day life [6]. HopStory explores the opportunity provided by such forms to link content to the setting in which the story is being experienced, allowing the space to express history and personality. In the following sections, we describe the implementation, technology and content that comprise the HopStory installation.

2   Hopstory

With HopStory we intended to create a historically inspired distributed story for a specific location such that physical navigation of the space by the audience becomes an editing process through which audience members realise their own version of the cinematic narrative. With this as our creative goal, we began our research into the history of the area and of the building that would host the installation. This research informed the development of the character-based story, which focused on four character's different points of view on the same events, taking place during a single day of work in the installation building, originally a brewery. This was then further analyzed to obtain a plot that maximized the continuity between the character viewpoints so that it could be filmed as forty-eight separate segments.

In the installation, the audience can collect story parts according to story time and character as they walk through the building. They then view their own edited version of the story, featuring the clips in the order that they collected them, at a designated playback station. Only in this moment of playback the viewers fully experience, their personally assembled story.

HopStory is novel in the way in which it marries physical navigation through the installation with character point of view. As Rokeby [7], points out, the story space can be conceived as a navigable structure or world: "The navigable structure can be thought of as an articulation of a space, real, virtual or conceptual. The author structures the space with a sort of architecture, and provides a method of navigation. Each position within the conceptual space provides a point-of view, defined and limited by the surrounding architectural structure. Exploring this structure presents the spectator with a series of views of the space and its contents. The sequence in which the spectator experiences these vistas forms a unique reading of that space". In the case of the HopStory the architectural metaphor can be taken literally.

Furthermore, the story connects to the audience's sense of time. As the story progresses, the characters move through the building, living out their day in the early 1900s. Similarly, as the audience wanders through the same building, experiencing the installation, they encounter the four characters at different locations and times. The audience encounters sculptures modeled after a brewery cat, a special character in the story. The sculptures indicate the locations where the story content is available.

Fig. 1. Cat sculpture in location

Using a simple physical object (described in section 2.2) for interacting with the sculptures the audience is able to collect scenes. When a scene is collected, an audio segment from that scene is played. Essentially, through contact with a cat, a participant receives a new scene and uncovers a character, who responds by revealing a part of his or her story. The instantaneous audio response may encourage audience members to seek out more scenes to add to their collection.

The audience controls the number of clips they collect but do not know what events they will witness before they make contact with a sculpture. Much like wandering through an actual building and choosing to eavesdrop on chance conversations, audience members edit their own movies by navigating the building space. However, rather than viewing each scene at the moment it is encountered, the audience saves up their collections for later viewing, allowing interaction with the system while carrying out other tasks, and experiencing the movie when it is convenient.

We found that the location-focused nature of the story provided a creative playing field for developing content. In the case of our installation, designed to be housed within a culturally significant brewery building, the historical inspiration was natural. Access to the physical setting of the characters' lives provided a concrete starting point for research, visualization of scene description, and conception of plot events. An additional character with a different role to play, a cynical brewery cat, wanders around the story providing historical anecdotes in what we called ambient scenes where no human character appears.

2.1 Installation

The installation was expressed by seven cat sculptures, which were embedded with small metal iButton receptors [8]. Six of the cats were spread through one floor of the building, and the seventh was seated on an armchair in a lounge area. The cats were designed to be eye-catching, and were around 1 meter in length.

The movie scenes collected by the participants were carried to the lounge area and projected onto the wall, for anyone nearby to view.

Participants were given a key ring, which contained a metal iButton for storing clips, and a card with brief instructions for navigating HopStory. When a cat was located, a participant was to connect his or her iButton to the metal receptor embedded within each cat, in order to 'store a scene' onto the iButton. When participants were satisfied with the collection they had stored, they could touch the iButton to the cat at the projection area and watch the movie they had collected. The instructions noted that a given cat could be consulted multiple times during the day, since the characters moved back and forth between different sculptures. During the demonstration, the story ran for the duration of one hour, with the scene advancing every seven or so minutes within each cat.

2.2 The Content

The story has been created with the purpose of providing the audience with a flavor of a day in the hop store when it was an industrial building. Four fictional characters bring the audience in four different journeys through the hop store during normal a day of work. The characters are informed by personal accounts of social conditions of the Liberties, the area surrounding the brewery, and the lifestyles of workers at the brewery in 1920 [9,10]. Plot events center around an accident caused by a combination of arbitrary actions from each character, providing many causal threads from which the audience build connections.

Each character can enter the building, and the story, at a different point in the day. Ambient scenes supplement the narrative, providing background historical information during the story times in which no character is present. Like traditional story forms such as the novel, play, or film, the form of HopStory imparts new constraints onto the creation of the content. The narrative was broken down into forty-eight fragments that illustrate the lives of the four characters as they progress through their day.

The HopStory narrative is ultimately portrayed in the style of traditional cinema, through a linear movie. The received movie is pieced together differently by each participant who interacts with the system, and each movie will posses a different number and combination of scenes, characters, or plot events. The constraints of such narrative assembly creates interesting challenges regarding the composition of story fragments. Each scene is somewhat anecdotal, so very short assembled movies will be meaningful. The story progresses in parallel with real time, insuring that the story will never go "back in time".

Simple themes are referenced in multiple scenes to unify the character's stories. For example, one recurring theme is that the character of the buildings foreman is very hungry, because he missed dinner the previous evening and then forgot his lunchbox. This is mentioned multiple times during his narration of the story, influencing his actions during the day of work. To connect to this theme, the other characters often refer to food and meals during the day, linking the story fragments narrated by the different protagonists. For example, the foreman's daughter starts her day by bringing a lunchbox to her father as shown in figure 2.

The characters do different things during the day, the foreman attends to the machinery, the foreman's daughter wanders through the building and sometimes they can be seen at the same time in the same location or dealing with the same event from a different perspective, giving the impression of a connected overall narrative. An example is the accident that happens in the hop store in the late afternoon. Each character experiences it in some form, even if just auditory. This technique is used to emphasize the differences in point of views of all the characters regarding the same incidents. The accident involves one of the characters, a boy falling on the ground and it can be experienced by the audience from each character's perspective: the boy falling from the stack; the foreman witnessing the accident and feeling guilty about having assigned the task to the boy; the girl scared by the noise but curious about what is happening; and the surprised planner, who hears the noise and wonders what's happening on the other floors of the building.

Fig. 2. Frame from the video showing the foreman's daughter delivering the lunchbox

The perception of the different story fragments as a whole is further facilitated by the presence of some characters in other character's scenes. For example the boy's character arrives late into the hop store building. As he sneaks inside, he sees the foreman character drinking a glass of beer with his men near a window. The viewer can see the men laughing at the window from the boy's point of view. At the same time, the story experienced from the foreman's side won't mention the boy, because they can't see him. While hiding from the foreman behind a wall, the boy is spotted by the planner. From the planner's point of view the fact is of minimal importance as he is completely absorbed in his work and barely notices the child. The boy would be just a shadow in the background for the planner, but from the boy's point of view, the incident is quite important. In the boy's scene, the planner walks by in front of him and stares at him for a second. The boy then puts a finger in front of his own mouth asking the planner not to tell the other workers about him hiding behind the wall. We believe that this way of recalling characters from other peoples perspective is quite effective in bringing unity to the whole story and suggesting continuity of place and time.

With these techniques, we attempt to ensure that an audience member receives a coherent and meaningful narrative regardless of the number of scenes collected and the order that they gathered them in, independently of the presence or absence of any specific scene.

2.3 The Technology

The technology used in HopStory enables audiences to collect and play back their story scenes through physical contact with the cat sculptures. The physical contact occurs with the use of iButtons, metal canisters the size of a coin made by Dallas Semiconductor which store small amounts of digital information. These were handed out to the audience on key rings before the demonstration. Figure 3 shows an iButton key ring and a cat sculpture.

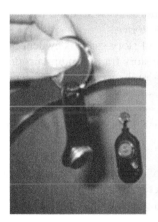

Fig. 3. iButton and iButton interaction with the receptor on the cat sculpture

The iButton receptors are small metal contact points, which were embedded in the cats. The receptors were plugged into the serial ports of six laptop computers attached to the cats. The audience roamed the space with their iButtons and then, as convenient, engaged with the sculptures to collect data. When the scene was acquired a short audio segment from the scene was played. At the same time data was uploaded to their iButton. Video clips associated with this data could then be retrieved and viewed at the playback station.

For each of the six locations, eight scenes were written, progressing through eight time slots in the story day. Each was tagged with a two-digit ID number indicating the time slot and location. This was the information stored on the iButton and used to reference the video clips at the playback station using custom software written in Isis [12].

3   Related Work

Research and installations relating to multi-viewpoint stories, place mediated histori-cal recollections, and tangible interaction provide the background to the HopStory system. For some time storytellers in a variety of formats have been exploring the use of multiple points of view as a way to structure narrative. In this context, authors have chosen to build characters who drive the narrative, to stimulate the audience to choose among different prospective on the same events. As Mazalek observes "One of the advantages of multiple viewpoint approach is that it leaves greater possibility for different viewers/readers to relate to different characters depending on their own personalities and preferences. Further more, events can take on a variety of meanings depending on whose perspective they are viewed from" [14].

The idea of buildings as containers for stories and place-related narratives was ex-plored in the Weirdview hypermedia project [15]. The audience is provided with a graphical interface portraying a row of houses in a street in Lucan Village in county Dublin. Real stories of people living on the street were collected and arranged using the houses as metaphoric containers of the stories.

Exploration of the physical navigation of story space is evident in Tamara, an in-teractive dinner play by Krizanc [16]. The story frames an upstairs/downstairs drama, taking place in the rooms of a large mansion house. Audience members start out in one room and are free to follow the actors when they move around the house as the story progresses. If there are two actors playing a scene in a room and one storms out, audience members must choose which actor the will continue to follow. The audience sees only a portion of the story relating to the characters they find most interesting.

Strohecker et al. describe [17] Tired of Giving, an interactive screen based story relating to the statement against racial segregation made by Rosa Parks in the United States. Viewers explore the story through the multiple perspectives of the different characters and a three-part chorus inspired from the ancient Greek theater.

HopStory was also influenced by previous work on tangible interfaces. In Genie Bottles, the audience explores a multi point-of-view narrative by lifting the corks of three glass bottles associated with three genie characters [18]. Each genie has a dis-tinct personality and background that affects how he or she talks about the events in the story. Each time the audience interacts with the bottles, they release slightly different perspectives based on which genie(s) they listen to, in what order, or for how long [14].

Spatial cinema has been the focus of several projects of the Interactive Cinema group at the MIT Media Lab including Elastic Charles (1987), Elastic Boston (1990), and Boston: Renewed Vistas. Most recently, Pan's describes M-Views which focuses on developing hardware and software to support the creation of location-aware mobile cinema [5]. In the current implementation, audience members carry iPAQs, equipped with a GPS or infrared sensors, and an 802.11 network card. "Another Alice", was the first cinematic experience developed for the M-Views system and was set within the MIT campus [6].

4 Evaluation and Future

We created the Hopstory as an exercise in designing a distributed story incorporating portable technology in the narrative process. The story develops in time, with a linear progression of the plot mapped to real time and unfolds in space using the architectural layout of the building as a navigation tool. Depending on the time and the space the audience is situated in when interacting with the Hopstory, they retrieve parts of the story from different characters points of view.

Hopstory was demonstrated at an exhibition held within our lab in January 2002. This event attracted a large and diverse group of academics and corporate representatives to our facility. Throughout the day of the event visitors entered, we handed them an instruction card and an iButton. Visitors could freely roam the floor, using this equipment with the cats of the Hopstory.

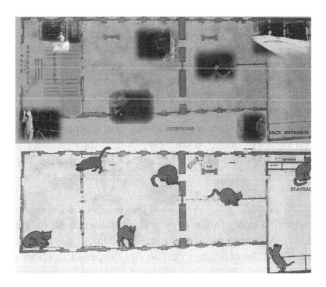

Fig. 4. Story and installation maps

We made a number of observations of audience behavior throughout the day and received a large amount of spontaneous commentary on various aspects of the Hopstory. These insights are briefly described below. The audience was interested and curious about the distributed structure of the narrative; they appeared to find the concept of a location based narrative fascinating. A variety of visual aids were used to explain how the story was distributed in space and time as shown in figure 4.

Very few audience members had problems with the technology. The interaction was simple enough that most users were able to interact with the system with no difficulties. The audience also responded well to the physical form of the sculptures, finding them appealing. The separation of story navigation and story viewing provoked mixed response among the users. While some had difficulty relating the collected fragments to the experience, others reported a relaxed experience. They pointed out that not having to stop and view the story at every node created a less disruptive experience that contributed to a more coherent plot.

Many visitors who kept the iButton with them collected story fragments in different ways, when they happened upon a cat sculpture. When these visitors came to the playback area to cash in on their story, we usually had to refresh their understanding of how the experience worked. Other visitors focused fully on the HopStory installation, actively searching for all the cats; these visitors collected story segments rapidly and then came to the playback area to review the story they had collected while navigating the floor. Few wanted to go back and experience more stories because they were aware the story was occurring in their time. Finally, the visitors passing by the playback area usually stopped and watched movies that others had collected and wanted to talk about the demo.

An advantage of using iButtons for interaction with HopStory was the non-intrusive quality of this technology. IButtons are portable and undemanding, leaving the user free to make choices about their level of engagement with the story at any given time. They could remain in a bag or pocket, easily accessed if a participant chose to engage with Hopstory. They stored story bits so that a conversation could be held during collection, and viewing could occur later when convenient.

The Hopstory experience has opened new research directions within the form of physically distributed interactive storytelling. The idea of linking a story to place can be taken further under the HopStory framework. The story content could be rigorously mapped to specific location- the scenes in the movie could depict the exact spots where the story fragments are available. The sculptural objects could also be enhanced to reflect story content, taking the physical form of objects or events in the narrative. We envisage our Hopstory installation as an exciting step forward in developing new forms of computational interactive narrative, which weds story content organically with enabling technology.

After testing the Hopstory, the evaluation pointed out the direction for future work. A seamless interaction between the story and the audience is being redesigned using Bluetooth technology instead of the iButtons. The content need to fit a broader space, the plot tightened and the characters personality deepened to foster engagement and curiosity about the story. From these findings a second iteration of the Hopstory sytem and installation is now under development.

Acknowledgments. We'd like to thank our actors, actresses, and voices: Giovanni Dini, Susi Harris, Steven Davy, Colin Harris, Mark Bent, Felix the cat, Eamonn Doyle, Ronan Swift, Jenny Langley, William Hederman. Also, for help with the audio production and postproduction: Eamon Doyle and Herve Gomez. For software counsel: Stefan Agamanolis, Cian Cullinan, Jamie Rasmussen, Matt Karau. For video advice and assistance: Michael Lew. Linda Doyle for being part of the initial brainstorming processes .

References

1. Kearney, R. On Stories. Routledge, London/NY, 2002, 156
2. Joyce, M. Afternoon. Electronic Hypertext. Riverrun, 1989.
3. Brondmo H.P. and Davenport G. Creating and Viewing the Elastic Charles – A Hypermedia Journal. Hypertext II Conference Proceedings (July 1989), 43-51.
4. Sparacino, F. Sto(ry)chastics: a Bayesian network architecture for combined user modeling, sensor fusion, and computational storytelling for interactive spaces. PhD Thesis, MIT 2002.
5. Pan, P. http://web.media.mit.edu/~ppk/Research.htm
6. Pan, P., Christina C., and Davenport, G. The Birth of "Another Alice." Computers and Fun 4, University of York, UK (November 2001).
7. Rokeby, D. Transforming Mirrors: Navigable Structures. http://www.interlog.com/~drokeby/mirrorsnavig.html
8. iButton Overview. http://www.ibutton.com/ibuttons/index.html
9. Byrne, A. Guinness Times: My days in the world's most famous brewery. Town House and Country House, Ranelagh, Dublin 6, 1999.
10. Johnston, M. Around the Banks of Pimlico. The Attic Press, Dublin, 1985.
11. Agamanolis, S. Isis, Cabbage, and Viper: New tools and strategies for designing responsive media. PhD dissertation, MIT 2001, 81-93.
12. Isis web site. http://web.media.mit.edu/~stefan/isis
13. O'Mahony, D. and Doyle, L. Architectural Imperatives for 4th Generation IP-based Mobile Networks. Proceedings, Forth International Symposium on Wireless Personal Multimedia Communications, Aalborg, Denmark (Sept 2001), 1319-1325.
14. Mazalek, A. Tangible Interfces for Interactive Point-of-View Narratives. MS Thesis, MIT 2001.
15. Nisi, V. and Briggs, J. "Weirdview", hypermedia interactive installation exibited at the Douglas Hide Gallery, Dublin, mscmm graduate show 2000.
16. Krizanc, J. Tamara. Stoddart Publishing Co. Limited, Toronto, Canada, 1989.
17. Strohecker, C., Brooks, K. and Friedlander, L. Tired of Giving In: An Experiment in Narrative Unfolding. http://www.merl.com/reports/docs/TR99-16.pdf
18. Mazalek, A., Wood, A,, and Ishii, H. GenieBottles: An Interactive Narrative in Bottles. Siggraph 2001.

Mobile Entertainment Computing

Christian Geiger[1], Volker Paelke[2], and Christian Reimann[3]

[1] University of Applied Science Harz
cgeiger@hs-harz.de

[2] University of Hannover, IKG, Appelstr. 9a, 30167 Hannover
Volker.Paelke@ikg.uni-hannover.de

[3] University of Paderborn, C-LAB, Fuerstenallee 11, 33102 Paderborn, Germany
Christian.Reimann@c-lab.de

Abstract. Constraints in hardware and context of use result in specific requirements for the design of successful mobile entertainment applications. To be successful, mobile games must differ in their gameplay to support intermittent use "on the move", the game presentation must be adapted to the limited output modalities of mobile devices and the interaction mechanisms should be suitable for the small and limited input modalities provided by a mobile device. In this paper we analyze the specific requirements of mobile game use and illustrate how they have been addressed in three mobile gaming projects.

1 Introduction

Advances in mobile computing and wireless communication technology [1] enable the creation of entertainment applications with appealing graphics and game-play on a variety of mobile devices ranging from smart phones over PDAs to wearable computing devices. As entertainment applications are targeted at a diverse user population that will employ them without previous training a highly usable interface design is as critical for their success as the narrative content itself [2]. The mobile context of use imposes additional requirements on entertainment applications: Typically, mobile applications are used for short episodes, possibly as one task among many. Game designers have to ensure that users can enjoy a pleasurable interaction experience under such circumstances. A common solution - seen in many current mobile games - is to create games that can be completed within a few minutes. It is, however, obvious that there is also interest in mobile games that enable deeper game-playing experiences over an extended period of time. The creation of such applications requires a platform that allows to make maximum use of the limited display and interaction capabilities provided by mobile devices. A suitable mechanism that supports intermittent use and appropriate means to support the creation of complex game content are other important requirements. In this paper we present exemplary solutions from three mobile gaming projects for: 1) High-quality 3D animations 2) Context refresh for intermittent use 3) Novel foot-based interaction techniques for mobile use based on computer vision.

S. Göbel et al. (Eds.): TIDSE 2004, LNCS 3105, pp. 142–147, 2004.

2   A High Visual Quality PDA Adventure: Squipped

An on-line study on requirements for mobile adventure games conducted by students of Hochschule Harz indicated that users prefer a high visual quality (compared to existing 3D games on PDAs like Quake), had problems with interaction on a PDA (compared to PCs) and are willing to spend about 10 minutes per game session. As a consequence, a prototype of a video-based adventure was developed (1 level, featuring about 15 min 3D animation), following game concepts from "Dragon's Lair" and "Rent a Hero". The use of pre-rendered 3D animations allows high quality images but requires a game engine that implements the game logic state transition graph, allows to render text, images and video on a PDA and handles user interaction. MediaPoint was developed to address these requirements. It integrates the PocketTV player SDK to play mpeg videos [6] and allows to render images and text as overlays. The logic of the state transition graph is captured in an XML format and executed by MediaPoint.

Analysis: The use of pre-rendered animation sequences enabled the intended high visual presentation quality but reduced interactivity to simple point and click. A key problem in the development was the monolithic story graph that resulted in a highly complex description (which prevented efficient execution on an Ipaq 200Mhz) and required a large number of try-and-error cycles. While a PC based emulation helped to decreased iteration cycle times a more efficient approach for content representation was developed for the following project.

Fig. 1. Data file and final game prototype (PC simulation)

3   Context Refresh with the Mobile Entertainment Engine

MobEE, the Mobile Entertainment Engine, addresses various requirements identified in the introduction: it supports structured creation of narrative application content, enables run-time presentation across a wide variety of mobile devices and supports context refresh for intermittend use.

To enable the use of an entertainment application across a variety of hardware platforms the story structure must be kept is a *device independent format*. Only the presentation format/media are adapted to the capabilities of the interaction device.

In MobEE the story structure is implemented by a set of finite automatons controlled by a central variable pool. Each hot-spot accessible by the user changes variables and thereby the states of the automatons. Each hot-spot and automaton-state-change can be linked to narrative information such as text, graphics, sound or animation which is displayed to the user upon activation. To avoid complex monolithic storystructures as in Squipped, a storyline in MobEE is segmented into an arbitrary number of small automatons, each representing a small segment of the story. Using this segmentation it is easy to debug game designs or to extend a story in later design phases. Activating a hot-spot can take effect on all other host-spots in terms of design, sound and information they provide. By carefully designing the automatons it is possible to represent almost any complex storyline in a format accessible to the MobEE game engine and change it easily afterwards.

To support the wide variety of mobile devices MobEE supports *exchangable representations* of the story content. MobEE can manage several textual, auditory or graphical representations of the same content and select the most appropriate presentation for the device in use. For 2D graphics scrolling images, sprites, 2D animations and video clips are suppored and 3D animation can be easily integrated into the architecture when mobile 3D accelerators become available.

As mentioned in the introduction, the use of mobile devices is often limited to short time intervals (e.g. waiting for a bus) and there may be longer periods between the uses of mobile entertainment applications. Therefore it may prove necessary to provide users with a *context refresh* of previous activities in the game.

Such a context refresh is realized in MobEE by keeping track of all user actions. By doing this it would be easy to show a user all his activities up to the point where he wants to continue the game. Since a complete history of all actions at every start of the program would be boring the context refresh has to be limited to significant actions. Unimportant detail and older actions that are no longer relevant can be left out of the context refresh. Since the application has no way of knowing which detail is important the developer has to provide this information when developing a game by applying values to key information that the application might show to the user. Based on this additional information the MobEE engine is able to sort out outdated information simply by looking at the number of facts provided to the user since certain information has been passed and using the importance of the information to calculate the necessity of showing this fact to the user in the context refresh.

If the application is using storytelling techniques to provide information for the user and the narration is using present time for its presentation it is necessary for the developer to provide the application with the same information placed in simple past for the re-narration. MobEE provides the user with a fast forward button to skip unwanted facts or even the whole refresh if he is still familiar with the content.

Example "Forgotten Valley", a PDA-Based Adventure with MobEE

The adventure "Forgotten Valley" demonstrates the capabilities of MobEE. Starting the adventure the user can start a new game or continue an old. When starting a new game he finds his Avatar in the middle of an unknown map, not knowing where he is or how he got here. Using the pointing device (which can vary between different mobile devices) the user can move around and explore in typical adventure fashion, solving little puzzles and talking to people populating the valley to find his way out.

Fig. 2. Starting Point and Riddles to solve

The behaviour of the non-player-characters as well as the overall logic of the game is realized by several automatons. Figure 4 shows the automaton, that controls the behaviour of the merchant's daughter. The daughter appears first when the player talks to the merchant, who asks him to rescue his daughter. The automaton then switches to an active state with an animation loop. The inactive state is reentered, when the daughter was successfully rescued.

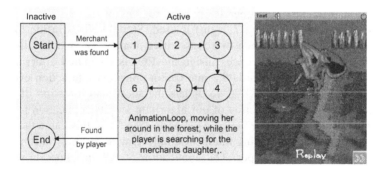

Fig. 3. Behaviour automaton for NPC and context refresh

Analysis: This project focused on gameplay features like context refresh, exchangeable representations and a suitable model for the story structure. Using MobiEE it is possible to create games that can be played in both text and graphics representations. The design of a story using a set of finite automata communicating via shared global variables proved to be much simpler than the Squipped approach and the context refresh was well accepted by users.

4 Vision-Based Interaction in AR-Soccer

Many games rely on a basic position input from the user as their central control paradigm. For example, in the classic game "Pong" two users try to position their paddles so that the ball is kept from leaving the playing area. Similar control paradigms are used in break-out games like the classic "Arkanoid".

In foot-based mobile interaction we propose to use the camera of video capable mobile devices to detect motion and position of the user's foot to effect the input required for such games. The camera facing towards the back of the mobile device (Fig. 5) is used to detect "kicking" movements of the user's feet. When a collision between the user's "kick" and an interaction object shown on the screen of the mobile device is detected, a corresponding interaction event for the application is generated. In games like "Pong" and "Arkanoid" the interaction object is the ball that is moving across the playing area. Depending on the specifics of the game under consideration either only the position of the foot is used (e.g. in "Pong") or the direction and speed of the detected motion can also be exploited.

The challenge is to analyze the video stream from the camera in real-time. Processing time and lag must be minimized for effective interaction with corresponding requirements on the processing power. We use the computer vision algorithm developed by Dirk Stichling [4,5] that calculates the motion of a "kicking object" (e.g. the user's foot) from the incoming video-stream and detects collisions between it and the interaction objects.

The results of the collision detection are used to calculate the new direction and speed of the interaction object, e.g. the ball. Since current mobile devices lack high-performance processors a simple and fast algorithm that combines 2D edge extraction and tracking and operates only in regions of interest (ROI) around the interaction objects (see figure 7, right) is used. Straight edges inside the ROI are vectorized and tracked between two consecutive images. The median direction and speed of the motions of all edges inside the ROI is computed afterwards. If the median direction points towards the interaction object an interaction event is generated and used in the game, e.g. to update the speed and direction of the virtual ball. To demonstrate the function of our algorithm and its application in games we have developed a small game called AR-Soccer (Fig.5). In this game the player has to kick a virtual ball (a moving interaction object) with his real foot into a virtual goal, bypassing the goalkeeper. The application of AR in games is well known since AR-Quake [3].

Analysis: The current prototype of our system was informally evaluated by more than 30 users. The overall feedback of the users was very positive. The users had no general problems with the CV based interaction and found it very intuitive. The main problem was the reliability of the computer vision, which was caused by the low frame rate. Current hardware limits our system (200 MHz ipaq) to processing 5-7 frames/second, suggesting its use as part of games where the interaction is part of the challenge. In the future we plan to use the wireless networking capabilities of mobile devices to extend the approach to two-player and multiplayer games, e.g. the classic two-player "Pong" and other mobile applications [7].

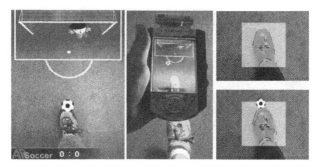

Fig. 4. AR-Soccer and the edge-tracking algorithm

5 Summary and Outlook

We addressed a number of requirements for mobile entertainment applications and described three projects that validate some of our concepts for games on PDAs. Current and future work is concerned how concepts for mobile games can be transferred to other mobile applications, e.g. edutainment applications.

References

1. Dunlop, M. D. and Brewster, S. A. (Eds.) (2001): Proceedings of Mobile HCI 2001: Third International Workshop on Human Computer Interaction with Mobile Devices, IHM-HCI 2001 Lille, France, September 2001
2. Johnson, C. (Ed.) (1998): Proceedings of the First Workshop on Human Computer Interaction with Mobile Devices, GIST Technical Report G98-1, University of Glasgow, Scotland
3. Piekarski, Wayne and Thomas, Bruce, ARQuake: The Outdoor Augmented Reality Gaming System, Communications of the ACM, 2002 Vol. 45. No 1, pp 36-38
4. Reimann, C., Paelke, V., Stichling, D.: "Computer Vision Based Interaction-Techniques for Mobile Games" in Proceedings of Game-On 2003, London, November 2003WMCSA (2002): Workshop on Mobile Computing Systems and Applications, IEEE, http://wmcsa2002.hpl.hp.com/
5. Stichling, D. and Kleinjohann, B. (2002): CV-SDF - A model for Real-Time Computer Vision Applications, in proceedings of WACV 2002: IEEE Workshop on Applications of Computer Vision, Orlando, FL, USA, December 2002
6. Pocket TV: www.pockettv.com
7. Paelke, V., Reimann, C., Stichling, D.: Kick-Up Menus. accepted as short paper, CHI 2004, Wien

StoryNet: An Educational Game for Social Skills

Leonie Schäfer[1], Agnes Stauber[2], and Bozana Bokan[3]

[1] Fraunhofer Institut FIT, Schloss Birlinghoven, D-53754 Sankt Augustin, Germany
leonie.schaefer@fit.fraunhofer.de
[2] Universität der Künste Berlin, Gesellschafts- und Wirtschaftskommunikation (GWK),
10595 Berlin, Germany
agnes.stauber@web.de
[3] Freie Universität Berlin, Center für Digitale Systeme (CEDIS), Ihnestraße 24,
14195 Berlin, Germany
bokan@cedis.fu-berlin.de

Abstract. This paper presents an approach combining concepts of digital storytelling and games with experiences in the field of social competence. This type of system has potential use for training seminars on soft skills and interpersonal communication. We introduce StoryNet, which combines a game-like experience with dynamic story generation. In this paper we outline a concept based on emotional intelligence, to navigate through stories.

1 Introduction

Digital storytelling presents a fascinating area with interfaces to several different research disciplines. Especially Games and Storytelling form closely related disciplines which combined offer a promising approach for a new type of edutainment applications. Games have always been used not only for pleasure but also for education. Digital games serve as a medium to teach natural sciences[1], to foster collaboration between and storytelling by children[2], or to train skilfulness in motion. However, most games focus on children, or train motion abilities or strategic thinking. Teaching soft skills, such as communication and interaction between colleagues at the workplace, still remains a challenge. People tell stories to entertain, this is the most popular notion of storytelling. Not so obvious but of the same importance is the preservation of memories[3] or transmission of tacit social knowledge[4]. Up to now, storytelling applications usually focused on the entertainment aspect rather than on memory or social knowledge. There is a place, then, for a new type of storytelling application that offers a game-like experience combined with training in social competence. StoryNet is an edutainment application which meets these criteria.

2 The StoryNet Idea

The idea of StoryNet is to combine a dynamically generated story for edutainment with coaching on social competence. The StoryNet narrative places the user in the

S. Göbel et al. (Eds.): TIDSE 2004, LNCS 3105, pp. 148–157, 2004.

Fig. 1. Scenes from StoryNet

context of an employee in a company. As an employee, s/he is in a tension triangle between colleagues, employer and goals to be reached. The achievement of personal aims which might run contrary to the interest of colleagues requires social competence, i.e. soft skills such as communication capabilities. The user can choose between different goals and define a strategy to reach his/her personal goal. The game story is presented to the user in a combination of images and text. The images show a scene from the workplace with different protagonists. The text explains the current context and asks the user a question.

Figure 1 shows two scenes from StoryNet. Both scenes show a conflict situation with two story characters. The user regards the scene in first-person view. The question related to the scene requires a user reaction to the conflict. The question posed does not require the user to solve a task or perform an action, but to use soft skills in communication and interaction. The game does not result in a definitive winning or loosing scenario. The user has to decide if s/he has achieved her/his personal goal. The idea of this game approach is to confront the user with typical scenarios which s/he will encounter in professional life. The user will meet typical types of personalities and has to find her/his own approach on how to deal with them. In contrast to real life or training seminars on social skills, the situation is repeatable and can therefore be better analysed and trained.

3 Related Work

StoryNet is inspired by Games, Storytelling and Education. Related work also can be found in the research areas of Virtual Humans, Artifical Intelligence[5] and developments in cinema and the Arts[6].

Klesen et. al.[7] present with CrossTalk a virtual character exhibition for public spaces. The characters interact using scripted dialogues, adapt to user feedback and react to the user in an emotional way.

Façade by Mateas and Stern[8] involves the user in an interactive drama by integrating believable agents in an interactive plot. In Façade the user can influence the story by means of text input, but remains a spectator while the drama evolves between the story's main protagonists. StoryNet takes a related approach in creating an interactive plot, but tries to adapt the course of the story by taking the user's profile into account. The virtual storyteller, developed by Silva et. al.[9], creates an interactive story in response to user input. While the scenarios differ between StoryNet and the Virtual Storyteller, the architecture shows a related approach: a range of values deciding on the sequence of the story scenes.

Justine Cassell and her group at MIT Media Lab are at present conducting research on Storytelling environments for learning purposes[10]. The storytelling environments are partly real, partly virtual and allow children to interact with their virtual counterparts. Storytelling and story listening is employed as a means to improve literacy in children.

The game 'The SIMS'[11] provides several features on social interaction. The player can create and control the life of virtual families which are represented by semi-autonomous avatars. The player remains in a god-like position. StoryNet also takes a game-like approach, but aims at confronting the user from a first-person view with scenarios which s/he might encounter in everyday working life.

4 Approach

StoryNet has an entertaining storyline, set in an exciting and fictional workplace. The game starts off with a tense situation; the choices made by the players during the game define how it will end. Plot development in StoryNet focuses on interaction with its characters, rather than on the definition of a sequence of events. As Berman[12] describes: "Your character´s need will create action as well as conflict, the basis of drama." In the centre there are the needs of the characters. Their conflicting interests are the basis of action, as there is no game without conflict. The reference to everyday work-life is represented in special tasks given by other game characters to the user, conflict situations between two or more characters and the user, and hidden goals or interests with which other game characters want to influence the user. When

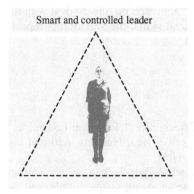

Smart and controlled leader

Feels under-
appreciated for
her work

Revenge
and unfair
pressure

Fig. 2. Character definition of a StoryNet protagonist

interacting with this game, the user has to decide on how to react to arising conflict situations; the user selects options of behaviour and emotions. These interaction options are based on knowledge about decision-making processes from psychological studies of conflict behaviour[13]. StoryNet contains a set of game characters, each standing for a special human stereotype based on socio-psychological theories about human interaction[14].

The ongoing action by the user influences the social relations between the user and the individual characters and the user and the group. After a StoryNet session, which takes about 20 minutes, the user is confronted with a relocation of social relationships. In an optimal instructional situation, the results of the game could be discussed by a group of learners and their trainer. Then the learner could be encouraged to repeat the game acting in a different way to realize and analyse different results of the story.

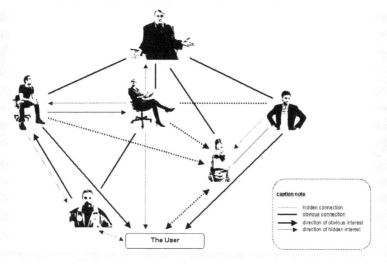

Fig. 3. Characters and their relations

In this game the user is confronted with different characters, who have certain roles in a fictional company, and who are predefined in their behaviour and in their relationship to each other. Figure 2 shows as an example the predefined characteristics of Ms. Smith. The character is represented as a triangle. A triangle is frequently used in scriptwriting to define the characteristics of a person in a story. Each point of the triangle refers to an attribute. Ms. Smith is the assistant of the managing director of the company. She is a controlled and smart woman, who is actually running the company. By being "only" the assistant, she permanently feels unappreciated and therefore often reacts unfairly in order to demonstrate her power.

In the first part of the game the user learns about the game story setting and certain events which occurred in the past, but not about the hidden goals of the game characters or conflicts in the company. The user has to find out about the real constellation and consider the effects of his/her reaction as in real life when the user has to act spontaneously and with social competence.

Figure 3 gives an overview of the constellation between the StoryNet characters and their relationships towards the user. The user's decision on how to interact with the characters decides on the next situation in the narrative and influences the relation of the characters to the user. The modelling of the interaction sequences and the inherent conflict situations, i.e. the encounters with the story's characters, follows the nine-step-model of Glasl[15], which contains the following phases: (1) effort for cooperation from both conflict parties, (2) polarization, (3) provocation, (4) doubt about agreement, (5) fight, (6) loss of objective problem in discussion, (7) systematic destruction, (8) "war of nerves", (9) destruction of the adversary even with the possibility of self-destruction.

5 Realisation

In the StoryNet architecture, as shown in Figure 4, a simple authoring tool enables the story writer to define scenes, story elements (images, text, sound) and a set of variables, which specify the position of the scenes in the plot and their relation to each other. The story-engine controls the flow of the story. It presents the story to the user, manages the user profile and decides which scene, i.e. process, to show next.

The story structure relates to the story model described by Bremond [16]. The story elements are described in XML. According to Bremond a story consists of a succession of processes, which subdivide into three functional parts and their combinations: possibility, acting and completion. Figure 5 shows an example of such a process in StoryNet. The first step called possibility describes the situation and allows the user to define her/his relation to two StoryNet characters, Ms. Smith and Ms. Mondano. The user has the choice between two different ways of acting, which leads to the completion of this process. For example the user can decide to become an ally of Ms.Mondano, and acts accordingly. Unfortunately, as a result he finds himself in conflict with the other character, Ms.Smith.

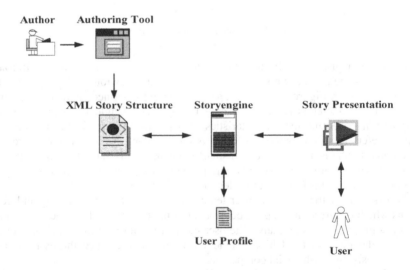

Fig. 4. StoryNet Architecture

POSSIBILITY:

Ms. Smith tries to create a good relationship with the user and solicits the user's support. Ms. Mondano, the daughter of the managing director, who also works in this company, brings coffee for the meeting. She happens to spill the coffee on the handbag of Ms. Smith.

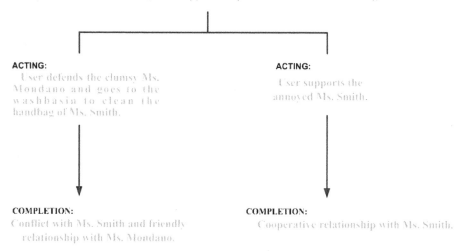

ACTING:

User defends the clumsy Ms. Mondano and goes to the washbasin to clean the handbag of Ms. Smith.

ACTING:

User supports the annoyed Ms. Smith.

COMPLETION:

Conflict with Ms. Smith and friendly relationship with Ms. Mondano.

COMPLETION:

Cooperative relationship with Ms. Smith.

Fig. 5. StoryNet Process

StoryNet is divided into two structurally different parts. The first sequence introduces the user to the story and during the course of events defines the profile of the user's story character. In the first sequence the user encounters the story's protagonists and, based on her/his decisions, sets the course for the development of the story. This part of the story uses a branching structure with a combination of interactive and non-interactive scenes. The story line starts with a scene as introduction, provides several choices on how to continue, and converges again in certain intermediate nodes and in the final scene. The design of the first part of StoryNet follows the approach on narrative guidance of interactivity proposed by Galyean[17]. Figure 6 shows an example section of the first phase of StoryNet. On the way through the story the user collects points on conflict and harmony and thus defines the user profile. The number of points is based on the user's decision in that particular scenario. The sequence of scenes depends on the user's reaction to the presented scenario and varies accordingly.

For example, in a scene the user encounters the secretary of his employer. The secretary is a moody type of person and obviously has a bad day. The user now can choose the option to interact with her in a friendly but neutral way, to pull her on his side in order to get an ally, or to ignore her mood and thus possibly provoke her to become an enemy. The last choice results in a high score on conflict and low number of harmony points. The first choice in the opposite. Neutral behaviour will result in an equal balance on points in conflict and harmony.

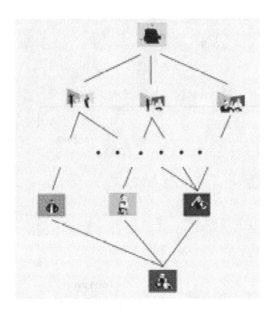

Fig. 6. StoryNet – Part of Phase I

The second part of StoryNet presents the results of the user's decisions as a dynamically generated story, which is played out without user interaction. The user profile, which has been defined during the first part, is evaluated and results in bonus points for conflict and harmony. The user profile defines the scenes which become part of the second phase of the story. The scenes of the second phase are organized in different slots. Each slot represents a sequence of the story. One sequence from each scene is selected for presentation. Figure 7 shows the structure of the second phase of StoryNet. The circles labelled with a 'P' represent the scenes, i.e. the processes, which are available for selection for this story sequence. The document icons represent the user profile, i.e. the score of points on conflict and harmony. The story for phase two is dynamically generated based on the relation of bonus points between the scenes and the user profile.

For example, in the second part of StoryNet the user will re-encounter all the characters of the story. A high score on conflict points will result in a selection of scenes which show the user in conflict with the characters of the story. An encounter with a character which resulted in conflict in the first part of StoryNet (see Fig.5), will result in the selection of a scene in the second part showing this character turning away from the user.

A balanced score of points on conflict and harmony, resulting from a more diplomatic and socially smart behaviour in the first part of StoryNet, might lead to a mixture of reactions. The user will have possibly gained some enemies but also have become an ally of other characters, and now might be able to reach his self-defined goal.

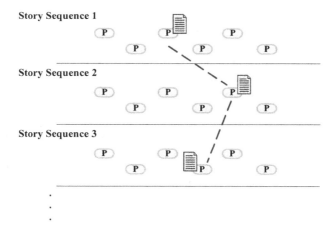

Fig. 7. StoryNet – Part of Phase II

StoryNet still is in the process of development. A first StoryNet prototype was real-ised in Flash. The story-engine is now being developed in ActionScript and Java. The StoryNet pictures were taken of participants at a StoryNet content workshop.

6 Scenario

The following scenario describes the initial scene of StoryNet and gives an impres-sion of the type of decisions the user has to make in course of the story. The StoryNet interface shows an image, a text describing the situation displayed in the image, and buttons marked with a decision. In the first scene the user is introduced to the story.

The user as a player takes the role of a male employee in a company. In the first scene the user finds himself in a meeting with the head of the company. The director tells the user some internals about the company and asks for his cooperation. In order to draw the user on his side, the director invites him to dinner. But the user as protago-nist in StoryNet also has a set of goals, which are assigned to him in the role of an employee. The user as an employee might aim at being supportive and so possibly acquire a higher status in the company. But the task he is asked to perform might contradict his moral attitude as well as his goal to marry his employer's daughter. The options for decision in this first scene, which are marked on the decision buttons, are: to accept the invitation to dinner, to decline, or to behave indecisively and postpone the decision to a later point in time. This is the initial scene in which the user has to decide on the personal goal of the employee. If the user as an employee decides on a career, he had better accept the dinner invitation and offer support to his superior's plans. If he is not career-minded, the user had better choose to decline the invitation.

In the course of the story the user will encounter other employees of the company. At each encounter the player will have to decide on the employee's reaction towards that character. For example, the secretary might be an useful ally even though she behaves like a dragon. It is up to the player to decide whether the employee should fight her, ignore her or to behave supportively towards her.

7 Results and Future Work

Interviews with seminar managers showed a high potential use of the game as an add-on to seminar programs on social competence. They especially valued the option to repeat situations and thus create a learning effect. StoryNet is still in a very early stage of its development. Therefore no user studies have been conducted so far. First user tests and system evaluation are planned for April and May '04 at open house events at Fraunhofer FIT. For future versions of StoryNet we are planning to enhance the set of characters in the story and the range of options for the user, thus allowing for different perspectives on the story. We intend to include other social factors as well as emotions for the generation of user profiles and story navigation. Furthermore we will extend our research on dynamic story generation based on indirect user interaction.

8 Conclusion

This paper presents a concept and first prototype for an edutainment application on social competence. We describe the psychological concept and illustrate the challenges with which the game confronts the user. We present our approach on realisation which relates to concepts of digital storytelling and employs story navigation by social factors. This type of edutainment application will be an important additional feature for training seminars on social competence and related topics.

Acknowledgements. We thank everybody who contributed to the development of StoryNet as well as friends and colleagues which provided helpful comments in preparation of this document.

References

1. Squire, K.: Video Games in Education, International Journal of Simulations and Gaming
2. Bayon, V., Wilson, J.R., Stanton, D.: Mixed Reality Storytelling Environments, Virtual Reality, 7(1). Springer Verlag Ltd., London (2003)
3. Schank, R.C., Abelson, R.P.: Knowledge and Memory: The Real Story, In: Knowledge and Memory: The Real Story, Robert S., Wyer, J., (ed.). Lawrence Erlbaum Associates, Hillsdale, NJ. (1995) 1-85
4. Linde, C.: Narrative and social tacit knowledge. Journal of Knowledge Management Vol.5(2) (2001) 160-170
5. Mateas, M., Sengers, P.: Narrative Intelligence, In: Narrative Intelligence, Mateas, M., Sengers, P., Editors. John Benjamins B.V., Amsterdam / Philadelphia (2003) 1-25
6. Rieser, M., Zapp, A., (eds.) The New Screen Media: Cinema/Art/Narrative. British Film Institute, London (2002)
7. Klesen, M., Kipp, M., Gebhard, P., Rist, T.: Staging exhibitions: methods and tools for modelling narrative structure to produce interactive performances with virtual actors. Virtual Reality Vol.7(1) (2003) 17-29
8. Mateas, M., Stern, A.: Integrating Plot, Character and Natural Language Processing in the Interactive Drama Facade. In Proceedings of: 1st International Conference on Technologies for Interactive Digital Storytelling and Entertainment (TIDSE) 2003. Darmstadt, Germany. Fraunhofer IRB Verlag (2003)

9. Silva, A., Raimundo, G., Paiva, A.: Tell Me That Bit Again ... Bringing Interactivity to a Storyteller. In Proceedings of: ICVS 2003. Toulouse, France. Springer Verlag Berlin Heidelberg (2003)
10. Cassell, J.: Towards a model of technology and literacy development: Story listening systems. Journal of Applied Developmental Psychology Vol.25(1) (2003) 75-105
11. Wright, W.: The Sims. Maxis/Electronic Arts (2000)
12. Berman, R.: Fade In: The Screenwriting Process, Michael Wiese Production (1997)
13. Schwarz, G.: Konflikt Management. Sechs Grundmodelle der Konfliktlösung. Wiesbaden Gabler (1990)
14. Hugo-Becker, A., Becker, H.: Psychologisches Konfliktmanagement. 3 ed. München Deutscher Taschenbuch Verlag (2000)
15. Glasl, F.: Konfliktmanagement, Diagnose und Behandlung von Konflikten. Bern Verlag P. Haupt (1980)
16. Bremont, C.: Logique du récit Seuil (1973)
17. Galyean, T.A.: Narrative Guidance of Interactivity. Massachusetts Institute of Technology (1995)

Inner Earth: Towards Interaction Patterns

Peter Stephenson[1], Keiko Satoh[1], Audrey Klos[1],
Diane Kinloch[2], Emily Taylor[2], and Cindy Chambers[2]

[1] imedia, 400 Westminster St, Providence RI, USA.
[2] Questacon: The National Science and Technology Center, Canberra, Australia.

Abstract. Inner Earth is a project to develop an online activity set to help children learn and think about what is inside the Earth. The child is taken on a ride in an elevator to the core of the Earth and they stop along the way to undertake certain activities involving plants, sewers, mines, fossils, convection and magma. The system was developed between imedia in Providence, Rhode Island, USA, and Questacon: The National Science and Technology Centre in Canberra, Australia. Communicating and implementing the project over such a distance was not problematic given the clearly defined roles of each team. The part of the project that required extensive negotiation and redesign was how the user interacts with each activity. Having a common systemic approach to design the interaction tasks, with established guidelines of what works in different situations, would have benefited the design teams. It is for that reason that we propose defining Interaction Patterns based on the design patterns that have been applied to software engineering, web applications, hypermedia and computer games.

1   Introduction

In schools, museums and online presentations, the ability to engage a person in an interesting and appealing activity improves information retention rates in students, visitors and the general public, well above that possible from static and oral presentations [9]. This fact is used by interactive science and children's museums to encourage, to entertain, and to educate their audiences. However, little attention has been given to develop tools for analyzing interaction styles and promoting what works best in different situations, for different students and ages especially within the context of on-line instructional design.

Formalising the interaction design process is a particularly difficult task that relies on personal experience and expertise in the context of the interaction. One evolving approach is the idea of applying design patterns [3] and anti-patterns [2], which are semi-structured formalisms that collect concepts that other designers have found useful (and useless). Design patterns have been applied primarily to software engineering. Other applications include designing web applications [8, 4], hypermedia [7] and computer games [6,1].

The focus of the Interaction Patterns project is on studying interactive instructional diagrams and activity sets in terms of interaction, components and

S. Göbel et al. (Eds.): TIDSE 2004, LNCS 3105, pp. 158–163, 2004.

design goals. The intention is to develop a process based on expert knowledge of best-practice that can guide the design process. Interaction patterns are intended to be a tool–set that structures the approach of a designer through levels of the design of an activity. When a specific interaction design problem exists, the pattern(s) dealing with this kind of interaction should offer solutions and approaches to the problem. Therefore, a designer can more efficiently develop a system by avoiding known pitfalls and using what has been identified to work well. This type of formalism is particularly important for interaction designers with minimal experience or expertise in the context of the interaction. We are therefore also interested in the use of interaction patterns to support education of the instructional design process.

2   Inner Earth

In a project with Questacon, The National Science and Technology Centre in Canberra, Australia, imedia, a school for interactive digital media in Providence, Rhode Island, USA, has been investigating the use of various interaction designs for online activities. The background of the work is an online activity set called *Inner Earth* designed for children of ages 7 to 12 and their parents. It is designed to take the visitor on a journey from the surface of the Earth to its core.

The surrounding story is that a child is digging in the back yard, when they are approached by their dog. The dog suggests they enter the kennel, which has been transformed into an elevator that can take the child to the center of the Earth. Along the way the child can stop at certain levels and explore what is found there.

The interface for the elevator is shown to the right in Fig. 1. Each elevator button takes the child to a different depth of the Earth, given by the depth meter, and a different activity. The current activity involves excavating dinosaur skeletons. To assist the child on their journey the dog becomes an avatar, who communicates remotely via the panel on top of the controls.

The dinosaurs activity is built on a hide–and–seek and a jigsaw interaction pattern. The child moves the brush over the screen and pushes the button to brush away dirt uncovering dinosaur bones. Once a set of bones is uncovered, the child moves each bone down to the model in the lower left of the screen to finish the activity.

Figure 2 describes the sewers activity. At this level, visitors connect the pipes from their house to drains that lead to the local river and the water treatment plant. By connecting the wrong pipe to the wrong drain, they either pollute the local waterways or they overload the water treatment plant. Figure 2(left) shows how connecting the shower to the storm drain results in contamination of the local waterways as shown in Fig 2(right). The activity therefore combines a process–chain and a cause–and–effect interaction pattern.

Figure 3 demonstrates two tamagotchi interaction patterns. Figure 3(left) involves a classic tamagotchi pattern in which the user keeps a daffodil in flower based on clicking buttons. By watering and feeding the daffodil and removing

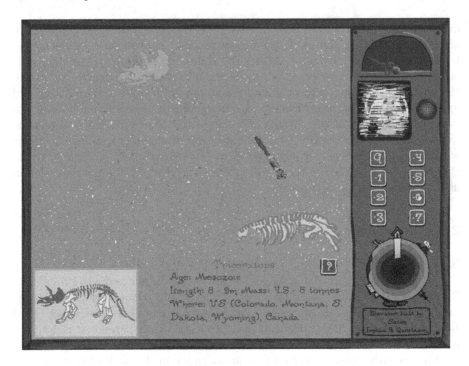

Fig. 1. The elevator interface and dinosaur activity.

weeds and harmful insects the daffodil signals its health by the height of its flower and the strength of its bulb. The volcano activity shown in Fig. 3(right) also involves a feeding interaction pattern. Students drag the rocks into the magma chamber to increase the pressure under the volcano. If enough rocks are placed quickly into the chamber the volcano will explode.

Figure 4(left) shows a mining activity built around a hunting interaction. In this activity, the visitor will guide the miner to collect the correct mix of minerals to make certain alloys. They will be timed and will have to avoid setting off the TNT and causing a mine disaster.

Figure 4(right) shows activity that had the longest design process. It was important for the Questacon team to include an activity on convection in the system. A considerable amount of time was spent on trying to identify how a visitor could play or interact with a convection field. Finally to help explain the idea of convection, we used an idea used to visualize flows. The visitor is given a blank screen onto which they place coloured dots. The dots move around the convection field tracing their path and developing a colorful design. While explaining convection to children is a difficult task, it is hoped that having visitors explore the shapes involved will enable them to identify convection in other real world scenarios.

The architecture for the Inner Earth activity set is straightforward and extensible. It was implemented using Macromedia's Flash software and therefore

Fig. 2. Investigating the sewers underneath your house.

Fig. 3. Tamagotchi style activities.

can be used as a stand–alone system or served over the Internet as a Shockwave file. The elevator serves as a container for each activity, which is completly self contained. When the visitor clicks on a elevator floor button, the activity attributed to that floor is loaded. The only communication between the container and the activity occurs when the activity informs the container to play the avatar animation or that the activity has been successfully completed. To add new levels to the activity set, only minor changes to the elevator container are required.

3   Conclusions

The development of online instructional material, such as *Inner Earth* involves a multi-disciplined team comprising educators and media developers. At first

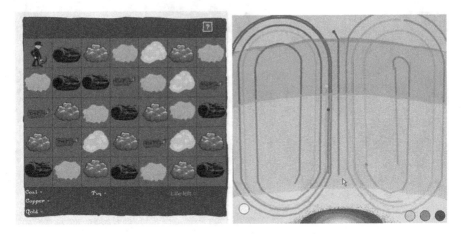

Fig. 4. Mining and convection activities.

glance, communication or disparate goals between these groups could be a problem, however this was not our experience. Even the global distribution of the teams did not lead to extensive problems with communication. The main aspect of the project that evolved considerably were the activities themselves and specifically how the visitors to the online exhibition interact with the activities. The interface to the system and background story were refined but did not change considerably after our initial discussions.

The initial design of the activities was based heavily on button–pushing and quiz-based interaction. Both of which we would now define as anti–patterns. Considerable effort was required to define interaction tasks and styles that could be understood by and were acceptable to everyone involved. Being able to base our initial designs and discussions on a template set of Interaction Patterns would have helped to structure and focus the initial development of ideas and reduce the effort required.

Often our aim was not to use solely goal-driven learning models but to also allow the visitor to experiment and explore different combinations and system states. A question that we now wish to answer is how successful were we in designing interaction tasks that engage different ages. While this paper is nearing publication so is the Inner Earth activity set. We soon hope to answer this question and to have more experience in which activities constitute Interaction Patterns and which Anti-Patterns.

As well as activity sets, we are currently developing and evaluating the use of Interaction Patterns to the development of interactive diagrams for in–class [10] and on–line [5] learning systems. Development of these systems is based heavily on practicum students from imedia's International Certificate Program of New Media (www.icpnm.org), such as Keiko Satoh. Therefore we are interested in developing Interaction Patterns as a teaching tool. Another possible direction includes using Interaction Pattern to assist designing game–based interfaces.

References

1. S. Björk, J. Holopainen, P. Ljungstrand, and K-P. Åkesson. Designing ubiquitous computing games: A report from a workshop exploring ubiquitous computing entertainment. *Personal and Ubiquitous Computing*, 6(5-6):443–458, January 2002.

2. W. Brown, H. McCormick, and S. Thomas. *Anti-Patterns and Patterns in Software Configuration Management*. John Wiley & Sons, April 13 1999.

3. E. Gamma, R. Helm, R. Johnson, and J. Vlissides. *Design Patterns: Elements of Reusable Object-Oriented Software*. Addison-Wesley, January 15 1995.

4. F. Garzotto, P. Paolini, D. Bolchini, and S. Valenti. Modeling–by–patterns of web applications. In P. Chen, D. Embley, J. Kouloumdjian, S. Liddle, and J. Roddick, editors, *Advances in Conceptual Modeling: ER '99 Workshops on Evolution and Change in Data Management, Reverse Engineering in Information Systems, and the World Wide Web and Conceptual Modeling, Paris, France, November 15-18, 1999, Proceedings*, volume 1727 of *Lecture Notes in Computer Science*, pages 293–306. Springer, 1999.

5. J. Jungclaus, P. Stephenson, D. Schmitz, , and L.M. Encarnação. The virtual study desk: Towards learning-styles based user modeling for content adaptation in online learning environments. In *E-Learn 2003*, November 7-11 2003.

6. S. Lundgren and S. Björk. Game mechanics: Describing computer-augmented games in terms of interaction. In *TIDSE 2003(1st International Conference on Technologies for Interactive Storytelling and Digital Entertainment)*. Comenius University, Bratislava, Slovakia, March 24–26 2003.

7. S. Montero, P. Dìaz, and I. Aedo. Formalization of web design patterns using ontologies. In *Advances in Web Intelligence: First International AtlanticWeb Intelligence Conference AWIC 2003 (Madrid, Spain, May 5-6)*, volume 2663 of *Lecture Notes in Computer Science*, pages 179–188. Springer-Verlag, Heidelberg, August 2003.

8. M. Nanard, J. Nanard, and P. Kahn. Pushing reuse in hypermedia design: Golden rules, design patterns and constructive templates. In *HYPERTEXT '98. Proceedings of the Ninth ACM Conference on Hypertext and Hypermedia: Links, Objects, Time and Space - Structure in Hypermedia Systems*, pages 11–20. ACM, June 20-24 1998.

9. J. Schenck. *Learning, Teaching, and the Brain*. Knowa Publishing, Thermopolis, WY, USA, April 2003.

10. P. Stephenson. Staying on the straight and narrow: The ideas behind iterative line digitization algorithms. *IEEE Computer Graphics and Applications*, 22(4):CDROM Project, July/August 2002.

Media Art Environment Geist: Integrating Traditional Painting into 3D AR Storytelling Scenario

Oliver Schneider[1], Stefan Göbel[1], and Christian Meyer zu Ermgassen[2]

[1] Zentrum für Graphische Datenverarbeitung e.V.,
64283 Darmstadt, Germany
{Oliver.Schneider, Stefan.Goebel}@zgdv.de
[2] 35041 Marburg an der Lahn, Germany
abc@strich-und-farben.de

Abstract. This paper describes an approach at ZGDV Darmstadt to combine experimental use of traditional means (paintings) and VR/AR technology for Storytelling based edutainment applications. The illusion of light and depth banned to paper or canvas was the mission of generations during history of art, when paintings and drawings were the only media to transfer the imagination of space and atmosphere to the beholder.

In the context of the edutainment application *Geist* providing a Storytelling based learning and gaming environment enabling users to become part of a story and interactively explore history of Heidelberg, our goal was to elaborate how painted images could serve as an effective surrogate of reality within a computer-generated 3D-world: Within the *Geist* demonstrator there are three locations where 3D-objects and virtual characters are surrounded by a texture that simulates a natural environment. It contains men, buildings, vegetation but also important phenomenons based on light, perspective and colour. So the virtual reality is enlarged by a second level of visual reality based on paintings. In order to embrace this sort of approach, it is necessary both to reflect reality and represent it in an artificial way. Because atmosphere in this case involves not only the reproduction and transforming of perception our eyes are used to but to create an adequate expression and prevailing mood: On the three locations the user is lead into the expectation of imminent occurrences that struck the town of Heidelberg during the 30 years war. The preliminary results allow to analyze the functional, cognitive and aesthetic nature of this crossbreed and to draw further conclusions concerning further developments. The first part of the paper provides an overview of the *Geist* project and the resulting demonstrator as reference example for an edutainment application. Afterwords the two major technologies Storytelling enhanced by VR/AR technology and traditional painting are introduced before the integration process of these two antithetic approaches is describes. Finally a short summary points out first results of this integrated approach and discusses further development directions.

S. Göbel et al. (Eds.): TIDSE 2004, LNCS 3105, pp. 164–170, 2004.

1   Introduction

By telling a story, *Geist* motivates you to go sightseeing in Heidelberg and learn about the Thirty Years War as significant time of the history of Heidelberg [6]. Users are supported to learn playfully, which awakens their natural drive to learn. Hence, this represents a typical environment for edutainment applications. To let users immerse themselves into the story (immersion), the ghosts (Geist) appears at several locations: The story presented with the help of *Magic Equipment*, which is based on augmented reality technology (see figure 1). Users are enabled to experience the story with all of their senses, without having to shut themselves off from reality. Interactive components encourage users to influence the course of events – the story – themselves. Because of the non-linear narration, the Geist system can always adjust to the user's needs and keep the story interesting. A *magic book* offers further historical information about the location and the circumstances of peoples life during the Thirty Years War. Hereby users such as common visitors or pupils and school classes are triggered by questions to start a dialogue with the avatars (chat) for interactive learning and satisfying their upcoming thirst for knowledge right away.

Fig. 1. Typical *Geist* scenario.

2   Approaches

From earliest civilisation mankind has used arches to place images. This has been left as archaeological evidence till today- may it be a cave deep under the earth or a cathedral towering in the sky. The beholder has been surrounded by the room and faced with images that are both the rooms limits and it's extensions into infinity. The stories depicted by such images are derived from hunting scenes (in the caves) to the Last Judgement (in the Sistine Chapel).

Today we have new kinds of rooms that have to be lined. They are merely screens and other surfaces, but the conditions to bring form and figure to virtual reality are related to those of the cave and the church. One can explore this space without dictation, without being confronted by a certain sequence of pictures as in the film and the visual angle likewise could be enlarged by painted images simulating a second level of extent [5].

The department for Digital Storytelling at the Computer Graphics Centre has conceptualized components for the story's content and its narrative form of representation. This includes components for various levels:

A *storytelling-environment* [2] is being developed for the portrayal of the story's runtime. It controls the story's cycle while considering the existing user-actions, keeps the line of suspense, builds up scenes, controls the characters, and sets the possibilities to interact.

Several authors have been working on creating the story's content based on historical data and a lot of discussions with historians, urban planner, tourist guides or pedagogues. They have written the story, specifying the order of events, and have designed the characters' looks and behaviour. Furthermore interactions have been created and the *magic equipment* has been designed and implemented with the help of mechanics.

Therefore Authoring Components are are used adjusting to the users' needs enabling users (authors) to write the story without an oversized tool in the technical manner [7,9].

The *storytelling-environment* presents the actual story by using several databases, which include both historical facts and fictitious content. A combination of GPS- and video tracking-procedures is used to determine the location of a user. The *magic equipment* enables both user input and output. It consists of AR-binoculars, audioplayback-units, and several props.

Additionally the *magic book* allows the possibility to directly use all connected databases.

Semi-autonomic virtual characters and a *scene-engine* [8], which is scriptable by the author allow and motivate interactions in the non-linear progression of the story. Explicit (ex. input) as well as implicit (ex. change of location) useractions and traits of the user himself (ex. age, sex) influence the course of the story.

2.1   Painting Texture

According to the saying "The proof of the pudding is in the eating" we decided to use textures evoking real settings to wallpaper the Geist-system (see figure 2).

Experience in designing and achieving large-size illustrations for museums and images for scientific use are the basic components for this task. The use of traditional or digital methods of figuration is worth considering. We came to appreciate the former for different reasons: it provides insight and access to the inspiring heritage of art history and we prefer the handling with tactile material and feel affirmed by the fact that the use of traditional means has become a rare but increasingly respected ability.

Apart from this, the realisation always requires an instinct in choice and moderate use of the suitable means. Skill is needed to deal with arrangement, composition, perspective, illumination, colouring, guidance of the beholders attention

Fig. 2. Matte for *Geist*.

as well as dramaturgy aiming to achieve the intended effect and to manage the numerous details.

The texture both presents several objects of natural environment and also important phenomena such as the effects of light causes on texture which determines our sense of reality. In order to embrace this approach, it is necessary both to reflect reality and represent it in a transcribed manner. This is because atmosphere in this case involves not only the reproduction and transformation of the perception that our eyes are used to but also the effort to create an adequate ambience, prevailing mood and attractive appearance [4].

2.2   Related Methods

The intention to surround the spectators with 3D-figures and -elements, pieces of scenery and painted backgrounds is applied by similar methods and it may be worth while to name a few:

Matte-effects are manipulations in film, in which parts of the range are complemented or replaced by painted images. From the very beginnings of film history to "Lord of the Rings" an advancing evolution of fancy technologies has been reached.

Remarkable in our context are at least Robert Wienes "Das Cabinet des Dr. Caligari" (1920) and Fritz Langs futuristic "Metropolis" (1927), that are based on the excessive use of 3D-models, artificial backgrounds and scenery. In order to enhance the expression of the story, the environment in "Dr. Caligari" is a dizzying empire of surrealism, like a cubistic painting that has come to life.

Panorama paintings were crowd pullers of 19th Century. The Bourbaki-Panorama (1881) in Luzern (Switzerland) remained until today. It depicts a memorable event of the Franco-Prussian War (1870/71): France's Eastern Army, under the command of General Bourbaki, crosses the Swiss border and gives up it arms.

The original dimensions of the painting corresponds to the panorama standard of the time: 14 to 15 metres in height, with a circumference of 114 metres! Circular paintings were often extended by means of a so-called faux-terrain, a 3D-foreground serving to create the illusionistic effect [3].

An emphatic example for a room where reality and illusion are interwoven is given by the baroque church. Besides illusionistic paintings on walls and on the ceiling, the visitor is unsettled by shiny gold platings and even 3D-figures [1].

2.3   Management of Narration

Important criteria for distinction of media is the quality in the management of narration. On the one hand, linear narration in film and literature and on the other hand media which does not fix the duration or direction of someones attention. Some paintings tend towards the latter.

Several Renaissance pictures of the Nativity indicate the adoration of the Christ child by the three kings of the Orient while simultaneously, behind the stable, the murder of the children in Bethlehem takes place and the angel appears to the shepherds nearby. Such interlaced narration managed within the pictures room provide a wide range of interpretations. While the action in a movie unfolds by numerous frames, it is managed within one frame in the art of painting.

The figuration and organisation of the Potemkin Village is much more complicated because the user might change his or her point of view and at least the nearby elements have to be turnable for each user movement. The price for this is a loss of creative access at the 3D-elements. However, the background and pieces of scenery in Geist are completed with painted texture, that also takes the effect of a narrative stabilizer within moving and turnable elements.

The result allow to analyze the functional, cognitive and aesthetic nature of this experiment and to draw further conclusions with regard to the realization phase of the Geist demonstrator to a really daily-in-use tourist attraction in Heidelberg.

3   Integrated Concept

In many ways, the destruction in Germany during the Thirty Years War was the most devastating experienced by any European country up to the 20th century. It has been conservatively estimated that about 50% of the population in the Heidelberg area died of military actions, plagues, hunger or disease directly resulting from 30 long years of war. When it started, people had forebodings about the things to come. Natural phenomenons were seen as forerunners of undefined disasters; of God's punishment. Leaflets printed in the 16th and 17th Century tell us about ghostriders, bloody swords or fighting armies appearing in the sky. These reports are complemented by woodcuts illustrating the incident: Beneath the apparition is the silhouette of the location as well as spectators to prove the authencity and to demonstrate the consternation caused by the event.

Geist tries a reinterpretation of those historic documents. On three locations the user is lead into the expectation of imminent occurrences that struck the town of Heidelberg (see figure 3).

Fig. 3. Integrated *Geist* scenario.

Therefore, we expanded the original *Geist* project to a combined integration of different content presentation codalities:

– Past vs. presence
– Historical facts vs. art
– Teaching vs. suspenseful narrative
– Illusion vs. reality
– 2D and 3D

4   Summary/Outlook

Functional, cognitive and aesthetic considerations could be the clincher for the use of painted images as supplements in interactive 3D-worlds in the future.

They could actually support a projects singularity, diversifying it's appearance and bringing variety by stressing the experimental character or enhancing the aesthetic pecurilarity of the virtual environment. Showing particular elements as either clearly defined and others as sketchily suggested helps to emphasize the main points. The traditional fields for paintings are images of urban or natural environement/landscapes, human society, historic events or daily life as well as surreal motifs. Without doubt, painted images are suitable for these and more applications, especially when other ways of creation are too wasteful or unsuitable.

By exchanging the story's content new subjects in the field of edutainment and tourism are possible – even theme parks and museums or fairs could use this system. In order to adopt the Heidelberg scenario concerning the Thirty Years War to other cities, places and application examples the creation of story content, virtual characters and a story instance based on predefined story models is neccessary.

A long-term development of the *Geist* concept could create a complete new genre, which would be located between traditional linear media and video games. Consequently, all together, *Geist* adresses the following markets:

- Education
- Information
- Entertainment
- Advertising/PR
- Eventmarketing

The Geist-Concept allows new forms of interaction and communication in the context of a story. First experiences allow new principles for the next generation.

Acknowledgements. The *Geist* project has been funded by the Federal Ministry of Education and Research (BMBF). The principal consortium members have been Fraunhofer IGD (GIS department), ZGDV eV (Storytelling department), both located in Darmstadt, and the European Media Lab (EML) in Heidelberg. The evaluation process has been supported by two subcontractors of ZGDV: University of Hannover and Lernteam, Marburg.

References

1. Bauer, H., Rupprecht. B. *Corpus der barocken Deckenmalerei in Deutschland*, Hirmer, München (1995)
2. Braun, N. *Automated Narration - the Path to Interactive Storytelling*, NILE, Edinburgh, Scotland (2002)
3. Finck, H. D., Ganz, M. T. *Bourbaki Panorama*, Werd Verlag, Zürich (2000)
4. Gombrich, E. H. *The image and the eye: further studies in the psychology of pictorial representation*, Phaidon Press Limited, Oxford (1982)
5. Gombrich, E. H. *The uses of images: studies in the social function of art and visual communication*, Phaidon, London (2000)
6. Kretschmer, U., Coors, V., Spierling, U., Grasbon, D., Schneider, K., Rojas, I., Malaka, R. *Meeting the Spirit of History*, Proceedings of: Virtual Reality, Archaeology, and Cultural Heritage (2001)
7. Schneider, O. *Storyworld creation: Authoring for Interactive Storytelling*, Journal of the WSCG, Plzen, Czech (2002)
8. Schneider, O., Braun, N. *Content Presentation in Augmented Spaces by the Narration of Interactive Scenes*, AVIR, Geneva, Swiss (2003)
9. Schneider, O., Braun, N., Habinger, G. *Storylining Suspense: An Authoring Environment for Structuring Non-linear Interactive Narratives*, Journal of the WSCG, Plzen, Czech (2003)

Conceptual Models for Interactive Digital Storytelling in Knowledge Media Applications

Ulrike Spierling

FH Erfurt, University of Applied Sciences,
Altonaerstr. 25, Erfurt, Germany
spierling@fh-erfurt.de

Abstract. This paper observes the way Interactive Digital Storytelling as participatory media can be conceived and perceived by authors who intend to build educational content. The suggestion of conceptual models and metaphors for semi-autonomous applications was motivated by experiences made with teaching Interactive Storytelling for knowledge media creation, realizing a lack of developing subsumable expectations of the outcome.

1 Introduction and Motivation

Can Interactive Digital Storytelling become a paradigm for better educational software? Current learning concepts focusing on constructivist methods severely criticize actual E-learning approaches. They demand an active, constructive role for learners enabling fun and "flow". Authors as Kafai [1] and Prensky [2] emphasize the big potential of interactive games for education. In schools, however, those situations still are preferred that guarantee the conveying of a defined factual information. Interactive storytelling then seems to be a technical solution to look for.

Teaching Interactive Digital Storytelling (IDS) concepts for educationalists and the purpose of knowledge transfer is still a rare endeavor. Here, first experiences were made in a joint academic initiative, performed with two groups of students from the disciplines of computer science and education science. It comprised the development of an IDS prototype targeted at the field of primary school mathematics, including the authoring of content for a real-time 3D learning environment. It also employed the definition of interaction through verbal dialogues with a group of virtual characters. In applying dramatic principles and storytelling techniques, characters were created with matching roles and individual knowledge capabilities in a fictional scenario that provided a learning mission (see Fig. 1). The practical work was carried out with a preliminary prototype of the interactive storytelling platform "art-E-fact". A description of the platform can be found in [3], a description of the educational project in [4].

During the progress of one semester, there has been a major turning point concerning the educationalist students' attitude towards the expected results. In the beginning, the potential was invisible because of the complexity of the task, and sceptical opinions were common. This had several reasons:

- Conceptualizing emergent dialogues with software agents is a rather complex and unintuitive task for novices, concerning the understanding of the model even more than technical programming issues
- 3D animated avatars led to a conceptual model very close to the metaphor of building a "Virtual Human", resulting in reluctance and acceptance problems, since educators were fearing the attempt of a replacement of the teacher

 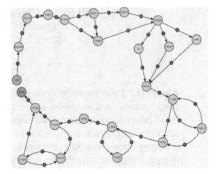

Fig. 1. Two conversing characters involving the learner *(left)* and a dialogue graph *(right)*

In contrast to that, after experiencing the first results at the end of the semester, positive expectations arose. First, it was noticed that by employing verbal language for interaction, the constructive process in e-learning situations might be supported in the future. In addition, a dialogue construction tool involving graph structures of conversations inspired the future elementary teachers to rethink the dialogue structures they currently used for their interaction with children in the classroom.

In summary, interactivity as well as learning occurred on both sides: teacher students in the "author"-role could construct and review dialogues in a god-mode like environment, and elementary school children experienced the interactive dialogues that were created for them as participants. The problem in the beginning was the lack of any accepted and suitable metaphor for each possible interactive situation.

2 Related Work

Conceptual models have been introduced by Norman [5] as a consideration for better interaction with designed artifacts. Within recent years, genres descriptions of computer games such as of Rollings and Adams [6] became a distinguishing feature among the variety of game artifacts. However, genre classifications for interactive storytelling still need to be fleshed out. Several transferred models of interactive situations for IDS are summarized by Murray [7] including the notion of agency, which is also discussed by Fencott [8] and Mateas and Stern [9]. The latter built a related system for interactive conversations "Façade", but with no educational purpose. Work on the modeling of interactive virtual humans and motivated agents as in [10] is relevant. However, the involved conceptual models are rather complex and need to be simplified for authors and educationalists, in order to provide models for controllable semi-autonomy.

3   Concepts of Interactive Storytelling and Knowledge Media

As existing classifications show, the existence of multiple genres for each Interactive Digital Storytelling and Computer Games make it hard to draw an exact line between both matters. Both can serve as knowledge media in the sense that knowledge can be represented through them. In most of all storytelling, there is a communication goal: A message being transmitted from an author to the audience, as well as entertainment by dramatic arcs. Stories can be considered as knowledge spaces with a formal structure that fosters the general acceptance and absorption of factual and emotional information. Games, in contrast, deliver no storyline of explicit information, but sets of rules that let agents behave in a certain way. The human player is the interacting agent who defines the course of actions. The knowledge space of a game may contain little factual knowledge presentation compared to the huge potential for acquiring system competence, used for example to learn about social systems in simulation gaming, all by exploration. Interacting with the two concepts leads to different dimensions in the experienced interactivity of a user (compare Fig. 2):

1) Human-to-Human (communication, via medium, storytelling paradigm)
2) Human-to-Self (exploration, via medium, fabrication of own thoughts)
3) Human-to-Computer (factual experienced actions, tangible or virtual)

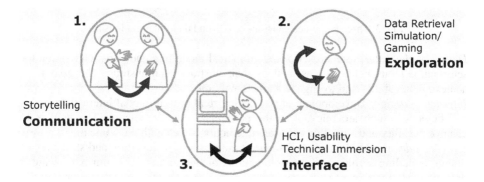

Fig. 2. Dimensions of interactivity in interactive knowledge media

In the primary school mathematics project, authors created a communication model, where interactions are possible but constrained to educational conventions. They in turn experienced a model of free exploration while using the authoring tool. The interface defines the resulting factual actions, for example unconstrained typing.

In the result, software agents conduct an interactive conversation with human agents. If "interactivity" is taken formally serious, both sides can interact, which means act reciprocally. This implies that the repertoire for the human actions exceeds choosing, selecting or collecting – there are possible speech acts, defined by natural language chatterbot technology. However, with a huge repertoire for the human, the resulting conversation is as unpredictable and complex as any emergent system. Non-programming authors or instructors, who want to deliver a message or knowledge-related factual information, have difficulty in describing such an emergent conversation. They need metaphors to understand and conceive agent interactions.

4 Conceptual Models for Interactive Storytelling

4.1 Premises and Constituents of Interactive Storytelling for Education

Beyond the issue of verbal interactivity, the following assumptions and definitions are taken as premises for the author's responsibilities in building successful applications involving *interactive storytelling*. As suggested by Crawford [11], IDS implies that the application has "to talk", "to think" and "to listen" to an audience. This constitutes three major design issues that have to be conceived by the creators: Output, Input and Processing (see Fig. 3). Moreover, these issues are interrelated, showing connecting edges of several levels of abstraction, which in total influence the experienced result:

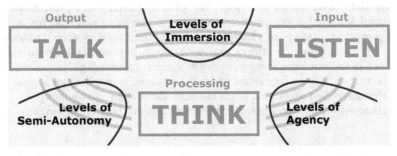

Fig. 3. Three major design issues of IDS and their interrelationships

Design of characters and story worlds: Graphical modelling and parameterization for semi-autonomous behaviour as well as their abstract relationships. The goal is to achieve believability and to engage learners with the content.

Interaction design: Development of physical, virtual or multimodal interaction modes and devices, which are relevant to the particular story or content. The goal is to achieve usability and smoothly integrate interaction styles with the content.

Structural design: Modelling of dialogue structures for conversation and structures of drama, including scripting of possible actions of the learner. The aim is to achieve didactic goals according to a learning concept, and to pace the content presentation.

Levels of agency: What is influenced by the user interaction? (Local agency affecting the verbal discourse vs. global agency changing major plot points)

Levels of semi-autonomy: To what extent is the outcome influenced by predefinitions or by rules? (Author-centred presentation vs. generated simulation)

Levels of technical immersion: What media and modalities are employed? (Virtual reality immersion vs. desktop metaphors)

4.2 Conceptual Design Levels for Clarifying Agency and Semi-autonomy

A major claim frequently made by visionaries of Interactive Storytelling is that an audience can influence the storytelling. However, there are different levels at which to affect the outcome. In Fig. 4 they are sketched as levels of agency applied to a level set of semi-autonomy further explained in [12]. The levels rather represent conceptual stages for authoring than elements of software architecture, though there are parallels to a number of existing systems. Semi-autonomy occurs on the edge between predefined factual information and rules for each level. The more rules on one level, the more agency can be experienced by potentially affecting the respective level. For factual knowledge transfer in a didactic lesson situation, the highest level might stay predefined, while the lower levels allow for conversational interaction, however constrained. If authors only provide a rule base with little pre-scripted structuring, they achieve a conceptual model more like an exploration or gaming experience depending completely on the action of the player.

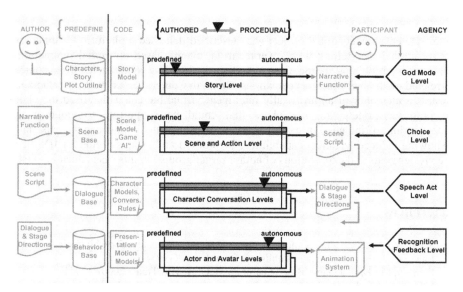

Fig. 4. Four levels of semi-autonomy including agency

4.3 Metaphors Used to Express Semi-autonomy

In a famous debate on agent software [13], the distinction between the interaction models of an agent and a tool for direct manipulation was made. The metaphors suggested here base on the assumption that there is no idealistic autonomous agent model representing a virtual teacher, because language processing is still error prone. Additionally, the metaphor of an all-knowing virtual agent scared the educators in the project. Suggestions for conceptual metaphors used to describe a mixture of scripted and interactive behavior are:

"Horse and rider": A metaphor for semi-autonomous agents in a unidirectional but highly interactive situation. The horse navigates by itself, but is used and directed by the rider. A savvy rider can challenge and completely control the horse, while a novice rider will still be carried home safely with a trained horse.

"Conversational dollhouse": A dollhouse as a toy or medium used for constructing interpretations of reality, enabling the "fabrication of thought" as well as communication among buddies. Looking at the conversing avatars as dolls provided a completely different perspective for most of the educationalists, as compared to a "Virtual Human" metaphor. They felt like speaking through them to their students.

"Regular's table": A metaphorical conception to describe the way several virtual characters would present a story as if staged for a play, and then turn to interact with the user. New participants in a buddies group (e.g. in a bar) don't stop running conversations; they learn a lot by just listening to the stories of the characters knowing each other, and get integrated into the conversation gradually over time.

5 Conclusion and Future Work

In this paper, an educational project was described that used a platform for emergent conversational storytelling with several virtual agents based on verbal interactions. The starting problems of the educationalists in building suitable learning content correlated with their fuzzy expectations about the outcome, as well as reluctance towards a metaphor of an artificially intelligent virtual human. This raised the claim for intuitive models and metaphors that could be supportive to enhance the understanding of intended or expected results of semi-autonomous agents, especially if showing reduced technical capabilities. Creators of authoring systems for IDS need to consider goals and expectations of author target groups, in this case educationalists.

References

1. Kafai, Y.: Minds in Play: Computer Game Design as a Context for Children's Learning. Lawrence Erlbaum Associates Publishers, New Jersey (1995)
2. Prensky, M.: Digital Game-Based Learning. McGraw-Hill Trade (2000)
3. Spierling, U., Iurgel, I.: "Just Talking About Art" - Creating Virtual Storytelling Experiences in Mixed Reality. In: Virtual Storytelling, Using Virtual Reality Technologies for Storytelling, Proceedings (ICVS 2003), Toulouse France (2003) 179-188
4. Spierling, U., Müller, W., Vogel, R., Iurgel, I.: Digital Conversational Storytelling Elements for Teaching Mathematics in Primary School. In: Proceedings of ED-MEDIA 2004, World Conference on Educational Multimedia, Hypermedia & Telecommunications, Lugano (2004)
5. Norman, D.: The Design of Everyday Things, Basic Books New York (1988)
6. Rollings, A., Adams, E.: A. Rollings and E. Adams on Game Design. New Riders (2003)
7. Murray, J.: Hamlet on the Holodeck: The Future of Narrative in Cyberspace, MIT Press, Cambridge MA (1998)
8. Fencott, C.: Agencies of Interactive Digital Storytelling. In: Proceedings of TIDSE 2003, Darmstadt (2003) 152-163
9. Mateas, M., Stern, A.: Integrating Plot, Character and Natural Language Processing in the Interactive Drama Façade. In: Proceedings of TIDSE 2003, Darmstadt (2003) 139-151
10. Gratch, J., Rickel, J., André, E., Badler, N., Cassell, J., Petajan, E.: Creating Interactive Virtual Humans: Some Assembly Required. IEEE Intelligent Systems, Issue 7/8 (2002) 2-11
11. Crawford, C.: Understanding Interactivity. http://www.erasmatazz.com (2000) 5-12
12. Spierling, U., Grasbon, D., Braun, N., Iurgel, I.: Setting the Scene: Playing Digital Director in Interactive Storytelling and Creation. In: Computers & Graphics (2002) 26, 31-44
13. Maes, P., Shneiderman, B., Miller, J. (Mod.): Intelligent Software Agents vs. User-Controlled Direct Manipulation: A Debate. Panel Outline, Extended Abstracts of ACM, CHI '97 (1997)

Experience the Antique Olympics!
An Interactive Educational Narrative

Anja Hoffmann and Birgit Riemenschneider

ZGDV Darmstadt e.V., Digital Storytelling Department,
Fraunhoferstr. 5, 64283 Darmstadt, Germany
{Anja.Hoffmann, Birgit.Riemenschneider}@zgdv.de

Abstract. In this paper, we describe a concept for a narrative e-learning application. We point out the enrichment of learning environments through stories and describe our approach to educational narratives. Furthermore, we present an interactive story plot to learn about the antique Olympic Games.

1 Introduction

E-learning is still fighting against high failure and dropout rates. Thissen sees the reason that educational applications often "metacommunicate dreariness and boredom, and they only address the cognitive part of learning." And Norman states: "For teaching to be effective, cognition and emotion must work together." [1]

In our opinion the use of stories enriches the design of engaging and motivating learning environments for many reasons: Stories are structured in a suspenseful way and foster emotional engagement. Experiencing a good story (e.g. within movies or novels) can cause total immersion in the imaginary world for the recipient, forgetting time and space. We can find essential functionalities for learning environments, such as focussing the learner's attention, provision of information and feedback about the learner's efforts. [2] In addition, stories are not limited to certain topic which means that a wide range of topics can be told in a narrative way.

Another fact is, that stories are fundamental to culture and human understanding. They have familiar structures which are recognizable and can easily be understood. In human tradition stories were means for information transmission and knowledge acquisition, e.g. within families and cultural communities. "Much true understanding is achieved through storytelling. Stories are how we communicate events and thought processes." [3]

In conclusion, we see great potential in the combination of Interactive Storytelling technologies for the design of e-learning environments. In this paper, we will describe a concept for an educational narrative game. Based on constructivism learning theory the learner will be able to explore the world of antique Olympia.

S. Göbel et al. (Eds.): TIDSE 2004, LNCS 3105, pp. 177–182, 2004.

2 Approach to Educational Narratives

2.1 Learning Model

Complex information is easier to understand when it is adopted to authentic situations. For this reason learning with "micro worlds" (such as simulations or role-playing games) contributes to clear understanding. [4] As known from constructivism theory the application should support active engagement with the topic in order to help the user to reflect and to construct his knowledge. Cognitive sciences point out the model of explorative learning and its motivational effects. [5] Furthermore a coach or tutor who consults the user is necessary to avoid frustration or annoyance.

Our concept combines elements of the described approaches to engaging learning applications: The story takes place in a virtual representation of antique Olympia incorporating virtual characters from former times, some of them acting as mentors or helper. Linear scenes alternate with interactive sequences in order to give the user the possibility to explore the situation and interfere without getting lost.

2.2 Game Play and Story

Within games one of the most motivating factors is the manipulation of the game world and the control over it. Therefore it must be open for interactive parts. Although stories are widely used in edutainment applications (e.g. Chemicus, Physicus [6]) there is still a lack of appropriate integration of story and instruction: "The instructional design was generally concentrated in an isolated instructional space that existed independently of the story arc." [7] The result is that the learning-supporting characteristics of stories are limited because of the interruption of immersion and engagement. To avoid this effect our approach aims at a full symbiosis of learning and story content, e.g. by integrating historic facts into dialogues.

2.3 Interactive Story Structure

The plot of a story consists of linear arrangement of events. In contrast to documentations narratives take previous events into account, create dependencies between actions and characters and give ideas of forthcoming events and the ending [8]

Following the argumentation of Crawford [9] we speak for a more abstract understanding of a plot. The basic story idea can be interactively varied with different characters, objects and events. For this we have adapted Vogler's Hero's Journey [10] – a model well known from Hollywood movies. The Hero's Journey consists of 12 modules and integrates 7 archetypical characters. These characters appear throughout the long human tradition of myths, folktales and stories. The Hero's Journey is suitable for an educational game because of its comprehensibility and its familiar course.

In order to allow a consistent and dramaturgical experience the game combines movie clips with interactive sequences. Fig. 1 shows the structure of the application.

Application Structure

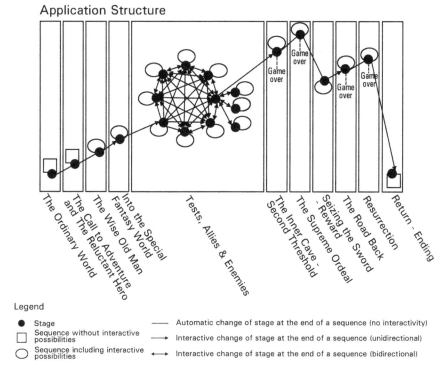

Legend

- ● Stage
- ☐ Sequence without interactive possibilities
- ○ Sequence including interactive possibilities

——— Automatic change of stage at the end of a sequence (no interactivity)

——→ Interactive change of stage at the end of a sequence (unidirectional)

←—→ Interactive change of stage at the end of a sequence (bidirectional)

Fig. 1. Structure of the application: Modules of the Hero's Journey

3   Concept

3.1   Curriculum

The antique Olympic Games took place in 4-year turns from 776 B.C. to 260 A.D. and have their seeds in religious rituals. The competitions were arranged to the honor of Zeus. Processions and oblations were also part of the Olympic culture which is one of the major differences to today's games. At that time, too, the event attracts many spectators: up to 40,000 people took part.

From content related view the user will learn about the origin of the Olympic Games, the relation of sport competition to religious and cultural circumstances and social and political relevance. He can virtually have a look at ancient Olympic places and meet with people from former times. Further can try out some disciplines and discover the differences to Olympic Games from today.

Concerning methodical perspectives the learner must be able to use the application and adopt novel knowledge in particular situations.

3.2 Target Group

The educational game addresses children and teenager older than 12 years. From this age children develop their ability from object orientation to think in more abstract ways. Symbolic and verbal elements become more relevant. Historic information about Olympia and its beginning will be transported through the design of an historic 3D environment, the visualization of objects and characters and – more abstract – dialogues.

3.3 Plot

The plot is based on the classic theme "rescue" [8] with a triangulation of characters: Hero, Enemy and Victim. The "good" is fighting against the "evil" and love will be approved in the end.

The hero is represented through the young athlete Alexis – the prospect winner of the Olympic Games. The role of the enemy takes his fierce rival Thanatos who grasps at the victory associated with glory and power. He let abduct Alexis' fiancée Helena to press the victory. In this situation Alexis is supported by Diagoras – the wise man and mentor.

3.4 User's Role

The user experiences the application from a Third-Person Perspective. Through mysterious circumstances he enters the game while the hero is desperately praying to Zeus for help. The user is represented through a virtual character with the look of modern times. He will support the hero through his journey.

3.5 Story, Instruction, and Interaction

The following paragraph gives an overview about story-related (s) and instructional (i) content as well as the interaction possibilities (ia) within different modules of Hero's journey:

1. *The Ordinary World*: (s) Alexis and his entourage arrive at Olympia - (i) Introduction to Olympic tradition - (ia) Movie clip, no interaction
2. *The Call to Adventure*: (s) Abduction of Helena, prayer to Zeus, appearance of user - (i) Impact of Olympic victory – (ia) Movie clip, no interaction
3. *The Reluctant Hero*: (s) Alexis' resignation – (i) Relation of Olympic Games to religion, reverence of Zeus – (ia) Movie clip, no interaction
4. *The Wise Old Man*: (s) Mentor Diagoras hands over some objects as oblations, encourages Alexis to follow Zeus' signs – (i) Meaning of Olympic truce – (ia) Receiving of different items
5. *Into the Special Fantasy World*: (s) Willingness to engage into the adventure, dialogue between Alexis and the user – (i) Relevance of different Olympic places, here: Leonidaion (guest house) – (ia) Short movie clip, transition to next module, no interaction

Fig. 2. Module *Tests, Allies & Enemies*

6. *Tests, Allies & Enemies*: (s) Different alternate scenes – (i) Olympic disciplines and differences to today's competition – (ia) User can choose between 11 different stages, make friends with other characters, collect items
7. *The Inner Cave - Second Threshold*: (s) Alexis and the user outflank the guardians– (ia) Use of collected items

Fig. 3. Module *The Supreme Ordeal*

8. *The Supreme Ordeal*: (s) Climax, capture of Alexis and his friends, confrontation with Thanatos who unfolds his plans, victory over Thanatos (cf. Fig. 3) – (i) Impact of Olympic victory to political power and social reputation – (ia) Dialogue between user and Thanatos as gamesmanship
9. *Seizing the Sword – Reward*: (s) Deliverance of Helena and escape – (i) Role of woman in former times – (ia) Use of collected items
10.*The Road Back*: (s) Finding way back through labyrinth – (i) Olympic area and buildings – (ia) Use of "magical Olympia guide"
11.*Resurrection*: (s) Obstruction of escape route – (ia) Solve last task
12.*Return – Ending*: (s) Punishment of Thanatos, return and victory of hero Alexis – (i) Award ceremony – (ia) Movie clip, no interaction

4 Conclusion

The concept of the educational narrative presented in this paper has been realized as an interactive demonstrator based on Macromedia Flash. It is suited to various environments from desktop-based applications to Mixed Reality set-ups. The structural model of the Hero's Journey is universal and can also be applied to various topics.

By using physical devices for interaction (e.g. similar to the project art-E-fact [11], [12]) the user's attention can be focused to relevant issues and it positively effects his motivation. Further it contributes to the immersion into the story, reinforces emotional feelings and improves the learning impact.

References

1. ACM eLearn Magazine, Education and Technology in Perspective: Feelin' Groovy. Retrieved Apr. 7th 2004 from http://www.elearnmag.org/subpage/sub_page.cfm?article_pk =10221 &page_number_nb=1&title=FEATURE%20STORY (2004)
2. Gagne, R. M., Briggs, L. J., & Wager, W. W.: Principles of instructional design. Fort Worth: HBJ College & School Division (1992)
3. Schell, J.: Understanding Entertainment: Story And Gameplay Are One. In: Jacko, J. A. , Sears, A.(eds.): The Human-Computer Interaction Handbook: Fundamentals, Evolving Technologies and Emerging Applications. Lawrence Erlbaum Associates, Inc., Mahwah, New Jersey (2002)
4. Holzinger, A.: Basiswissen Multimedia, Band 2. Vogel Verlag, Würzburg (2001)
5. Schulmeister, R.: Grundlagen hypermedialer Lernsysteme: Theorie – Didaktik – Design, Addison-Wesley, Bonn, Germany (1996)
6. Klett-Heureka. Retrieved Apr. 7th 2004 from http://www.klett-verlag.de/heureka/ (2004)
7. Noah, D.: An Analysis of Narrative-based Educational Software. Retrieved Nov. 15th 2003 from http://naturalhistory.uga.edu/narrative_paper.htm (2003)
8. Tobias, R. B.: 20 Master Plots: And How to Build Them. Walking Stick Press (2003)
9. Crawford, C.: Plot versus interactivity. Retrieved Apr. 7th 2004 from http://www.erasmatazz.com (2004)
10. Vogler, C.: Die Odyssee des Drehbuchschreibens (A Writer's Journey), Second Edition. Zweitausendeins, Frankfurt a. M., Germany (1998)
11. art-E-fact, Generic Platform for Interactive Storytelling in Mixed Reality, EU-Funded Project (IST-2001 37924 ART-E-FACT). Project website. Retrieved Apr. 7th 2004 from http://www.art-e-fact.org/
12. Spierling, U., Iurgel, I.: Just Talking About Art. In Virtual Storytelling. In: Proceedings Second International Conference, ICVS 2003, Toulouse, France (2003), (LNCS 2897), p. 189-197

Narrative, Game Play, and Alternative Time Structures for Virtual Environments

Craig A. Lindley

Institutionen för Teknik, Konst och Nya Medier,
Högskolan på Gotland, Cramergatan 3, SE-621 57 Visby, Sweden
craig.lindley@hgo.se

Abstract. Computer games are the most popular and successful virtual environments. However, computer games are usually not simply either games or digital storytelling systems, but involve three primary types of formal semiotic system bearing upon time structure: games, models and narratives. Strong narrative structures depend upon an a priori time-structure, but there are less specific alternatives, including rhetorical, categorical and poetic structures blending into the general higher order time structures of games and simulations. Experience within a virtual environment may be based upon only one of these systems, but more commonly the systems are integrated using a variety of strategies to create rich and multi-layered temporal experiences.

1 Introduction

Computer games include elements of a variety of formal systems that can be analysed and realized autonomously. The concept of *ludic space* captures the realm of these experiences variously incorporating concepts of game or game play together with elements of narrative, simulation, and non-narrative principles for structuring temporal experience.

Ludic systems are fundamentally time-based, and temporal structure is a major determinant of the perception of ludic form. Ludic systems involve four levels of temporal structure. The temporal structure of the experience of the player, that can be referred to as the *discourse* level, corresponds in pure narrative systems with the level of narration. This is the level at which a plot is revealed via one or more discursive episodes, and for which the sequence of revealing episodes within the players temporal continuum may not necessarily correspond with the sequence of temporal events within the revealed plot; that is, the order of events within the revealed world may not be linear in the time order of that world, but could include flash-forwards and flash backs (hence the players time order and that of the revealed world may not be isomorphic).

The actual events revealed to the player as part of the play experience may be referred to as the *performance* level. This is the level at which the player is not simply an active viewer, but an interactive participant within the ludic world, having an influence on the nature and shape of the events manifested within the game world dur-

S. Göbel et al. (Eds.): TIDSE 2004, LNCS 3105, pp. 183–194, 2004.
© Springer-Verlag Berlin Heidelberg 2004

ing the "playing of a game". The performance level includes only those parts of the virtual world directly experienced by the player. In purely narrative systems this is the *plot*. Ludic systems may not have a sufficiently strongly pre-specified plot structure to represent progress within a strongly preconceived (ie. authored) conception of a narrative, so the performance level may or may not constitute an experience strongly characterisable as a plot.

Whether the player has a strong sense of plot or not, their (inter-)actions are likely to have consequences that are only manifested in an implicit why, implying a game world beyond that which is explicitly represented to the player. In pure narrative systems this is the *story* level. In computer games, the temporal system may not be as precisely pre-structured as traditional narratives, and so can more appropriately be referred to as the *model* level; this is the level at which the authored logic and parameters of a game together with the specific interactive choices of the player determine an (implied) diegetic world, some of which is made available to the player via the experiential zone created by a virtual camera, a virtual volume of audio reception, and a surface of virtual haptic reception (eg. a virtual body that receives damage or health).

Beneath the model level is the level of the *generative substrate*, the system of rules and constraints constituting a space of possible worlds of experience created by the designers of the game. In the traditional semiotics of language these distinctions may be equated in terms of the discourse level corresponding with speech (the semiotician Saussure's *parole*) and the generative substrate corresponding with the system of a language (Saussure's *la langue*). Narrative theory posits semantic levels including the diegesis (the world represented by discursive acts) and the discursive order of presentation of the time order within the diegesis (the narration level). Since ludic systems may have time orders that are not dominated by strong narrative models, a different terminology is required to characterize these various levels. Hence it is possible to distinguish: the discourse level, the performance level, the model level, and the generative substrate.

This paper disregards the discourse level and considers the time structure of the performance level as experienced by the player. This level is the primary focus of game design, requiring different approaches at the model and generative levels for realizing particular patterns of time structure within the player's performative experience of a game. This differs from (but is compatible with) the temporal genre distinctions proposed by [2], who focus on pragmatic and discursive issues involving distinctions between mimetic versus arbitrary narration/presentation times, real time versus turn-based interaction cycles, and the discourse-to-model level issue of overall finite versus infinite persistence of the ludic space. Similarly, the formulation of game semiotics presented by Klabbers [9] also appears to be compatible with the formulation presented here. However, Klabbers emphasizes atemporal aspects of game semiotics (their *synchronic* semiotics) in relation to simulation, while the framework presented here emphasizes the temporal semiotics of games (their *diachronic* semiotics) in relation both to simulation/modeling and to narrative together with other non-narrative time structuring principles. Ultimately these approaches should be integrated and further developed to provide a rich semiotics for ludic systems supporting both analysis and design. The principles of generative temporal structure described here can be used for analyzing ludic systems, and also as a foundation for implementing systems, since the different sequencing strategies have different associated technical data structures and algorithms that may be combined by various strategies within digital systems supporting the experience of narrative.

2 Games, Models, and Linear Temporal Structures as Independent Formal Subsystems of Ludic Space

Ludic systems may involve three different kinds of formal semiotic system determining the temporal structure of the play experience at the performance level. Each of these types of formal system can be realized in ways that operate independently of the others, although any given ludic system may involve more than one of these formal types to varying degrees and using different strategies of interrelationship or integration. It is their potential independence that suggests the identification of these systems as usefully separated high level areas of analysis and design concern. The three types of formal system are: the formal system of games, the formal system of the model, and the formal system of the narrative. In Lindley [11] this trichotomy was expressed in terms of game, narrative and simulation, respectively. However, to be more accurate, simulation must be considered together with *fabrication* in the case of systems for which correspondence with an external system is of limited concern, and the concept of the model captures this more effectively than that of simulation.

3 Games and Game Play

Computer games encompass a vast range of different kinds of interactive media productions. In the broadest possible sense we call all of these things games. However, this is not useful for understanding the different time-structuring systems operating within games. It is much more useful to adopt a narrower definition of game, particularly one supporting analysis and design methods very distinct from those of other formal ludic semiotic subsystems. Hence a game will be defined as follows:

A game *is a goal-directed and competitive activity conducted within a framework of agreed rules.*

This can be referred to as the *ludic* or *ludological* definition of game, the kind of definition at the heart of traditional game theory (this definition captures many features of the definitions considered by Juul [8], but omitting criteria based upon issues of pragmatics that are highly subject to external accidents of history and context). Single player puzzle games represent an interesting case in relation to this definition. In particular, it is not so clear who the player is competing against, and it is not obvious that a puzzle should be regarded as a game. Taking the stance that a puzzle *is* a game, by the adopted definition, then the competitor can be interpreted as one or more of: the player themselves (competing against oneself, or one's own limitations), other players trying to solve the same puzzle, or the author of the puzzle.

It is often said that learning to play a game involves learning the rules of the game (eg. [10]). However, the above definition does not require this; it only require that activity obeys the rules, and that players implicitly or explicitly agree to those rules. As Juul notes, one of the advantages of computer games is that the machine enforces the rules, relieving the player from the need to know all of the rules in detail and supporting rule sets far too complex for purely manual operation.

The rules establish what as a player you can or cannot do, and what the behavioral consequences of actions may be within the game. Successful play does *not* necessarily require learning all of the game rules, but only those necessary to support a particular playing style, and perhaps none at all. Learning to play a game, making progress within a game and completing or winning a game are a matter of learning how to interact within the game system and its rules in a way that supports progress. This is a matter, not necessarily of learning the game rules, but of learning a *gameplay gestalt*[1], understood as a pattern of interaction with the game system. Playing the game is then a matter of performing the gestalt. It is what the player does, within the system and as allowed by the rules of the game. In computer games, where the machine enforces the rules, this may lead to players having very poor conscious appreciation of what the rules actually are; instead they have learned successful (and unsuccessful) patterns of interaction by trial and error.

A gameplay gestalt can have many forms for a particular game, capturing different playing styles, tactics and approaches to progressing through the game and (perhaps) eventually winning. In general, it is a particular way of thinking about the game state from the perspective of a player, together with a pattern of repetitive perceptual, cognitive, and motor operations. A particular gameplay gestalt could be unique to a person, a game, or even a playing occasion. Recurrent gameplay gestalts can also be identified across games, game genres, and players. Some examples of gameplay gestalts in computer games include:

☐ *Action games*: shoot while being hit, strafe to hiding spot, take health, repeat
   RPGs: send fast character to lure enemy from group, all characters kill enemy, take health, repeat
☐ *Strategy Games*: order peasants, send to work, order soldiers, send to perimeters, repeat while slowly expanding the perimeters (up to the point of catastrophic win/lose); OR: move x archers to tower y every n minutes to head off the enemy camel musketeers from the east who arrive every n minutes
☐ *In General*: confront barrier, save if successful, reload and retry if unsuccessful

Patterns like these may or may not be explicitly designed for by the creators of a game. If designers do take them into account, it may be in supporting the development and emergence of these patterns in play, rarely by forcing them on the player. It may also be that a game has a single winning gestalt. This may not be a simple re-

---

[1] A *gestalt* may be understood as a configuration or pattern of elements so unified as a whole that it cannot be described merely as a sum of its parts.

petitive interaction pattern, but perhaps the performance of one very specific pattern, or a generic pattern performed repetitively in variable instantiations.

3.1 Temporal Structure in Games

The rules and ludic medium of a game (at the generation level) imply and support a range of different types of valid actions at the performance level, typically with scope for variations in how those actions are performed, and how and when different actions are selected and sequenced. A *move* within a game is an abstraction over player action, mapping it to an abstracted action of significance within the rule set and independent of local, personal and idiosyncratic variations in performance; a move is a connotation of a physical action allowed and facilitated by the framing of the game (I can move a chess piece on the board at any time, but I only make *a move* in the game of chess when I'm playing the game). Hence a player performs actions having conventional connotations as moves within the formal system of the game. Those actions are likely to be highly stylized according to the game, and actions too dissimilar to the stylized set will be regarded as fouls or cheats if their performer intends them to have in-game significance, or as *extra-ludic* actions potentially frustrating other players if they are not intended to have in-game significance. A gameplay gestalt, as described above, is a player's pattern of move performances.

Player engagement within a game experience is strongly associated with the choice and performance of game moves. The potential for choosing moves results in a very loosely predefined time structure such that games are not strongly a priori time-structured in their design. A specific type of move is likely to have some time structure at least implicit within the rule-derived constraints bounding valid ways of performing it. But this is minimal, and the temporal structure of gameplay gestalts is an emergent structure developed during play by a player. Even games like *Snakes and Ladders*, in which progress is a matter of very constrained movement across a highly structured grid, supports a very large space of possible combinations of moves on the board, corresponding to an equally large space of possible time structures (choice in this case being realized in the performance of an act having a probabilistic outcome, ie. the throwing of dice).

For this reason, the purest examples of game form cannot be regarded as heavily time-structured systems. However, there are larger scale time structures specific to game form. These larger scale structures are reflected in the language of rounds, bouts, matches, tournaments, seasons and campaigns. The most primitive complete game experiences, at which a point of win or loss is reached, are bouts or rounds. Significantly, higher level game structures tend to be highly repetitive patterns of these simple game experiences. They are largely concerned with the organization of opponents and extension of the simple competitive situation of a game to include a broader field of opponents with a view to obtaining a global performance or game play ranking obtained by accumulation of the results of many bouts.

In order to discuss these higher level structures more clearly, the following somewhat arbitrary working definitions are proposed:

☐ a *bout* or a *round* is the single performance of a game between opponents resulting in a win/lose state[2]

☐ a *match* is a series bouts or rounds of the same game between the same opponents

☐ a *contest* is a series of rounds of different games between the same opponents

☐ a *league* is a series of rounds of the same game between different opponents

☐ a *tournament* is a series of rounds of different games between different opponents

These structures may be nested in hierarchies, lattices or networks. For example, performances within a tournament may each have the form of a match. High level game structures have their own rules, these being rules for the accretion of the results of bouts and rules for matching competitors in ongoing events. A multi-game structure requires a *principle of accrual of results*. That is, various formulae may be used for accumulating wins and loses, and degrees of win/loss, into an overall competitive ranking, or for the identification of a set of *champions* across various categories. The structure may also include *elimination events* in which losing competitors are eliminated from further competition, or the game system may include *principles of handicap* by which differences in demonstrated game play expertise are compensated for to provide for less predictable outcomes in ongoing competitions.

These are match, contest, league and tournament rules that have no impact upon low level game rules or the abstract form of moves within each specific game type. The time structure among these higher level game groupings at the performance level is incidental to the essential performance of the players. Even more strongly, it can be stated that the high level structures of game forms have little to no dependence on specific time orders. Their primary meaning is the ranking of player competence; time-ordered competitions are a convenience for identifying this ranking. In principle it doesn't matter at all what the sequencing of competitions is, as long as it leads to an order of player competence (hence the common freedom to choose the sequence in which one defeats one's opponents in a computer game level). So at this level, too, games are not primarily time-structured designs, and the high level time structure does not impinge upon low level game rules or the basic experience of play. This is a critical distinction between the temporal form of games and those temporal ludic experiences that have a strong a priori linear time structure at the performance level that is pre-specified by their designer. In many computer games, instances of combat are individual bouts (these are experiences of playing single games, by the definition above), while levels may be seen to be organized as a series of matches, contests, leagues or tournaments. If a higher level game structure is designed to present players with a specific sequence of game experiences, activities and opponents, serving to shape the emotional tone and intensity of the experience, the form is starting to move away from pure game form, more strongly integrating variants of authored narrative as manifested in the pre-specified sequential design.

---

[2] There may be more than two opponents, and each opponent could either be an individual or a group; opponents may also be synthetic, eg. the NPCs of a computer game.

4 Narrative Time Structure

Narrative structure within ludic systems may be either pre-authored at the performance level, or an emergent pattern based upon combinatorial principles built into the generation level. Narrative in the strongest sense is perceived when a structure conforms to a very specific narrative pattern, such as the three-act restorative structure described below. However, strong narrative structure is not the only pre-specified linear time-structured experiential mode possible at the performance level; in ludic systems, as in cinema (see Bordwell and Thomson, 1997), we can design for other high level temporal structures including rhetorical, categorical and poetic forms[3].

4.1 Strong Narrative Structure

A common and strongly determined narrative structure used in computer games, borrowed from film scriptwriting, is the *three-act restorative structure* (see [5]). The three-act restorative structure has a beginning (the first act) in which a conflict is established, followed by the playing out of the implications of the conflict (the second act), and completed by the final resolution of the conflict (the third act). The three-act restorative structure includes a central protagonist, a conflict involving a dilemma of normative morality, a second act propelled by the hero's false resolution of this dilemma, and a third act in which the dilemma is resolved once and for all by an act that reaffirms normative morality. Each act within the three-act structure culminates in a point of crisis, the resolution of which propels the plot into the following act, or to the final resolution.

In computer games incorporating a prespecified three act restorative structure at the performance level, the central conflict form often manifests recursively (ie. the structure is repeated at different levels of temporal scale). For example, the overall restorative three-act model may be applied to the game experience as a whole, with the dramatic arch being completed when the user finishes the game. At this level the story is usually not interactive, since act one, key scenes within the story of act two (ie. primary plot points), and the playing out of the consequences of the final resolution in act three are typically achieved by cut scenes, sequences of non-interactive, pre-rendered video or non-interactive animation sequences. The next level down within the recursive structure is that of the game level. The game level is designed for the pursuit of a goal, that of the player reaching the end of the level, which progresses the player through the second act of the higher level three-act structure of the game narrative. There is rarely if ever a one-to-one correspondence between game levels and acts; more typically, the first act and the end of the third act are presented via cut scenes, with playable game levels summing to form a highly extended second act

---

[3] Bordwell and Thomson [3] suggest narrative, categorical, rhetorical, associative and abstract forms for cinema. We take the associative to be a general supercategory, and refer to poetic rather than abstract form in order to distinguish between issues of structural form and issues of external representation.

followed by the final resolution of the third act as the end of game play (eg. by over-coming the final and toughest enemy, usually a demonic character at the heart of the central conflict in the story). Although experience within a level typically has much of the structure of a match, a contest, a league or a tournament, the sense of level-specific narrative development can be enhanced by increasing difficulty through a level, or by an internal dramatic structure that emphasizes the point of completing the level, such as the defeat of a level boss, the big barrier creature at the end of the level. The false resolution that drives act two of the three-act restorative model at the high-est structural level may be seen manifesting repetitively with each game level: when the game level is resolved (completed), the player finds themselves at the beginning of the next game level full of conflicts.

At the next level of the recursive decomposition of game structure, there is often a series of smaller scale conflicts and challenges within a game level, which may in-clude monsters to be defeated or avoided, puzzles to be solved, or treasures, clues or keys that must be found in order to progress in the current or future game levels. Usually it is only this lowest level of the game plot that is highly interactive; these are actually the individual games played by the player (by the definition above). The linear and non-interactive cut scenes framing game play are revealed in a predefined order, and within a level all players usually start in the same place and must have completed the same set of tasks in order to complete the level. The low level and interactive parts of the game are played by performance of a gameplay gestalt, a re-petitive pattern of moves by which the player progresses through the individual games of a level. Hence game play usually has little if any bearing on the story being told; the story is for the most part a structure imposed on top of, and different from, game play.

The three-act restorative structure is described in detail here due to its prevalence as a model for commercial story writing in time-based media, being used by both writers and prospective funders. Dancyger and Rush [5] describe the systematic vio-lation of the model as a method for writing less familiar narratives. However, more radically different liner time-structures are possible, corresponding to weaker con-ceptions of narrative but also functioning in very different ways to narrative. Before describing these alternatives, we consider why there may be a perceived tension (eg. [1]) between narrative and game play in computer games.

4.2 Narrative and Gameplay

Given the definitions above, the question of the relationship between gameplay and narrative can now be phrased more clearly. In particular, the apprehension of an expe-rience as a narrative requires the cognitive construction of a *narrative gestalt*, a cog-nitive structure or pattern allowing the perception and understanding of an unfolding sequence of phenomena as a unified narrative. The three-act restorative structure is a narrative gestalt pattern that people understand and expect, and will often be disap-pointed if it is not satisfied (eg. if the story ends before the central conflict is resolved, or if the hero dies permanently during the story). In playing a computer game, one must learn and then perform one or more gameplay gestalts in order to progress through the tasks of the game. To experience the game as a narrative also requires the apprehension of a narrative gestalt unifying the flow of game experiences into a coherent narrative structure. The tension between gameplay and narrative can be viewed as a competition between these respective gestalt formation processes for perceptual, cognitive, and motor effort. Within the range of effort required for immersion and engagement, if gameplay consumes most of the player's available cognitive resources, there will be little scope left for perceiving complex narrative patterns (eg. we forget the motivation behind the character's battles, and what *was* the uber-villain's name again?). More than this, the narrative adds little to player immersion and engagement (who cares, it's fun anyway!). Conversely, focusing on the development of the sense of narrative (eg. in the case of multipath movies or branching hypertexts) reduces the player's need and capacity for a highly engaging gameplay gestalt.

Despite various strategies for integrating narrative and game play, at the lowest level of the dramatic structure of a game the conflict within the detail of the gameplay experience is never usually one concerning the player-character's survival, but one involving tradeoffs between the player's cognitive, emotive, and performative efforts. Is it worth trying to jump over a ravine at the risk of falling and having to reload a past game state for the sake of a health pack that may help me to get past the tough enemy ahead without then having to reload and retry when the enemy defeats me? The conflict is an ergonomic one in terms of the player performing gameplay gestalts. And this has *nothing* to do with the higher level narrative context. So the tension between gameplay and narrative is more fundamental than being a simple competition for cognitive and performative resources: the player's investment in the low level conflict as an active participant is disconnected from any deep narrative significance understood in terms of the shape of higher level narrative gestalts framing the performative experience. This explains the perceived tension between narrative and game play and suggests strategies for overcoming this tension by developing game play mechanics that are fundamentally dramatic, in that their consequences *do* affect the higher level narrative patterns of the game. While the three-act restorative structure is a useful heuristic for writers wishing to determine a high level story structure, it is too high level for effective integration with game play. For this, the basic game mechanics must when played constitute narrative action on the part of the player. This suggests a strategy for achieving narrative game play by moving away from high level predefined narrative pathways at the model and generative levels towards a more detailed integration of principles for narrative generation within the mechanics of player interaction. That is, narrative game play requires a more object-oriented approach (see [6]), in which game characters encapsulate narrative potential, and the specific narratives that emerge over time are a function of the players' history within a ludic world.

4.3 Rhetorical, Categorical, and Poetic Structure

While narrative represents a strong time structuring principle at the performance level of a game, rhetorical, categorical and poetic structures may also be incorporated, representing weaker forms that function very differently from narrative. *Rhetorical* form presents an argument and lays out evidence to support it with the aim of persuading a reader (or player) to hold a particular opinion or belief. Rhetorical design principles may function as the foundation and primary structural principle of ludic time (eg. Based upon Rhetorical Structure Theory, or RST, see http://www.sil.org/~mannb/rst/). RST models can be effectively used at the generation level as a substrate for the production of rhetorical sequences at the performance level of a ludic systems.

Categorical media productions use subjects or categories as a basis for their syntactic organization (see Lindley, 2001). Contests and tournaments, as defined above, are simple examples of categorical organizations, having categories constituted by different game types. Many computer games use a categorical structure for level design, where levels are differently themed. For example, the player of a game may begin in a wrecked spacecraft, then enter a jungle, then a system of underground caverns, then a secret laboratory, then a city, and so on, where each location sets the theme of a game level. Categorical structures can in principle be nested to any level, and ludic components can belong to any number of potentially orthogonal classification systems.

Poetic structure may be said to be structure that emphasises formal patterns above rhetorical or narrative function. These patterns help to define different written and verbal poetic styles (further examples may be found at http://www.english.uga.edu/cdesmet/class/engl4830/work/projects/brent/poetfm&na. htm and at http://fox.rollins.edu/~phelan/PoeticForm.html). In ludic systems poetic form may be manifested not only in text but also in the patterns of rhythm or flow that a game player feels in performing gameplay gestalts and moving through the game space.

Narrative, rhetorical, categorical and poetic structures are often found simultaneously within individual ludic systems. Strategies for integrating forms include the use of different forms at different levels in the hierarchical construction of temporal order; and the use of different forms at the same level of temporal scale. It is also possible to combine sequencing techniques and principles to create hybrid sequence mechanisms.

5 The Model

Much has been made of the view of games as simulations (eg. [7]). But what exactly is a simulation, such that it's different from a narrative or a game? A simulation can be defined as: *a representation of the function, operation or features of one process or system through the use of another.* For game worlds, it must be possible for the simulation model to be a model of a system or world that is a fiction or *fabrication*. This makes *model* a preferable term, since it does not need to be a model of any aspect of reality, while a simulation is more typically understood as representing some aspect of a real system.

As noted above, all computer games involve a level of modeling at which the performance space of the game is fabricated. The experience of the game for the player as a game in the strict sense, as a narrative and/or as a simulation at the performance is then a matter of the degree to which the performance is structured by the formal systems of a game or narrative. If there is little or no prestructured game or narrative form shaping the performative experience, the simulation system becomes the dominant structure informing the shape of the player's experience. The presence of game or narrative forms within the performance level tends to push the sense of the ludic system as a simulation into the background, since game play and narrative provide strong imperatives of purpose motivating player action. For a simulation, play is much more of a matter of exploring the space of possible experiences supported by the simulation, in which case teleology in the performative level is provided much more strongly by the player. Authored and prespecified time structures are then typically manifested by:

☐ discrete event modelling of temporal phenomena, such as the motions of physical objects within a 3D space subjected to modelled gravitational forces
☐ growth and decay of game world objects (eg. buildings within zones in *Sim City*)
☐ events manifesting probabilistically, such as arrivals or departures of game objects (eg. wandering monsters or enemies)
☐ functional modeling of complex systems (eg. vehicle simulators and models)

A model-based ludic system may involve *no* specific repetitive and goal-oriented activities (there may be no obvious end state, other than the player getting bored), and *no* large scale predefined patterning of the performance level. Performance level time patterns emerge over the course of running a model, can be completely different for different runs, and may never have been anticipated by the designers of the model. Repetitive action may be used to operate a model, but may not be directed to any specific final goal by the player/operator.

The extent to which a ludic system is structured and experienced predominantly as a model is reflected in the ability of players to define their own narratives, temporally structured experiences and/or games and game systems within the modeled world. In this sense a model provides a *field of play*, within which it is up to the players to define *how* they will play. Integration of more specific time structuring forms into the performance level, such as narrative and game play patterns, provides more ready-made purposes for interaction, but the model substrate of ludic systems always makes it an option for the player not to play the provided games or not to follow prestructured narratives.

6 Conclusion

This paper has presented a number of different types of possible semiotic systems that may be used to structure performative experience in ludic spaces. A high level distinction is made between the forms of the game, the model, and the linear time-structured experience. The temporal organization of games has been considered and several different systems for generating linear time-structured experience have been described. These systems, of narrative, rhetoric, categorization and poetics, may be the only organizing system for temporal experience in a given ludic system, but most systems involve more than one type of temporal semiotic organisation, and there are numerous strategies for integrating these systems.

References

1.   Aarseth E. J. Cybertext: Perspectives on Ergodic Literature, The Johns Hopkins University Press, 1997.
2.   Aarseth E., Smedstad S. M. and Sunnanå L.: A Multi-Diemnsional Typology of Games", Proceedings, Level Up Digital Games Research Conference, pp. 48 - 53, Copier M. and Raessens J. Eds., 4 – 6 November 2003, Utrecht.
3.   Bordwell D. and Thompson K. Film Art: An Introduction, 5th edn., McGraw-Hill,1997.
4.   Damer B., Gold S., Marcelo K. and Revi F.: Inhabited Virtual Worlds in Cyberspace, Virtual Worlds: Synthetic Universes, Digital Life, and Complexity, Ch. 5, Heudin J.-C. ed., 1999. 127 – 152.
5.   Dancyger K. and Rush J.: Alternative Scriptwriting, Second Edition, Focal Press, 1995.
6.   Eladhari M. Objektorienterat berättande i berättelsedrivna datorspel ("Object Oriented Story Construction in Story Driven Computer Games"), Masters Thesis, University of Stockholm, http://zerogame.interactiveinstitute.se/papers.htm. 2002.
7.   Frasca G.: Videogames of the Oppressed – Videogames as a Means for Critical Thinking and Debate, Masters Thesis, Georgia Institute of Technology, 2001.
8.   Juul J.: The Game, The Player, The World: Looking for a Heart of Gameness, Proceedings, Level Up Digital Games Research Conference, pp. 30- 45, Copier M. and Raessens J. Eds., 4 – 6 November 2003, Utrecht.
9.   Klabbers J. H. G.: The Gaming Landscape: A Taxonomy for Classifying Games and Simulations, Proceedings, Level Up Digital Games Research Conference, pp. 54 - 67, Copier M. and Raessens J. Eds., 4 – 6 November 2003, Utrecht.
10.   Kücklick J.: Literary Theory and Computer Games, Proceedings of the First Conference on Computational Semiotics for Games and New Media (COSIGN), Amsterdam, 10-12 September 2001.
11.   Lindley C. A.: Game Taxonomies: A High Level Framework for Game Analysis and Design, Gamasutra feature article, 3 October 2003, http://www.gamasutra.com/features/20031003/lindley_01.shtml.

Telling Stories with Dialogue Boxes to Retrieve Documents

Daniel Gonçalves and Joaquim Jorge

Computer Science Department, Instituto Superior Técnico, Av. Rovisco Pais
1049-001 Lisboa Portugal
djvg@gia.ist.utl.pt, jorgej@acm.org

Abstract. Nowadays, it is common for users to handle large numbers of documents. Organizing and retrieving those documents is extremely difficult using the tools commonly provided for those tasks. The use of document-describing narratives constitutes an alternate, easier way of allowing the users to do so. Narratives can help them remember important information about documents and are a natural way to convey that information to computers. In order to develop this approach, it is necessary to understand what shape do document-describing stories have. To this end we interviewed 20 users and collected 60 stories about documents. Analyzing these stories yielded a thorough characterization of their contents and structure and to extract guidelines on how to deal with them. We then validated those results by creating and evaluating two low-fidelity prototypes for possible story-capturing interfaces. We found that stories told to computers can be very similar to those told to humans, if the interface is properly designed. These results seem to suggest that structured text entry is a promising design for this interface.

1 Introduction

Computers are part of most people's everyday life. It is now common for typical users to have access to several different machines, both at home and in the workplace. Furthermore, many common tasks are now performed with the help of computers, from purchasing goods on the Internet to turning in tax forms. All this has caused most users become swamped in documents.

The usual ways to organize and retrieve documents, usually based on hierarchies, are becoming harder to use as these trends progress. Such hierarchical approaches require users to explicitly classify their documents. However, this is a problem-laden task. Two of the most common difficulties appear when a document seems not to fit any of the existing categories (and might not justify the creation of a new one by itself), or when more than one category seems to apply. The users are aware that their ability to later retrieve the document is strongly dependant on this classification, causing undue cognitive loads. In fact, once stored into the hierarchy, the documents become invisible until found again, the only clue to their whereabouts being the aforementioned classification. Thomas Malone [4] found that many users try to avoid

S. Göbel et al. (Eds.): TIDSE 2004, LNCS 3105, pp. 195–206, 2004.

classifying their documents, just storing them in undifferentiated collections (*'piles'*) and resorting to additional clues, such as their location, to find them. More recently, while looking at the usage of email tools [10], Whittaker et al witnessed that some people use those tools not just to read and send email, but overloading them with other functions for which those tools were not designed for, such as managing their agenda or storing their documents. This occurs because email messages are not hierarchically classified. Instead, they have associated to themselves all sorts of specific context-dependant information, such as the sender, date, or subject. Using this information instead of an explicit classification helps the users to find the messages or documents stored therein.

Several approaches have appeared that try to make use of additional information for document organization and retrieving. For some, time is the most relevant factor. It is the case of Lifestreams [2], in which all documents are organized on a temporal stream that can be navigated or filtered. In the Timescape system [9], the desktop displays collections of objects bound to a certain time period, and can be moved to past or future states. These approaches have the disadvantage that, by giving time a special role, they can disregard other potentially useful information.

More general are the approaches based on Gifford's Semantic File Systems [3]. In them, there are no directories or folders per se. Instead, the user faces virtual directories whose contents are the result of queries for specific values of certain properties of the files. More recent approaches that embody this idea are Dourish et al's Placeless Documents [2] and Ricardo Baeza-Yates et al's PACO [1]. These approaches, however, shift the burden from classifying the documents to the need for the user to remember the names and possible values of an arbitrary set of properties.

We argue that narratives can provide a better way to retrieve documents taking advantage of autobiographic information. In fact, humans are natural-born storytellers. We start our life listening to stories told by our parents or grand-parents, and tell them to others on a daily basis. On human-computer interaction research, it is common for storytelling to be investigated as a way for the computer to interact and convey information to a human user. Here, we explore the opposite notion, that using stories to convey information to the computer is also a useful form of interaction. In fact, stories help us to remember related pieces of information. Thus, rather than the effort required to remember unrelated properties, stories will allow the users to naturally and easily remember a wealth of information about their desired documents that can then be used by the computer to find them.

To better understand how interfaces for document retrieval using narratives can be built, we performed a study in which twenty users were asked to tell document-describing stories. Sixty such stories were collected and analyzed, allowing us to understand what story elements are more common and what structure is to be expected in such a story. From this data we were able to extract several guidelines on how narrative-based interfaces for document retrieval can be built. However, those stories were told to a human interviewer. Would stories told in a structured environment, like a computer interface, share the properties we had just found? To answer this question we used the guidelines to create two low-fidelity prototypes of possible story-based interfaces and, again, asked twenty users to tell their stories, but this time using the prototypes. Both resorted to dialogue boxes for the introduction of the several story elements, and one represented the story as a set of graphically separate elements, while the other was based on structured text entry. For several reasons we chose not to consider an interface allowing unrestrained natural language interaction with a software agent. First, it would be hard to simulate such an interface on a low-fidelity-prototype without falling back to telling the stories to a human. Second, given the wide range of sentences the users can utter, such an interface would have a hard time establishing meaningful dialogues, given the current state of speech recognition. Third, the document-retrieval task should be performed as efficiently and robustly as possible within the current technological constraints. Finally, we want to take advantage of the users' familiarity with existing solutions to the retrieval problem.

We found that stories told to computers can be as rich as those told to humans and share a similar structure. However, for this to happen, the interface must be designed with care.

In the following section, we describe the first part of the study, in which the stories' contents and structure were analyzed. Next, we'll show two possible approaches for capturing document-describing stories and their evaluation. Finally, we'll discuss overall results and possible future work.

2 Analyzing Stories

This part of the study aims at getting answers to two important research questions: 1) what is the expected content of document-describing stories, and 2) what structure is typical of such stories. In order to answer those questions, we conducted a set of interviews in which 20 users were asked to tell stories about their documents Given that we did not know what to expect, we chose a semi-structured interview method.

2.1 Procedure

The subjects could tell their stories in any form they chose, but the interviewer had a set of questions prepared to keep them on track if they started digressing. The interviews were recorded with subject consent. Participants were asked to tell three stories, describing three different document types: Recent Documents, created by the user up to two weeks ago; Old Documents, created by the user over six months ago; and Other Documents, which the users had read but not created. Special care was taken to find a diverse user sample. They were balanced in gender, with professions ranging from computer programmer to social sciences professor. Ages varied from 24 to 56. We also accounted for a wide range of computer expertise from casual users to nerds.

2.2 Analyzing the Interviews

All interviews were transcripted and submitted to a formal Contents Analysis [7,11]. We coded for the elements in Table 1, the only ones found during the analysis phase.

The coding was made by hand rather than automatically, which would require a dictionary of words belonging to the several elements, forcing the researcher to anticipate all possible relevant words. This is an impossible task on our study given the open nature of the users' responses. We coded for frequency rather than for occurrence to be able to understand not only what elements occur more frequently, but also if they are repeatedly in a story. Finally, we took note of whether a particular element was *spontaneous* (occurring normally in the course of a story) or *induced* (remembered by the users after some intervention from the interviewer).

Table 1. Story Elements

Time	Place	Co-Authors	Purpose
Author	Subject	Other Docs.	Personal Life
World Events	Doc.Exchanges	Doc. Type	Tasks
Storage	Versions	Contents	Events
Name			

We also conducted a Relational Analysis. A transition between two elements was considered to have occurred when they immediately followed each other in a story. No transition was recorded when the destination element was induced, since in that case no real connection between the elements existed on the user's mind. This analysis allowed us to estimate how the stories are structured.

2.3 Results

The stories usually took five minutes to be told. Their transcripts averaged two to three plain text pages, although some users told longer stories. A typical story might start like this translated excerpt from a real interview:

Interviewer: So, now that you have thought of a document, please tell me its story...
Interviewee: It's a paper I had sent to my supervisor. We had sent it to a conference some time ago. It was rejected... meanwhile I had placed the document on my UNIX account...

The data collected from the Contents and Relational Analysis was submitted to statistical tests in which the values for the different document kinds and story properties were compared. All results are statistically significant with 95% confidence. A detailed technical report describing this part of the study and its results can be found in [5].

We found stories to be 15.85 elements long, on average (st.dev.=5.97). A significant difference was found between documents created by the user and Other Documents (17.7 and 12.15, respectively). Story length seems to be independent of age, but women tell longer stories than men (16.81 vs. 14.67 elements).

Since a transition between two elements was considered only when the second one wasn't induced, comparing the number of transitions with the total elements number gives us an estimate of how spontaneous the story was. We found that 47% of stories were spontaneous, regardless of document type.

Each continuous sequence of spontaneous story elements was called a story train. The entire story is composed of several of those trains, separated by some induced element. Over 75% of the elements in a story are contained in just three different story trains: the first two, containing 50% of the story, and the last (another 25%), where a final burst of information exhausts the available data. Stories have 2.87 trains, on average, regardless of document type.

Table 2. Element frequencies and avg. percentage of induced occurrences in stories

	Element	Recent	Old	Other	Overall	Element	Recent	Old	Other	Overall
Frequency	Time	38	34	28	100	Exch.	25	18	23	66
Induced per story (avg%)		35.0	54.2	59.6	49.6		47.7	56.3	34.2	46.0
Frequency	Storage	31	27	25	83	Place	27	27	6	60
Induced per story (avg%)		47.9	43.3	40.0	43.8		65.4	60.0	22.5	49.3
Frequency	Purpose	34	32	14	80	Personal	12	13	11	36
Induced per story (avg%)		16.7	23.3	11.3	17.1		17.5	12.5	21.7	17.2
Frequency	Tasks	31	24	22	77	Version	15	16	0	31
Induced per story (avg%)		45.8	45.0	34.2	41.7		46.3	35.0	0.0	27.1
Frequency	Content	26	29	21	76	Author	4	4	15	23
Induced per story (avg%)		23.8	37.5	5.8	22.4		5.0	15.0	22.5	14.2
Frequency	Other Doc.	24	29	21	74	Name	8	5	5	18
Induced per story (avg%)		40.0	52.5	57.5	50.0		0.0	10.0	1.7	3.9
Frequency	Subject	28	17	25	70	World	8	5	2	15
Induced per story (avg%)		35.0	40.0	21.7	32.2		12.5	5.0	5.0	7.5
Frequency	Co-Author	30	33	5	68	Events	2	5	0	7
Induced per story (avg%)		55.2	66.3	10.0	43.8		2.5	7.5	0.0	3.3

2.3.1 Story Elements

The most common overall story elements were *Time, Place, Co-Author, Purpose, Subject, Other Documents, Exchanges, Type, Tasks, Storage* and *Content*. (Table 2). Some were mentioned more than once in the stories (100 occurrences of Time in 60 stories, for instance), whenever the user felt the need to clarify some information. Elements such as *Authors, Personal Events, World Events, Versions, Events,* and *Names* were the least often mentioned.

Among document types, the larger differences were found comparing documents created by the users and Other Documents, namely regarding *Co-Authors* (usually only the main author of Other Documents is remembered), *Author* (taken for granted when describing own documents), and *Version* (hard to know for documents of other authors). *Place* and *Purpose* were also different appearing to be easier to remember for documents created by the users, with which they closely interacted.

Less often induced were *Purpose, Author, Personal Events, World Events, Events* and *Name* (Table 2). With the exception of Purpose, these are the least frequent elements. Thus, they are rarely and spontaneously mentioned, suggesting that no amount of persuasion can make the users remember them. Purpose is a frequent element, showing it to be important and easy to remember. The more often induced elements are *Time, Place, Co-Author, Other Documents, Exchanges, Tasks* and *Storage*, all of which are very frequent, suggesting they are important but require external stimuli to be mentioned. Few noteworthy differences in the percentages of induced elements were found when comparing the several document types.

2.3.2 Element Transitions

We verified that some transitions do occur more frequently than others, suggesting an underlying structure. Only 36.7% of all possible transitions occurred more than once, the most common being *Time-Purpose, Tasks-Content, Subject-Time, Type-Purpose,* and *Storage-Type*, and also the reflexive transitions involving *Content, Place, Time,* and *Storage*. Normalized transition frequency values were calculated, accounting for the relative frequency of the involved elements. This was done to look for biases when infrequent elements appearing together, causing the transition not to be significant. No such bias was detected. With few exceptions, most transitions have low probabilities of occurring, enough to have some expectations but no certainties.

2.4 Discussion

There was little dependency of personal factors such as gender or age to the way in which the stories were told. *No user customization will be necessary in relation to what to expect from a story.* The interface might still need to adapt to specific needs of the users, but not regarding the stories themselves. We did find some differences among stories describing different document kinds. *It is important to determine early in the narrative what kind of document is being described, in order to correctly form expectations about what can be found ahead in the story.*

Several elements appearing in stories are induced, the result of an intervention by the researcher. Since those generally occurred as the result of the storyteller being at a loss for what to say next, it becomes evident that the listener plays an important role, by encouraging the storyteller to continue and remembering more information. *It is important to establish dialogues with users in order to obtain all information they can actually remember.* To know what the storyteller might still add to the story, the data about the frequency of the story elements and whether they were induced or not can be used. That data and the expected story structures can also be used to build expectations about the stories, help disambiguate them, and know how better to encourage the storyteller go on. Particularly relevant in this regard is the fact that events occurring during the interactions with the documents mentioned. *They appear not to be relevant in the stories.* Also important is *a model of the users and their world,* to understand some context-dependent information the usually for granted when telling the stories.

Stories are inherently ambiguous and inaccurate. The precision of the data can vary a lot. For instance, Time information ranged from specific dates and times ("last Friday at 14:00") to vague references such as "around summer last year". Also, the re-membered information is often incomplete. *Some level of ambiguity must be tolerated by narrative-based interfaces.* A particular aspect of this inaccuracy occurs when the users often remember the overall look of a document rather than specific images of phrases therein. *Some technique that identifies the overall structure or visual appearance of a document and can use that information to differentiate among several documents would be useful.*

Often, the users describe documents related to the ones they want to find, in the form of short recursive stories. *Those stories must be captured and analyzed, taking care to prevent the users from digressing from the main story.*

3   Telling Stories in Structured Environments

At this point, we have a thorough characterization of document-describing stories and a set of design guidelines for interfaces that make use of them. However, it is neces-sary to validate those findings, and verify if stories told to a computer are similar to those told to a human listener. Hence, we developed two low-fidelity prototypes that embody the guidelines above and collected new stories using those prototypes. Those stories were then compared with the ones previously collected.

3.1   The Prototypes

Prototype A (Fig. 1) is based on the sequential entry of story elements using dia-logues. The screen is divided into three different areas. In Area 1 the several dia-logues, one for each possible story element, appear. The order in which they do so reflects the structure found in the previous part of the study. A drop-down list can be used to select a different story element. In Area 2 each story element is displayed as a small box that can be edited, dragged, and deleted. That area is divided into three sections representing, from left to right, the past, present and future. It is possible to drag a story element to those areas establishing a temporal restriction.

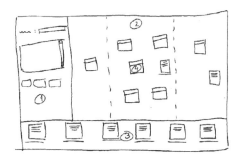

Fig. 1. Prototype A   **Fig. 2.** Prototype B

In Area 3 the interface present a list of candidate documents that, from the story told so far, could be the one sought by the user. Those documents can be dragged to the main story area if they seem somehow related with the target-document (written by the same author, at the same time, etc.).

Unlike Prototype A, Prototype B (Figure 2) represents the story in a textual manner. Instead of just presenting the dialogues to the users, it displays, on Area 2, incomplete natural-language sentences. The blanks in those sentences can be filled with the help of dialogues similar to those used in Prototype A (Area 1). For instance, the computer could present the user with the following sentence:

> **This is a document I read** `time`

At the same time, the dialogue where information about Time can be entered will be visible. If the user specifies July 2003 as the relevant time period, the sentence would change accordingly. At the same time, the next element would be requested:

> **This is a document I read** | last July |. **Its author is** `author`.

This will go on until the target-document is found. In Area 3, promising documents are shown to the user, as in Prototype A. Finally, although the order in which the several story elements are asked to the users reflects the expected story structures, they can control it with the help of the buttons labeled 4 to 6. The first one, "I don't remember", can be pressed when the user can't remember the element being asked at the time. The interface will just ask the next one. The second, "It didn't happen", is used to indicate that something being asked didn't take place (a document didn't have co-authors, for instance). The third, "I want another", shows the users a list of all possible story elements allowing them to select the element to be mentioned next.

Both these interfaces follow the guidelines found above, albeit in different manners. Time is given an important role, especially in Prototype A. Dialogues with the user are inherent to both prototypes, as is the easy access to other documents and ways to relate them to the target document. The dialogues themselves are built in a way that takes into account possible ambiguities and uncertainties. More details can be found in the technical report that describes this study [6].

3.2 Procedure

A Wizard-of-Oz methodology was used when evaluating the prototypes. Two researchers were present in all interviews. The Wizard was responsible for simulating the prototype's reactions to the users' actions. He possessed a list of sentences to be used in Prototype B, and knew the order in which the several elements were to be asked to the users. The Observer took note of the users' reactions, comments, and all other relevant information, including the order in which the story elements were told, their values, what features of the interfaces were used, and at what time.

The users were asked to tell stories about the same document kinds considered previously (Recent, Old, and Other). Afterwards, they were asked to fill in a small questionnaire, allowing us to evaluate their subjective satisfaction with the prototype.

3.3 Prototype Evaluation Results

Again, the user sample was fairly diversified, to prevent biasing the results. Ten users evaluated each of the prototypes, allowing us to collect thirty stories for each. All results are statistically significant with 95% confidence, unless otherwise stated.

Regarding story length, we found that they were, in fact, longer than the ones previously analyzed! For Prototype A they were, on average, 16% longer, regardless of document type, and those told using Prototype B were 20% longer for documents created by the users, and 35% longer for Other Documents! We attribute this increase in story length to the fact that the dialogues presented to the users help to them to remember more information, as does the story itself, visible at all times.

The elements were presented to the users in an order that directly reflected the underlying structure found in the previous study. Hence, changes in that order are a good estimate of how structure differs from stories told to humans to those told using the prototypes. We found that although 50% of the users of Prototype A chose new elements 1.23 times per story, on 43% of stories, only 10% of the users of Prototype B did so, for 3% of the stories (0.07 times per story). This is a surprising result, considering that the order in which the elements were presented to the users was the same for both prototypes. We see that the form of interaction favored by Prototype B is better suited for storytelling, better mimicking the experience of telling stories to humans. We can, thus, conclude that if the interface is build correctly, the element order found in the previous study remains valid.

We found some differences in the frequencies in which story elements were mentioned. With few exceptions (such as Tasks, found less often when using the prototypes), this is consistent with the longer stories.

Also important is the relative order of the different story elements. We divided them into two categories, for each document type: frequent and rare. In fact, it was noticeable in the occurrences of story elements in the previous study that some were mentioned very frequently, and some were rarely referred to. There is a gap of at least 20% between the two groups. We did this division for the stories told to the prototypes and compared the groups in which the story elements were placed in both story sets. With few exceptions, the relative importance of the elements remains the same. *Name* seems to become somewhat more important in Recent and Old Documents. *Personal Life* information becomes even more infrequent. For Other Documents, the differences are larger, with *Place* and *Version* given more importance.

3.3.1 Comparing the Prototypes

With the help of a questionnaire, we were able to compare the prototypes in terms of the quality of the subjective user experience they produce. The users were asked to rate a set of sentences with a value from "1-Strongly Disagree" to "4-Strongly Agree". From those ratings, we were able to infer their opinion about the prototypes. Given the low (ten) number of users of each prototype, the usual statistical significance tests could not be used. However, some values can be directly compared to provide insights into the users' subjective feelings.

Both prototypes were considered equally *satisfying, flexible,* and *complete,* in terms of the information they allow the users to mention (with averages of 3.35, 3.2, and 3.05, and standard deviations of 0.58, 0.61 and 0.82, respectively). This is unsurprising, since similar dialogues were used to collect information in both prototypes.

Although both prototypes were considered *simple* and easy to use, Prototype B was considered the simpler (3.7 vs. 3.3 with a std. dev. of 0.48 in both cases). It would seem that the textual representation of narratives is felt as more natural by the users. In terms of *novelty,* Prototype B was also the winner (3.9 vs. 3.6 with std. devs. of 0.52 and 0.32, respectively). The approach followed in Prototype A was perceived as more similar to existing solutions. Finally, with respect to *understandability,* Prototype B is, again, superior to Prototype A (3.7 vs. 3.3 with std. devs. of 0.82 and 0.48). This leads us to conclude that presenting the story using natural language sentences is less demanding, cognitively-wise, than graphically separating the story into its elements.

On Table 3 we find a summary of the usage of the main features of both interfaces. As we had already mentioned above, half the users of Prototype A chose different elements than those suggested by the interface 1.27 times per story, and for Prototype B that value is of only 0.07. This reflects the fact that Prototype A is more confusing, making it hard for users to see how certain elements fit in the stories.

The values are much more similar regarding the number of times the users just let the prototypes choose a new element for them. The decisive factor here seems to be only the users' memories, and not the prototype in use. Virtually never in both prototypes was the ability to correct an already introduced story element used. It seems that users have great confidence in what they remember. In a real system it is conceivable that, after failing to find a document, this feature could be used.

Dragging documents from the suggestion list to the main area of the interface was seldom done in Prototype A (0.4 times per story for 23% of stories). This could be due to the fact that no real documents were used. In a real usage situation, those documents could elicit better responses from the users in this aspect. Even less used was the ability to move elements to the past and future areas of the interface. In fact, this was considered to be one of the most confusing aspects of Prototype A.

Table 3. Average usage frequency of interface features (per story)

		Rec.	Old	Oth.	Over all	Stdv	%Stories	%Users
PA	**Chose**	1.40	1.30	1.10	1.27	0.15	43.33	50.00
	Moved On	2.44	2.80	5.20	3.48	1.50	76.67	80.00
	Correct Element	0.00	0.10	0.00	0.03	0.06	3.33	10.00
	Drag Document	0.60	0.40	0.20	0.40	0.20	23.33	50.00
	Drag Past/Fut.	0.27	0.18	0.18	0.21	0.05	23.33	40.00
PB	**Chose**	0.00	0.00	0.20	0.07	0.12	3.33	10.00
	Moved On	2.70	3.50	3.44	3.21	0.45	93.33	100.00
	Correct Element	0.00	0.00	0.00	0.00	0.00	0.00	0.00

3.3.2 User Comments

From the users' comments and reactions, it was possible to detect important limitations of the prototypes. First of all, although there was a dialogue for entering information about Other Documents, the users felt it was not enough. Some true support for recursive stories is required. It was also mentioned that the Personal Life Events, World Events, and Events story elements are confusing and even useless. It was hard to tell them apart, and they were often confused with other story elements. They were explicitly described as "superfluous", "unnecessary", and "useless" by some users. Some users did like them, though, as the frequency of their occurrence shows. It would seem that their usefulness is highly dependant of the user.

Many users of Prototype A complained about the order in which the story elements were suggested to them. Not even one user of Prototype B did so! We can conclude that Prototype A is not mimicking the storytelling process adequately.

Some users felt that some of the dialogues became redundant, in some situation. Overall, several suggestions were made regarding the improvement of the dialogues, a full account of which can be found in the study's technical report [6]. Notably, there were complains about the lack of better support for recursive stories about related documents, and some confusion between Purpose and Subject.

3.3.3 Discussion

The most important conclusion that this study allows us to achieve is that, indeed, *stories can be told in structured environments just like they are told to humans*. The differences are, if anything, advantageous. For instance, stories told to the prototypes were larger than those told to humans, conveying more information. Story structure remains largely unchanged, and the elements maintain their relative importance.

For this to happen, it is important to maintain the illusion of storytelling with an adequately conceived interface. Prototype B, based on text-represented stories, was clearly better suited for that task. Not only were the stories told using it longer but also the users hardly felt the need to choose different story elements just "going with the flow", as if telling a real story. This means that the elements were easier to recall in that prototype, reinforcing the conclusion that it is simpler and easier to understand.

4 Conclusions

We verified that, indeed, narratives can be a natural, efficient way for users to remember important information about their documents, and to convey it to a computer. This makes stories an important alternative to traditional document retrieving approaches which are quickly becoming ineffective given the ever growing document numbers the users must face nowadays.

After collecting sixty document-describing stories, we were able to devise a thorough characterization of those narratives, identifying not only their overall structure, but also what elements they contain, and which were more important (Time, Purpose, etc.). From this we extracted a set of user interface design guidelines.

When trying to retrieve a document, the stories will be told to a computer, and not to a human. Hence, we performed another study in which the previous findings were validated using two low-fidelity prototypes. The stories collected using them were, indeed, similar to those told to humans. We soon verified that it is important to maintain the illusion of telling a story in the users. If that illusion shatters, the stories immediately suffer in terms of quality. This explains the differences found when comparing both prototypes. Prototype A, where the different story elements were separately represented, was clearly unable to maintain that illusion, resulting in a worse user experience. Prototype B, based on structured text entry and presenting stories in a textual manner, better mimicked the experience of telling stories to human listeners. In short, it is important for the interface to be correctly designed and tested with the users' help.

The next step in our research will be to build a functional prototype based on Prototype B and improved with the help of the suggestions made by the users. This will allow us to further validate or findings, and to answer some important research questions that have yet to been addressed, regarding narrative-based document retrieval. The most important unresolved issues concern the accuracy and discriminative power of stories, so far unexplored since no real documents have been considered in our studies, allowing us to validate the stories in a real situation.

References

1. Baeza-Yates, R., Jones, T. and Rawlins, G. A New Data Model: Persistent Attribute-Centric Objects, Technical Report, University of Chile, 1996
2. Dourish, P. et al. Extending Document Management Systems with User-Specific Active Properties. ACM Transactions on Information Syst.,18(2), pp 140-170,ACM Press 2000.
3. Freeman, E. and Gelernter, D. Lifestreams: A Storage Model for Personal Data, ACM SIGMOD Record,25(1), pp 80-86, ACM Press 1996
4. Gifford, D., Jouvelot, P., Sheldon, M. and O'Toole, J. Semantic File Systems. 13th ACM Symposium on Principles of Programming Languages, October 1991.
5. Gonçalves, D. Telling Stories About Documents, Technical Report, Instituto Superior Técnico, 2003 (http://www.gia.ist.utl.pt/~djvg/phd/files/telling_stories.zip)
6. Gonçalves, D. 'Telling Stories to Computers'. Technical Report, Instituto Superior Técnico, December 2003.
   http://narrative.shorturl.com/files/telling_stories_to_computers.zip.
7. Huberman, M. & Miles, M. Analyse des données qualitatives. Recuil de nouvelles méthods.. Bruxelles, De Boeck 1991.
8. Malone, T. How do People Organize their Desks? Implications for the Design of Office Information Systems, ACM Transactions on Office Information Systems, 1(1), pp 99-112, ACM Press 1983.
9. Rekimoto, J. Time-machine computing: a time-centric approach for the information environment. In Proceedings of the 12th annual ACM symposium on User interface software and technology, pages 45-54, ACM Press, 1999.
10. Whittaker, S., Sidner, C. Email overload exploring personal information management of email. In Conference proceedings on Human factors in computing systems, pages 276-283, ACM Press, 1996.
11. Yin. R. Case Study. Design and Methods. London, Sage Publications 1989.

Mediapark:
Presenting the Media Docks Luebeck with the Digital Storytelling System *Jeherazade*

Peter Hoffmann, Tim Eggert, Lia Hadley, and Michael Herczeg

IMIS Institute for Multimedia and Interactive Systems
Willy-Brandt-Allee 31a, Media Docks
D-23554 Luebeck
http://www.imis.uni-luebeck.de
{hadley, herczeg}@imis.uni-luebeck.de
tim@froggologic.org

Abstract. This article presents the first implementation results of a storytelling system called *Jeherazade*. The *Jeherazade* system is based on the idea to enhance the classical theory of Aristotle to the new form of digital storytelling. The article describes the ideas and the results of a example implementation, *mediapark*. *Mediapark* is a presentation done for demonstration purposes. It shows the functionality of *Jeherazade* and gives an idea of its future possibilities. Included to this storytelling demonstration, *mediapark* also shows the integration of a speech and dialogue based interaction API.

1 Introduction

Digital storytelling is the latest step in the progression of presenting content in form of a narrative. Usually it follows the same well-known strategies similar to classical storytelling. The most frequently used strategy is the one which follows the course of suspense in a poetic story as Aristotle described it long ago. He dissects the story into four parts: exposition, ascension, climax, and conclusion [2, 8]. This idea worked as long as stories followed a linear construction and there was no interaction possible by the reader.

Since modern technologies offer readers the possibilities of interaction, as well as non-linear navigation (e.g. in information sites, web sites etc.), it is not easy to design stories with a classical course of suspense. Due to the fact that the readers can choose their own individual way through information sites, the author has less control on how the suspense is built and, as a result, how the readers will experience "their" story. The *Jeherazade* concept uses Aristotle's concept as a cornerstone to develop a new digital storytelling method [5].

The basic idea of *Jeherazade* is to expand the story line from linear to non-linear, or from two to at least three dimensional. So the story line becomes a story site [5, 4]. The reader is free to navigate through his story site on his own individual story paths.

S. Göbel et al. (Eds.): TIDSE 2004, LNCS 3105, pp. 207–212, 2004.

It would be ideal if the course of suspense of those individual story paths would follow the classical course. If non-linear navigation is used it is nearly impossible to guarantee an intense course of suspense. The reader has to be guided with hints and clues. This is the task of the storyteller. The storyteller makes suggestions at different decision points in the story about which way would bring about the most exciting developments in the story path (Figure 2).

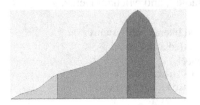

Fig. 1. Classical story line

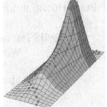

Fig. 2. Story site with a story path

2 *Jeherazade*

The *Jeherazade* system is an interactive digital storytelling system which is based on the idea that readers are story chasers [5, 4]. Analog to classical readers the story chasers experience narratives by choosing individual story paths in story sites. They adopt active roles in the narrative. They choose their individual story paths and meet characters who give them information, hints, and clues. This information allows them to interact with the story line by making decisions.

2.1 Characters and Equipment

Characters in the *Jeherazade* system have the task to present the information stored in the story site. This is the way *Jeherazade* tells the story and gives hints and clues for the forthcoming story path.

There are two kinds of characters in the *Jeherazade* system. The first one is the story chaser: this character represents the reader and is totally free to follow own individual paths through the story site. It does not present the stored information but informs the *Jeherazade* system about the story chasers actions and choices. The other kind of characters in the *Jeherazade* system are actors in the narrative: their task is to present the narrative's content. They can be personalized characters like 2D and 3D avatars as well as abstract characters like video or audio players, text or image windows and so on [5].

Equipment used in the Jeherazade system has the task of providing the interaction between the story chaser and the story site. This is the way the story chaser "tells" the story site what story path he wants to choose or what information he needs before he continues.

The equipment is also divided into two categories. The first one is the equipment which builds the environment in which the story takes place, comparable to the scene or the stage in theatre or film. The other category of equipment are interaction utilities. Presently, this kind of equipment consists of simple interaction devices (e.g. keyboard, mouse and joystick). A speech input device is also integrated into the system.

As the *Jeherazade* system has a modular software architecture, it is possible to connect new and other kinds of characters and equipment to the system easily. It is planned to integrate several kinds of sensors (e.g. light and movement) as well as an image-processing tool for the recognition of pointing gestures [7].

2.2   Grid Layers

In the *Jeherazade* system the content of the story is separated from interaction and presentation. It is possible to use the same information in several plots which are adapted to a special audience or target group. For example, the same text can be used by a comical character for children, as well as for a realistic character for grown-ups. To provide this idea of flexible usage of information, the content and the plot in the *Jeherazade* system is arranged in a grid layered architecture.

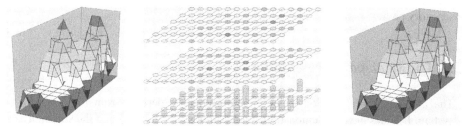

Fig. 3. Different courses of suspense for the same information site: yellow: i-grid layer; blue-red: s-grid layer (without sub-grids)

The lowermost grid layer is the i-grid layer (information grid layer). This layer contains the basic information which will be presented in the plot of the narrative and is stored in form of files of any format. Each nodal point in the grid layer can carry a different number of information files. This creates a flexible support for navigating in the depth oh information. The position of the stored information in the i-grid layer has nothing to do with any kind of physical location in an exhibition site.

The ec-grid layer (equipment & character grid layer) is arranged separately. This layer defines, which equipment and characters are available for interaction and presentation of the story's content. It only defines the default settings for each piece of equipment and character on the story site. More specified settings are designated in other grid layers.

The story plot is designed in the s-grid layers (suspense grid layers). The number of s-grid layers on a story site depends on how many different target groups exist. An s-grid layer itself consists of two sub grid layers: the s-ec-grid layer and the s-s-grid layer.

The s-ec-grid layer gives the specifications for the settings of the equipment and characters defined in the ec-grid layer to give characters and equipment their final shape (appearance) and behavior adopted to the specific target group.

Even more important is the s-s-grid layer. In this sub grid layer the suspense is specified in reference to the information and the specific target group. The information itself is neutral and offers no suspense: it is only as suspenseful as the amount of interest awakened in the target group.

2.3 Storyteller

A character's behavior and appearance, the equipment, and the various grid layers of information are used for presentation, interaction, design of the story grid site, and exploring individual story paths. To tell a real story, a core is needed in form of a storyteller. This is the task of *Jeherazade*. It gives the story chasers hints and clues where to go next to experience a suspenseful story. *Jeherazade* encourages the story chaser to follow a certain story path; it doesn't prevent the story chaser though from choosing any path e.g. by hiding options of possible ways. It only gives hints if one choice at a decision node "fits" in the course of suspense better in that particular chosen story path.

3 The *Mediapark* Presentation

The *mediapark* presentation is the first presentation derived from the *Jeherazade* system. It is designed to demonstrate *Jeherazade*'s functionality and the simplicity of implementing the concept.

Fig. 4. Comic-figure avatars, representing likeness of IMIS staff, guide through the media docks and the IMIS Institute.

The media docks, which is the home of the Institute for Multimedia and Interactive Systems (IMIS), is used as the scenery for this *Jeherazade* presentation. The story in the *mediapark* presentations introduces the reader to the Media Docks Luebeck and the Institute for Multimedia and Interactive Systems (IMIS). The story chaser follows an information trail through the "media docks" building and receives historical anti-dotes, information about its restoration, and information about present usage.

Another trail contains specific information about the Institute for Multimedia and Interactive Systems (IMIS): who works there, what research is done, which seminars are offered for the students of the University of Luebeck, etc.

3.1 Nonrealistic Rendering

The idea to use 2D comic figures as avatars was taken after several impressions of realistic rendered 3D avatars proved to be too artificial [1]. For example, motion and facial expressions of 3D avatars made it difficult to accept 3D avatars as realistic dialogue partners.

The figures of the comic TV series "Southpark" were used as archetypes for the 2D comic *mediapark* characters in the *Jeherazade* demonstration. Those figures are a good example for simplicity and effectiveness. They move, change their facial im-pressions, and talk in a manner that is easy for the reader to relate to, even though they are not natural.

3.2 Synchronous Speech Interaction

As the only "not basic" equipment and characters a speech and dialogue API was integrated into the present *Jeherazade* system. This API (SADi-J) supports both, speech input and speech output. Furthermore it manages dialogues between speakers.

The speech input part of the new developed API is used in the *Jeherazade* system as a piece of equipment. Its is comparable with the function of buttons in the GUI or mechanical sensors etc..

The SADi-J API extends the Java Speech API to a better handling of managing dialogues between two or more speakers. In the *Jeherazade* system this functionality is used for the possibility to speak longer dialogues in one story nodal point without burdening the storytelling core of *Jeherazade*. Such dialogues include the texts to be spoken, events for facial animation and commands for the character animation

The events (i.e. speech and dialogue) stay within the story renderer of *Jeherazade*. A dialogue gives the information at a story nodal point and defines the next story segment. This segment is atomic and can not be divided anymore.

4 Conclusion and Future Prospects

The *mediapark* project has two goals. The first goal of the *mediapark* demonstration was to show the feasibility of the *Jeherazade* concept. The second goal is to show the functionality of the newly developed speech and dialogue API SADi-J.

The API SADi-J extends the existing Java speech API to a dialogue managing API. The demonstration shows that SADi-J is able to handle dialogues between two and more speakers including switching the voices and emotional expressions in the voices. Even if the main focus in the development of the SADi-J API was the handling and managing the flow of speech dialogues, it also supports and integrates the functions of the Java Speech API for speech recognition. The *mediapark* demonstration showed that both sub-goals for the speech input and output were reached.

The second, even more important goal of the *mediapark* demonstration was to show the feasibility of the *Jeherazade* concept. This was accomplished by expanding the classical story line into a story site and giving the story chasers the possibility of exploring their own individual story path. Furthermore, it shows the feasibility of the *Jeherazade* software architecture. This architecture splits the story into grid layers for the information and for the plot and the technical system with the equipment, which provides the interaction, and the characters, which present the current information, and the storytelling logic.

The *Jeherazade* system and the SADi-J API will both be extended to include new options. The concept for a museum exhibition in Castle Eutin has already been completed [5, 4]. The next step is to create an extended story site which includes the grid layers introduced above.

A challenge that has to be met is how to facilitate authors in the process of story site design [5]. They need to be provided with easily accessible and comprehensible authoring tools. For more comprehensible presentations it is planned to use XMendel, a web-based semantic web tool, developed in the Institute for Multimedia and Interactive Systems at the University of Luebeck [3, 6].

References

1. Baptistao, Alceu: Making Of Kaya. http://www.vetorzero.com.br/kaya/kaya1.html. 2002
2. Fuhrmann, Manfred: Die Dichtungstheorie der Antike. ISBN: 3534054695. Wissenschaftliche Buchgesellschaft, Darmstadt. (1992)
3. Hartwig, R.; Herczeg, M.; Hadley, L.: "XMendeL - A web-based semantic Web Tool for e-Learning Production Processes" In: Proceedings to ICCE 2003, Hong Kong, ISBN: 962-949-144-3, pp. 556-56
4. Hoffmann, P.; Herczeg, M.: Distributed Storytelling for Narrative in Spacious Areas. In: TIDSE, 1st International Conference on Technologies for Interactive Digital Storytelling and Entertainment (Hrsg.). Darmstadt, 24. – 26. März 2003
5. Hoffmann, P.; Herczeg, M.: Expanding the storyline. Museums and the Web 2004. 24. – 26. June 2004 (to appear)
6. Schön, I.; Hoffmann, P.; Herczeg, M.: Changes in the Production Process for E-Learning-Systems Using the Combination of Instructional and Narrative Models. In: Proceedings of the ED-Media 2003, Honolulu, Hawaii, (2003)
7. Spierling, Ulrike, Schnaider, Michael: Info zum Anfassen - der digitale Messestand. In: ZGGDV Jahresbericht 2001, Darmstadt (2001). 57 – 58
8. Staehle, U.: Theorie des Dramas. ISBN: 3150095034. Reclam, Ditzingen (1973)

Scene-Driver: An Interactive Narrative Environment Using Content from an Animated Children's Television Series

Annika Wolff[1], Paul Mulholland[1], Zdenek Zdrahal[1], and Richard Joiner[2]

[1] Knowledge Media Institute, The Open University, Milton Keynes, MK7 6AA, UK
a.l.wolff@open.ac.uk
[2] Department of Psychology, University of Bath, Bath, BA2 7AY, UK
r.joiner@bath.ac.uk

Abstract. Narrative theories are often employed to provide coherence to collections of resources as well as in the creation of models of interactive drama. Scene-Driver is an interactive narrative system which combines these two approaches in the form of a game. The game reuses scenes from a children's animated television series called Tiny Planets. A child interacts with a Scene-Driver narrative by selecting "domino-like" tiles, the right-hand side of which dictates certain properties of the next scene to be played. Narrative coherence is maintained by ensuring that a certain ordering of scenes is adhered to, regardless of a child's choice of tile, e.g. a conflict resolution cannot be shown prior to that conflict being introduced. This ordering is based on narrative principles and analysis of the 65 episodes of Tiny Planets.

1 Introduction

Pepper's Ghost production company have produced a children's animated television series called Tiny Planets. The show tells of the adventures of two space aliens called Bing and Bong, who travel amongst a group of "tiny planets" on a large white sofa and embark on adventures with the local inhabitants of the planets. In total, there are 65 Tiny Planets episodes, each containing approximately three minutes worth of novel animated content. Animated television series incur high production costs which necessitate additional merchandising, since the costs are difficult to recoup solely through selling the series.

An option for producing this extra merchandise is to reuse the existing content from the television series to create a novel narrative. Some games based on children's television series have "viewing galleries" where children can select and view their favourite clips from the programme. However, it was our intention to extend this approach by structuring the content using narrative principles in order to provide a coherent experience. Scene-Driver was developed to enable the construction of novel narratives, using canned content in the form of scenes from a television show, whilst enabling a child to interact with and thereby influence the narrative flow. It has been developed and tested using the Tiny Planets content. Since the intended users are 5-7

S. Göbel et al. (Eds.): TIDSE 2004, LNCS 3105, pp. 213–218, 2004.
© Springer-Verlag Berlin Heidelberg 2004

year old children, a further requirement was to develop a suitably intuitive interface for use by children of these ages.

2 Potential Approaches to Interactive Narrative

Figure 1 shows the potential approaches to creating an interactive narrative using the content of the Tiny Planet's television series. Considering the "passive-generated" category, there are arguments as to why this approach is unfavourable. When developing an episode of Tiny Planets many creative decisions are made which produce dramatic effect and which can enhance the entertainment value of an episode (e.g. which camera angle to use and how to edit between shots). To formally capture knowledge at this level such that it can be used computationally is by no means a trivial task and the benefits of doing so are unclear. The child would merely be a passive observer of a novel, but potentially second-rate, episode of Tiny Planets. For this reason it would seem that the second category, in which the child interacts with the narrative as it progresses, is the more favourable approach. The current version of Scene-Driver falls into the "Active - canned" category, using the existing scenes from the series which are joined together by activities involving the child. This has enabled the development and testing of the "narrative" aspect of the model, whilst future work will move the model into the Active-Generated category by replacing the canned scenes with novel plot-level scenes.

	Content	
	Canned	Generated
Passive	TV Show	Unfavourable
Active	Scene-Driver	Future....?

Fig. 1. Potential Approaches to Creating Interactive Narrative

3 Using the Content of the Tiny Planets Television Series

The 65 episodes of Tiny Planets were analysed in order to devise a means for identifying and describing scenes in terms of narrative principles. We devised a plot description based on narrative theory and this analysis. We believe that this form of description would be applicable for describing a broad range of television series, for the purpose of implementing them within Scene-Driver. The analysis suggested that each episode could be viewed from several different levels, most notably a *plot level* and a *directorial level*.

The plot level contains elements that are commonly thought of as being integral to a narrative. Each Tiny Planets episode has a theme which tells the viewer the general purpose of the story, by way of a voice-over at the start of each episode. The theme introduction element of the plot-level is the introduction of the characters and props of the theme at some point in the episode. Within each episode there is at least one conflict which must be resolved, through a successful resolution attempt, before the story can end. However, rather than ending the episode immediately a conflict has been resolved, there are one or more "postcompletion" events.

The directorial level is the level at which events occur to provide dramatic effect, such as increasing anticipation or to provide entertainment value. The success of the directorial level, such that the enhancement of the enjoyment value of an episode is achieved, depends on the creative choices made in the edit and written into the storyboard. For this reason, the directorial level is more difficult to formalise.

The analysis of the episodes informed the design of planning algorithms to support engagement and coherence, such that the most basic narrative must follow the structure "theme-introduction -> conflict-introduction -> conflict-resolution -> postcompletion-event" to ensure coherence, with comedic elements included for entertainment value.

4 Playing Scene-Driver

As mentioned previously, it is desirable that the child is an active participant in the narrative. It is therefore necessary to implement a child-friendly interface that the child can use to respond to clips they have just seen and to exert some influence over what is shown next. In Scene-Driver, the interface is based around the idea of dominoes which, instead of the usual "dots", depict elements such as "characters" (other examples include props or actions), from the television series. The child interacts with the system by placing a tile that has a left-hand side which matches the scene they have just seen. The right-hand side of the tile specifies what will appear in the next scene. In this way, the child is able to manipulate the direction of the narrative, whilst a "scene-supervisor" module ensures that the narrative adheres to the principles of conflict introduction, resolution, comedic moments etc. The scene-supervisor also ensures coherent transition from one scene to the next by way of "transitional scenes", such that if a character that was not in a previous scene is to be in the next scene, that character is seen to "arrive". Conversely, if a character was in the previous scene and is not to be in the next, then the character must be seen to "leave". A theme (e.g. "shapes") and a "difficulty level" can be chosen prior to starting a game. This refers to the matching type, of which there are three possible options. These are described below, assuming that a character tile set has been chosen.

In a complete match game, the left-hand-side of a tile matches a scene if the characters shown on the tile were present in the scene. The right-hand-side then determines which characters are present in the next scene. In this scenario, a question arises as to whether the matching should be based on the characters that are physically present on screen in the final shot of the scene or on those characters assumed to be present (e.g a scene may finish with a close-up of a character, whilst other characters have been present right up until the close-up). We refer to these two distinct methods of matching as either implicit (matching to all characters present throughout) or explicit (matching only to characters that are present at the start and end of scenes).

In a rewrite rule game, the left and right-hand sides of the tile have a different meaning to that of the complete match game. In this game, whichever character(s) are depicted on the left-hand side of the tile are to be "voted out" and then "replaced" – in the next scene - with the character or characters on the right-hand side of the tile. Take a scene involving Bing, Bong and a "triangle local" (a "local" is a geometrically shaped character with eyes). If a tile depicting a "triangle local" on the left-hand side and a "round local" on the right-hand side is placed against that scene, this has the meaning "in the next scene, replace the triangle local with a round local". So instead of a scene involving Bing, Bong and a triangle local, there will be a scene involving Bing, Bong and a round local.

5 Scenario: Playing the Game

When starting the game, a scene is played on a "television" in the centre of the screen. In figure 2 this scene involves Bing and 3 flockers trying to push a ball up a ramp. In the top-left of the screen is an "inter" tile that are used in both the complete explicit and rewrite games for continuity and to aid the child in matching tiles to scenes. In a complete-explicit game this takes the form of a different coloured tile that matches the start and end state of the scene which has been played. In a rewrite game, it takes the form of a "cast-tile" which shows the cast that had been present within the previous scene and which characters are therefore available to be "replaced" in the next scene. At the bottom of the screen is a set of 8 available tiles. The child must choose a tile that has a left-hand side that matches the right-hand side of the tile at the top of the screen.

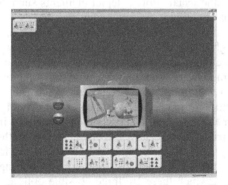

Fig. 2. Starting the game (taken from Complete Explicit)

6 Algorithm for Tile-Set Construction

Each scene in a "scene-library" is described according to an ontology. Examples of attributes used to describe the scenes are "has-characters", "has-props", "has-themes", "has-plot-level-descriptors". The first stage in tile-set construction is to create a sub-set of scenes which are consistent with the chosen theme. The theme may be intrinsic to the clip or may further reflect the theme of an episode or the theme of the particular planet the episode was set on. For example, a clip involving pushing a ball could be described by the themes "moving heavy objects", "shapes" and possibly "comedic".

The second stage is to ensure plot coherence. The simplest plot structure must have the plot elements "theme introduction" "conflict introduction" and "conflict resolution" in this order, to maintain plot coherence. More complex plot structures must still maintain this ordering, but could have additional plot elements such as "comedic events" to provide directorial consistency.

Therefore, in this stage, the sub-set of selected scenes are classified as being one of the above four plot element types. The scenes that fall into the categories "theme introduction" and "conflict introduction" are part of a "theme phase" (TP) and "conflict phase" (CP), respectively.

From the set of conflict resolutions matching the theme, one is selected to be used within this particular game (CR). This will be the successful solving of the task by the character(s) displayed if the child succeeds in creating a chain of dominoes. The rest of the set of potential conflict resolutions are discarded.

From the set of scenes in the conflict phase, the one which is the corresponding introduction of the conflict resolution chosen in the previous step (i.e. from that same episode of Tiny Planets) is selected. This will be the first scene shown in the conflict phase during any playing of the game. We refer to this scene as the conflict anchor (CA).

Of the scenes in the theme phase, one is selected as the scene to be shown before the child plays the first domino. This scene is called the theme anchor (TA). Once these have been selected all possible legal pathways between the scenes can be generated (see figure 3). Arrows show possible paths between the scenes. Some arrows are uni-directional to maintain the appropriate order in which scenes are shown, such that a child progresses from TP, through CP before reaching CR. Comedic scenes can be associated with both phases.

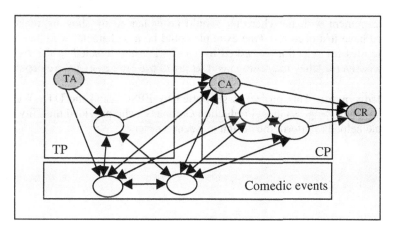

Fig. 3. Representation of the scene-subset during tile-generation

The final stage of tile-set generation is to prune this search space to eliminate tiles which would enable illegal moves during a game. Examples of illegal moves are:

- The possibility that a tile is placed in the theme-introduction phase that links only to a scene in the Conflict introduction phase other than the Conflict introduction anchor.
- The possibility that a tile can be placed which necessitates playing the conflict resolution before the conflict introduction has been played.
- The possibility that a tile can be placed in the conflict phase that links only to a scene in the Theme Phase
- A tile is available that can be placed after the conflict resolution has been played.

7 Conclusions and Future Work

Scene-Driver is a tool that enables the creation of novel narrative from existing broadcast content. It demonstrates the potential for using narrative principles in the creation of new engaging narratives, with which a child can interact as the narrative progresses. Whilst the system has been implemented with content from the Tiny Planets television series, it is anticipated that the same principles and software infrastructure could be easily applied to alternative broadcast content. A second version of Scene-Driver is under development. The main difference between the current version and the later version will be at the point of interaction. Whilst in the current version the interaction occurs at the end of a scene, the interaction for version two will occur within dynamically generated scenes. There are also possibilities for introducing variability into the presentation of remaining tiles by having different characters present the tiles in different fashions, according to principles such as novelty (e.g. if they are present at the end of a scene and have yet to present tiles within that narrative) and by different methods (e.g. producing them from a hat or bag etc.). It is anticipated that further directorial elements will be introduced into transitions. For example, emotional engagement with the characters could be enhanced by showing reactions to events that have just occurred. One example could be if a character who has just presented the tiles for selection is "asked to leave" (i.e. not depicted in the right-hand side of a chosen tile) they may shrug, as if to say "I tried my best" before departing.

Acknowledgements. This project is supported by EPSRC and the DTI. We would also like to thank Peppers Ghost Production Company, who provided the Tiny Planets content and helped to inform the design of Scene-Driver.

On Distributing Interactive Storytelling: Issues of Event Synchronization and a Solution

Stefano Ferretti, Marco Roccetti, and Stefano Cacciaguerra

Department of Computer Science, University of Bologna, Mura Anteo Zamboni 7,
40127 Bologna, Italy
{sferrett,roccetti,scacciag}@cs.unibo.it

Abstract. Interactive storytelling represents an emerging application in the field of computer entertainment that enables the dynamic creation of complex virtual stories. In some sense, Interactive Storytelling may be seen as a form of multiuser role-playing game where different evolutions of a given cyberdrama may emerge from activities performed by virtual characters, controlled either by intelligent agents or by humans. The demand for providing a distributed support to the generation of a cyberstory is converting the Web into an interactive storytelling central. Unfortunately, the classic distributed schemes employed to synchronize events on the Web introduce large delays, thus impairing the interactivity in the cyberdrama generation. To surpass this problem, we have devised a new event synchronization service to support the distributed cyberdrama generation activity. According to this proposal, events generated by distributed agents may be discarded when they become *obsolete* according to the semantics of the story. Dropping obsolete events brings to the positive result of speeding up the story generation, thus gaining interactivity while maintaining the consistency of the distributed state of the plot. Actual measurements from a deployed simulation show that our approach can implement a responsive event synchronization service for distributed interactive storytelling.

1 Introduction

Character-based interactive storytelling represents one of the emerging applications in the field of computer entertainment. These applications enable the dynamic creation of complex virtual plots which emerge from the interactions among characters. Users are able either to watch the evolution of a plot, as simple observers, or to control one or more characters by direct interventions on the story. Interactive Storytelling (IS) aims at generating a cyberdrama where human users, with the collaboration of synthetic entities (e.g. synthetic agents), are in charge of governing virtual characters. Each character has its own role and specific goals; during the plot evolution, each character performs tasks with the aim of reaching its specific targets. As each character is allowed to perform autonomous actions during the generation of the plot, the global state of the story emerges as a result of the interaction of tens, hundreds, of characters engaged in a variety of processes such as, for example, information ex-

S. Göbel et al. (Eds.): TIDSE 2004, LNCS 3105, pp. 219–231, 2004.

change, cooperation and competition for resources. An important effort has been devoted to identify relevant dimensions and major problems for the implementation of IS. There is an important debate on the roles played by narrative and interaction in the IS framework. Interaction typically requires user involvement at the detriment of the story evolution; on the other hand a strong influence of the narrative may relegate the user to a simple spectator rather than been actively involved [1]. In this sense, our interest for IS goes towards the direction of developing mechanisms for augmenting the interaction dimension. Even though we are aware that narrative plays an important role in IS, we are more attracted by the multiuser role playing game aspects of IS. In this respect, to the best of our knowledge, the most noteworthy aspect of IS is that IS prototypes are usually implemented based on a centralized scenario where synthetic agents (governing virtual characters) are hosted in the same, unique machine. To drastically alter the trajectory of the nature of these applications, our claim is that IS developers should crank out new distributed software solutions that accelerate the diffusion of this kind of multiuser role-playing games. Also reflecting the industry's momentum (take, for example the cases of Playstation2, Xbox and Game Cube), networked and distributed technologies should come into the IS picture. Indeed, IS researchers and developers should be pushed to devise new distributed solutions where the orchestration of the activities performed by users (and synthetic agents) may be deployed over a network.

In essence, several advantages may derive from such a kind of Distributed Interactive Storytelling (DIS) including, for example:

1. the possibility of enabling a large amount of dispersed users to interact with each other, also by means of a plethora of portable devices, such as laptops, cell phones, PDAs and game consoles (massive multiuser IS);
2. the possibility of maintaining a persistent state of the cyberdrama even when users disconnect to perform other activities;
3. the possibility of enabling proactive advertising/advising software mechanisms employed to invite users to play the game.

Typical solutions adopted to distribute the state of a cyberdrama may be based on the idea of resorting to a distributed architecture where several servers are geographically distributed over the network [2, 3, 4]. Following this approach, each server maintains a local, replicated representation of the state of the cyberdrama (*Cyber-Drama Servers* or *CDSs*). Users and agents, hosted in machines which are possibly different from those where their *CDS* runs, communicate to it their generated events. In turn, each *CDS* collects the events generated by its connected users, updates the cyberdrama state, and finally, notifies these updates to each other *CDS* over the network. Needless to say, sophisticated event synchronization schemes have to be adopted so as to maintain the consistency of the distributed cyberdrama state among *CDSs* [3]. To govern the problem of maintaining the consistency of the cyberdrama state, traditional event synchronization schemes may be exploited that are based on the idea of ensuring a totally ordered reconstruction of all the generated events at each *CDS*. Unfortunately, the problem with these schemes is that they typically introduce large computational and communication delays [5]. This kind of temporal overheads, plus possible network latencies, may disrupt the interactivity of DIS applications.

Instead, an important requirement for DIS systems is that of providing players with an interactive fruition of the story evolution. This requirement arises from two principal motivations: first, users expect to enjoy a life-like (or a movie-like) evolution of the plot as it is dynamically generated by a real-time interaction among DIS entities. Second, smart agents may take a full advantage of interactivity, as they may quickly react to the external stimuli generated during the plot evolution, and win for the competition for shared resources against other agents.

With this in view, we have recently proposed an approach for the design of an event delivery service which may be used to synchronize events for distributed games [3, 5]. In this paper, we show how our interactive event delivery service may be adapted to distribute IS activities over the Web. Our approach rests upon the idea of using the cyberdrama semantics to relax the request for total order (and reliability) that arises during the delivery of the generated events at each *CDS*. This allows to speed-up the interactive generation of a cyberdrama, thus ensuring an augmented interactivity among users.

In essence, our mechanism exploits two different schemes based on the notion of *obsolescence* and *correlation*. With the term of *obsolete*, we denote those events that lose their importance as time passes. The idea is that of dropping obsolete events to react to loss of interactivity during the game. Essentially, the time difference elapsing between the generation of each event and its delivery to a receiving *CDS* is measured. If this value is above a predefined interactivity time threshold, then our mechanism reacts by dropping obsolete events. Our strategy guarantees that state inconsistencies are not caused as only obsolete events are discarded to guarantee interactivity.

Further, we have devised an additional mechanism to process incoming events at each *CDS* based on the semantics of *correlation*. Summing up, the notion of correlation corresponds to the idea that only those events which are semantically correlated need to be processed according to a totally ordered scheme. Instead, non correlated events may be processed following different orders at different *CDSs*. Following this scheme, as soon as an event arrives at a given *CDS*, it may be processed without any need of synchronization with those events that result non correlated to it. Measurements taken from a deployed simulation show that our approach can implement a smooth, low latency, interactive event synchronization service for DIS systems.

The reminder of this paper is organized as follows. Section 2 presents a distributed architecture suitable for supporting DIS prototypes based on autonomous characters. In Section 3 we describe the event synchronization service we have devised. Section 4 reports on some simulation results obtained in an experimental study we developed. Finally, Section 5 concludes the paper.

2   On Distributing Interactive Storytelling

Traditional IS systems are devised to work based on a centralized scenario where all agents are hosted in a single machine. In this case, interaction among agents is a simple task as all newly generated events are instantaneously perceived by all the agents present in the cyberdrama. Prominent examples of IS are discussed in [6, 7, 8, 9, 10, 11, 12, 13] where a typical character-based architecture is described which is suitable for interactive storytelling applications as composed of several agents/characters. Agents incorporate a behavior engine representing the mind of the character that is in charge of planning a set of target actions to be accomplished in order to reach a specified goal. To take decisions, each agent uses reasoning and planning strategies; in particular, the agent builds plans based on its beliefs about the story evolution. Beliefs are obtained as an outcome of the interactions with other characters. Beliefs are essentially used to derive the preconditions to plan new target actions.

Several AI-based solutions have been proposed in the IS literature to implement agents' strategies [6, 7, 9, 11]: the most commonly adopted approach is that of representing agents' plans by using Hierarchical Task Networks, which are typically based on the use of AND/OR graphs. According to this approach, when generating plans, the agent decomposes its main goal into a set of sub-tasks; each sub-task is, in turn, dynamically refined until the finally derived sub-task represents a primitive action to be performed in the virtual scenario of the story. Simply put, a primitive action corresponds to a sort of *animation* of the character which has as final effect that of updating the global state of the cyberdrama. In essence, each performed action corresponds to an IS event leading to a modification of the global state of the cyberdrama. Possible events performed by virtual characters are, for instance, movements in the virtual world as well as specific interactions with other characters or with some resource (e.g. a character tries to pick up an object).

A well-known example representing the decomposition of a main goal into a set of primitive actions has been presented in [8]. Based on this example, two virtual characters (i.e. Ross and Rachel) are represented who interact in the virtual story. The main goal of Ross is to "*ask Rachel out*"; to this aim, the agent representing Ross decomposes the goal into a set of sub-tasks aimed at: i) acquiring general information about Rachel's preferences, and ii) talking to her. To accomplish the first sub-task (i.e. acquiring information about Rachel), Ross has several possible alternatives as, for instance, reading Rachel's diary or asking for suggestions to her friends. Suppose that among these possible alternatives Ross decides to "*read Rachel's diary*"; then, this objective may be, in turn, decomposed into the following primitive actions: "*locate the diary*", "*go to the diary*", "*pick up the diary*" and "*read the diary*". Each of these primitive actions corresponds to events which modify the state of the cyberdrama as soon as they are processed. It is worth pointing out that we will use Ross and Rachel as a basis to develop a working example that will be exploited throughout the paper to illustrate our proposal for distributing and synchronizing the activities of story generation on the Web.

With the aim of distributing the state of the story among different *CyberDrama Servers (CDSs)*, a basic solution has emerged where each *CDS* maintains a local, replicated representation of the state of the cyberdrama [2, 3, 4]. When users/agents perform primitive actions, the corresponding events are collected by the *CDS* to which those users/agents are connected. This *CDS*, in turn, updates the state of the story and, finally, initiates an event exchange activity whose final result is that of spreading the story update to each other *CDS* over the network. Sophisticated synchronization schemes have been proposed to maintain a consistent state of the plot evolution among different, interconnected *CDSs*. Obviously, this is a very critical task, as inconsistencies and different orders in the delivery of events to different *CDSs* may cause different stories for different users. Take, for example, the case when (the agent controlling) Rachel generates the event "*Rachel writes in her diary that she loves Ross*" and (the agent representing) Ross generates the event "*Ross reads Rachel's diary*". Suppose also that the character Ross runs on a *CDS* (say CDS_A) while the character Rachel runs on a different *CDS* (say CDS_B). It goes without saying that possible different stories may emerge if these two events are processed in different orders at the different *CDSs* which record the state of the plot. For example, if the event generated by Rachel is processed at CDS_A prior to the action generated by Ross (diary read), then Rachel presumably considers that Ross is aware of her love. Instead, if at CDS_B the event generated by Ross is processed prior to the action performed by Rachel then, consequently, a state of the story is recorded at CDS_B where Ross does not know that Rachel loves him.

Summing up, the delivery of the generated events among distributed *CDSs* assumes a remarkable importance during the plot generation, as state consistency must be guaranteed. Further, event delivery/processing must also take place as quickly as possible, as users expect to enjoy a plot evolution like in a real-life situation. To provide support to the event exchange activity carried out among different *CDSs*, we have devised an event synchronization delivery strategy that guarantees an "approximate" consistency of the story evolution while ensuring a high degree of interactivity.

3 Event Synchronization for Interactive Storytelling

This Section presents an event delivery service devised to support the event exchange activity among *CDSs*. In particular, we report here a simplified discussion on the formal concepts that are at the basis of our work; the interested reader may find a detailed discussion on this concept in [3].

3.1 Interactivity

As to interactivity, we observe that DIS applications may be considered as well supported only if the time difference between the generation of an event at a given *CDS* and its delivery (to other *CDSs*) is kept within a specified threshold during the story lifetime. In essence, we propose to take into account that a time threshold may exist representing the limit above which interaction among DIS entities (agents/users) is not guaranteed. We term it as *Interaction Threshold* (*IT*). It is obvious that this parameter may be tuned depending on the specific DIS application and on the required interactivity degree. We denote the *event generation time* of an event e with $T_g(e)$. We denote with $T_d^p(e)$ its *event delivery time* at a given CDS_p. Finally, we term *Time Difference* (denoted $TD_p(e)$ or simply *TD*) the difference among the event generation time of e and its event delivery time at a given CDS_p. It is easy to observe that this measure provides an estimation of the interactivity degree given by the system during the evolution of the virtual life in a cyberdrama. As a consequence, interactivity may be provided by assuring that the *TD* of the delivered events is maintained within the *IT* at each *CDS*. There is no need to say that all the time measurements expressed above need that all the clocks governing the functionality of each *CDS* are kept synchronized. We assume that all clocks in our system may be kept synchronized by resorting to some clock synchronization algorithm, such as, for example, those proposed in [14].

3.2 Correlation and Obsolescence

We have already mentioned that a totally ordered event delivery is sufficient to ensure state consistency across different *CDSs*. Unfortunately, a total-order based approach may drastically slow down the evolution of a cyberdrama, thus impairing interactivity. Based on this consideration, we propose a novel approach that allows to relax the totally ordered delivery for augmented interactivity. Our scheme rests upon the idea of exploiting the event semantics in the cyberdrama. Indeed, relevant information extracted by the plot may be used to alter the delivery order of events. Take, for example, the case of the two following events: *"go to the Central Perk café"* generated by the agent that controls Ross and *"write in the diary that Rachel loves Ross"* generated by the agent controlling Rachel. As these two events are semantically independent, they may be processed by different *CDSs* following different orders, without affecting the state consistency. The novelty here is that total order is not always necessary for consistency maintenance. Based on this consideration, we have devised a formal relationship suitable for identifying events to be processed in the same order at all the *CDSs*. We called this relationship *correlation*. In essence, an event e_1, generated by an agent A, is correlated to an event e_2 generated by B, if the execution of e_2 after e_1 drives to a different state of the story with respect to the case when e_1 is processed after e_2. In essence, the event e_1 (is correlated with the event e_2 and) has an influence on the plan of agent B. Consequently, e_1 and e_2 need to be processed in the "right" order. It is clear that different delivery orders at different *CDSs* do not cause inconsistencies if the performed actions correspond to non correlated events. Instead, executing correlated events in different orders at different *CDSs* may lead to different stories. Obviously, the management of correlated events requires a formal specification of the actual state of the story being generated (i.e., the semantics of the story). A typical approach to specify the state of the story may be that of associating state variables to the entities of a given story (e.g., characters' actions and objects). Based on this approach, for example, two events representing certain actions performed by some characters may be considered as correlated simply by verifying if they modify the value of the state variables associated to a given object. This approach has the great advantage of allowing to detect correlation dynamically during the story generation.

Obviously, an event synchronization delivery strategy must ensure that only correlated events are delivered in the same order at all the *CDSs*. Instead, the order requirement may be completely relaxed when non correlated events are delivered. We have devised an event synchronization mechanism which implements a *correlation-based* ordered processing strategy built on the top of a simplified version of the Time Warp algorithm. Simply put, all the events (both correlated and non correlated) are processed according to an *optimistic approach* at each *CDS*. This means that events are processed at a given *CDS* as soon as they are received. Then, in the case when two or more correlated events are identified that have been processed out of their correlation-based order at a given *CDS*, a rollback procedure is invoked, that is, a rollback is processed only if correlated events are identified which have been processed out-of-order. This approach has the great benefit of reducing the number of rollbacks performed at each *CDS*, thus reducing the computational overhead. It is worth pointing out that our optimistic correlation-based ordered event processing strategy is performed at each *CDS*. Final events are transmitted by each *CDS* to its connected players only when those events are no longer subject to possible rollbacks. In essence, our rollback strategy does not affect the game evolution being perceived by the players. Taking the decision if a given event is no longer prone to rollbacks is carried out by means of a synchronization mechanism described in [5].

Besides the order according to which events are processed, another important aspect to be investigated is whether events may be discarded that have lost their relevance during the plot evolution. This may be the case when "fresher" events make irrelevant "older" events. For example, knowing the position of a character at a given time may be no longer important when the position of this character changes. Essentially, events may exist in a story whose significance is restricted only to a given time interval, as their effectiveness may be annulled by subsequent events. We call these events *Timed Events* (or *TEs*). Our idea is to devise a delivery strategy that allows one to discard *TEs* when their interval of validity is expired.

Obviously, also a large amount of events exist in a cyberdrama that must be eventually delivered (at each *CDS*), independently of their delivery time. Take for example the case of Ross that generates the event *"kiss Rachel"*; it is clear that this event must be eventually delivered at all the *CDSs*, as this is a central event in the plot. We call these events *Persistent Events* (or *PEs*). Summing up, *PEs* represent important elements in the generation of the plot and account for important interactions among characters in the cyberdrama. Instead, *TEs* are events that do not constitute strong interactions. In particular, the importance of a given *TE* diminishes when a new event is generated that annuls it. We have denoted this kind of relationship among events as *obsolescence*. A possible obsolescence example is the following. Denote with e_1 the event *"move Rachel's diary to the bedroom"* and with e_2 the event *"move Rachel's diary to the living room"*; both events are generated by Rachel, and $T_g(e_1) < T_g(e_2)$. Suppose that a given *CDS* does not receive e_1 (and does not process it) but receives e_2 straight after. In this case still a consistent state is maintained at that *CDS*, since the execution of e_2 (without the execution of e_1) brings to the same final state. Essentially, e_2 has made e_1 as *obsolete*. However, it might be the case when a further event e^* (correlated to e_1), temporally interleaved between e_1 and e_2, breaks the obsolescence relationship between e_1 and e_2. As an example, consider the case when Ross is trying to pick up the diary from the bedroom ($e* =$ "*pick up the diary*") and $T_g(e_1) < T_g(e*) < T_g(e_2)$. In such a case it is obvious that no obsolescence relationship can be established between e_1 and e_2, as the correct execution of $e*$ alters the state of the plot. Based on the notion of obsolescence, we devised an approach that guarantees that only each *PE* (and each non obsolete *TE*) is reliably delivered at all the *CDSs*. Instead, in the case when a *TE* e has become obsolete due to the occurrence of further events, then our strategy ensures that either e, or the event that has made obsolete e, is delivered at each *CDS*. By exploiting this notion of obsolescence we may gain interactivity. The idea is as follows: the *TD* value is measured at the receiving *CDSs* for each delivered event. If this value exceeds *IT* at a given *CDS*, then obsolete events are automatically dropped as their execution is no longer important. Dropping obsolete events speeds up the execution of "fresh" events, thus obtaining interactivity.

```
Event e₁:                              Event e*:
 <event>                                <event>
   <issuer> Agent_A </issuer>             <issuer> Agent_B </issuer>
   <character>Rachel</character>          <character> Ross </character>
   <action>move_object</action >         <action>pick_up_obj</action>
   <object> diary </object>              <object> diary </object>
   <object> … </object>                  <object> … </object>
   <location>                            <location>
     <to> bedroom </to>                    <to> bedroom </to>
   </location>                           </location>
   <time> t₁ </time>                     <time> t* </time>
 </event>                               </event>

Event e₂:
 <event>
   <issuer> Agent_A </issuer>
   <character>Rachel</character>
   <action>move_object</action>
   <object> diary </object>
   <object> … </object>
   <location>
     <to> living_room </to>
   </location>
   <time> t₂ </time>
 </event>
```

Fig. 1. An XML-type Event Description

Representing correlation and obsolescence may be performed adopting one of the traditional methods employed in traditional IS prototypes such as a formal syntax [8, 13]. As an example, we provide in Figure 1 an XML-type definition of three possible events drawn by the story where Ross tries to pick up the Rachel's diary. From an analysis of this Figure, it is easy to understand that the use of an XML-based syntax can make easy the task of implementing relationships between characters (and their actions). Stated simply, a direct analysis of the XML fragments of Figure 1 tells that

e_2 makes e_1 as obsolete. In fact, all these events have as <object> the diary, and $T_g(e_1) = t_1 < t_2 = T_g(e_2)$. Based on the notion of state (semantics of the story) provided in Section 3.2, it is easy to understand that e_1 and $e*$ are correlated as they all perform actions on the same common <object>, the diary.

4 An Experimental Evaluation

We report on some results obtained from an experimental evaluation we conducted to assess the efficacy of our approach. In particular:

1. we evaluate the benefits derived from the use of our correlation-based event processing strategy. We measure the number of rollbacks needed to maintain the consistency of the story with correlation. Further, we contrast this value against the amount of rollbacks needed whit a traditional synchronization algorithm;
2. we assess the benefits derived from the use of our obsolescence-based delivery strategy. We measure the number of obsolete events that must be dropped at a given *CDS* to maintain the level of interaction below a predefined *IT* value (150 milliseconds).

Table 1. Ping Statistics

	Avg RTT	*Std Dev*	*Max RTT*	*Min RTT*
Bologna	15.232	9.047	74.908	5.807
Milan	192.590	112.329	478.312	24.423
Turin	27.788	10.281	96.773	13.272
Trieste	103.626	41.968	191.643	19.977

To evaluate our correlation-based event processing strategy, we simulated a distributed scenario comprised of five *CDSs*. The values of the network latencies among these five *CDSs* where drawn based on a lognormal distribution where all the parameters (average delay, delay standard deviation, minimum and maximum delay) were obtained from measurements taken by running the ping application on a *CDS* hosted in the Computer Science Laboratory of Cesena (Italy). The four Web servers exploited for experimentation were located as shown in Table 1. The values of these distribution parameters are reported in Table 1. The choice of using a lognormal distribution to model network delays at the application level was based on recent research results discussed at length in [15]. As to the frequency according to which events are generated at a given *CDS,* we took the decision of adopt a lognormal distribution with an interarrival time of subsequent events of 62 milliseconds and a standard deviation of 12 milliseconds. Also this choice was based on recent results drawn from the games literature [16]. Further, we conducted our experiments with event traces containing as many as 1000 events, where the average size of the messages representing an event was equal to 200 Bytes. This choice was motivated by the literature [16]. As to the experimentation we have carried out to assess the efficacy of the notion of correlation, we have evaluated four different scenarios, namely, *scenario₁*, *scenario₂*, *scenario₃* and *scenario₄*. In essence, within the *scenarioₓ*, the XML-based representation of each event in the trace contained exactly x <object> tags ($x=1,...,4$). Each <object> tag contained up to ten different real objects (diary, cup,...). Obviously, the larger the amount of <object> tags within an event, the larger the possibility of occurrence of correlated events. For each of these four different scenarios we conducted ten different experiments. In each experiment the probability of having the same <object> (e.g. the diary) shared between two subsequent events (correlation) was set equal to 0.1, 0.2, 0.3, 0.4, 0.5, 0.6, 0.7, 0.8, 0.9. All these four scenarios were contrasted against the execution of an event trace performed without any correlation check. The measurements taken are reported, respectively, in Figures 2, 3 and 4. The most important consideration which is common to all the three Figures is that our approach reduces the number of events subject to rollback compared to a classic optimistic approach.

In particular, Figure 2 reports the rollback ratio for each given scenario, that is the total number of rollbacks in the system divided the total number of generated events. As expected, the higher the correlation probability, the higher the rollback ratio, as only non correlated events may be processed with different orders at different *CDSs*. Further, the smaller the number of <object> tags, the lower the rollback ratio. Figure 3 reports the total number of events subject to rollback. Note that different rollbacks may be comprised of different amounts of rolled back events. It is easy to understand that the number of events subject to rollback decreases when the probability of correlation decreases. Moreover, during a rollback, a smaller number of events is typically subject to rollback if the number of <object> tags in the rolled back events decreases. In Figure 4 the average number of events subject to a single rollback is reported. Obviously, our approach brings to a reduction of the computational delay due to the containment of the number of rollbacks. This delay reduction allows an augmented interactivity degree.

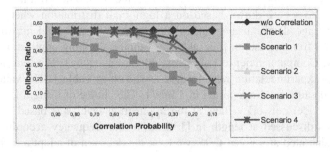

Fig. 2. Rollback Ratio

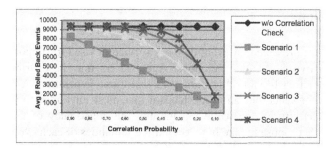

Fig. 3. Number of Rolled Back Events

A final experiment was conducted to assess the efficacy of our obsolescence-based delivery strategy. We measured how many obsolete events must be dropped to maintain the *TD* value below the *IT* value. This experiment was carried out with only two *CDSs*, as well as simulating an *IT* violation rate varying in the following range: [0%, 15%]. For example, an *IT* violation rate of 10% means that the 10% of the total number of events have a *TD* value above the *IT* value. Results are reported in Figure 5 where the amount of obsolete events is shown which are dropped to report the *TD* value below the *IT* value after a violation of the interaction threshold has been experienced.

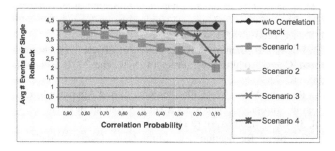

Fig. 4. Number of Re-Processed Events within a Single Event

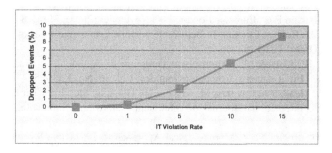

Fig. 5. Dropped Events

5 Conclusions

In this paper we presented an event delivery service devised to support the distribution of interactive storytelling activities. Agents/users may be distributed over the Web and interact each with other during a cyberdrama generation. A critical role is that of the event synchronization mechanism that must guarantee to players an acceptable interactivity degree while maintaining the consistency of the state of the cyberdrama. We propose to take into account the semantics of each event in the story. Thus, by exploiting event relationships such as, obsolescence and correlation, we may first drop obsolete events, and then, allow different processing orders at different servers. As these activities are carried out without causing inconsistencies in the replicated representation of the cyberdrama, we may safely obtain an augmented interactivity. We have reported experimental results that confirm the efficacy of our approach.

Acknowledgements. We wish to thank the Italian M.I.U.R. (Interlink) and Microsoft Research (UK) for the partial financial support to our research.

References

1. Cavazza, M., Charles F., Mead S.J.: Characters in Search of an Author: AI-based Virtual Storytelling. Proc. of First International Conference on Virtual Storytelling, LNCS 2197, Avignon, France, (2001) 145-154.
2. Cronin, E., Filstrup, B., Jamin, S., Kurc, A.R.: An Efficient Synchronization Mechanism for Mirrored Game Architectures. Proc. of NetGames2002, Braunschweig, Germany, April, (2002) 67-73.
3. Ferretti, S., Roccetti, M.: A Novel Obsolescence-Based Approach to Event Delivery Synchronization in Multiplayer Games. International Journal of Intelligent Games and Simulation, Vol. 3, No. 1, March/April (2004).
4. Griwodz, C.: State Replication for Multiplayer Games. Proc. of NetGames2002 Braunschweig, Germany, April, (2002) 29-35.
5. Ferretti, S., Roccetti, M.: The Design and Performance of a Receiver-Initiated Event Delivery Synchronization Service for Interactive Multiplayer Games. Proc. of the 4th International Conference on Intelligent Games and Simulation (Game-On 2003), Q. Mehdi, N. Gough, S. Natkin Eds., Eurosis, Londra, UK, November (2003), 211-218.
6. Bates, J.: The Role of Emotion in Believable Agents. Communications of the ACM, Vol. 37, No. 7, (1994) 122-125.
7. Blumberg, B., Galyean, T.: Multi-Level Direction of Autonomous Creatures for Real-Time Virtual Environments. Computer Graphics, Vol. 30, No. 3, (1995) 47-54.
8. Charles, F., Mead, S.J., Cavazza, M.: Generating Dynamic Storylines Through Characters' Interactions. International Journal of Intelligent Games and Simulation, Vol.1, No. 1, (2001) 5-11.
9. Grasbon, D., Braun, N.: A Morphological Approach to Interactive Storytelling. Proc. of Artificial Intelligence and Interactive Entertainment (CAST'01), S. Augustin, Germany, (2001).

10. Louchart, S., Aylett, R.: Narrative Theory and Emergent Interactive Narrative. Proc. of the 2nd International Workshop on Narrative and Interactive Learning Environments, Edinburgh, Scotland, August (2002).

11. Mateas, M.: An Oz-centric Review of Interactive Drama and Believable Agents. Technical Report CMU-Cs97-156, School of Computer Science, CMU, Pittsburg (1997).

12. Perlin, K., Goldberg, A.: Improv: A System for Scripting Interactive Actors in Virtual Worlds. Proc. of the 23rd Annual Conference on Computer Graphics (SIGGRAPH '96), New Orleans, LA, USA, August, (1996)205-215.

13. Sobral, D., Machado, I., Paiva, A.: Managing Authorship in Plot Conduction. Lecture Notes in Computer Science, Vol. 2897, O. Balet et al. Eds, Springer Verlag, (2003) 57-64.

14. Cristian, F.: Probabilistic Clock Synchronization. Distributed Computing Vol. 3, No. 3, (1989) 146-158.

15. Park, K., Willinger, W.: Self-Similar Network Traffic and Performance Evaluation. Wiley-Interscience, 1st Edition, January, (2000).

16. Farber J.: Network Game Traffic Modelling. Proc. of NetGames2002, Braunschweig, Germany, April, (2002) 53-57.

Interaction and Expressivity in Video Games: Harnessing the Rhetoric of Film

Laurent Cozic, Stephen Boyd Davis, and Huw Jones

Lansdown Centre for Electronic Arts, Middlesex University, Barnet EN4 8HT, UK
{l.cozic,s.boyd-davis,d.h.jones}@mdx.ac.uk

Abstract. The film-maker uses the camera and editing creatively, not simply to present the action of the film but also to set up a particular relation between the action and the viewer. In 3D video games with action controlled by the player, the pseudo camera is usually less creatively controlled and has less effect on the player's appreciation of and engagement with the game. This paper discusses methods of controlling games by easy and intuitive interfaces and use of an automated virtual camera to increase the appeal of games for users.

1 Introduction

The film-maker benefits from more than a hundred years' development of expressivity in the medium, using viewpoint, editing and other means to affect the way the action of the story is perceived. Video Games designers have attempted to imitate some of these devices, but several difficulties arise in trying to adapt the language of film to an interactive context. It might seem that the best solution for games is simply to show the action as simply and straightforwardly as possible; we therefore discuss the benefits that a more inventive approach potentially confers. Our interest particularly is in seeing how far the demands of interactivity and the expressive possibilities of film-making can be reconciled in a game. This work is relevant not only to video games design but also to the visual presentation of virtual environments and to the automated construction of extended CGI sequences.

Bares *et al.* [2] describe a constraint-based approach to camera planning. The camera settings are generated from a set of visual constraints on the objects of a scene in the same way a camera operator move the camera according to the constraints of the story board. Drucker and Zeltzer encapsulate camera tasks into "camera modules" that "can be used as the underlying framework for controlling the virtual camera in widely disparate type of graphical environment". [6]

He *et al.* use "idioms" to describe the behaviour of the camera for each type of scene. The rules of cinematography "are codified as hierarchical finite state machine" which "controls camera placements and shot transitions automatically". [9]

Halper *et al.* discuss the importance of having a good balance between constraint satisfaction and frame coherence in order to have "smooth transition and appropriate

S. Göbel et al. (Eds.): TIDSE 2004, LNCS 3105, pp. 232–239, 2004.
© Springer-Verlag Berlin Heidelberg 2004

cuts". They also propose a new method to deal efficiently with occlusion based on projective shadow casting algorithm. [7]

De Loor *et al.* [10] describe a virtual camera that has many features controlled by human interaction but with some drawbacks when it is set into automatic activity.

In this paper, we discuss our approach to implementing more cinematic features and 'seamless' interaction in a system for 3D video games. In section 2, we explain what we mean by expressive cinematography and outline the aspects of camerawork that have implication in game design. In section 3 we review the different type of third-person viewpoints in adventure and action games. Section 4 discusses briefly a game engine, devised to illustrate the features discussed elsewhere through creation of a prototype game, 'The Intruder', written in an OOP scripting language. We sum up in section 5.

2 Cinematographic Concepts in Games

Two aspects of camerawork in film-making have implications for the deployment of virtual cameras in a video game: the target of a given shot and the attributes of the shot such as angle and framing. The techniques discussed in this paper deal with aspects of the first and second issues, which are closely interconnected, and the extent to which practices derived from film-making may be useful in games design. We also touch on the third issue of the relationship between shots, in our discussion of camera selection.

2.1 Information and Affect

Film-making works at two levels. It provides visual (and aural) information, and it does so in such a way as to impact psychologically on the viewer. For these reasons it has been called a form of *rhetoric*, a mode which aims not just to inform but also to influence and persuade [8]. More than a hundred years of film-making have seen the development of a mature 'language' for this purpose. In the design of video games, the designer similarly needs not just to inform the player about the game events but also to afford some particular perception of them. Different games may require different approaches but a first step is the investigation of techniques which, once developed, might be customised to the requirements of particular game genres.

In the simplest model of film-making, the camera needs to be pointed at the place where the action occurs. Since actions may occur in several places, some rule needs to determine what should be shown. The depiction will often need to show the context of an action, which may be provided by adjacent shots, or it may be provided within the shot itself, for example by a medium or long shot. As described so far, the camera might be thought of as depicting a pre-existing drama. This is the position taken for example by He *et al.* [9] in devising an automated cinematography system for use with virtual environments. They aim to ensure that the significant event is always in view. This is the simple principle of what we have called the *optimal view* [3]. But the camera has a crucial role not just in presenting, but also in articulating the drama. Armes [1] remarks that the slippage between the events and the depiction has in itself significant interest for the viewer. This slippage may take the extreme form of denying viewers the view that they feel they need, a technique dating back at least to *The Birth of a Nation* [15, 12]. Or in framing a shot a viewpoint may be chosen which partly conceals the object of interest. In *Rosemary's Baby* [16], Ruth goes to use the phone in an adjoining room. Polanski uses the doorway as a frame for this action, so that Ruth's face is concealed from view – the viewer yearns (and expects) to see her expressions, but cannot. The resulting frustration leads to intense engagement with the action. Such examples suggest that there are limits to the 'optimal view' approach for virtual cinematography. Significant benefits may arise from choosing the target more subtly and framing the shot in other ways.

2.2 Shot Selection, Virtual Cinematography

All we have said up to now concerns continuous camerawork. The other aspect potentially useful to the games designer is shot selection. Whereas in film-making this is divided into two phases of activity, the capturing of action to film and the subsequent temporal organisation of that material by editing, in the live environment of the game we might think of this as a single process. It is in some ways therefore more akin to the selection of cameras in televising a live event. However both the requirements and the opportunities differ. The requirements differ for the reason already set out above: the aim is not always, as it might be in televising a football game, to choose cameras merely to achieve the 'optimal view' – the one which affords the clearest picture of the event – but also to affect how the events are perceived. The opportunities also differ, since the game designer has greater foreknowledge of what will occur under a given set of circumstances and of its significance in the development of the 'story'. Cameras can be positioned with a view to affecting the relationship between the viewer and the events.

3 Third Person Views in Video Games

Two of the most widespread third person view games are the adventure and the action game. By adventure game we mean those based on the resolution of puzzles and on an elaborated plot. The possible actions and movements of the player's avatar are in general very limited as this kind of game mostly expects reflection from the player. Typical examples include the *Resident Evil* [21] or the *Monkey Island* [20] series. Action games by contrast appeal to the player's dexterity and reflexes. The main character has many more possible movements. The plot is poor or nonexistent as it is not the main concern of the game. Typical examples include *Super Mario Sunshine* [24] or *Tomb Raider* [25]. Finally we will review the way games that mix these two genres handle the camera.

3.1 Adventure Games

Most of the camera systems of these games track the character using static cameras with a position and an orientation set during the making of the game. The main advantage of this technique is that it allows precisely describing each scene by showing the player what he is supposed to see under an angle that is coherent with the story. For example, in *Resident Evil 2* [22], the first encounter with one of the creatures is prepared by a series of carefully chosen shots that aim at creating suspense. First, as the player moves towards the place where the creature is located, a shot shows a window through which the player can see a form that appears briefly. The next shot shows the character through a window in a subjective view. The wooden window – which can visibly be easily broken – is at a few centimetres from the character; thus making it very vulnerable. The shot just before the encounter shows blood drops falling from the ceiling in the foreground. This example shows that predefined viewpoints can be used to create a dramatic impact in games without having to use cut scenes.

However it is often difficult with this technique to make views that are both functional and dramatically relevant. A viewpoint should not hinder the player's actions because, as he does not control the camera, he will not be able to choose a better one. The risk is of making the game artificially difficult by masking a hazard he should have seen. Thus, the narrow shots of *Resident Evil* [21] sometimes do not show the player the enemies that can nevertheless be very close; thus forcing the player to shoot randomly in the direction of the footsteps.

Another problem with this type of display is that it may be difficult to understand the link between successive shots. Thus in *Fear Effect 2* [17] the game cuts from shot A to shot B without any visual link between shots except for the presence of the central character. This can give the strange feeling of arriving suddenly in a completely new place although the character is still in the same room.

3.2 Action Games

The most commonly used camera in this type of game is the tracking camera. As well as the default following mode, in some systems the player can freely zoom or rotate to choose the most useful view. The level of control depends directly on the level of precision required by the game play. In *Super Mario 64* [23], the player has four buttons to control the camera, to allow precise positioning. The game can indeed require great precision to avoid obstacles or to jump from one platform to another. In comparison, only one button is used to control the camera in *The Legend of Zelda: Ocarina of Time* [18]: it resets its position so that it points in the same direction as the character.

Although giving a lot of freedom to the player, the free camera has the disadvantage of being difficult to control in narrow spaces. It tends to "knock" against the walls or to be obstructed by objects of the scene and, finally, it does not allow seeing the scene with as much efficiency as with predefined views.

Finally, as the camera is only driven by the player's movement and never by the plot or by the characters' emotions, this type of camera system only provides dramatically neutral viewpoints. Thus in *Ocarina of Time* [18], the fight between the main character and his worst enemy will be "filmed" in exactly the same way as any other common fight.

3.3 Mixing the Genres

Games that mix action and adventure generally have two alternatives: whether they use a camera system with several modes — one for each type of situation, or they leave the player complete control over the camera.

In *Ocarina of Time* [18], the player has to explore the virtual world, talk with characters and collect various objects to resolve puzzles; but to progress in the game he also has to defeat enemies using swords, bows or other weapons. These different phases of the game each use a different camera style. When the player is exploring the houses or the town, the views are predefined and cannot be changed by the player. However, when the player is on the outside world or in a castle infested with enemies, the game switches to a tracking camera. As this example shows, mixing genres can simply mean mixing the corresponding camera styles.

Another solution found in some games is to give the player complete control over the six degrees of freedom of the camera as it has been done recently in *The Legend of Zelda: The Wind Waker* [19]. This could be considered as a universal camera system as it could theoretically fit any situation. Indeed the player can always translate and rotate the camera to find the 'optimal view'. However, we think this solution should be avoided because it forces the player to consider too many parameters at the same time which can lead him to lose concentration on the game-play itself. Besides the task of controlling the camera is arguably not as entertaining as controlling the character. Steven Poole remarks that "controlling the camera should not be the player's job" [11] but it should be the developer's goal to devise a fully automated camera system.

4   The Intruder's Camera System

In this section we briefly discuss features of our camera system used by our prototype game 'The Intruder'. Greater detail of implementation will form the core of a later paper to be submitted for publication. [4]

4.1 Shot Selection

Each scene comprises several cameras with a predefined position. The game switches from one to another according to the position of the character. When the character is occluded by an object for more than a second, the system attempts to find a camera under which the character is visible. If it is visible under several cameras the system will select one under which the character is not too big or too small on screen.

Continuity is handled by positioning the camera in such a way that it is not possible to cross the line of action. Each shot is also selected so that it shares some visual features with its previous and successive shots. This helps the player to make sense of the virtual world easily.

4.2 Tracking Modes

Each camera can track a character in three different modes: #simple, #anticipate and #watcher. In the #simple mode (cf. Fig. 1.) the camera is locked on the character and re-frames without delay as soon as it moves. This view shows the player too much useless information as it uses half of the screen to show the player what he has already seen, i.e. the space behind the character.

The second mode (cf. Fig. 1.), commonly used in films, anticipates the motion of the character so there is more space in front than behind [14]. In this respect this view provides more useful information to the player than the previous mode. As the character is on the left or the right of the screen, the player's centre of interest is also more likely to be on the centre of the screen. Therefore by showing the player what he wants to see and by getting rid as much as possible of the useless information, we achieve an 'optimal view' as described previously. It is also the most playable view as it allows the player to anticipate his movements. However this view can be dramatically weak: by showing the player everything he wants to see, potential dramatic effects such as those described previously are lost. It is to deal with these issues that a last mode has been implemented.

The #watcher mode (cf. Fig. 1.) makes the camera follow the character as if seen by an external observer who cannot anticipate character movements, so adjusts the shot with a small delay. The fact that it leads to more space seen behind the character than in front can be used to support the dramatic purpose of a scene. For example we can imagine a scene where the player just heard a call for help coming from somewhere near his character. He decides to run towards this scream. Here by activating the #watcher mode, the camera will very slowly follow the character in such a way that the player will see what he is looking for only when he will be right in front of it. By playing on the contrast between the emergency of the situation and the slowness of the camera, some suspense could be achieved. This view, as its name shows, can also be used to simulate an external observer: for example a journalist followed by his cameraman. In The Intruder, which unfolds in a kind of ghost house, this view can also enhance the narrative by being used to draw the player's intention to the invisible presence that observes the character.

The different character of the latter two modes is crucial to the distinction we wish to make. The #anticipate mode provides the so called 'optimal view' – that view which provides the best information – but the #watcher mode offers the more expressive view, chosen for its rhetorical effectiveness. The more expressive view, as we have implemented it, does not conflict with the demands of usability.

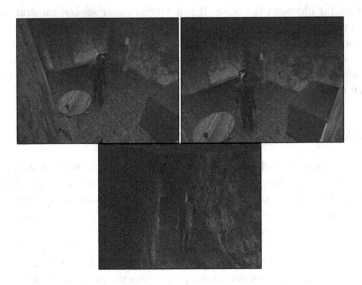

Fig. 1. Examples of shots generated by the #simple (left), #anticipate (middle) and #watcher (right) modes.

5 Conclusions

We have reviewed different ways of 'filming' a character for dramatic effect. We consider a free camera under control of the player to be dramatically poor in most circumstances, though such a system can be suitable for action games. Predefined viewpoints can be used to add more meaning to a given scene and are seen as dramatically more interesting. However, they can create usability problems because they do not always show the player what he or she wants to see. In particular in this paper, we have discussed what is needed for an autonomous virtual camera system to generate more expressive shots.

We do not believe that videogames should become an ersatz cinema. Boyd Davis and Jones say, 'it is not a matter of simply transferring existing spatial practices to the newer medium ... There is a need to rethink inherited pictorial and spatial practices to suit the demands made on the artefact. It is useful to remember ways in which digital interactive media are unlike their antecedents'. [3]

We have presented work in progress that will continue for at least a further year with the aim of producing an engine that will support games that are intuitive to play, engaging and dramatically illustrated. Davenport enunciates our aims, 'Gradually, these smart tools will gain the expertise and knowledge of their human masters, and their utility (and complexity) will increase.' [5]

References

1. Armes, R., 1994, Action and Image: dramatic structure in cinema, Manchester University Press, Manchester, UK
2. Bares, W. H., Thainimit, S., and McDermott S. A model for constraint-based camera planning. In Smart Graphics. Papers from the 2000 AAAI Spring Symposium (Stanford, March 20--22, 2000), pages 84--91, Menlo Park, 2000. AAAI Press.
3. Boyd Davis, S. and Jones, H., Screen Space: Depiction and the Space of Interactive Media, in J.A. Jorge, N.M. Correia, H. Jones and M.B. Kannegai (eds.), Multimedia 2001, Springer, Vienna, 2002, pp. 165-176.
4. Cozic, L., The Intruder: Expressive Cinematography in Videogames, Working paper, Lansdown Centre for Electronic Arts, Middlesex University, 2003.
5. Davenport, G., "Smarter Tools for Storytelling: Are They Just Around the Corner?", IEEE Multimedia, 3(1), 1996, pp. 10-14.
6. Drucker, S. M., and Zeltzer, D. CamDroid: A system for implementing intelligent camera control. In 1995 Symposium on Interactive 3D Graphics, pages 139--144, Apr. 1995.
7. Halper, N., Helbing, R., Strothotte, T., Computer games: A camera engine for computer games, Computer Graphics Forum 20 (2001)
8. Harrington, J., The Rhetoric of Film, Holt, Rinehart and Winston, New York, 1973.
9. He, L., Cohen, M. F., Salesin, D. H. The virtual cinematographer: a paradigm for automatic real-time camera control and directing, in Proceedings of SIGGRAPH 96 (August 1996), Computer Graphics Proceedings, Annual Conference Series, 217-224
10. de Loor, P., Favier, P.A., and Tisseau, J , Programming Autonomous Entities with Purposes and Trends for Virtual Storytelling, International Conference of Virtual Storytelling, Avignon, Sept 2001, pp. 40-43.
11. Poole, S., Trigger Happy, Fourth Estate, London, 2000.
12. Reisz, K., and Millar, G., The Technique of Film Editing (2 ed.), Focal Press, 1982.
13. Thompson, R., Grammar of the Edit, Focal Press, 1998.
14. Thompson, R., Grammar of the Shot, Focal Press, 1998

Computer Games and Films
15. *The Birth of a Nation*, D.W. Griffith, 1915.
16. *Rosemary's Baby*, R. Polanski, 1968.
17. *Fear Effect 2*, Kronos Digital Entertainment, 2001.
18. *The Legend of Zelda: Ocarina of Time*, Nintendo, 1998.
19. *The Legend of Zelda: The Wind Waker*, Nintendo, 2002.
20. *Monkey Island*, LucasArts, 1990.
21. *Resident Evil*, Capcom, 1996.
22. *Resident Evil 2*, Capcom, 1997.
23. *Super Mario 64*, Nintendo, 1996.
24. *Super Mario Sunshine*, Nintendo, 2002.
25. *Tomb Raider*, Core Design Ltd., 1996.

Exploring Narratives for Physical Play:
A Pop-Up Guide to an Interactive Playground

Kyle Kilbourn, Larisa Sitorus, Ken Zupan, Johnny Hey, Aurimas Gauziskas,
Marcelle Stiensta, and Martin Andresen

University of Southern Denmark, Mads Clausen Institute,
Grundtvigs Allé 150, 6400 Sønderborg, Denmark
{kyle,larisa,aurimas,ken,johnny}@itproducts.sdu.dk
marcelle@mci.sdu.dk
andra00@student.sdu.dk

Abstract. In this paper, we discuss a conceptual project in which students from the University of Southern Denmark combined the elements of physical play with interactive technology to create an 'Interactive Playbook' as a new medium for children's storytelling and play. Through the application of moving parts and computing technology in a pop-up book, we sought to simulate a playground on a smaller scale. We expect that through this technology, the notion of play can be enhanced in two ways. A narrative is introduced enabling the user to learn the games as they play. Second, the mechanics of the game allow for exploration of game possibilities that can be adopted into children's play cultures.

1 Introduction

To learn a board game by just using a paper description is a rather difficult task. Although visuals often can provide an additional layer of information, having someone present who has played the game before is a more fruitful way to learn about the rules of the game. It provides a knowledge base to start from, and – at a later stage – to adapt the rules to personal preference. When computing power is embedded inside the game board, the interactivity supported by it adds an extra layer of complexity to the game. To explain such 'enhanced' games using more conventional media such as paper guides becomes a real challenge.

In the Interactive Playbook project, students of the Mads Clausen Institute at the University of Southern Denmark explored the possibilities to create a 'play guide' that both explains games that can be played with digitally-enhanced playground equipment and allows for exploring new games. A consortium of Danish companies and research institutes developed the playground equipment, for which the play guide had to be designed [1].

S. Göbel et al. (Eds.): TIDSE 2004, LNCS 3105, pp. 240–245, 2004.

1.1 The Body Games Project

The Body Games Project is a research project funded by the Danish government that investigates the possibilities for the integration of digital technology in outside playgrounds as a method to increase interest in physical activity among children [1]. Prototypes consist of interactive soft tiles that contain LED-lights, which change color or turn on/off when stepped on. The tiles can be placed as a grid on the playground surface and support a variety of games. Both tiles and games have been developed in cooperation with children.

1.2 Communicating Physicality and Interactivity

The goal of the Interactive Playbook project was to create an engaging playbook that would spark the imagination of the players about the games one could play on such an interactive playground through explanation and exploration of possible tile-games. On a basic level there was the need to introduce and explain the game concepts that would provide the players, in our case children, with a framework for playing. As the game concepts were based on games familiar to children (e.g., 'tag'), children should be able to rely on skills they have already mastered.

Additionally, support should be given for further exploration and modification of the basic game concepts to the players' preferences. For a playbook to achieve both goals it would need to inspire children to go beyond the examples presented and come up with game concepts of their own. This way, the interactive playbook should encourage the development of a child's play culture as it supports both the acquisition of skills and further exploration of gaming possibilities [2].

1.3 Creating an Interactive Playbook

In this paper we will explore the use of storytelling in interactive media and its relationship to playing physical games. Others have shown the power of stories to explain tacit (or physical) knowledge by triggering preexisting knowledge [3]. Working with narratives became an important aspect to this project as we investigated the nature and qualities of media in which to present game concepts. Our design for an interactive playbook combines physical mechanisms with digital components and takes the form of a pop-up book with an embedded touch-screen. After introducing the design, we will end with a reflection of the playbook as it was developed for this project.

2 How to Demonstrate a New Playground Concept?

When introducing novel play concepts that merge reality with computing technologies, there have been varying levels of success in the player's understanding of the game mechanics [4]. One problem is that the virtual game concepts do not always relate to the physical play equipment. Another danger that especially holds to implementing gaming techniques into physical playgrounds is that the novelty may wear off quickly because the possibilities are not all understood and the interactivity is seen as adding relatively little value[1]. Therefore it makes sense to be sure that the interactive game concept is well presented.

When entering the Body Games playground, the interactive tiles are a blank canvas that will be activated when stepped upon. We felt that this would be precisely the problem when players experience such a playground for the first time. When faced with a brand new playing environment, players need a strong motivation to start playing. A good narrative could act as a springboard to encourage physical action. Environmental storytelling can be the precursor of an immersive narrative experience by becoming the staging ground where narrative events are enacted [5].

3   Exploration of the Nature and Qualities of Media

Properties of an interactive environment we took into consideration were, among others: *procedural* where setting is shaped by the rules of behavior and *participatory* where environment allows the person interacting to bring out these behaviors. Together these give a sense of *agency* if a user gets the correct action from the digital artifact [6]. We explored narrative styles in traditional and new media that followed these two characteristics. The products we experienced for traditional media included instruction manuals, information graphics, comic books and pop-up books. In general paper-based media allow the reader to interact in a physical manner with the narrative. As for new media types, we played video games and interactive animations. While playing these games, we clearly understood that the rules must clearly be laid out so that users can understand them. Some approaches to instructing video game users included: *screen tips*, where time or spatially triggered pop-ups briefly appeared to guide game play, *tutorials* that required viewing before playing the game, and *character guidance* that let actors in the game get help while interacting with them.

4   Design of the Interactive Playbook

Our interactive playbook called *Adventures in Tileland*, combines physical/tangible elements with digital components to tell the story of the main character, Mudds, as he completes his journey through the imaginary world of Tileland.

---

[1] Personal communication with a playground manufacturer, 2003.

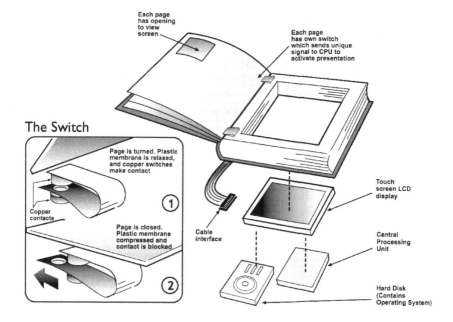

Fig. 1. Technical overview of the Interactive Playbook

4.1 The Concept

Housed in the form of a traditional book, the interactive playbook becomes a tool that oscillates between explanation and exploration. It utilizes a pop-up book and an interactive touch screen because we felt that the product had to have physicality and not be composed of just pixels on a computer screen. Pop-up books encourage movements, which might reinforce interest in physical activity considering the importance of tangibility for children, as well as the development of their motor skills.

The touch screen allows for explanatory video showing various games being played by children. A switch embedded in the page activates the movie corresponding to the game presented on the page. The movie starts when the user touches the screen. Although our prototype playbook mainly used a wizard-of-oz approach, we envision that the playbook will be based on modified existing technologies (fig. 1). The last page of the playbook is a touch screen that allows interactivity with game pieces played on a game board mimicking the tiles on the interactive playground.

4.2 The Narrative and Content Description

The story for the interactive playbook revolves around the protagonist Mudds and is set in the imaginary world of Tileland. Mudds engages with the landscape of Tileland by jumping and accomplishing various tasks as they relate to the game concepts being presented on a page. The environment taps into existing knowledge about the country of Thailand (elephants, floating market boats, food) and gives a more immersive and compelling experience than a wholly imaginary world.

The story is presented in a non-linear fashion. The first page sets the context in which the story enfolds (fig. 2). A conventional narrative describes how Mudds receives a letter from his Aunt Con and Uncle Crete proposing a visit to Tileland City. Mudds' mission is to find them. Boxes on the adjacent page open up to either a LCD screen or a picture preview of the corresponding pages. This allows readers to freely jump to different points within the book.

Fig. 2. The first two pages of the Interactive Playbook introduce the character and his history. It also shows a table of content on the right side in the form of boxes

Exploration of Mudds' adventure continues in pages that follow. The pop-up elements are used to visualize the actions described in the narrative. For example, the pulling of a paper tab activates Mudds' jumping. An LCD is integrated in the top right corner of each page spread. The screen functions as a mediator between the playbook fantasy and the real world, as it is used to present video clips of the physical interactive tiles and software games played by children.

The plot of Mudds' adventure not only captures physical actions that can be done in the playground. It also hints game strategies. Here the narrative works as a guide for children allowing them to play games exactly as presented by the playbook or inventing related games. For example, by hiding behind elephants, Mudds can stay cool while working his way through the hot days in Tileland. Sliding rotational tabs move his position. To do this readers use the slider to move Mudds behind an elephant.

To encourage self-created narratives, game pieces are provided, while the LCD acts as the contextual starting point for game creation. For instance, on the last page Mudds is introduced to a board game (fig. 3). Here players can act out stories, play games, or get more help with a tutorial.

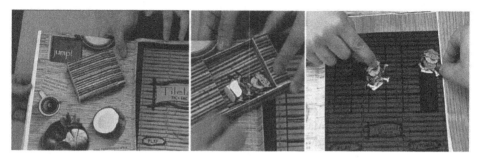

Fig. 3. The last pages of the book showing one example of a game that can be played called tic-tac-tile. Players can use the figurines to play the game on the touch screen (right)

5   Conclusion and Reflection

In this project, we investigated the physical dynamics of children's game playing and how combining computer technology and the traditional pop-up book can enhance it. Using the playground as a model, we discovered the possibilities to present game concepts and the physicality of the interactive playground through the use of moving parts and a narrative-based play guide. Through the design of the book, readers are encouraged to extend their imagination in endless scenarios and outcomes. Like the interactive outdoor playground, but on a smaller scale, readers can relate and mimic the actions of children's physical play.

Though the project is still in progress, our first impressions confirm that the combination of conventional and digital narratives supports children learning and exploring game concepts for new technology-based play environments. The next phase of the project would be to present the book to children to gather their feedback.

References

1. http://www.bodygames.dk
2. Mouritsen, F. (1998). Child Culture - Play Culture. Working Paper 2. Child and Youth Culture. Odense University, Denmark
3. Thomas, J. C. Story-based Mechanisms of Tacit Knowledge Transfer, retrieved 28 February 2004 from http://www.unite-project.org/ecscw01-tkm/papers/thomas-ecscw01.pdf.
4. Ishii, H., Orbanes, C. W. J., Chun, B., and Paradiso J. (1999). PingPongPlus: Design of an Athletic-Tangible Interface for Computer-Supported Cooperative Play. ACM Conference on Human Factors in Computing Systems (CHI 99), Pittsburgh, PA.
5. Jenkins, H. (2004). Game Design as Narrative Architecture. First Person: New Media as Story, Performance, and Game, MIT Press.
6. Murray, J. H. (1998). Hamlet On The Holodeck: The Future of Narrative in Cyberspace, MIT Press.

Beyond Manzanar:
Creating Dramatic Structure in Ergodic Narratives

Tamiko Thiel

Center for Advanced Visual Studies
Massachusetts Institute of Technology
265 Massachusetts Avenue, N52-390
Cambridge, MA, USA
tamiko@alum.mit.edu

Abstract. Interactive narrative requires new techniques in order to truly exploit the dramatic possibilities of the ergodic, first person experiential viewpoint. In the interactive 3D virtual reality installation Beyond Manzanar the author used concepts borrowed from music theory to focus dramatic development on the emotional states evoked in the user by interactions with the virtual environment. The piece explores parallels between the imprisonment of Japanese Americans at Manzanar Internment Camp in Eastern California during World War II, and Iranian Americans threatened with a similar fate during the 1979-'80 hostage crisis. Users experience the space in the perspective of the immigrant, their own movements triggering the dramatic inevitability of their own imprisonment.

1 Introduction

Beyond Manzanar is an interactive 3D virtual reality installation (finished in December 2000) by the author and her collaborator Zara Houshmand. A realist reconstruction of the Manzanar Internment Camp in California, USA, becomes a framework for surreal visions of the betrayal of the American Dream. Users experience the virtual space in the role of internees, their own explorations explicating parallels between the situation of Japanese American families interned at the camp during World War II and Iranian Americans threatened with a similar fate during the 1979-'80 Iranian Hostage Crisis. [1] The physical environment of Manzanar, strikingly similar to the landscapes of Iran, creates a poetic bridge between two groups linked by the experience of being "the face of the enemy." Imagined landscapes of Japanese and Iranian gardens explore the healing processes of memory and cultural grounding.

Beyond Manzanar uses 3D computer games technology but is exhibited as a room installation in a gallery or museum setting. Users can enter and leave at will, the piece loops continually and has no true beginning or end. We wished however to create a dramatically satisfying experience accessible even to novice users in order to reach the elderly audience of former internees. The techniques of interactive narrative that we developed for Beyond Manzanar can be applied to a wide range of artistic and educational uses of the technology in order to reach a broad general public well beyond the stereotypical "3D gamer."

Manzanar, an oasis in the high desert of Eastern California, was the first of over 10 internment camps erected during WWII to incarcerate Japanese American families

S. Göbel et al. (Eds.): TIDSE 2004, LNCS 3105, pp. 246–251, 2004.

solely on the basis of their ancestry. The US military and President Roosevelt claimed there was secret and classified evidence of "military necessity" to intern all people of Japanese descent living on the West Coast, suppressing countless military and intelligence studies that maintained the contrary, even in the face of Supreme Court challenges. [2] In 1979 during the Iranian Hostage Crisis there were physical attacks on Iranian Americans and calls to intern and deport them regardless of their personal political views "like we did to the Japanese." [3]

Beyond Manzanar is exhibited as a room installation with the image projected life-sized (3m x 4m) on a wall. It runs on WindowsXP PCs using the blaxxun Contact 5.1 VRML browser plug-in. Users navigate in first-person viewpoint through the virtual space via a simple joystick, which is easy to use even for the elderly and handicapped, and all interactivity is based on the movement and position of the user. For a more detailed descriptions of the installation please see the Beyond Manzanar website: http://mission.base.com/manzanar/.

2   Creating Dramatic Tension in Ergodic Narrative

In contrast to the first person *narrative* viewpoint of traditional media, interactive narratives use an ergodic [4] first person *experiential* viewpoint. The user is at one and the same time audience, main character (which may or may not be visible as her "avatar") and a "silent narrator" of the events that occur to her in the course of the piece. Although this may seem to be merely a new variant of Joseph Campbell's classic "hero's journey," [5] it puts a new onus on the author/designer: even if the designer creates the total framework of virtual spaces and possible experiences that the hero/user can encounter, she has very little control as to what her hero will actually do. Additionally, when the piece loops or branches its dramatic structure becomes episodic, with a concomitant flattening of the overall dramatic experience.

This requires a subtle but important shift from traditional ways of thinking about creating audience engagement. In traditional media dramatic tension is typically focused on characters in a story plot, or on the interactive challenges of gameplay. In ergodic narrative however the user is truly the hero: the most important character development happens, so to speak, in the user herself. Rather than focusing on the characters and the linear buildup and resolution of a plot, it is helpful to look at techniques derived from music theory, focusing more on the series of moods and emotional states that each scene in the piece should evoke in the user. [6]

In Beyond Manzanar, for example, each scene (or in game terminology "level") has an emotional "ground note." This could be a negative feeling, for instance of confinement and alienation, or a positive feeling, for instance of peace and security. The sequence of emotional states is carefully chosen to build dramatic tension as music composers do with the phrases and movements of a symphony, complementing or alternating emotional states, building suspense or releasing it dramatically.

In the camp scene the ground note is a lonely emptiness, underscored by sounds of ghostly footsteps and the incessant, mournful wind. In the sky, headlines and anti-Japanese signs slowly fade in and out to literally fill the air with hate and foreboding. Through the barracks windows the user sees historic photographs of the crowded and rough conditions of internee life at Manzanar, but when she enters the barracks herself, they are empty but for the murmuring of the vanished crowds.

Fig. 1. Camp Scene: Signs of Antipathy

Beyond the ghosts, however, is a Japanese room leading into a paradise garden. The internment camp disappears, the eye sweeps out over a pond, continues over trees and through a pass in the far mountains.

Fig. 2. Japanese Paradise Garden Scene

In the garden scene these mountains, which had formed such a formidable barrier in the camp scene, unite the man-made garden with the timeless beauty of the natural world. This sense of unity with nature is deceptive and temporary, a momentary dream in the dull reality of camp life. Once users begin to explore the garden, they inevitably trip a trigger that throws them out of the garden and back into camp. The mountains return to their role as a natural barrier. Users are left with the feeling of responsibility, however inadvertently, for having destroyed the dream of the garden.

This cat-and-mouse play with constraints versus freedom, the apparent ability to see or move endlessly versus a sudden blockage of view or path, play with the user's feelings of frustration or empowerment, creating a powerful tension and release cycle that add to the feeling of drama. The barbed-wire fence, for instance, is invisible from the middle of the camp it. The space is oppressive but seems unbounded. If however users try to "escape," the fence materializes in front of them. To turn the user's feeling of frustration into empathy for the internees' condition, the fence is enhanced with poems of exile written in English, Farsi (Iranian) and Japanese, some actually written by internees in the camps, some from classical Japanese and Iranian literature. The user stands at the fence, confronted with a narrative voice that underscores the visual and physical message of the fence: You too are a prisoner.

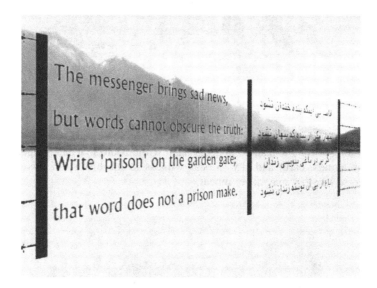

Fig. 3. Camp Scene: Rumi Fence-Poem

Sequential scenes are linked by open doors or paths that function as portals into the next scene, an intuitive clue that works even for inexperienced users. When users cross such a threshold, the portal slams shut or disappears behind them, creating a feeling of loss, entrapment and frustration – just as it did for the internees. As in real life, there is no going back. As in the Internment, even if there was no real alternative users must live with the consequences of their actions.

Although the looping structure of Beyond Manzanar provides no true beginning or ending, it still has a point of maximum tension followed by a period of quiet resolution. In the "video war" scene we play on the origins of interactive 3D technology in flight simulators developed by the US military, and its current use in computer games – and also on Iranian American fears that the American fighter jets used in the Gulf War against Iraq could also be used in some future conflict against Iran. Users are swept up out of an Iranian paradise garden by an F-15 fighter jet. Tumbling in the air, they see the garden now framed by an internment camp - and by the sights of the F-15. Rather than becoming the all-powerful gunner, however, the user has no control whatsoever: once war starts you lose control of your own destiny.

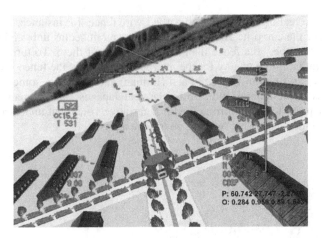

Fig. 4. Video War Scene

The F-15 finally passes, leaving users high in the air. They spiral down to earth and a poem, "Mandala for Manzanar" appears against the Manzanar landscape. It asks the mountains, winds, earth and sky to bear witness to the history of this place called Manzanar, so its story may never repeat.

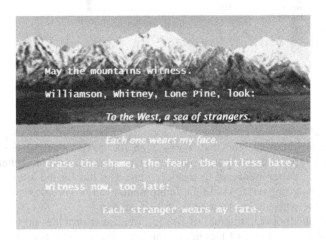

Fig. 5. Verse 1, "Mandala for Manzanar," by Zara Houshmand

Acknowledgements. Beyond Manzanar was made possible by generous support from: Gifu International Academy of the Media Arts and Sciences, Japan, Intel Corporation, blaxxun Interactive, Inc., WIRED Magazine and the Asian American Arts Foundation of San Francisco.

Parts of this text were taken from a longer paper published in the conference proceedings for COSIGN2001: Computational Semiotics for Games and New Media. That paper is online at: http://mission.base.com/manzanar/articles/cosign/cosign.html.

References

1. WWII internment of Japanese Americans:http://bss.sfsu.edu/internment/documents.html. Threats to Iranian Americans: "Carter Cracks Down: Iranian Students Face Deportation," Seattle Post Intelligencer, Nov. 11, 1979, p.A-1, and Grabowicz, Paul. "Acts Against Iranian Students Disturb Japanese-Americans," Washington Post, Nov. 23, 1979, p. A21.
2. Robinson, Greg. *By Order of the President: FDR and the Internment of Japanese Americans*, Harvard University Press, Cambridge, MA, 2001 See http://biotech.law.lsu.edu/cases/pp/korematsu_II.htm on ruling that Internment was "not justified." Also see Rep. Norman Mineta's remarks in the Congressional Record: http://bss.sfsu.edu/internment/Congressional%20Records/19850219.html#n13
3. Fogarty, John. "Hayakawa to Seek Internment of Iranians," San Francisco Chronicle, March 12, 1980, p.1. Reactions to Hayakawa's bill from the Japanese American community: Eastham,Tom. "Hayakawa's 'seize Iranians' plan attacked," San Francisco Examiner, March 12, 1980, p.?.
4. Aarseth, Espen. "Cybertext: Perspectives on Ergodic Literature," Johns Hopkins U. Press, Baltimore, 1997.
5. Campbell, Joseph. "Hero with a Thousand Faces," Princeton U. Press, 1972.
6. Meyer, Leonard. "Emotion and Meaning in Music," U.of Chicago Press, 1956.

Poetics of Voicemail:
The Tree-Structured Narrative of *BirthData*

Marlena Corcoran

Barer Strasse 54A,
80799 Munich, Germany
corcoran@anglistik.uni-muenchen.de
http://www.marlenacorcoran.com

Abstract. Voicemail is an everyday form of interactive narrative that structures my multimedia performance work, *BirthData*. This literary, theatrical work raises questions about interactivity in genres other than forms of computer gaming. It provides examples of ways to make a hierarchical logical structure more artistically complex, through a better understanding of levels of lag, and through the use of images, sounds and performative gestures that conceptually link disparate levels of the voicemail tree. In *BirthData*, the structure is the content.

1 *BirthData*: The Structure of Time

BirthData is a multimedia theater piece that I created and performed onstage in the Black Box of the Gasteig in Munich, Germany in 2001. The performance was carried live by streaming video on the website of Location One, a gallery in New York that specializes in online/offline performance.[1] *BirthData* is comprised of very short, poetic narratives dealing with birth, rebirth and resurrection. They are linked by a hypertextual structure not usually recognized as such: the voicemail tree. *BirthData* begins as if an anonymous caller, in the position of a user, had dialed the Department of Health for a copy of a birth certificate. The recording begins reasonably enough:

Welcome to the Fiction Department of the New York City Department of Health.
If you are calling about the West Nile virus, press one.
If you are calling about rodents, press two.
If you are a mobile food vendor, press three.
If you are calling about the results of a restaurant inspection, press four.
If you are calling about documents pertaining to *BirthData*, press five.
For all other inquiries, press six.

---

[1] I wrote *BirthData* in English and performed it in a German translation by Günter Zöller. It was sponsored by the Kulturreferat München. Complete credits for *BirthData* and a link to streaming video can be found on my website: www.marlenacorcoran.com.

S. Göbel et al. (Eds.): TIDSE 2004, LNCS 3105, pp. 252–257, 2004.

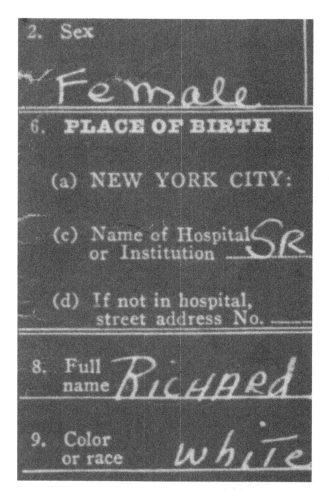

Fig. 1. Marlena Corcoran, *BirthCertificate*, 1997, Cibachrome print, 30 x 19 in. Fragmented images of a birth certificate recurred in animated video projection as the stage set of *BirthData*, as we struggled with categories we once thought were fixed, such as race, place, gender or parenthood.

It is worth noting that a voicemail tree is not merely passive, as I realized when I first called the actual Department of Health.[2] New Yorkers are a cantankerous lot, and by categorizing their most frequent questions and complaints, the designer of the real-life tree provided a snapshot of their concerns at a given moment; from the perennially popular rodents to the mayor's crackdown on street vendors selling food. These concerns were broadcast by, and not only received by, the Department of Health. A real-life voicemail tree is in fact interactive in two senses. Obviously, it immediately responds to the user's choice of button. Less obviously, the tree itself—its units and their order–will be altered in response to caller volume: how many people call in

---

[2] The voicemail tree of *BirthData*, it must be stressed, is a work of fiction.

about a given topic, or about a new topic. The levels of interactivity take place in different time frames, however: one is fast and automated, whereas the other is slow and mediated by human interpretation. This results in different degrees of lag, which might be exploited in more complex rhythms than the usual rapid-fire computer game. I decided to experiment with the genre in both form and content. For example, the final stage set of *BirthData* shifts the time frame from pre-recorded video to live, as the performer turns the video camera on herself.

Fig. 2. The interplay of person and text is a main concern of *BirthData*. The mask, worn by the performer and projected as stage set, is made of fragments of the story manuscripts. Mask by Marlena Corcoran. Photo by Peter Graf

The second level of the voicemail tree of *BirthData* directly addresses time: it asks the caller to specify the time period of the birth in question. A new voice, differing from the first in gender, age and local accent, announces: "If you were born between 1900 and 1949, press two," etc. One hears a beep, signifying that the anonymous caller has chosen a time. The next level of choices is apparently designed to direct a call to the appropriate database, depending on the circumstances in which the caller was born. The choices in *BirthData* become increasingly strange:

If you were born in a hospital or institution within the five boroughs, press one.
If you were born at home, press two.
If you were born again, press three.

If you were born in a public conveyance, on land or on sea, or on a street or waterway within the jurisdiction of the City of New York, press four.
If you were born within the jurisdiction of the Board of Correction, press five.
If you were adopted and would like information on searching our records, press six.
If you wish you had never been born, press seven.
If you were born too late, press eight.
If your birth was not reported, press nine.
If you were born under circumstances we cannot imagine, press star.
If you are sure you can somehow make us understand, press . . .
If you believe in the resurrection of the body, and the life of the world to come . . .

This list has internal narrative development, in that it begins with the expected circumstance, namely, a birth in a hospital. With a slight foreshadowing jog to the spiritual, it progresses from the accidental to the unfortunate. By number five, I would say: I may have problems, but I was not born in jail. Six is a metacategory, which comments on the structure of the database. It is informed by the experience of a friend of mine who was adopted, and tried to find his birth certificate. Apparently the records from that era were designed precisely not to help but to foil such a search. If you wish you had never been born, you should probably be calling a different department. The next three grow increasingly desperate and difficult to categorize. The list moves from past physical birth through current feelings about one's birth to, in this performance, a chorus of all the recorded voices, expressing—albeit in the conditional—our belief in a future birth: the hope of the resurrection.

2   Where's the Joystick?

I would like to address the objection that a voicemail tree is both simplistic and rigidly hierarchical: compulsory in just the sort of way we hope will be subverted by interactive narrative. To this I have two replies. One is that interactivity as it is currently promoted seems to me to obscure our awareness that our choices in such projects are limited indeed. The limitation extends to the time frame, which tends to be very short. Second, and I hope more fruitfully, I would like to suggest ways in which the voicemail tree of *BirthData* is rendered more artistically complex by complementary, sometimes contradictory, structures of sound and image.

A voicemail tree is indeed typically a two-dimensional, top-down structure: certain choices exclude others as one works one's way down into the categories. Once you're down at IV.D.i.b., you are far removed from, say II.C.ii.b. The artistic challenge is to not only allow, but foster, connections among far-flung units. To this end, imagine a Roman-numeral outline that did not keep its categories separate; that did not lie inert on the page. Imagine picking up that sheet of paper and twisting it on itself so that unit x is now right up against unit y. This structure would look less like a logical tree and more like an oak—an oak that could be twisted anew at will. This turns a two-dimensional thought structure into a three-dimensional one.

Fig. 3. Shifting images of a baptismal gown (*left*) and a birth certificate (*center*) continue the meditation on water and writing, as the performer writes with a quill pen, acting out one of many forms of record-keeping in *BirthData*. Photo by Peter Graf

This can be accomplished by artistic or poetic means. In *BirthData*, there are two main, recurring categories of images, sound and actions: 1) running water, and 2) textual composition. They link story to story and moment to moment in nonverbal structures that differ from that of the voicemail tree. Briefly: The sound of typing groups itself in our minds with the sound of the performer crumpling paper on which she has performed the act of writing. A dreamy series of almost abstract images of a crumpled baptismal gown relates to the crumpled paper, or to the sound of running water. The video animation of a child's handwritten story about a girl who disappears brings us back to the performer's projected act of handwriting, or to the first story, about a missing girl who drowned. The relentless linear narrative of a Roman-numeral outline is thus subverted by organizational structures of sight, sound and action.

3 Structure Is Content

It is intellectually and aesthetically desirable in an artwork that the navigational structure not seem alien to the work, but rather an integral part of the concept. In the case of *BirthData*, the humble voicemail tree, a structure from the practice of procuring a birth certificate in real life, provides a navigational device that is plausible, robust, and artistically flexible. It has the potential to work across genres, moving from an enacted choice onstage to a functional choice, should I construct *BirthData* as an interactive installation, as I had originally planned. In its openness to poetic reformulation, its complex responsiveness over time, and its adaptability across genres, voicemail proves to be a sophisticated case of interactivity.

Fig. 4. Marlena Corcoran, *Fisher 7*, 2001, Cibachrome print. The first story of *BirthData*, "The Real Susan," is about a young woman who drowns, and the fate of her body on Resurrection Day. Sound and image, too, establish the motif of the ocean.

Libro Vision:
Gesture-Controlled Virtual Book

Horst Hörtner, Pascal Maresch, Robert Praxmarer, and Christian Naglhofer

AEC Ars Electronica Center Linz Hauptstrasse 2
A-4040 Linz Austria
{horst.hoertner,pascal.maresch,robert.praxmarer,
christian.naglhofer}@aec.at

Abstract. LibroVision is a new way to provide access to information, one that is oriented on the metaphor of a book and engineered by means of an intuitive interaction interface. The aim of the approach described here is to utilize books to take advantage of acculturated patterns of communication for the purpose of digitally propagating information. In going about this, prime consideration has been given to the development of an intuitive and convenient system of user-computer interaction, and to the accompanying increase in efficiency with respect to understanding the content to be disseminated. To achieve this, content is presented in the form of a digital book. A video camera registers the movements of the user standing before it and translates them into navigation commands. This work is one of the focal points of the Ars Electronica Futurelab's R&D program: the evaluation, development and application of ephemeral interfaces.

1 Introduction

Over the last two decades, there have been intense efforts to conduct interaction with computers in ways that increasingly resemble patterns of interpersonal communication. Up to now, the mouse and keyboard have been the most practical devices for most applications, but they presuppose certain knowledge and skills, and thus limit the population of potential users. Touch screen user interfaces have been utilized primarily in public spaces and for interaction with the general public; they certainly do simplify matters but always require users to conform their behavior to computer technology. Developments in the field of computer vision now make it possible to completely eliminate any physical contact with hardware since a computer can be taught to "see" and "understand" the humans it encounters. This provides the basis for the development of an ephemeral interface that reacts to users' natural gestures.

One objective of this work is to show that user acceptance of a system is heightened when the technology recedes into the background. The users come to the fore as active agents; they are free and unencumbered, though they do indeed keep the invisible reins of control firmly in their hands. This feeling of immediate reaction to users' own movements and presence endows the system with a new experiential quality. The immersion of the users is enhanced since their behavior is more natural in the absence of artificial linkages to the system. The user is perceived by the system and receives immediate feedback; in this way, the system directs attention to itself. Here we see the

S. Göbel et al. (Eds.): TIDSE 2004, LNCS 3105, pp. 258–263, 2004.
© Springer-Verlag Berlin Heidelberg 2004

advantages of ephemeral interfaces—systems that intelligently react to the presence of visitors and transport them into a narrative that they recognize as the upshot of their own reality. With the possibilities of computer vision, a broad spectrum of parameters can be analyzed and incorporated to control the narrative flow.

The concrete physical manifestation of the LibroVision prototype constitutes an attempt to use the above-described interface design to implement the tried-and-true "book" metaphor in digital form as well as to create a natural and attractive mode of information retrieval that is well suited to the dissemination of information in the form of texts and images.

2 Computer Vision

Computer vision refers to the analysis of certain parameters of digital graphics files (for the most part, real-time video files). Computer vision systems usually work with filters that reduce the video signal to relevant information. For LibroVision, it is necessary to differentiate between a user's movements and motion in the background of the image in order to thus be able to translate movement within the camera's field of view into navigation commands. The key here is that the user, upon entering the camera's field of view, be able to perceive on the monitor screen a reaction that is directly associated with his/her movement. LibroVision constitutes a simple demonstration of ephemeral interaction, but our future R&D efforts will be expanded to include more complex interconnections between analytical parameters and reaction patterns of the system in order to make for more subtle and, at the same time, "truer-to-life" control of the system. The user ought to get the feeling that the type of movements he/she makes (quick/slow, expansive/restrained, etc.) engenders a commensurate reaction on the part of the system. Such a system can then be implemented for interactive and even generative storytelling

3 Virtual Books

Actually, visualizations in book form are nothing new. Such applications are often found in the context of museums and exhibitions to present especially precious artifacts or works of art. Most examples utilize commercially available software like Macromedia Director or Flash, and they typically consist of the same elements: a Macintosh platform, high-resolution digital scans, touch sensors or buttons, and, in some instances, animation sequences to simulate the turning of the pages. Virtual books are also used to direct attention to static objects that would otherwise be easily overlooked. The sense of fascination generated by the animated movements of the pages of a book has proven to be particularly effective in the process of focusing attention. The best-known examples of virtual books are those in the "Turning the Pages" project developed at the British Library in London. Historical documents were digitized and lavish 3-D animation sequences were produced for the visualization of the turning of the pages in order to provide library visitors with virtual access to the priceless originals. A number of variations of "Turning the Pages" utilizing a variety of different interfaces has since been developed. In contrast to the approach we have been pursuing, prime emphasis in "Turning the Pages" is placed on the faithful reproduction of books that actually exist. Furthermore, the terminals in the British Library are operated via touch screen.

4 LibroVision

LibroVision combines a virtual book with an ephemeral interface based on image recognition. As originally conceived, its primary area of application was the digital presentation of printed matter (the prototype was developed for presenting SAP's Innovation Report 2003); however, instead of just faithfully reproducing such documents, the graphic material would be accompanied by complementary video material and interactive elements. The initial LibroVision prototypes have ultimately shown that this platform is an appropriate one for disseminating and mediating the encounter with a broad spectrum of content. Throughout the process of development, though, attention was not focused chiefly on content but rather on intuitive interaction with the medium. Accordingly, the only functions that have been implemented are those that are self-explanatory in the context of the encounter with the installation.

The book metaphor instantly evokes on the part of users a series of impressions and patterns of behavior that have been learned through the process of dealing with real books and are also solidly rooted on a subconscious or emotional level. This begins with the book's cover. A closed book arouses curiosity. It is immediately clear

Fig. 1. User Interface

that this book contains content or information that the individual encountering it is called upon to discover. And by means of suitable labeling, these expectations can be channeled even more precisely. Whether the front or rear cover is visible indicates the direction in which the text is to be read—at least in Western cultures.

A consequence of this visualization in book form is an upgrading of the status of mere information by endowing it with an emotional quality that can bolster the process of disseminating the respective content. This emotional quality is further enhanced by the distinctiveness of the interaction. In contrast to other forms of visualization, users can virtually grasp the individual pages of the book in their hands. As absurd as it may appear, the absence of a tangible interface seems to make the connection to the virtual object considerably more real than, for example, in the case of a touch screen solution. When observing how users deal with LibroVision, we notice that many of them instinctively perform a grasping motion with their thumb and index finger although this has absolutely no impact on the interaction.

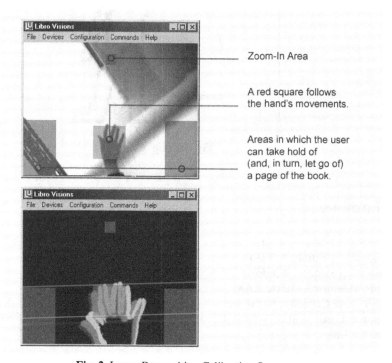

Fig. 2. Image Recognition Calibrating Screen

5 Interaction

For interaction purposes, two different modes are available. Gesturing with the hand from left to right (or vice-versa) turns the page in the virtual book. But when the user's hand slowly approaches a page, the page is registered and remains linked to the user's hand until the user moves his/her hand to the opposite page. In standard mode, the user can activate the zoom function by positioning the arrow symbol (cursor) directly on top of a button located at the top of the screen. However, this also takes place automatically when the user gets very close to the screen—thus corresponding to a natural reaction to an indication of wanting to observe something in greater detail.

6 LibroVision Setup

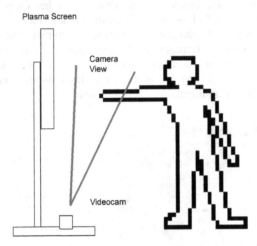

Fig. 3. Setup

7 Hardware

1 PC
Processor: Pentium 4, 3 Ghz
Operating System: Windows 2000/XP
Main Memory: 1 GByte RAM
Hard Drive Capacity: 80 GByte
Graphic Card: ASUS V9950 Ultra, 256 MB (nVidia GeForce FX5900 Ultra-Graphic Chip)

1 Camera
Philips ToUCam Pro II

1 Display
PIONEER 50'' PDP-503MXE professional plasma display

Cables
1 USB extension, 1 long cable with a 3.5 mm stereo jack plug on each end, 1 long VGA DSUB monitor cable, 1 long power cable

References

1. "Turning the Pages" – British Library. http://www.bl.uk/collections/treasures/about.html
2. Forsyth D. A, Ponce J.: Computer Vision – A Modern Approach. Prentice Hall, 2003
3. Norman D. A.: The Design Of Everyday Things. Basic Books, 1988
4. Hofmann J.: Raumwahrnehmung in virtuellen Umgebungen – Der Einfluss des Präsenzempfindens in Virtual-Reality Anwendungen für den industriellen Einsatz. Deutscher Universitäts Verlag, 2002
5. Wardrip-Fruin N., Montfort N.: The New Media Reader. MIT Press, 2003
6. Johnson S.: Interface Culture. Basic Books, 1997

DinoHunter: Platform for Mobile Edutainment Applications in Museums

Axel Feix, Stefan Göbel, and Rene Zumack

ZGDV Darmstadt e.V., Digital Storytelling Department,
64283 Darmstadt, Germany
{Axel.Feix, Stefan.Goebel, Rene.Zumack}@zgdv.de
http://www.zgdv.de/distel/

Abstract. Based on the global DinoHunter scenario this paper introduces "DinoPick" and "DinoQuiz" providing Storytelling based Edutainment applications for museums using mobile devices (PDA's). Both applications are realized as interactive learning applications enabling museum visitors such as kids or pupils to learn about the world of Dinosaurs via picking on dinosaur images or via a multiple-choice quiz game. Initially these applications have been realized as fat client applications and currently are being transmitted to thin client applications using W-LAN and the Ekahau positioning engine for locating users and streaming Open GL data of animated dinosaurs from a rendering server to clients.

1 Motivation

The global aim of DinoHunter is to develop integrated concepts for mobile edutainment applications for museums. From the technical point of view, Dino Hunter combines computer graphics technology with interactive Storytelling, user interface and user interaction concepts such as Kids Innovation or momuna (mobile museum navigator) [2],[3],[5]. Recently a set of DinoHunter applications such as "DinoSim Senckenberg" or "DinoExplorer Senckenberg" have been developed and realized for the Senckenberg museum in Frankfurt, Germany [6]. These applications provide local interactive applications placed on info terminals in front of dinosaur skeletons within the museum (DinoSim Senckenberg) or freely available for download on the museums website (DinoExplorer Senckenberg).

The next development step of the DinoHunter series provides methods and concepts to transmit these local scenarios to mobile applications in the form of rallye-like learning and quiz-games enabling users to learn about the world of dinosaurs using mobile devices, walking around in the museum and getting additional information.

S. Göbel et al. (Eds.): TIDSE 2004, LNCS 3105, pp. 264–269, 2004.

2 Mobile Scenario

The mobile scenario consists of three major components: Firstly a rendering and animation server is used as basic platform for the generation of walking dinosaurs such as T-Rex and Diplodocus for DinoSim Senckenberg. The generated Open GL data of walking data is streamed on W-LAN basis to mobile devices (PDA's) and thirdly the Ekahau positioning engine is used to locate museum visitors within dinosaur halls via access points: Hence, the position of visitors is used to stream selected data corresponding to dinosaur skeletons placed in front of the users view point.

In principle the Ekahau Positioning Engine is primarily used for indoor tracking, but could be also used within outdoor apllications. The complete architecture of the positioning server contains a PC, PDA and provides asset TAG location coordinates (x, y, floor) and tracking features to client applications. EPE includes a stand-alone Manager application for drawing the Ekahau Tracking Rails, recording site calibration data, tracking wireless devices on map, and statistically analyzing the positioning accuracy. The main advantages are usage in any W-LAN scenario, the possibility to locate over 100 devices per second (mulit-user), a pure software solution (no additional hardware needed) and the fully integration in one standalone-server. Altogether EPE guarantees ~ 1m accuracy and enables visitor tracking within both indoor and outdoor environments.

Fat Client Scenario: Wihtin the client/server architecture the fat client has all its information and application on board and performs the bulk of data processing operations. Despite of the user-tracking via Ekahau no W-LAN functionality is necessary. The main advantage is that each client is independent and doesn't need to take care about network capacity overload. Further on the used technology is much more simple. On the other hand, the main disadvantage is, that there is no change to establish collaborative environment using communication among different users/visitors of a museum. Additionally, the complexity and functionality of fat client applications is limited to the capacity and performance of PDA hardare.

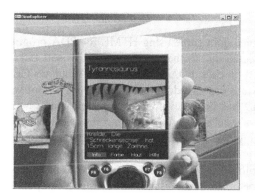 

Fig. 1. "DinoExplorer Senckenberg" and "DinoSim Senckenberg" developed for the Senckenberg museum in Frankfurt, Germany.

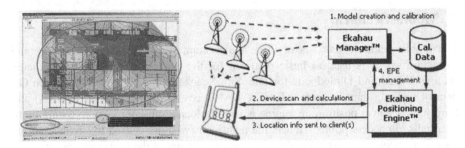

Fig. 2. Ekahau Positioning Engine – global scenario (right) and access points for computation of position of user (left).

Opposite to the fat client scenario, the thin client scenario allows complex applications shifting computation capacity to a server and streaming exclusively temporal data (results of computation) to the client. Although the term thin client usually refers to software, it is increasingly used for computers, such as network computers and net-PocketPCs that are designed to serve as the clients for client/server architectures. Thin clients could occur in the peculiarites of network PDAs or mobile phones without expensive hardware. Hereby, all these clients have the ability to receive information such as web-sites, images, movies or even 3d-animations via streaming.

From the practical point of view and with regard to possible bussiness models for museums the currently the thin client scenarion is more favorable due to limited hardware costs allowing visitors to bring their own devices such as PDA's or mobile phones.

The following section describe „DinoQuiz" and „DinoPick" as representatives of mobile museum applications in a technical manner.

3   Reference Applications

DinoQuiz is realized as multiple choice quiz game using HTML for PDA programming purposes. HTML has been selected due to the fact that the Microsoft Internet Explorer initially (default) is installed on each PDA/Pocket PC and Windows CE as operating system and no further extensions or additional installations of software have been necessary. Thus, DinoQuiz has been developed and tested within a very short development phase in a couple of weeks. Development changes or extensions of DinoQuiz are easily to integrate using WYSIWYG editors for GUI programming. Further on, various style sheets and predefined stories and story frameworks for the different user groups (kids, pupils with different ages and knowledge background or elderly people with more or less experience in the usage of "high-tech equipment") are provided by DinoQuiz enabling museum pedagogues or teachers to build their individual stories adopted to the individual and specific situation and user needs.

Fig. 3. "DinoPick" for learning about Dinosaurs via picking parts of the Triceratops with a pen (left, middle) and "DinoQuiz" (right) realized as multiple choice game on a PDA.

On the other hand DinoPick has been realized as interactive learning game using a pen as "picking device". DinoPick has been implemented with embedded Visual C++ and the Game API (GAPI) provided by Microsoft. Figure 3 shows the basic principle of DinoPick: Users can select regions of a Triceratops (skeleton) and those regions are highlighted and textured with images available in a little database.

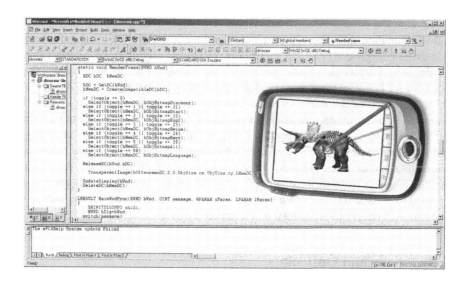

Fig. 4. Development of DinoPick using embeddedVisualStudio 3.0 and GAPI.

In addition, predefined audio sequences (voices generated with AT&T speech software) provide auditive impressions and explanations about anatomic components of the dinosaur. The DinoPick demonstrator bases on a collaboration between the Storytelling group and ZGDV Darmstadt and ATIP [4] as specialists for speech technology providing a multimodal platform.

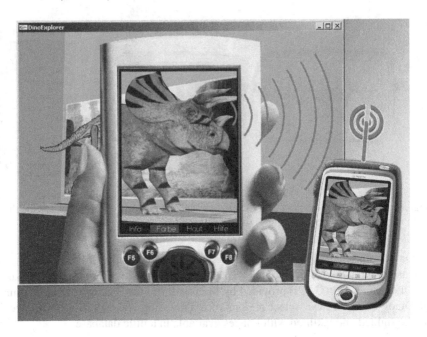

Fig. 5. "DinoMobile" streaming "DinoExplorer" OpenGL-data via W-LAN to PDA's.

Both DinoPick and DinoQuiz are configurable for different user groups (age, knowledge background, cultural metaphors, etc.) and languages (currently German and English). Further developments include the extension of the underlying knowledge base for DinoQuiz and story models enhanced by methodic didactic aspects.

The next step in the multi-spreaded DinoHunter development process is the implementation of an interactive client Interactive Client to view a reconstructed dinosaur from all sides with "flesh and skin" [1]. To archieve this goal it is necessary to establish a broadband streaming of a real-time rendered virtual dinosaur model augmented to a real dinosaur skeleton. Hence, visitors can walk around the skeleton and view the dinosaur from various point of views. The scene is rendered on a server and streamed to a PocketPC or even a modern mobile phone. This enables the user to use all shader technology implemented on the server-hardware on its own mobile device.

4   Summary and Outlook

DinoPick and DinoQuiz describe the latest applications developed within the wide range of DinoHunter scenario. Based on the local terminal application DinoSim and DinoExplorer as 3D search game in a virtual museum, both developed for the Senckenberg museum in Frankfurt, DinoPick and DinoQuiz provide methods and concepts for mobile dinosaur applications. First demonstrators for those mobile applications have been realised and successfully tested. In addition to feasibility tests, further usability tests will take place during spring and summer 2004.

Further trends of DinoHunter developments aim at collaborative scenarios for visitor groups such as families or school classes. Thus, a new genre of edutainment applications for museums combining traditional, linear museum education and (collaborative) video-games might be created in a long-term.

References

1. Bimber, O., Gatesy, S.M., Witmer, L.M., Raskar, R. and Encarnação, L.M. Merging Fossil Specimens with Computer-Generated Information. IEEE Computer Graphics (2002) 45-50
2. Feix, A., Hoffmann, A., Osswald, K., Sauer, S.: DinoHunter – Collaborative Learn Experience in Museums with Interactive Storytelling and Kids Innovation. In: Göbel, S., Braun, N., Spierling, U., Dechau, J., Diener, H. (eds.): Technologies in Interactive Digital Storytelling and Entertainment. Fraunhofer IRB Verlag, Stuttgart (2003) 388-393
3. Göbel, S., Sauer, S.: DinoHunter – Game based Learning Experience in Museums. In: Proceedings ICHIM'03, École du Louvre, Paris. CD-ROM. Archives & Museums Informatics (2003)
4. Reininger, H., ATIP Moderne Technologien zur Informationsverarbeitung GmbH. Web-Site: http://www.atip.de
5. Sauer, S., Göbel, S.: Focus your young visitors: Kids Innovation, Fundamental changes in digital edutainment. In: D. Bearman & J. Trant (eds.): Museums and the Web 2003, Selected Papers from an International Conference. Toronto: Archives and Museums Informatics (2003) 131-141
6. Sauer, S., Osswald, K., Göbel, S., Feix, A., Zumack, R.: Edutainment Environments: A Field Report on DinoHunter Technologies, Methods and Evaluation Results. In: D. Bearman & J. Trant (eds.): Museums and the Web 2004, Selected Papers from an International Conference. Toronto: Archives and Museums Informatics (2004) 165-172

An Example for Location Sensitive Media Integration: Re-discovering the Place Itself as a Medium by Adding Technology

Jens Geelhaar[1], Lars Wieneke[1], Peter Mende[2], and Jens Wille[2]

[1] Bauhaus Universität Weimar, Berkaer Strasse 11, 99423 Weimar
{jens.geelhaar, lars.wieneke}@medien.uni-weimar.de
[2] transformat, Helmholtzstrasse 15, 99423 Weimar
{p.mende, j.wille}@transformat.de

Abstract. In this paper we would like to introduce our approach towards the integration of place and media technology. It should serve as a proposal, that takes into account the significant role of the place itself as a medium and discusses the possibilities and tasks of media integration in this context. We would like to call this approach location sensitive, because in our point of view, the characteristics of distinctive locations demand for sensitive technological integration as well as sensitive selection of displayed information.

1 Introduction

Scientific research proved to be very successful in combining state of the art technology with historical sites and places [2, 3, 5, 7] Without evaluating the respective findings any further, at least two hypotheses could be drawn from this:

- The combination of location sensing technologies and information delivery systems has a potential that goes far beyond the application of in-car navigation systems.
- Sites and places contain more than there is obvious.

While the first thesis might prove itself in the near future, the latter became a strong stimulus for our work while facing the question: "If the distinctiveness of a place matters, what surplus could be generated by the integration of technology?"
Since the antique, historical and mythological notions of place and its accredited effects to human thought relate closely to the term 'genius loci' – undoubtedly this metaphysical connotation avoids itself from being defined in scientific dimensions. Nevertheless, the term addresses an inherent property of a distinct place to be perceived without further mediation [10]. Therefore the concept of the 'genius loci' might seem inappropriate for the integration of technology – no specific surplus could be created as the place itself tells or enables everything that could be told or enabled. Anyhow, a slight possibility exists in this case: If mediation through means of technology is unnecessary or even impossible, the combination of place and technology

S. Göbel et al. (Eds.): TIDSE 2004, LNCS 3105, pp. 270–276, 2004.

could have the potential to pave the way for the creation of the essential attention that is necessary for such experience.

Another point of departure for setting up a concept to the renaissance of the place under the light of technology could be found in the work of the philosopher and social scientist Walter Benjamin. Although larger parts of his work remained a fragment, his ideas and thoughts are still a precious source for a manifold of scientific disciplines [6]. A detailed introduction or even overview to the work of Benjamin would go beyond the scope of this exhibition paper - although further contemplation might prove to be very fruitful and will be taken into account for future projects.

Besides his often cited publication "The Work of Art in the Age of Mechanical Reproduction" [4] and the interrelated concept of the 'aura', Benjamin spent about 16 years of his life to finish his opus magnum: The arcades project [1]. Challenged by the distinctiveness of the place - in his case Paris as the capital of the perished 19th century - Benjamin tried to work out the features of the place from the perspective of his presence, the 1930s. A process quite similar to what we want to achieve. Paris itself became for Benjamin, as Schlögel puts it, a single place with a three-fold meaning: "the place of inspiration (or awakening), a place of remembrance (the traces of the perished capital of the 19th century) and the place, where the work of realisation could be accomplished " [9]. Again, no plans for mediation are given, instead Benjamins concept of the virtual Paris denies, according to MacLaughlin, the possibility to be represented or planned by any means of technical reproduction, because Benjamin "[...] describes an experience of Paris itself as a virtual medium" [8].

In contrast to the idea of a 'genius loci', obstacles for mediation are not founded in a mythological concept, but besides other aspects also in the sheer complexity of the subject. The present place is formed by the course of time, the change of its parts in time as well as the change in combination of its parts – the loss, reconstruction and transformation of its parts – and the history of this change itself. What becomes vital is not mediation but initiation, an assignment for which Benjamin chose another place and its functions: The Bibliothèque Nationale, where he spent years of shifting through the evidence of a past still present, working out his way to the place. Neverteless, this initiation is determined by the way one chooses for an intellectual approach and becomes therefore subjective.

Taking into account these two examples, our second thesis needs to be refined: If the place itself becomes the medium, the statement "Sites and places contain more than there is obvious" becomes obsolete. An appropriate shift in the right direction might be given by defining "The content of sites and places is evident to those who are willing and prepared".

2   Towards Location Sensitive Media Integration

Based on these findings and the refined thesis, a few postulates for location sensitive media integration can be displayed. In our approach towards location sensitive media integration four distinctive, but highly interconnected elements are combined.

2.1 Narration

Central task of the narration is to guide the visitor in such a way, that he becomes capable to realize the specific distinctiveness of the place. Emphasis has to be put on unobtrusive scratches and slight marks, as they embody hints on the past in the present. A successful narrative approach seduces the visitor to commit eye-work – to disclose the parallelism of past gone layer by layer. As soon as the visitor starts with this work, the narration has to retreat in the background, although willing to give information if asked for.

2.2 Representation

If the place itself is the main medium, the representation has to be as gentle and obtrusive as possible while still capable to illustrate the narration. Less becomes better. Large scale Monitors and highly afflicting media distract far too much from the place and its features. A careful selection of "calm" media becomes necessary.

2.3 Interaction

Following the characteristics of location and space, interaction has to take place in a way that it almost vanishes behind the eye-work task of the visitor. At its best, interaction follows the behaviour of the visitor without requiring additional input.

2.4 Production

The element of production involves in this case the process of setting up the narrative and its corresponsive parts as well as the required methods of selection, edition and refinement. An adequate production would also include procedures for the integration of subjective contributions of visitors, therefore enhancing the value of the place by additional meanings and interpretations – reflecting the manifold and plurality of denotations of the place.

Depending on the task – the place and its characteristics as well as the desired accentuation – various ways of integrating the described elements could be found in our exhibits and their features. Always emphasising one of the elements, but nevertheless with a combination of the four.

3 Exhibits

All exhibits were realised by the usage of transgo, a software solution developed by transformat. The overall system is based on a specific "context management system". By this approach, space and content can easily be merged. The interface lets e.g. the curator of an exhibition drop audio- or video files on special locations or exhibits. The visitor finds media in space; he has nothing to do but to walk through the exhibition. No machine needs to be operated or activated – the content becomes context sensitive.

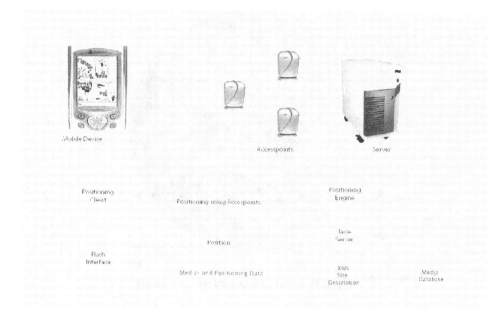

Fig. 1. Scheme of client/server infrastructure. content server strems media according to the acquired location by the positioning engine

The fundamental technology transgo uses is a WLAN positioning engine, patented by ekahau. The site has to be covered at all places by (at least) three standard WLAN access points (ap). They deliver the content to the visitor and their signal strength is analyzed for the positioning. After calibrating the site, the PDA sends the received signal strength of all three ap´s to the positioning engine, which interprets it to a local position and hands it over to the content server where from the content is sent back to the PDA. After once chosen a specific tour the visitor gets the content according to this choice. Interaction does not take place on the machine but in space. The visitor interacts by walking through the room.

The TIDSE exhibit shows three different examples that all make use of the same technical framework while trying to demonstrate our concept of location sensitive media integration.

3.1 Interact

Being one of the first applications developed under usage of the transgo framework, this example acts as a sample for the possibilities of user interaction and user based production. The visitor is asked to participate. He can easily drop notes, leave comments or start a location-based discussion. Shown as an experimental university project "pinworld" represents the idea of a Geographical Weblog Interface.

In contrast to the mobile phone location based services this prototype opens up the feedback channel, communication takes place! The license free network shows new connections and possibilities of local communication.

Fig. 2. Pinworld - a geocoded note community

The touch screen interface opens up special ways of using the machine and interacting with it. Also the type of communication with each other is used in another way, small handwritten notes let the system appear as a non digital post-it box, same time anachronistically and personally.

Using the Network for positioning, content distribution and peer-to-peer communication shows the basic idea of a framework for mobile gaming applications and collaborative platforms.

3.2 Documentation

The second example makes use of the transgo framework in the *haus am am horn* application, shown as it is running in Weimar in the first bauhaus building. The PDA screen shows for example furniture design as it was at this place in 1923 but got lost during 2nd world war. In one room the visitor finds a video of an interview with the architect Georg Muche also the inaugural address of an exhibition is stored right beside the paintings.

The application makes a virtual tour in real space possible. The Visitors gets an impression of the story of the house and the functionality of the transgo system. Implementing the Media Layer shows history in place and enables new experience. As a side effect, the museum is able to gather useful information about the visiting time and the routes the visitors take inside the house. On a next step further buildings will be integrated to one Weimar walkabout.

The transformation of this application from its original place to the TIDSE04 exhibition makes apparent, that the displayed narration, interaction and representation demand for their intended context, therefore creating a certain longing to reunite the now broken connection between place and technology.

Fig. 3. WLAN positioning enables locative media

3.3 Experimental

The third example of the exhibit shows media collages of sound, image and video. They are brought to special locations or so called islands, represented by small modular intervention spread over the room. Content is generated by experimental artist work, during workshops and traveling.

Fig. 4. A media layer over public spaces contains background information

This experimental layer is showing the diversity and flexibility of the transgo system and its careful approach towards production. Storylines virtually link different locations and can be followed by using the PDA. By choosing special route, the visitor can interact and affect the story. Narration and interaction correspond in a new way of storytelling.

4 Conclusions

In this paper we have presented an approach towards location sensitive media integration that takes into account the features of the place as a medium of its own. Three examples for this approach have been set up to demonstrate its strengths and virtues. Future efforts will be put on developing this framework towards a reliable and adaptive theoretical approach.

References

1. Benjamin, W.: The Arcades Project, translated by Howard Eiland and Kevin McLaughlin; prepared on the basis of the German volume edited by Rolf Tiedemann, The Belknap Press of Harvard University Press, Cambridge Massachusetts, and London, England 1999
2. Chalmers M, (2001) Place, Media and Activity. ACM SIGGROUP Bulletin, 22(3):38--43, December 2001
3. Ciolfi, L. (2003): Towards a Localized Experience of Technology. A proposal to enhance interaction design for ubiquitous computing systems, Short paper In Proceedings of HCI2003: Designing for Society, Vol.2, Bath (UK) September 2003
4. Geulen, E.: Under Construction:Walter Benjamin's „The Work of Art in the Age of Mechanical Reproduction", In: Benjamins ghosts: interventions in contemporary literary and cultural theoriy. Edited by Gerhard Richter, Stanford University Press, Stanford, California 2002: 121-141
5. Harrison, S. and P. Dourish (1996). Re-Place-ing Space: The Roles of Place and Space in Collaborative Systems. In proceedings of: CSCW 96. Cambridge, MA., ACM Press: 67-76.
6. Koepnick, L.: Aura Reconsidered: Benjamin and Contemporary Visual Culture, In: Benjamins ghosts: interventions in contemporary literary and cultural theory. Edited by Gerhard Richter, Stanford University Press, Stanford, California 2002: 95 – 117
7. Kretschmer U., Coors V., Spierling U., Grabson D., Schneider K., Rojas I.and Malaka R. (2001): Meeting the Spirit of History. In proceedings of: Virtual Reality, Archaeology, and Cultural Heritage 2001.
8. McLaughlin, K.: Virtual Paris: Benjamins Arcades Project, In: Benjamins ghosts: interventions in contemporary literary and cultural theoriy. Edited by Gerhard Richter, Stanford University Press, Stanford, California 2002: 204- 225
9. Schlögel, K.: Im Raume lesen wir die Zeit. Über Zivilisationsgeschichte und Geopolitik, Carl Hanser Verlag, München, Wien 2003: 128-136
10. Sollod, T. Ellen.: Spirit of Place,. http://www.arcadejournal.com/Vol16/16-3/16-3spirit.htm

Monotony:
An Experimental Interactive Narrative

Deneva Goins and Janine Huizinga

Hogeschool Voor De Kunst Utrecht, Facult of Art Media and Technology,
Oude Amersfoortseweg 131, PO box 2471
1200 CL Hilversum, The Netherlands
deneva_1@bgnet.bgsu.edu, janine@waag.org

Abstract. In theme, this experimental artwork deals with a journey of interaction between disembodied thoughts, memories of a situation in which a person undergoes devastating mental and emotional changes to accommodate the repeated loss of loved ones to uncontrollable circumstances. The overlying theme is evaluating the struggle for control of the uncontrollable. The story uses experiential user-driven plot concept, a plot model based on the philosophical theory of deconstruction as a basis for designing the interactive scenario.

1 Introduction

In theme, this experimental artwork deals with a journey of interaction between disembodied thoughts, memories of a situation in which a person undergoes devastating mental and emotional changes to accommodate the repeated loss of loved ones to uncontrollable circumstances. The overlying theme is evaluating the struggle for control of the uncontrollable. The story uses experiential user-driven plot concept, a plot model based on the philosophical theory of deconstruction as a basis for designing the interactive scenario.

2 Story Concept

Monotony is an interactive story in which the user has a meaningful experience through cognitive interaction with redundant symbols, text, sound, and imagery. These elements represent a story which has been desconstructed into pieces which the user can then interpret. This story was devised as a demonstration of a creative solution to the problem of interactive narrative. The concept was to utilize the philosophical idea of deconstruction as a metaphor for interactivity. Rather than presenting a linear story, the completed work attempts to present elements of the story in a disembodied fashion so that the user can experience them and interpret the story by through association. The goal was to create a storyspace which allowed the user to understand meaning through a continuum rather than the more traditional way of directly being

S. Göbel et al. (Eds.): TIDSE 2004, LNCS 3105, pp. 277–283, 2004.

told the meaning through linear, multi-linear techniques or narration. The total effects of interacting with the story should yield an emotional response within the user.

2.1 Reasoning

The reason this approach has been taken was to push the limits of the medium, not necessarily in a technological sense, rather as a medium of interpretation. The nature of interactive media is unique in that it can be used with a new philosophical framework. Deconstruction is the most appropriate approach to interactive media because it exploits the nature of the medium by advocating continuous interpretation and free exploration. Regardless of the many attempts to combine the two, interactivity and narrative are two concepts that do not mix in a meaningful way. The result of mixing interactive narrative is often a domination of either interactivity or narrative. When utilizing new media, artists and designers must recognize that in order to exploit it, a change in perception is required. Older philosophies such as the structuralist constraints of narrative must be released in order to allow for such an aesthetic to develop.

2.2 Significance

Understanding the creative possibilities is conveying meaning within new media is important because these media represent a language for culture to be communicated. All forms of stories and communication are encoded with ideas, tradition, and entertainment aiding in the socialization process shaping the way people identify with themselves and their environment. New media has mechanized the storyteller into data that is easily copied, distributed and absorbed transcending historical barriers of time, and geography. Journeying into to storyspace encased by information networks involves partaking in a world of simulation or pseudo reality. With a dismembered storyteller, cultural memory is fragmented into what may seem as meaningless data floating throughout. It is the responsibility of new media designers to understand and adjust themselves to the philosophical paradigm shifts in culture to make use of the qualities of new media storytelling.

3 Traditional Narrative

Traditional narrative plot structure involves: exposition, rising action, climax, falling action and resolution. These are typically most important elements of story and must be adhered to sequentially. Monotony was first written using this plot structure, then it was deconstructed in order to convert it to an interactive story. The story was deconstructed into 4 basic scenes plus one starting interface. The emotional elements of the story were deconstructed from their 'literal' representations to more abstract representations consisting of sound, animation, text, metaphor and color. The characters, timeline, language and plot have been deconstructed (disassembled) into basic colors, sound an animation. Many metaphors have been utilized to allow the user interpret the story though association. Deconstructing the initial story broke down the linearity and narration of the story to allow for interpretation of the deconstructed pieces.

4 Deconstruction Process

Deconstruction is a complex theory, but can be simplified into 4 requirements: reversal, displacement, un-closure and re-deconstruction. Reversal means that things that are binary opposite (such as good vs. evil) and the hierarchy of beliefs that support them must be revealed. This reversal should reveal the ironies and inconsistencies within the hierarchy thus, transforming the perceived relationship of the binary opposites. This continuous transformation allows for many reversals resulting in a break down of the hierarchy therefore exposing the assumptions that support it. Following this, one must return to the story with a new perspective. At this point, the hierarchy has been displaced and can no longer return to its original fixed structure. No new conformity can be inherent. While traditional narrative perceives binary oppositions as stable things within narration, deconstruction sees them as a 'organized' within transience. In order for the reversal to occur, deconstruction must remain un-closed. This un-resolution is a continuum allowing for infinite interpretations. Nuncio describes, "There is no movement from beginning to end but every point could be a beginning and end and even viewed at the same point in every direction." Re-deconstruction is then the principle that allows deconstruction to take place all over again."

4.1 Experiencial User Driven Plot Concept

When this theory was applied as a model for interaction, some terms were changed for clarity. The new model is referred to as Experiential User-Driven Plot. It involves six possible stages comparable to deconstruction: exposition, association, discovery, reversal, re-exposition, and exit.

Exposition is when the user enters the story space for the first time in order to explore its contents. In the above diagram it is represented by the largest red arrow on the left. This stage can be regarded as the beginning of the story. All points of the story can be considered exposition because it is the container for the story. This phase is primarily making observations in the story such as imagery, sound, text, etc. *Association* is when the user begins to 'make sense of' or apply logic to the elements they have observed. This logic is applied through associations between the information they have observed and creates foundations for the story they will experience. Naturally, the user will discover incomplete pieces of information which creates conflict in the their mind. This sense of unclosure will prompt the user to solve the conflict by searching for more information or inventing their own resolution. This stage is *discovery* because the user feels they have resolved a portion of the information in the story. Reversal is the point after the user has uncovered a perceived a 'truth' or solution in the story which changes their perspective on the information that they have already gathered, however, this truth raises other questions. The user has some sense of resolve from the initial discovery but does not have a complete picture of the story. Then the user must move into the Re-Exposition phase, where they re-evaluates the initial information and may return to the initial scenes in order to make observations again or discover new information based on the truth uncovered in the discovery phase. From here the process of association, discovery, and reversal will unfold again in their respective orders. At any time the user can choose to Exit the story when they are content with the information they have unraveled. Exit is a variable stage , where the entry is not.

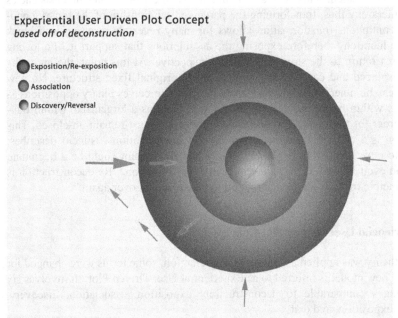

Experiential User Driven Plot Concept
based off of deconstruction

Exposition/Re-exposition

Association

Discovery/Reversal

Fig. 1. The point of entry is represented by the largest arrow on the left. The different colored regions represent different stages of the user's experience while the arrows represent the order in which they are experienced.

4.2 Pacing the Story

Essentially, the pacing of the story is determined by the user's motivation to discover new things. The navigation is both exploratory and user friendly where the user continuously goes over the same scenes looking for more information. The information is exploratory because the user can continuously rediscover the same elements, but with new perspective. The information is user friendly because in and of itself it remains consistant. If the user returns to a scene, they will find the same "stuff" but upon their return, will understand it in a new way where the items will contain a new-found significance.

4.3 Thematic Control

The key to guiding the user and maintaining thematic control over the story is to present redundant information in different ways. For example, if there is important text in the story, perhaps this text could be presented in several forms: 1 as written, 2 as dialogue, 3 as reavealed through symbolism within the story on several different scenes. This technique was applied to Monotony using the poetry. In one scene, a voice of a character states the emotional effects of cancer, whereas in another scene, images of different types of cancer cells displayed. Still yet, another scene involves a poem, written in text about the effects of cancer. All 3 of these representations are the same thematically, but will engage the user in different ways.

4.4 Relation to Traditional Plot

Experiential User-Driven Plot borrows from traditional narrative plot in that it has observation stages and discovery, but the dramatic arc is driven by the user, not the sequence of events. In addition, it has been modified to include the ideas of deconstruction therefore making room for interactivity. These modifications are necessary to realize and exploit new media.

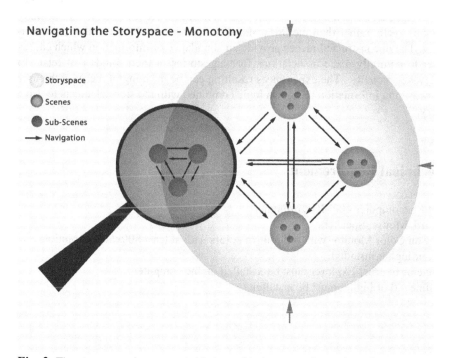

Fig. 2. The story space is represented below with the gray sphere where the scenes are represented by green spheres.

4.5 Interaction Scenario for Monotony

Upon entering the story space the user is faced with an interface that allows them to access any of the scenes initially. Within each scene, are sub scenes as depicted in the enlargement, that only reveal themselves through interaction.

Within the sub scenes, the user is allowed to reverse at anytime back to the initial screen and to other scenes, but they must keep exploring if they want to uncover additional information within that scene. Navigation and plot have been depicted separately to emphasize that the Experiencial User-Driven Plot model can occur at any point of interaction. It is not to be confused as navigation itself, rather it is a cognitive model.

5 Conclusions

In combining the Experiential User Driven Plot Concept with the interaction model discussed, the result was an artistic story which could be interpreted only through interaction. The meaningfulness is derived from the largely self guided experience of the user making associations between metaphoric scenes assigned by the story designer. Engaging in new media is found through interactive discovery, a potentially continuous cycle, rather than the linear dictation that occurred with traditional narrative plot. The deconstructed pieces provide an abundance of information which causes the user to naturally make associations forming stories in their minds that relate to themselves personally. The experiences resulting can be meaningful, because the user must draw upon information their own logic combined with the story elements to drive the story.

6 Technical Requirements

Macintosh Computer 400MHZ or higher
Keyboard, Mouse, Speakers
Display on Color Monitor with millions of colors with at least 800x600 resolution
OS 9.x or higher installed.
Netscape or Internet Explorer must be installed on the computer.
Quicktime 4.0 or higher must be installed.

References

1. Nuncio, Prof. Rhode V, *The Text and the Logos - Launguage Debate in Jacques Derrida's Deconstuction* (2000) Retrieved April 16 2003 from San Beda College.
2. Kolstrup, SÆ ren. "Narratives: Different Narratives, Different Theories for Different Media?" <u>Virtual Interaction: Interaction in Virtual Inhabited 3D Worlds</u>. Ed. Lars Qvortrup. Springer 2001.
3. Stigel, JÆ rgen. "The Limits of Narration" <u>Virtual Interaction: Interaction in Virtual Inhabited 3D Worlds</u>. Ed. Lars Qvortrup. Springer 2001.
4. Lawrence, D, I Amado, and C. Sanders. "Digitization - An Agent for Creativity, Expression and Interaction?" <u>Digital Content Creation</u>. Ed. Rae Shaw and John Vince. Springer-Verlag 2001.

The Fabulous Adventures of MC Walker: Conceptual Videogame

Maarten Deville[1], Hugues Huygens[2], and Vincent Regent

Transmedia Postgraduate, Graduation Project for 2003.
1030 Brussels, Belgium.
[1] oz@doublegum.be
[2] Hugues.Huygens@pandora.be

Abstract. Transmedia is a 2 year Postgraduate Art/Design/Media course in Brussels. Previously I had studied Graphic Design, graduated in Multimedia with an interactive story/play on PC for two players + audience, based on a story by Paul Auster. Transmedia offered a steppingstone to go further. It was a logical next step to make a conceptual videogame. The game is a conceptual, music driven, socially inspired, abstract adventure, where walking cubes meet and socialize. We recently started preparations for a more elaborate sequel to this game, but I will focus on the finished product for now.

1 Introduction

Let me tell you something about my background concerning games: I'm 25 years of age, and I've been playing games since we bought our first Personal Computer - an IBM compatible of course, with optional hard drive (!) -, which was somewhere around 1986. My brother in law had copied tons of games for me to play. We're talking 'Digger', 'Pac-Man', 'Paratrooper', 'Lode Runner' and Sierra adventures like 'Space Quest', 'Police Quest' and 'Kings Quest'.

Although these weren't my first encounters with video or computer games -I had an occasional blast with a friend's 1982 MB Vectrex, and his 1977 Atari 2600- I spent quite an amount of hours a week on our PC, for several years. However, entering the overly hyped Playstation era, I lost track of 'the scene'. The last 24 months however, my life has taken a serious turn towards videogames, again. Where I used to spend all of my spare time in bars, pubs and clubs or simply behind my pc, I know was sitting behind my TV playing games and borrowing others people's console to play games I couldn't play on mine.

The time I didn't actually spend in front of my TV, I was scavenging the internet for more and new details on recently released or upcoming titles with a different perspective. I think I never read as much in my entire life, jumping from one games site to another as a daily routine. Not that there was something new to report on a daily basis, but I couldn't afford to miss it if it did turn out worthwhile. The easiest way to stay up to date, was to subscribe yourself on a huge international Forum,

S. Göbel et al. (Eds.): TIDSE 2004, LNCS 3105, pp. 284–289, 2004.

where people were constantly posting interesting news they had found somewhere on the net, and referred to it with a link. After a while, you have gathered your own bunch of interesting sites and go from there. However, thinking about these forums and the insane amount of posts being fired at it every minute, one has to wonder. Weren't gamers supposed to be anti social, and lack any skills of communication?

2 Concept/Brainwork

The concept that was the basis for the game was actually present in an interactive dossier/website I made (http://www.doublegum.be/transmedia). You have a small space (a square) with a form bouncing up and down, left to right, at a random pace in this square. This form changes shape when it enters a new sector (I had the square divided into four sectors) the new shape is equal to the shape of that sector (every sector has a shape: a square, a triangle, a circle and a line). In the mean time there is a very repetitive sound, like a sort of humming sound, that accompanies the shape shifting form. This sound also changes in pitch, while the form shifts from one form to another, from each sector to the next; giving every sector/shape its own humming sound. You now have an interactive form that bounces in between sectors, but in the meantime, changes its identity: sound and shape. You can drag the form to each one of the sectors, changing its shape and sound, to create an 'opening' to a next level (Read: a link). The form is still doing the same thing, bouncing; but the sectors' links have become different links in their own place and time. So you have a double lay-ered way of interactivity, providing information on top of information, all brought together by an interactive humming shape shifting form. The state of this form will provide information of its own, since its shape and sound is tied to the sector it cur-rently is in, and thus the link that is currently enabled. The fact that the form is bouncing in a never ending way, also provides the fact that it is living a life of its own. Therefore, the little artificial 'intelligence' it has, makes it the perfect screen-saver.

Two strange ideas came to mind in the past year however. Well, one at least, the other one's not really thát strange: When you're walking down the street, and it's crowded as you have to find your way dodging other people, you quickly walk past a couple of hundreds of people, in say five minutes time? Ok, assuming nobody pushes you out on the road, or steps on your toes, how many people will you remember after those five minutes? One? Two? None?

On the other hand, when you actually do notice someone, someone you find inter-esting, doesn't matter why -because of the way he or she looks, walks, dresses,...- and you're rather intrigued by this person, do you ever just walk up to a perfect stranger, and start communicating? -"Hi, I'm Maarten. I must say, you have this really funny way of walking and I was wondering if I could get to know you better. I'm serious, the way you walk really intrigues me"- You'd be happy to walk away without getting slapped in the face or getting yourself arrested. There are social boundaries, people do not easily.

Ok, second thing that rattled my mind was the fact that when you're watching a movie, the viewer (the camera) is always following the main character around. You can not escape this situation. The only thing you can do is change the channel, walk out of the theater, go to bed or whatever. So what if you are following this main character in a movie, and he comes across a character that has nothing to do with the story of the film, just a drunk leaning against the counter, or an old lady walking by. You're not interested anymore in the film's main theme, but you want to know where this old lady lives, and where she's going to. You want to know what her story is and how she happened to end up on your screen. You want the camera to leave the other character and start following this one. But there's nothing you can do, and two seconds later, she's gone. What if you actually could do something? It's all about perception, freedom and social barriers.

I started asking myself the following questions, in order not to make the same mistakes many game developers were making: "Why did the videogame not evolve alongside its graphic evolution? Why was the conceptual design of the videogame in general not following the 3D graphics? Why were game designers still thinking in a one dimensional way?" The videogame has virtually no limitations, yet it seems as if even the use of sound and visuals in an intelligent way, is even too much to ask for.

The idea grew, however, that I was not going to be able to make a videogame, in terms of scenario, depth and gamespace. So I had to make something where I could make my point, I had to make the part of the game, where most game developers failed.

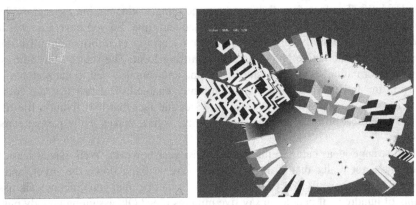

Fig. 1. The interactive dossier/website (*left*) is in many ways comparable with the final gamespace. The world for 'The Fabulous Adventures of MC Walker' (*right*) may look completely different, but don't let looks fool you.

It would have to be the way you interact with your environment and where this interaction equals information. Hundreds of elements are being put in videogames, yet they all fail to 'add' value to the game. The way information is being handled in videogames is hardly interactive. The only way you can call this interactivity is when you consider reading a newspaper to be interactive. If you do, then I'm not making my point, but on the other hand, if you do, then what's the use of digitalizing a game? We should all go back to playing cards.

So this is what I was going to try, make an interactive gamespace, where the information you need, comes in elements of gameplay. The game would not have a story; it would not have a goal to it. Basically, it might not be a game. But it would provide a way of thinking and interacting, a space where you could easily apply various types of games to.

3 Practice/Handiwork

I applied for Criterion's Renderware, the worlds leading middleware development tool for games. Renderware had been used by 'Grand Theft Auto', by 'Tony Hawk's Pro Skater' and by 'Burnout' to name a few. After a lot of waiting and miscommunication, I could freely download it from Criterion's site. -They had a special policy for students. And so I started looking for a programmer to write the code. Luckily I found one, free of charge; and he liked my idea, so we were off.

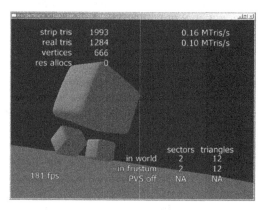

Fig. 2. The inhabitants of the virtual world all look like this: two cubes (the feet) beneath one big cube (the body), shown here, walking, in a Renderware Visualizer.

All my ideas were beginning to take shape. I had designed a character, consisting out of two cubes - the feet - and one big cube on top - the body -. Since the game was going to be some abstract form, rather than be a real game, it seemed appropriate. I started the character's animation, which was one of the most intense occupations. Even for a simple character consisting of three cubes, we needed dozens of animation files. Take into account that this was my first game animation, so naturally I made some errors.

The character will have its own identity (just like the shape shifting form in the interactive dossier) consisting of a color, and a deep-house loop, divided in up to five channels. The Character will walk in a world filled with similar characters, all having their own identity - meaning color and tune -. But just as in real life, you do not know the identity of the people you pass by when you walk down the street. So your character will not see the color - meaning, they will all appear grey, nor hear the tune these other characters have (he plainly will not know their identity). But not unlike real life, you will get an impression about someone, when you pass by. So whenever your character is near another character, this other character will 'lighten up' to some extent (you will be able to get a glimpse of the character's color, coming through the shade of grey) and you will hear one or two sound channels of the other character, instead of your own channels of the same sort (your beat may be replaced by his beat) giving you an idea of what kind of character you're passing by. You get an impression.

Of course, this interaction between music loops should not just start at any given point but exactly in the rhythm of the beat. This is not only to prevent it from being annoying, but creates a new element of gameplay: As you walk you will make your own music. When you start walking you get to hear one of your music channels. As you keep walking the other channels will randomly drop in, but always into the rhythm. When you stop moving, channels will randomly disappear, leaving you with only one loop if you remain still. Now, with the interaction between your music and the other character's music as you pass them, you will always be creating your own soundscape, not only providing you with an impression of the character's identity, but also giving a new dimension, a new reason to play the game.

Furthermore, when you like somebody's color or tune, you can choose to interact with this character of choice. In this state of interaction, you will be shown his full color, and also hear more of his music channels, despite some of your own, giving you new, more profound information about the character's identity. If you then wish, for obvious reasons (you like the other character better) you can swap characters, and continue the game in an entirely new identity. Since the character you previously inhabited is no stranger to you (you know his identity, you once were him/her) this character will be walking around, with its full color permanently shown, making it easier for you to find him/her back if you would happen to need him/her again.

This last element had me fulfill all the goals I was aiming for, all but one. As you might remember, I mentioned the use of a screensaver.

Well, this feature is also present: When you stop playing the game, your character will wait a while, before taking matters in its own hands. Your character will start to wander around on its own, but will still be causing an abstract visual work, as it passes other characters and so causes them to lighten up. You'll also listen, to a randomly-based ever-changing soundscape. The camera will follow his every move, just the way he would do yours.

The game is being made in full 3D, and given the game's abstract form, I didn't want this to be any other way when it came down to 'level design'. The world you walk upon is a small one, yet, it is also a sphere. Buildings are big cubes, all very much alike; except for the bigger buildings, situated in the upper and lower part of the world. These buildings have the shape of letters, spelling the identity of the building. For instance, the bank will be a building shaped in the word 'BANK'. The upper part of the world is the 'daytime' area; the lower part is cast in darkness. You can walk from day to night and back again.

4 Please Insert Coin

I hope that when you read this, you can see the possibilities this way of working can offer, and can immediately be applied to a new style of 'role-playing' games, 'adventure' games, or even 'party' games. You gather more and more information, thus coming closer to your goal, as you switch through characters. You could create a party game where you have to collect as many samples as quick as possible, but all from the same color. Etc...

My goal was to create something where critical information about the game was part of the game itself, rather than having an annoying sidekick 'suggesting what you should or shouldn't do, and rather than having text fragments pop up every two minutes. I tried to make a closed concept, which offers an open game.

Of course, I could have put more into it, and I wanted to, but there wasn't enough time. The element of 'weather' as an interactive way of dealing with information (it could start raining whenever you encounter a bad person, or the sun starts shining when you get closer to your objective,...). Considering we're all rookies, who worked on this game for only a small number of months, I think we did pretty well. Keep in mind that regular videogames take up to 4 years to produce, with a team of dozens of people.

As a final word, I would like to thank Vincent Regent, who has been working on the music with me, and offered quite an amount of enjoyable tracks; also Huug Huygens who's been doing the coding for the game. Both helped a great deal, also in giving me some feedback about games - being hardcore gamers - and providing some ideas. Without them, I wouldn't have had much of a game to show.

Maarten Devillé 2004

Janus – Keeper of the Gate to the Otherworld

Finula Biermann[1] and Hugo Binder[2]

[1] Hochschule für Gestaltung, Offenbach, Germany
finula@gmx.de
[2] Computer Graphics Center,
Digital Storytelling Department, Darmstadt, Germany
hugo.binder@web.de

Abstract. Often presentations scare off through their complexity. An immense amount of new information overwhelms and intimidates the spectator. Taken by the hand, the attention drawn to novelties and accompanied and supported on a journey into new areas, the adventure may begin. The theme of our project is a physical avatar (circa 50cm tall), who guards a small door into the unknown. The figure was developed based o roman God of the gate, Janus. The physical avatar acts as a mediator between the worlds. He guards the border between our world and the unknown. Although he stands in our world he knows what exists behind the door. When approached by a person, the Janus program starts. He awakes to life and draws the attention to himself and the door. But the door is not easily opened. First a few questions have to be answered. Wherein Janus may aid the spectator or deny entrance. In addition to this presentation large photographs will be exhibited, which deal with variations of the theme guard/gate.

1 Introduction – Lure in, Help, Deny

This project was developed in close relation to the diploma of Finula Biermann in 2003, which dealt with the „Gate to the Otherworld". Especially the doorkeepers and the helpers who accompanied the voyager in the unknown dimensions appeared very fascinating throughout the research. The space behind the door seems to be a magic place, a fairytale place with wish-come-true-magic. Everything could exist behind that door. The doorkeeper (in our case Janus) has the classical function of a wise leader/ manipulator, a mediator for travels into the „other" room. Should an incomprehensive i.e. a technical world be behind that door, Janus will know about it and he will be able to help us understand with his familiar sympathetic appearance. In our presentation Janus will first ask the visitor a few questions and then grant or deny entrance. A real interaction could later be realised but at first we want to play with the expectations and the curiosity. What will happen next? What is behind that door? This project is supposed to create a symbiosis between the technical and the art world. The human does not enter the virtual reality with the aid of technical but the otherworld approaches us in form of a sympathetic mysterious creature.

S. Göbel et al. (Eds.): TIDSE 2004, LNCS 3105, pp. 290–292, 2004.

Fig. 1. Janus the Doorkeeper

2 Background – Boarder Guard and the Roman God Janus

In many cultures the border is known to be inhabited by an own protective ghost. Guards of the border, which has to be overcome before one can enter the holy space, are dragons, snakes, monsters, dogs, scorpio-people, lions and so on. Our figure Janus was inspired by the double faced roman god of the door, Janus. He was able to look in-and outside surveying the arriving and the departing. All gates were sacred to him for the commencement of an action was to be seen like the passing through a gate, and determining a good outcome.

3 Initial Idea – Physical Avatar as a Teaser

An unusual, closed door alone will awaken curiosity, but if in addition it is guarded by a creature from a fairytale which speaks to us the curiosity is enhanced.
Ideally Janus would become a leader into a new world who adjusts to his protégé communicates with him and prepares him for the otherworld. (Similar to "the diamond age, or a young lady's primer" by Neal Stephenson). Since this would only be possible if at all with an immense technical effort we want to play with the subject in our presentation. With a relatively small technical effort we want to trigger maximum curiosity and astonishment that awakens an appetite for more.

4 Technical Realisation

Janus is an animated puppet with expressive mimics, its movements are synchronized with the prerecorded text and sound. The puppet with its servomotors is controlled by a microprocessor interface which is connected to a pc. A special software links the animation sequences to the audio stream and processes the sensor input. Actually there is a motion detector designed to be the only interaction device for the user, that starts and ends the presentation.

5 Conclusion

Due to the design of the puppet and its actions the curiosity and phantasy of the visitor shall be addressed. The physical avatar Janus takes playfully the role of the helper and companion in a unknown, virtual world. Through the dialog he imparts knowledge about the interface to the otherworld and increases the joy of use for the visitor while using the interface.

Oral Tradition versus Digital Storytelling: On Educational Effects of Middle European Folk Tales and Their Value for Digital Storytelling

Harald Kibbat

wirklich wahr, An der Schwemme 5,
38527 Meine, Germany
andrascha@t-online.de, harald.kibbat@autostadt.de

Abstract. Digital Storytelling Projects seen by an old-fashioned oral story-teller. The author writes about old storytelling techniques and the influence it may have on future programs, about the psychological background of folk tales, their origins and their purposes. Also included is a brief view into the future of both oral and digital story and fairy tale telling.

1 Introduction

My first reaction to the kind invitation of the ZGDV was – thoughtfulness.

State-of-the-art technology, reflections on Digital Storytelling like the exciting information I read about the GEIST project in 2003, and, in contrast with it, the old oral tradition of story and fairy tale telling, a sort of tradition I try to keep alive as one of only about 600 German native speakers in Germany, Austria and Switzerland.

An antagonism? I don't think so. Being a storyteller myself, I can share my humble hoard of experience with a clear conscience with the attendees. The noble claim Digital Storytelling technologies lay to their use for mediation of information and knowledge is shared with the old oral traditions of folk tales.

1.1 Educational Effects and Psychological Background

Fairy tales have been told at all times. In Germany, oral story telling traditions can be found until the beginning of the 20th century. They were used as means of transportation for knowledge, experience and ethic values between adults. Fairy tales come in handy for crisis management and conflict mastering; they are a social tool for difficulties in reaching maturity.

Publishing the *Kinder- und Hausmärchen* 1811-15, the Grimm Brothers opened the European folk tales for children as an additional recipient group. Since then, folk tales are thought to be a valuable educational medium.

S. Göbel et al. (Eds.): TIDSE 2004, LNCS 3105, pp. 293–296, 2004.

Fig. 1. Old-fashioned fairy tale telling at work

Nowadays, I do use folktales from the Grimm Brothers [1] and Ludwig Bechstein [2], and artificial fairy tales from Wilhelm Hauff [3] and Richard von Volkmann-Leander [4] and others to take the interest of recipients of all ages to the ways and paths of fairy tales and story telling. The archetypical symbolism of folk tales, their non-elastic structure, its over-enhancement into the unreal in all its facets and, resultant to it, the implicitness of the wonderful is particularly suitable to arrest the attention of recipients of all ages.

For psychological purposes, folk tales reach their recipients in the child-ego state. While receiving a folk tale, everyone remembers instantly and unconscious moments of his/her own childhood, including sitting haimish on the lap of a familiar adult. At the same time, recipients of folk tales experience unconscious processes which can be helpful in personal conflict mastering. Experiences like *I am not alone/the first with that problem* are beneficial.

Meanwhile, the experienced story teller can almost always read out the reaction of his recipients by watching their body language. This is the main and great advantage of free story telling in comparison to a text read aloud, because a direct, face-to-face-dialogue is happening. A text read aloud or a digitally mastered story is rather a monologue. In this way, an experienced story teller can read the emotional state of the recipients and react accordingly by tuning his story telling.

2 Folk Tale Telling and Digital Storytelling

I do believe that the structuring of folk tales is transferable to multimedia storytelling projects. The rhythm of trinary elements which is ruling the structure of many fairy tales (e.g. three bothers, three tasks, three riddles) is highly recognizable and could be of use for further projects. The repetitions that are contained in this rhythm can also be of value for the transport of information and knowledge, not only because repetitions are loved by children.

Fig. 2. The audience is listening

Fig. 3. Fascinated young audience

The immense contrast included in folk tales (good/evil, hard-working/slothful, poor/rich, alive/dead, etc.), too, seems ideal to me to wake, enthrall and hold the attention of an audience, whether by oral or digital means.

Considering interactive and multimedia oriented story telling projects, I see a great potential for using and merging new and old technologies. Avatars could try to catch the user's eye to mimic a face-to-face interaction, magical assistants, talking animals or the like, can enhance and ensure the enchantment of the recipients. The linking of traditional, 'fabulous' folk tale techniques and structures with state-of-the-art technologies displayed here at Darmstadt seems to be very attractive to me. Developments for museums and science centers, exhibitions and computer games and art, learn and teaching programs for school and academic purposes are pointed out to me.

Future fields for developments can be found on enhancing the abilities to identify the emotional state of users by avatars.

3 Conclusion

Digital storytelling gives an almost boundless spectrum of possible uses.

Using traditional, old-fashioned structures, the methods of folk story telling, embedded in modern technologies, can reach a greater attention. Thus we can get a win-win situation for both my profession and discipline and the new media systems and developments.

References

1. Rölleke, H. (Ed.): Kinder- und Hausmärchen der Brüder Grimm. Ausgabe letzter Hand mit den Originalanmerkungen der Brüder Grimm, 3 Bände. Stuttgart (1982)
2. Bechstein, L.: Ludwig Bechstein Märchenbuch/Neues deutsches Märchenbuch. Diederichs, München (1997)
3. von Steinsdorff, S., Koopmann, H. (Eds.): Wilhelm Hauff, Sämtliche Werke, 3 Bände. München (1970)
4. von Volkmann-Leander, R.: Traeumereien an franzoesischen Kaminen, Maerchensammlung. Verlag Artemis u. Winkler (2000)

Antiziganism and Persecution of the Sinti and Roma from the Late Middle Ages to the 20th Century

Josef Behringer[1], Udo Engbring-Romang[2], and Stefan Göbel[3]

[1] Verband Deutscher Sinti und Roma, Landesverband Hessen
64293 Darmstadt, Germany
verband@sinti-roma-hessen.de
http://www.sinti-roma-hessen.de
[2] 35039 Marburg, Germany
udo@engbring.de
http://www.engbring.de
[3] ZGDV Darmstadt e.V., Digital Storytelling Department,
64283 Darmstadt, Germany
Stefan.Goebel@zgdv.de
http://www.zgdv.de/distel/

Abstract. Based on the studies published by Udo Engbring-Romang and the experience of the mobile exhibition "Hornhaut auf der Seele" (Horny Skin On the Soul) this paper describes development plans of a permanent exhibition on "antiziganism" located in Darmstadt, Germany. Here, Interactive Digital Storytelling methods and concepts as well as Computer Graphics technology for interactive artifacts are used to enhance the planned exhibition from the technical point of view.

1 Motivation

For more than 600 years Sinti and Roma have been living in Central Europe, and since the 15th century they have been objects of prejudice and persecution. The following project intends to make clear that there is a connection between antiziganism (sometimes called anti-gypsysm) as pictures made about „gypsies", the segregation from the society of the majority und the persecution executed by the police. Within a center for democracy and anti-rassism the authors want to establish an exhibition in Darmstadt enhanced by computer graphics and interactive storytelling technology. Hereby, important elements of the exhibition will be an information kiosk and interactive artifacts enabling visitors to interactively explore history of the persecution of the Sinti and Roma in Europe.

The following sections describe the scenario and historical aspects of the planned exhibition, a first prototype of the exhibition in form of a mobile exhibition indicating the motivation and historical background of the planned exhibition and technical possibilities to enhance the exhibition with current innovative methods, concepts and approaches in interactive storytelling and computer graphics.

S. Göbel et al. (Eds.): TIDSE 2004, LNCS 3105, pp. 297–302, 2004.

2 Scenario

The idea for the establishment of an exhibition on antiziganism was initiated by the Hesse subsidiary of the German society for Sinti and Roma. The global aim was the improvement of the communication between majority and minority within the German society. Therefore, the foundation of an educational institution for democracy and anti-rassism should be founded in Darmstadt. Hereby, a permanent exhibition on the affections of antiziganism and on the history of the persecution of the Sinti and Roma from the Middle Ages up to the time after World War II is supposed to build the central component of the planned educational institution.

From the content related point of view, the information and knowledge transmission about the persecution of the Sinti and Roma means and requires informing about the reasons of antiziganism and the effects for the majority and the minority. Hereby, the society of Sinti and Roma wishes to inform visitors of the exhibiton in an intellectual way, they should be emotionally affected and should be directly integrated into the concept of the exhibition.

Apart from traditional and well-known exhibition techniques, emotional aspects and approaches are in the focus of current exhibition plannings. Visitors are supposed not only to be confronted with poster boards and traditional media, but should be affected by the objects and innovative installations created by artists. Furthermore they should begin a real und virtual dialogue about the history of persecution of the Sinti and Roma using interactive Storytelling techniques.

Fig. 1. View to Poster Boards – Architectural Design by Claus Brunner

Altogether, the exhibtion will provide the opportunity to inform about the history of the Sinti and Roma implying a history with prejudice and segregation. Concerning comprehensive and multi-faceted knowledge transmission it is necessary to inform about the genocide committed by the Germans between 1943 and 1945, too. Another aspect concerns the information about the conditions of the origins of antiziganism. In order to follow and integrate all these aspects, the exhibition will analyse and discuss the function of antiziganism in different contexts (referring to religion, literature, arts or science) and will use various information and knowledge transmission techniques and media. For example, history is primarily presented with pictures and documents, furthermore clips of interviews with survivors of the genocid are added.

From the architectural point of view, the planned exhibion will irritate the visitors – to effect emotions: darkness and brightness, crooked poster boards and unevenness of the floors. This kind of irritation will be intensified by means of artificial presentation enhanced by computer based dialogue systems, virtual characters or interaction and discussion among virtual characters or between virtual characters and visitors.

3 Mobile Exhibition Prototype

The investigations and studies by Engbring-Romang [2,3] as well as his filmed interviews, published by Josef Behringer [1] and the texts of the mobile exhibition „»Hornhaut auf der Seele (Horny Skin On The Soul)«"- Die Geschichte zur Verfolgung der Sinti und Roma in Hessen are the basis for the historical part of the planned, permanent exhibition. This mobile exhibition primarily addresses schools and other educational institutions.

Fig. 2. Mobile Exhibition titled "Hornhaut auf der Seele" – Poster and Visitors in Wiesbaden

For the first time, on January 19th, 2004, the mobile exhibition has been presented to the public in the town hall in Wiesbaden, the capitol city of the state of Hesse. Chief mayor Hildebrand Diehl opened the exhibition in presence of Norbert Kartmann, president of the diet in Hesse. From January 20th to February 14th citizens and school classes had the opportunity to regard the poster boards.

The first feedback shows that the visitors stayed more than an hour in the exhibition. Most of the visitors were affected because they did not know much about the persecution. But pupils expected more than to read – longer – texts or to look at documents. They want to hear, to listen und to learn interactively about the history of the Sinti and Roma.

Fig. 3. Opening of the Mobile Exhibition in Wiesbaden

Following these user needs, interactive storytelling techniques briefly described in the next paragraph will be integrated into the conceptual phase and development of the permanent exhibition.

4   Technical Exhibition Enhancements

Immersion represents one of the most important factors with regard to the acceptance of human-computer interfaces. Content, which is presented in an exciting and diversified way, is indispensable to bind users to a system. In order to overcome this obstacle, the Digital Storytelling department uses interdisciplinary approaches settled in the fields of multimedia, media design, TV/movie, or literature and myths, and it develops narrative environments for both knowlege transmissions and learning scenarios. Similar to films or plays in theater, content and dramaturgically designed scripts are generated by authoring tools and transmitted by multi-modal interfaces enhanced by natural conversation and dialogue forms.

Referring to innovative interaction metaphors for the man-machine dialogue, within its strategic research project IZA ("Info zum Anfassen", engl.: tangible information) ZGDV has developed a novel concept to present information in a compelling way while keeping track of intuitive forms of interaction. The basic idea is to involve the user in a natural conversation with the presentation system. This is done in two interlocked ways: One way is to adapt approaches from the scientific domain of interactive, digital storytelling together with intuitive state-of-the-art multimodal interaction schemes; the other way is to correlate the tangible, hence physical, environment with the virtual presentation environment.

The IZA concept has been implemented as a generic platform for mixed reality information kiosk systems and will be adopted to an appropriated physical set-up fitting the user needs and ambience of the permanent exhibition on antiziganism. Based on an underlying story model and conversation strategy, users are involved in a story-driven conversation and interact with the system.

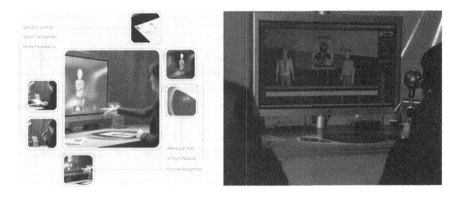

Fig. 4. IZA information kiosk – Technical scenario & interaction metaphors (left) plus application scenario with virtual characters talking about art (right)

Apart from information kiosks and multi-modal interfaces the storytelling group will develop an comprehensive authoring and run-time environment enabling authors or historians to enter historical facts and background information or any available media and providing predefined stories and learning scenarios for visitors, pupils oder school classes. Here, teachers can use those environments and infrastructure to prepare the visit of the exhibition and to create their individual story custom-tailored to the curriculum and knowledge background of their pupils.

Fig. 5. DinoHunter applications developed for the Senckenberg museum in Frankfurt: DinoExplorer Senckenberg provides a searching and learning game within a 3D environment (left). DinoSim Senckenberg is realized as touchscreen application on a terminal showing appearance and behaviour of various dinosaurs such as the famous T-Rex (right).

Examples of storytelling based environments for museums and exhibitions provide the art-E-fact project [7] and DinoHunter applications developed for the Senckenberg museum in Frankfurt [4,5,6].

5 Summary and Outlook

It is the aim of the Association of the German Sinti and Roma in Hesse to establish a permanent exhibition within an educational institution in cooperation with the historian Udo Engbring-Romang, with the artists Ritula Fränkel and Nicolas Morris and ZGDV Darmstadt providing methods and concepts for computer graphics and interactive storytelling.

Based on underlying concepts provided by the different partners and first experience of a mobile exhibition the development phase for the permanent exhibition is scheduled for a project phase of 3 years.

References

1. Behringer, J, Mettbach, A: „Wer wird die nächste sein?". Die Leidensgeschichte einer Sintezza, die Auschwitz überlebte/"Ich will doch nur Gerechtigkeit": Wie den Sinti und Roma nach 1945 der Rechtsanspruch auf Entschädigung versagt wurde. Brandes & Apsel Verlag, Frankfurt (1999)
2. Engbring-Romang, U.: Die Verfolgung der Sinti und Roma in Hessen zwischen 1870 und 1950. Brandes & Apsel Verlag, Frankfurt (2001)
3. Engbring-Romang, U.: Bad Hersfeld – Auschwitz. Zur Geschichte der Verfolgung der Sinti im Kreis Hersfeld-Rotenburg. Brandes & Apsel Verlag, Frankfurt (2002)
4. Feix, A., Hoffmann, A., Osswald, K., Sauer, S.: DinoHunter – Collaborative Learn Experience in Museums with Interactive Storytelling and Kids Innovation. In: Göbel, S., Braun, N., Spierling, U., Dechau, J., Diener, H. (eds.): Technologies in Interactive Digital Storytelling and Entertainment. Fraunhofer IRB Verlag, Stuttgart (2003) 388-393
5. Sauer, S., Göbel, S.: Focus your young visitors: Kids Innovation, Fundamental changes in digital edutainment. In: D. Bearman & J. Trant (eds.): Museums and the Web 2003, Selected Papers from an International Conference. Toronto: Archives and Museums Informatics (2003) 131-141
6. Sauer, S., Osswald, K., Göbel, S., Feix, A., Zumack, R.: Edutainment Environments: A Field Report on DinoHunter Technologies, Methods and Evaluation Results. In: D. Bearman & J. Trant (eds.): Museums and the Web 2004, Selected Papers from an International Conference. Toronto: Archives and Museums Informatics (2004) 165-172
7. Spierling, U., Iurgel, I.: „Just Talking about Art" – Creating Virtual Storytelling Experiences in Mixed Reality. In: Balet, O., Subsol, G., Torguet, P. (eds.): Virtual Storytelling. Springer-Verlag, Berlin Heidelberg New York (2003) 179-188

Author Index